The Encyclopedia of
HERBS
&
SPICES

The Encyclopedia of
HERBS & SPICES

Pamela Westland

Marshall Cavendish

Published by Marshall Cavendish Books Limited
58 Old Compton Street
London W1V 5PA

First printing 1987
3 4 5 6 7 8 9   99 98 97 96 95 94 93 92 91

© Marshall Cavendish Limited 1975–1987

ISBN 0 86307 815 X

Printed and bound in Singapore by
Times Offset Private Ltd.

CONTENTS

HERBS

SPICES

HERBS

14

INTRODUCTION

Throughout history and throughout the world, herbs have played an important part in the development of mankind. Providing us with food, medicine and cosmetics, herbs can cure, kill and nourish us.

The first part of the book describes their history from ancient civilizations to the present day, with reference to mythology, botany, medicine, horticulture and cosmetics. Where possible, we have provided the necessary information to enable you to reproduce the herb gardens, beauty aids, traditional folk remedies and pot-pourri that enhanced the lives of those who lived in a less complicated age than our own.

The flavour, scent and medicinal and nutritional properties of fresh herbs are inevitably superior to those of herbs which have been dried or frozen. What better way to provide yourself with a constant supply than to grow them yourself? In the second section of this book we have chosen the most useful herbs and explained how they should be planted and cultivated. It does not matter if you do not have a garden; most herbs grow quite successfully in pots and window boxes. A herb garden will also provide you with a colourful and sweet-smelling array of plants that more than compensate for the small amount of time and effort involved in growing them.

In cooking, particularly, herbs come into their own. Mass-produced foods, although convenient, tend also to be bland and boring. The judicious addition of the right herb can help to counter this and add the difference to your cooking which will make it worthy of the best restaurant. The final section includes a selection of recipes which are comprehensive in their ability to provide meals for the family and also for special occasions.

The submergence of many traditional crafts and lores by the development of modern technology is now ending. Partly because scientific research has now authenticated what was previously assumed from experience, and partly as a reaction to our machine-governed lives, much knowledge that has been ignored for years is finding new value in our search for simplicity and self sufficiency.

HERBS THROUGHOUT HISTORY

As long as man has existed, herbs have been an integral part of his life. Evidence of their use and the traditions which sprang from their consequent importance is still being discovered all over the world.

Before he learned to hunt animals, primitive man depended on plants for both food and medicine. Even after meat became an addition to the human diet, it was for many centuries a luxury and the staple foods were bread and other grain-based products. The only way to give such a regimen variety or savour was by the addition of wild plants—the cultivated vegetable is a comparatively recent introduction. Apart from improving the flavour of food, herbs also helped to preserve it and make it more digestible.

Through experience, a tremendous amount of knowledge on the subject of herbs was gradually accumulated and passed on from one civilization to another. Occasionally this became interwoven with superstition, but even then it was usually based on sound plant lore.

One of the earliest known records of the use of herbs is on an Egyptian papyrus dated about 2000 BC which mentions the existence of herb doctors. Garlic is known to have been fed to the builders of the pyramids to keep them healthy, and other documents illustrate their importance in cooking and religious rites, such as the embalming of the dead. Their knowledge was passed to the Greeks and then to the Romans. Further confirmation of their importance can be found in both the Old and New Testaments of the Bible.

The works of famous Greek philosophers and physicians such as Aristotle and his pupil Hippocrates (in the third century BC), and later of Dioscorides show an extensive knowledge of the botanical nature and medicinal use of hundreds of different kinds of herbs. These works and their influence on the herbals of later botanists *cum* physicians such as Galen, Tusser, Gerard and Culpeper are discussed in greater detail in the chapter on medicinal herbs, but their influence was far-reaching.

By the time the Romans were making themselves rulers of the world, they depended so much on herbs for cooking and medicine that the Roman armies carried herbs in their baggage on all campaigns and journeys. In the process, sometimes intentionally and sometimes accidentally, they introduced the planting and use of some previously unknown herbs in every part of the Roman Empire. At the same time they also acquired many new herbs themselves from their colonies and incorporated them into their own way of life.

Pliny (23–79 AD) wrote eight books on medicinal plants. Although herbs were used to keep soldiers healthy and treat illness they were by no means restricted to healing. The patrician Romans, particularly, made heavy use of herbs in the rich sauces in which they tended to smother their food. This was in an attempt to disguise the flavour of food which was preserved by salting and drying, often not very satisfactorily. This use of herbs remained until the twentieth century, when refrigeration was invented and had such a radical effect on our eating habits.

While all this was going on in the west, large reference books had also been written in a similar vein in countries such as India and China, where traditional herbal remedies are still prescribed along with more orthodox medicines.

Even after the Roman Empire collapsed, people everywhere continued

Opposite page, above *The herb elecampane is named after Helen of Troy. One legend relates how the plant sprang from the tears she shed after being abducted by Paris.* Opposite page, below *A street vendor selling groundsel.*

16

· 5591· THE RAPE OF HELEN BY PARIS: BY A FOLLOWER OF FRA ANGELICO ACTIVE 1417 - DIED 1455 ·

to rely on herbs for their flavour, scent and curative properties. Although, in Britain, it took the introduction of Christianity to revive herbs to their former importance after they had fallen into relative obscurity. As monasteries sprang up in Britain and throughout Europe, the monks developed large herb gardens, whose plants were used to cure the sick and revive ailing pilgrims.

Eventually herbs were grown in the gardens of both rich and poor. They were used in the preparation of food, beer, wine, cosmetics, perfumes, candles and insect repellents as well as of medicine. The rich lord would use potions and ungents prepared by his lady to staunch the bleeding and heal the wounds of the men in his private army. The lady herself would strew aromatic herbs among the reeds which covered the floors in an attempt to counter the odours which constantly assailed one in the days before indoor plumbing and sanitation. Herbs used for this purpose were known as 'strewing' herbs.

These early herb gardens were very beautiful as they included plants that we now connect simply with colour and scent, such as carnations, peonies, foxgloves and roses, although in those times every plant had a purpose. For example, as honey was the only form of sweetener, stress was laid on those plants which attracted bees; bergamot, hyssop, balm, lavender, thyme and savory.

By the mid-sixteenth century, the use of herbs was so common that they

17

A sixteenth century apothecary mixing his herbal potions and medicines.

were grown everywhere and the monastery gardens ceased to be so important. Large herb gardens, however, established for the general public for the benefit of their health, such as that in Padua, still survive from this time.

As well as their more functional use, the value of herbs in sometimes determining the difference between life and death, gave them considerable significance in magic and superstition. Astrology was used to work out the most propitious times for the planting and harvesting of herbs. Certain of them were thought to be under the influence of a particular planet—chives, for example, belonged to Mars, and chervil to Jupiter. Even today, some people still plant herbs during the waxing of the moon just to be on the safe side.

Because people knew the power and usefulness of herbs in their everyday life, they turned to them for help against evil and harmful magic. They believed, for example, that rosemary, lavender, dill, hyssop, angelica and southernwood, would protect them from witchcraft and the evil eye. The leaves of the elder were gathered on the last day of April and fixed around doors and windows to protect the inhabitants from charms and spells. The elder was a magic tree, all herbs were under the protection of the elder mother and, although it was full of love for mankind, it was wiser to ask its pardon if forced to cut one down. On the positive side, certain herbs, such as *Artemesia abrotanum* (southernwood), were used to make love potions and charms.

Practical uses, however, included not only their addition to food and medicaments, but their inclusion in pot-pourri and pomanders. These were used to scent yourself and your surroundings and act as a disinfectant. More details about such objects are given on page 26, where we also tell you how to prepare them for yourself.

Oils from the seeds of herbs were used from Roman to Tudor times and beyond to polish wooden floors and furniture. People fortunate enough to posses a bath would add home-made herbal bath additives and the lady of the house would also prepare her own herbal hair rinses and tooth washes in her still room.

The influence and use of herbs was spread from Europe to the New World by the settlers who brought herbs and spices to America from every part of Europe. The Shakers, a sect of Quakers, were among the first to make a commercial success out of growing, drying, packaging and selling herbs.

The popularity of herbs remained reasonably constant until the eighteenth and nineteenth centuries. At this point scientific knowledge became sufficiently advanced for man to evolve synthetic substitutes for many of the properties previously derived from plants. Consequently the use of a vast number of herbs declined and many were cultivated for their beauty and fragrance alone. Perennial favourites such as mint and parsley survived this decline, but generally herbs passed into oblivion.

In recent years, science has helped reverse this situation by proving the nutritional and medicinal value of plants and incorporating them into modern medicines and cosmetics. Simultaneously, although food has ceased to necessitate the use of herbs to preserve and disguise its flavour, mass production and its consequent detrimental effect on the taste of food, has ensured the revival of herbs in the kitchen. All the information needed to grow herbs for these purposes is contained in the Concise Herbal section of this book, while the final section is devoted to recipes in which the herbs have been chosen to complement the main ingredients.

Socially, along with our increased capacity for self-destruction, there has evolved an increasing awareness of our ecology and environment, leading to a greater appreciation and reliance on natural products. Interest in herbs is consequently reviving as people return to the cultivation and use of plants in every aspect of their lives.

HERBS FOR HEALTH

Herbs have always contributed a great deal to human health, and they still do. Their most obvious value is as the source of some of the drugs and medicines used in modern remedies. For example, pyrethrum is made from a member of the chrysanthemum family. From the poppy comes opium and heroine and the pain-killer morphine. Digitalin, the drug used for heart disorders, is derived from the leaves of the foxglove. Indeed until comparatively recently herbs were the major source of medicines, for when antibiotics and other such modern drugs were unknown, people were forced to rely upon natural tried and tested cures.

Herbalists

The first known important work, however, dealing specifically with medicinal herbs was written by a Greek physician, Dioscorides. In about 60 AD he compiled a herbal called *De Materia Medica*. The book described the properties of some six hundred plants. The information was so complete and so accurate that the herbal was used as a standard text for centuries afterwards.

One of those who used Dioscorides' herbal as a work of reference was Willian Turner, who lived from 1508 to 1579. Turner, a Protestant clergyman, a doctor of medicine and the pioneer figure in English botany, was a scientist by training. The *Herball* he wrote shows the mixture in him of curiosity and strict caution.

John Gerard, who was born in 1545 in Nantwich, Cheshire, England, and wrote what is probably the most famous of all herbals, did not have Turner's strictness. His book expresses above all his enthusiastic love of plants. Even so, its warmth does not diminish Gerard's scientific insight and discipline. During his lifetime he was a surgeon, the superintendent of Lord Burghley's gardens (Lord Burghley was Elizabeth I's Chief Secretary of State) and an apothecary to James I. And as a physician and gardener he made a collection of seeds and plants from gardens throughout Europe, even employing a plant collector to find new items.

Below A *detail of the poppy plant, from which opium, heroine and morphine are extracted.* Bottom left A *woodcut showing the stylized nature of early herbal illustrations.* Bottom right A *detail of the foxglove from which the drug* digitalis *is extracted for use in the treatment of heart conditions.*

The frontispiece and some of the illustrations from Gerard's Herbal, published in 1597.

A later herbal, which makes fascinating reading, is that published by Nicholas Culpeper in 1649. His book is particularly interesting because at that time medical treatment was extremely expensive and poorer people were forced to treat themselves by using simples, or remedies made from herbs gathered wild or grown outside their cottages. Culpeper's book was intended to supply these people with all the information necessary to treat themselves without recourse to doctors.

Culpeper linked herbs with astrology and tended to exaggerate the medicinal claims to be made for each plant. He was also an advocate of a system of natural healing, still found all over the world, called the Doctrine of Signatures. This system works on the basis that 'like cures like': yellow plants cure liverish conditions, such as jaundice, which tinges the skin yellow; plants with heart-shaped leaves are good for the heart; plants with red flowers or blotches of red on their stems or leaves are good for the blood, and so on. This doctrine resulted in many herbs being named after the specific medicinal properties they were held to have, such as eyebright, liverwort (agrimony) and heartsease.

In 1694, nearly a hundred years after Gerard's death, John Pechey published his *Compleat Herbal of Physical Plants*. He, too, was a doctor who had absorbed both the old learning and the new explorations in botanical science.

For these men, and for many others like them with a rigorous scientific training, there was an obvious connection between herbs and health.

Herbal medicine has, of course, never disappeared. There are still homeopathic pharmacies and certainly people still use traditional herbal cures. In China there have grown up two entirely separate schools of medicine, one centred around modern western drugs and surgical techniques and the other based upon acupuncture and traditional mainly herbal medicines—some of which have remained virtually unchanged for 2,700 years. Recently, too, in the west there has been a drift back to 'natural' cures and herbal medicines in reaction against the ever-increasing complexity of modern drugs.

Medicinal teas

The various herb teas are really the safest, easiest and best ways of getting the benefit from aromatic leaves and flowers of herbs. The majority of these teas are also anti-indigestive and relaxing—the preparation and merits of herbal teas, or tisanes, are given in detail on page 36.

Herbal medicines

Making your own medicines can be a complicated and somewhat hazardous occupation because many of the herbs have dangerous or unexpected side-effects. So anyone interested would be wise not to attempt to it but to investigate the stock of the nearest herbal or homeopathic supplier. Among other things a number of creams and ointments are made from herbs, one well known one being comfrey ointment which has quite amazingly good effects in cases of back strain. (In medieval times this herb was called boneset or knitbone, and recommended for sprains and strained backs.)

Herbal medicine becomes further confused because each herb was used to cure innumerable ailments. Rue, for example, which is dangerous taken in large quantities, was used for putting on bee and wasp srtings, as an antidote for poisons, as a cure for dizziness and to take away warts and pimples.

Some herbal cures

Many of the herbal cures do now seem rather fanciful. The very few listed below are included for their interest value, you are not really advised to try them.

Asthma sufferers, even as late as the first quarter of the twentieth century, were advised to 'mince garlic, spread it on thin bread and butter, and eat just before going to bed'.

At the same time a dandruff cure, which unfortunately is not specific about the quantity of sage in a packet, or how to dissolve it, recommended that you 'Take one packet and a half of sage, and dissolve it in one pint of boiling water. When cold, strain into a bottle and brush into the scalp every night'. (If you do consider trying this be careful, the sage liquid will stain walls and clothes, and may, like some hair-colourants, temporarily stain your scalp!)

Two particularly odd herbal cures state that to improve a bad memory you should drink sage tea, sweetened to taste, and that garlic sliced and worn in the socks will cure rheumatism.

To keep your skin clear some herbalists advise you to boil elder flowers in water, strain and then drink the liquid. And a nice seventeenth-century recipe for 'An excellent water for Ye sight' says: 'Take fennel, anniseed

Part of a homeopathic dispensary, where herbs are used, among other naturally available plants and minerals, to make remedial medicines.

and elecampane, dry and powder them, mix in good brandy, dry it again; every morning and evening eate a pretty quantity, it is excellent for sight'. While another of the same period tells you to 'Take a good white wine, infuse eyebright in it three dayse, then seethe it with a little rosemary, drink if often, it is most excellent to restore and strengthen the sight. Also eate of the powder of eyebright in a new laid egg rare-roasted every morning'.

A Welsh antidote for a spider's bite was to mix garlic, treacle and ale—unfortunately the quantities are not given. But you were supposed to drink freely of the mixture so ale probably predominated.

There are many complicated and expensive recipes for removing freckles and sunburn, mostly dating from the times when a pale skin was the sign of a lady. Rather more useful ones are those which tell you how to stop sunburn hurting. One such advises washing the affected part with sage tea. Finally, a delightful recipe for 'Comforting the head and the braine' which says: 'Take rosemary and sage of both sorts of both, with flowers of rosemary if to be had, and borage with ye flowers. Infuse in good Canary wine for three days, drink it often.'

The medicinal herbs

The medicinal properties of herbs were second in importance only to the culinary qualities. Below are listed the traditional medicinal usages and beliefs attributed to various herbs—obviously not all the reputed curative properties are to be relied upon or tested.

Agrimony This is an ancient medicinal herb. The Greeks used it to cure cataract. In Britain, many centuries later, it was made into a spring tonic and a blood purifier which was 'good for them that heave naughty livers'.

Agrimony was also made into an ointment called *arquebused* and applied to wounds inflicted by an arquebus, a hand-held gun.

Bergamot Because, like all the mints, it contains thymol, bergamot used to be made into an infusion for colds and sore throats.

It is only quite recently that its qualities as a tea have been discovered in Europe, but they have been famous for centuries in the northern part of the United States, and in Canada. The Oswego Indians must have been the first to use its leaves to make a tea, for in North America this plant is named after them. After the 'Boston Tea Party', (December 16, 1773) patriotic American colonists drank it instead of Indian Tea.

Its fragrance when it is growing makes it a good bee plant and one of its American names is bee balm.

Betony This was ground into an ointment with hog's grease and used to soothe burns.

Borage Even in Roman times, borage had the reputation of being a cheerful, encouraging plant, one that, in Pliny's words, 'brings always courage'.

Centuries later, the great Elizabethan gardener and herbalist, John Gerard had the same praise for it in its use 'for the comfort of the heart, to drive away sorrow'. He—and many other people—had found that the effect of its leaves in a salad was 'to exhilarate and make the mind glad', and the idea of an exhilarating salad is delicious in itself.

Borage was grown, too, for the beauty of its vivid blue flowers—Louis XIV had some planted in the gardens of Versailles—and they have been much copied in embroidery for centuries.

Catmint, Catnip The true catmint is *Nepeta cataria* which, said John Gerard, cats love so much that 'they rub themselves upon it, wallow or tumble in it, and also feed upon the branches and leaves very greedily'. People like it very well too—as a medicine. It was regarded as 'a present helpe for them that be bursten inwardly of some fall received from a high place'. That makes it sound more a miracle than a medicine, but 'bursten inwardly' was just a vivid version of 'bruise'.

Below Aniseed, *mixed with fennel, elecampane and brandy, was recommended to be taken twice a day to improve the sight.* Bottom *Sprigs of flowering borage, added to sage and rosemary and infused in* Canary *wine, was said to comfort the head and brain.*

Chervil This is yet another herb which the Romans brought into Europe from the shores of the Mediterranean and the Levant.

In England in the fifteenth century it was an essential plant, and it stayed in favour. For John Gerard, chervil made salads that excelled 'in wholesomeness for the cold and feeble stomache'. The boiled roots were a preventative against plague. It could be eaten to cure the hiccups, and its leaves soothed the pain of rheumatism and bruises.

Chives One of the most ancient of all herbs, chives were a favourite in China as long ago as 3000 BC. They were enjoyed for their mild, delicious onion flavour, and used as an antidote to poison and to stop bleeding. For a herb, chives came late to the gardens of Europe, arriving in the sixteenth century.

Coltsfoot Its odd country name, son-before-father, was given to it because the flowers appear before the leaves. For many centuries coltsfoot (or coughwort) flowers have been valued for their use in treating various chest complaints, particularly bronchitis and asthma. They were dried and then inhaled or smoked, and have been used as a substitute for tobacco, too.

Comfrey There is a tradition that comfrey was much grown in the herb gardens of monasteries. That may have been because monks so often had to care for the sick and injured, and one of the old names for comfrey was knit-bone.

It was believed to mend broken bones, and to heal such things as bruises, sprains, swellings and backache. One Elizabethan recipe is for comfrey root, boiled in sugar and liquorice, and mixed with coltsfoot, mallow and poppy seeds to make an ointment for curing bad backs and strains. But its use was not confined to muscular troubles, people also made comfrey tea for colds and bronchitis, using 25g/1oz of dried leaves to 600ml/1 pint (2½ cups) of boiling water.

Dill The common name comes from the Norse word *dilla*, meaning 'lull'—dill was believed to be good for insomnia. The seed is used as a mild medicine for flatulence, good for soothing a 'windy' baby.

Elder Elderflower water has been taken as a remedy for colds for several centuries.

Elecampane The botanical name, *Inula Helenium*, comes from Helen of Troy. There is a legend that the plant sprang from her tears, but John Gerard says that her hands were full of it when Paris took her away from Greece.

Elecampane looks like a sunflower, and in Germany there was an ancient custom of putting a bunch of it in the centre of a nosegay of herbs to symbolize the sun and the head of Odin, the greatest of the Norse gods.

The Romans, in their practical way, used the roots in a medicine for the cure of over-eating, and Tudor herbalists candied them to use for the treatment of coughs, catarrhs, bronchitis, and chest ailments generally.

Eyebright The botanical name, *Euphrasia officinalis*, comes from Euphrosyne, one of the three Graces, whose name is the Greek word for gladness, and the common name comes from its use as an eye lotion. Milton in *Paradise Lost*, speaks of how it was used with rue to restore Adam's sight.

Long ago, country people used to use it, too, for an early morning drink, and in some places they made wine from it. In the north of England, where it grows on Hadrian's Wall, it was used to treat hay fever.

Fennel The Greeks thought very highly of fennel and used it for slimming and for treating more than twenty different illnesses. The Romans ate it—root, leaf and seed—in salads and baked it in bread and cakes. In Anglo-Saxon times it was used on fasting days, presumably because, as the Greeks had already discovered, it stilled the pangs of hunger. Even in later centuries it was 'much used in drink to make people more lean that are too fat'.

In the Middle Ages fennel was a favourite strewing herb, for, apart from

Below *An infusion of dill water has been a traditional remedy for flatulence for centuries.* Bottom *As well as having a mild and delicious oniony flavour, which makes the chive a great asset in cooking, it has also been used as an antidote to poisons and to stop bleeding.*

Below *The origin of the common name for* Marrubium vulgare, *horehound, is derived from its use as an antidote to the bight of a mad dog.* Bottom *An old manuscript showing an illustration of vervain.*

being fragrant, it kept insects at bay. It had a high place in the kitchen, too, lending its flavour to food that was often far from fresh to make it palatable. The royal household of Edward I, who reigned in England towards the end of the thirteenth century, used fennel at the rate of 3.8kg/8½lbs each month.

Fennel even had power against witches. If it were hung over the doorway on Midsummer Eve it would keep them away. And people who put it in the keyhole of their bedrooms made sure that nothing dangerous would disturb their sleep.

Garlic This is one of the oldest and most valued of all cultivated plants. It may have come into southern Europe from the east. Certainly it was known to the Ancient Egyptians who used it as a food and a medicine and thought so highly of it that it seemed almost a god to them. The builders of the pyramids ate it; the Children of Israel ate it; the Romans—needless to say—ate it and encouraged other people to do the same. It was an ingredient in medicine for leprosy—the term for a leper in the Middle Ages was pilgarlic, because he had to peel his own.

The antiseptic quality of garlic is not just a matter of faith—in World War I, sphagnum moss soaked in garlic juice was used for wound dressings. Garlic was valued in other medicines, too, for the digestion and for colds, coughs and asthma, and an old country remedy for whooping cough was to put a clove of garlic in the shoes of the whooper!

Horehound The Greeks thought highly of it and used it as an antispasmodic drug. It was an antidote, too, for the bite of a mad dog, and this, of course, is how it got its common name.

Lemon balm *Melissa offinalis,* the botanical name for this herb, comes from the Greek word for 'bee' and the Greeks believed that bees would never go away from a hive if it grew nearby. The hives were even rubbed with it to make the bees welcome.

Lemon balm had valuable qualities for human beings, too. It soothed tension. It was a dressing for wounds, especially sword wounds, and in the Middle Ages it was believed that a sprig of lemon balm placed on an injury was enough to staunch the blood. It was good for the ears, toothache, and sickness during pregnancy. It was held to cure mad dog bites, skin eruptions and crooked necks. It prevented baldness. And when made into an amulet in a piece of linen or silk, it caused the women who wore it to be beloved and happy.

With all these powers to its credit, it is not surprising that the Ancient Greeks believed that it promoted long life, and that a Prince Llewellyn of Glamorgan drank 'mellissa tea'—so he claimed—every day of the 108 years of his life.

Lovage The Greeks used lovage for a medicine and so did the Romans. It was they who brought it to Britain and spread it about Central Europe.

Lovage was grown all through the 'Dark Ages'. It is yet another of the almost-all-purpose medicines: it was taken for sore throats, quinsy, and for eye ailments; for indigestion and stomach-ache, and for getting rid of boils, spots and freckles. It was also added to baths, most probably as the earliest deodorant.

In Central Europe, when girls went to meet their lovers, they wore lovage in a bag hanging round their necks, and perhaps it was its use as a perfume that led to lovage being put into love potions which were guaranteed to awaken everlasting devotion.

Pennyroyal The Romans gave pennyroyal the name *Mentha pulegium* for it kept away fleas, and *pulex* is the Latin for flea. The great John Gerard called this pudding grass. In Tudor times it was gathered in London among the marshy parts of 'Miles end . . . poore women being plenty to sell it in London markets'.

Maybe the 'poore women' of Gerard's day found a ready market for it because it had so many uses. Gerard himself claimed that it would purify

24

'Corrupt water' on sea voyages, and that it would cure 'swimming in the head and the paines and giddiness thereof'. And in dried and powdered form it was made into medicine for coughs and colds.

Rocket This must have been an early form of anaesthetic. The Romans—who sometimes sound like travelling herbalists in chariots—ate both the leaves and the seeds, and the Elizabethans were also extremely partial to it. One herbalist recommended its being taken before a whipping, so that the pain would not be felt, and another praised its use against the biting of the shrew mouse 'and other venomous beasts'!

St. John's wort St. John was the patron saint of horses and this herb was reputed to cure equine ailments.

Sage Sage was yet another traveller to Britain and northern Europe in the Roman baggage train. Its Latin name, *salvia* means 'health', and from very early times people believed that it was a source of well-being, both physical and mental.

The Greeks used it to counteract all manner of afflictions, including ulcers, consumption, snake bites and grief. The Romans ate it. The Chinese at one time preferred sage tea to 'tea' tea, partly for its tonic properties. It was held to be good for the brain, the senses and the memory—it strengthened the sinews; it was good for palsy and cured stitches; it made a good gargle and mouthwash and kept the teeth white. And Gerard recommended its use in the brewing of ale!

Savory Savory was grown in Egypt in ancient times, and used in love potions. The Romans liked it, too, but they used it in a spicy sauce. When it became at home in Europe, it was used chiefly as a medicine, for cheering people up, for tired eyes, for ringing in the ears, for indigestion, for wasp and bee stings, and for other shocks to the system.

Tansy This herb was used as a popular cure for worms and also to bring on abortion.

Tarragon *Artemisia dracunculus* is the botanical name and *dracunculus* means, charmingly, little dragon. In ancient times, the mixed juices of tarragon and fennel made a favourite drink of the rulers of India. In the reign of Henry VIII, the little dragon made its way into English gardens, and the diarist John Evelyn described it as 'friendly to the head, heart, and liver'.

Thyme A tisane made from the leaves of this herb is supposed to cure insomnia.

Wormwood Its grand name first, according to tradition, was *Parthenis absinthum*, but Artemis, the Greek goddess of chastity, had so much benefit from it that she gave it her name and it became *Artemisia absinthum*. There is even more to its name, for its bitter taste is proverbial, and *absinthum* means 'destitute of delight'.

Wormwood was well thought of as a medicine for a number of complaints. It was used to cure quinsy, prevent drunkeness, and heal the bites of rats and mice, and, mixed with wine, rosemary, blackthorn and saffron, it had a reputation for keeping people in good health. Wormwood had its magical qualities, too. If it was hung beside the door, it kept away evil spirits. And, back in the everyday world, if it was added to ink, it stopped mice from eating old letters.

Valerian Also known as 'all heal', a tisane made from this herb is supposed to act as a general panacea.

Yarrow The botanical name of a herb very often tells much of its early history—or maybe its early legend. Yarrow got its botanical name, *Achillea millefolium*, because it was the herb used by the Greek hero Achilles to heal his warriors in the Trojan War. An old country name for it is 'soldiers' woundwort', and it was chiefly famed and used for its healing qualities, probably in the form of an ointment. In infusions it was taken as a tonic and a cure for feverish colds. People did try it, too, as a cure for baldness, though its efficacy is not proven.

An illustration from a thirteenth century manuscript showing a man suffering from the bite of a mad dog, below him, and on the right, henbane, the plant used to cure him.

HERBS FOR BEAUTY

Herbs have been used in cosmetics for thousands of years—even the ancient Egyptians developed their own rouge and lip-reddener from plant extracts. Unfortunately, however, they were largely superseded by mass-produced synthetic products which could be manufactured with greater speed and economy but were inevitably less pure.

Recently there has been a return by commercial cosmetic firms to incorporating herbs in their products, reflecting a general trend towards a more natural, uncomplicated way of life. But although it is possible to buy many herbal beauty aids, it is so simple and economical to make them yourself that it is worth experimenting with a few recipes.

It has been possible to rediscover the original formulae for many of the old beauty preparations because careful houswives wrote them down in their family recipe books, many of which have survived to this day. As you experiment with them you will be able to invent new concoctions suited to your individual requirements.

Whether you grow your own herbs or buy them makes little difference, although the fresher they are the better. Some cosmetics require whole herbs, while others are based on herbal infusions or herbal oil, that is the essential or volatile oil contained in the leaves and/or flowers. These oils have the property of improving the circulation of the blood, encouraging the production of white corpuscles and acting as a disinfectant. Where a concentrated oil is required, this must be bought from a herbalist as the quantity of herbs necessary to extract oil makes this an impractical project for the home herbalist. Although initially these may be expensive, the quantities needed in the preparations are so minute that the oil becomes a long term investment.

It is worth remembering that herbal cosmetics only work externally. It is equally important to eat properly and take regular exercise. The use of herbs and good fresh vegetables and fruit in your diet is as important to beauty as the use of them in cosmetics.

How to make a herbal infusion
Pour boiling water over the appropriate herb and leave to infuse as you would if making tea. The proportion should be either 3-4 tablespoons of fresh herbs, or 1 teaspoon of dried herbs, to 300ml/10floz (1¼ cups) of boiling water. Use an earthenware or china pot but not one made of metal and leave the infusion to steep for at least 30 minutes before straining and bottling in screw-top jars. An infusion will keep in the refrigerator for a week. Never waste it, if you have made more than you require for a specific recipe, the remainder can be added to your bath water.

The face
The three basic steps to keeping your skin firm and supple are cleansing, toning and moisturizing. Cleansing entails removing the grime and dirt from your skin, which accumulates every day, especially if you live or work in a city. This tends to open the pores slightly. Consequently, the next step is to tone the skin. Toners, or tonics, are mildly astringent and close the pores up again and firm the skin. Inevitably both cleansers and tonics tend to dry the skin slightly and remove some of the natural oils. These are replaced by moisturizers which keep the skin supple and help to prevent wrinkles. Once a week you should clean your face thoroughly. This can be achieved either by a facial steam bath or by using a face pack or mask. Do not use these methods too often, unless you have some persistent blemishes, as they dry the skin.

Facial steam baths

Put two cups of herbs in a bowl with 1 litre/2 pints (5 cups) of boiling water. Hold your face over the bowl and cover your head with a towel to make a tent. Steam your face, keeping it about 30cm/1ft from the bowl for 4 to 8 minutes. Chamomile, elder flowers, yarrow, fennel, sage and lime flowers are suitable for this purpose.

Face packs

Method 1 Chop three or four handfuls of fresh herbs, put them into a pan and just cover with boiling water. Simmer for about 10 minutes or until the leaves combine to make a thick mash. Set aside to cool a little. While

The increase in the popularity of herbal cosmetics reflects the general trend towards a more natural way of living. Although commercial herbal products are available, it is much cheaper to make your own. Pure cosmetics, applied regularly, will help your skin and hair, but remember to eat properly as well.

Chamomile flowers made into a shampoo or herbal rinse not only act as a conditioner but also lighten fair hair.

it is still warm, spread it over a pad of sterile cotton (available in boxes) and apply this to your face, avoiding the eyes and mouth. Leave on for 10 to 15 minutes. Rinse off with lukewarm water.

Sage, or a mixture of dandelion and nettle leaves, are both particularly good for this sort of pack, but any of the herbs recommended for a facial steam bath would be suitable.

Method 2 Mix a small carton of yogurt, 150ml/5floz ($\frac{1}{2}$ cup), with 1 teaspoon of infused fennel seeds and 1 teaspoon of fresh, chopped fennel leaves. Spread evenly over your face, avoiding the eyes and mouth. Leave for 10 to 15 minutes and then rinse off with lukewarm water.

Fennel acts as both a tonic and a wrinkle smoother.

N.B. As when using any form of face mask or pack, be careful to protect your eyes with cotton wool balls soaked in cold water.

Cleansers

These should be used every morning and evening. A good basic cleanser is an investment.

Basic cleansing cream The cleansing agent in this cream is the lanolin. Both lanolin and beeswax are obtainable from dispensing chemists (drugstores). Use this cream to clean your skin night and morning: apply a small amount, massage it well into the skin, then remove all traces with a clean tissue.

	Metric/U.K.	U.S.
Beeswax	14g/$\frac{1}{2}$oz	1 Tbs
Lanolin	25g/1oz	2 Tbs
Avocado or olive oil	75ml/3floz	$\frac{3}{8}$ cup
Herbal water (infusion of the appropriate herb)	2 Tbs	2 Tbs
Essential herb oil (for scent)	2 drops	2 drops

Melt the beeswax with the lanolin in a double saucepan over low heat. When they are completely liquid stir in the oil. Remove the saucepan from the heat and stir in the herbal water and essential oil. Stir constantly until cool. Keep the cream in a screw-top jar.

Skin toners

Face tonics or toners are basically cold teas, the 'infusions' described at the beginning of this chapter. They should be patted on to the cleansed skin with a tissue or cotton ball and left to dry. Apart from closing the pores, some herbs have other beneficial effects.

Chamomile Tones up relaxed muscles.

Comfrey An infusion of comfrey, especially if mixed with witch hazel water helps smooth wrinkles and is a tonic.

Elder An infusion of the leaves or flowers has a slight bleaching effect and helps fade blotches and freckles.

Fennel An infusion of leaves or seeds helps clear spots as fennel has healing properties.

Lady's mantle Particularly good for sensitive skins.

Lemon balm Helps smooth wrinkles.

Lime flowers Helps smooth wrinkles.

Mint An infusion of mint sprigs is quite a strong astringent and is excellent for cleansing ingrained dirt and spots. If your skin is particularly sensitive only half the amount of herbs should be used to that recommended in the introduction to this chapter.

Nettle An infusion of nettle leaves is good for tired skin as it is astringent and gives a refreshing tingle.

Rosemary A tonic which brightens up sagging skin.

Tansy Infused with buttermilk instead of water, tansy has a slight bleaching effect and helps fade freckles.

Thyme Reasonably astringent and helps to clear spots and acne.
Yarrow Astringent, good for greasy skins.
For a stronger astringent effect, any of these herbal infusions may be mixed with witch hazel water.

Moisturizers

Having cleansed and toned your skin, you should then apply a moisturizer. Any plain, unscented cold cream can be easily turned into a fragrant herbal cream. You can just add chopped herb leaves to the cream—but you may find it difficult to remove the little pieces of herb from your face! Or you could heat the cold cream up gently in a pan and add a little herb oil to it. Alternatively for the more adventurous you could try the following recipe.

Night moisturizing cream
Use a very little at a time and leave it on your face overnight.

	Metric/U.K.	U.S.
Beeswax	50g/2oz	¼ cup
Cocoa butter	25g/1oz	2 Tbs
Avocado oil	5 Tbs	5 Tbs
Distilled water	4 Tbs	4 Tbs
Wheat germ oil	1½ Tbs	1½ Tbs
Borax	¾ tsp	¾ tsp

Melt the beeswax, cocoa butter and avocado oil in a double saucepan over low heat. When they are completely liquid and well blended, stir in the distilled water, wheat germ oil and borax. Whip the mixture until it cools to prevent granules forming.

Eye lotions

Eye baths are restoring to tired eyes and helpful in cases of conjunctivitis and eye strain. A cold infusion of any of the following herbs will help clear bloodshot eyes; parsley, elderflowers, dried cornflowers, verbena, fennel and eyebright. If you can find or buy eyebright, it is by far the most effective.

Teeth

Fresh sage leaves, rubbed on the teeth, whiten and cleanse them, as well as strengthening the gums. Eating fresh strawberries also whitens the teeth because of the acid they contain.

Hair

Herbs can help give lustre and body to the hair and may be incorporated into both shampoos and conditioning rinses.

Herbal shampoos One of the most natural and refreshing ways of washing your hair is to use a home-made herbal shampoo. Herbal shampoos are made quite simply by pouring boiling water over fresh or dried herbs, leaving them to steep for 24 hours, and then straining off the liquid. The usual measure is about one heaped teaspoon of herbs (or more if using fresh herbs) to one cup of water, but a slightly stronger brew will do no harm at all. Add the infusion to a mild baby shampoo.

However, if you want to make an entirely home-made herbal shampoo, you will need another herb—soapwort. This common and attractive perennial grows in hedges, by streams and on damp waste ground. The pink, scented flowers appear in late summer and the leaves, from which the soapy substance is drawn, are broadly elliptical and strongly veined.

For centuries before the advent of commercial soap, the plant was used by country people for all washing purposes—and at one time it was particularly recommended for washing delicate silks because it gave them a sheen which could be achieved in no other way. The strongest concen-

Below Rubbing fresh sage leaves on the teeth helps clean and whiten them as well as strengthening the gums. Bottom Most commercial shampoos contain detergent, which does little good to your hair and the only purpose of which is to produce vast quantities of foam. By making your own shampoo you can ensure that this undesirable substance is removed and that only the health-giving qualities of whatever herb you have selected are present.

tration of the soapy substance is in the root, but it is not very practical to use it because you will destroy the whole plant. The leaves and stems should be sufficient—and are available dried.

Although herbal shampoos can now be bought it is much cheaper and more satisfactory to make your own, and you will be sure that, unlike commercially-made shampoos, they contain no detergent.

When making the shampoo avoid using metal containers as these will mar the fragrance. Use small china or pottery vessels with tight-fitting cork lids, a wooden spoon and a nylon strainer.

Be sure to buy purified borax (available in chemists and drugstores) and not the kind recommended for laundering or cleaning sinks.

Basic shampoo If you are using fresh herbs—which are always preferable if available—gently bruise the leaves before making the infusion to allow as much of the essence as possible to mingle with the water.

	Metric/U.K.	U.S.
Dried soapwort (or one handful of fresh leaves and stems)	2 Tbs	2 Tbs
Chamomile flowers	1 Tbs	1 Tbs
Borax	1 tsp	1 tsp

Divide the ingredients equally into two china or pottery jars. Fill each jar with 300ml/10floz (1¼ cups) boiling water. Wedge the corks in tightly and leave the mixture to steep for about 24 hours. Give the jars a good shake from time to time. Pour the mixture through a nylon strainer and discard the herbs.

Variations

Anti-dandruff shampoo If you are troubled by dandruff add an infusion of one part stinging nettle and one part parsley to the shampoo above.

Perfumed shampoos A few lime flowers or two sprigs of lavender added to the basic shampoo before corking will give your hair a delicate, natural fragrance.

Bear in mind that this natural shampoo will not be nearly as 'soapy' as a commercial shampoo. People tend to believe that a shampoo will only clean their hair properly if it produces a tremendous lather, which is why so many commercial shampoos contain detergents which do just that (and little else). A mild and gentle herbal shampoo cannot compete so far as froth goes—but its cleansing and aromatic qualities are undeniable.

Herbal rinses and conditioners

Herbal rinses are simply made by infusing the herb of your choice in water as described at the beginning of this chapter. All of the herb rinses mentioned, if poured over the hair as a final rinse after shampooing, will make your hair shine, but some of them have additional properties.

An infusion of nettles, lime flowers, fennel or sage will act as a good general conditioner.

A parsley rinse helps clear dandruff, and is also reputed to restore thickness to thinning hair.

A rosemary rinse darkens dark hair and imparts a delicious fragrance.

An infusion of chamomile flowers brightens fair hair and has the reputation of stimulating hair growth.

It is, of course, possible to combine one or more herbs together, such as nettle and rosemary, and infuse them to make a hair rinse to suit your individual requirements.

Feet

An infusion of marigold or lime flowers or lavender leaves added to a hot foot bath will refresh tired feet. After the bath, dry your feet and rub them with the essential oil of marigold petals to get rid of any soreness.

Hands

Always try to remember to wear rubber gloves for washing up and rub hand cream into your hands whenever they have been immersed in water or exposed to inclement weather. Below is a recipe to enable you to make your own herbal hand cream.

Hand cream

	Metric/U.K.	U.S.
Glycerine	50g/2oz	¼ cup
Elderflower water	75ml/3floz	⅓ cup
Essential oil of lavender, roses or bergamot	12 drops	12 drops
Lemon juice	8 drops	8 drops

Mix together the glycerine and elderflower water. Stir in the herbal oil and lemon juice and store in a screw-top jar.

Bathing

Any aromatic herb added to the bathwater in oil, vinegar or bag form, will scent and refresh the body. Particular herbs, however, have special

Left Fresh or dried herbs may be used in the preparation of shampoos, handcreams and bath oils. Right, below The essential oil extracted from lavender makes a sweet-smelling additive to herbal hand cream. Right, bottom Any aromatic herb added to bath water will scent and refresh the body.

properties, and it is from these that we suggest you make your selection:

Agrimony and **ragwort** are both recommended for aching muscles.

Lovage has a pleasant aroma and acts as a mild deodorant.

Angelica acts as a skin stimulant.

Comfrey and **rosemary** Prolonged immersion in bath water infused with either of these two herbs is said to rejuvenate the skin.

Valerian and **chamomile** have a soporific effect and are ideal for evening baths.

Southernwood, with its lemony tang, **nettle** leaves or well-boiled **juniper** roots are all invigorating.

Eucalyptus leaves, **rosemary, lavender, elderflowers, rose, geranium** leaves and **violets** will all provide a particularly fragrant bath.

There are many ways to add herbs to the bath, which incidentally is a very ancient tradition, the point to remember is *never to throw herbs directly into the water*, or you will have to spend hours trying to clean the bath out and the waste pipe may become blocked.

Infusions Prepare as specified in the introduction to this chapter and add directly to the bath water in whatever quantity you like.

Essential oils may be bought and added directly to the bath water drop by drop until it is sufficiently scented, or make your own oil.

Bath oils Prepare according to the following recipe and add directly to the bath water.

For the oil use either olive, sunflower, safflower, sesame seed, avocado or almond. Choose herbs from the recommended list or use mint or pine needles for a particularly invigorating bath. Pour 600ml/1 pint (2½ cups) of oil into a large pottery or china bowl. Add as many fresh flowers or leaves as it will take and cover. Soak for a couple of days. Remove, strain, squeeze out and discard the flowers or leaves. Add as many fresh herbs as possible to the remaining oil and leave for a further two days. Repeat the removal and addition of herbs until you have used about ten batches. (This is why herbal oils are so expensive to buy.) Always keep the bowl covered. Finally strain the oil, squeezing the herbs firmly and then discarding them, and store the oil in tightly capped or corked bottles in a dark cool place.

Bath vinegars

These are more astringent than bath oils and are more suitable if you have a greasy skin. Select herbs from the recommended list with the addition of bergamot and balm. Take two cups of fresh leaves or flowers and when they have been washed and dried, pack them loosely in a wide-mouthed glass jar. Pour over 1 litre/2 pints (5 cups) of wine or cider vinegar. Cover tightly and place the jar where you will remember to shake it, or stir the contents with a wooden spoon, every other day. After ten days, rub a little on the skin and smell. If it is not herby enough, drain the herbs away and replace with fresh leaves or flowers and repeat the process. When the vinegar is ready, strain it into bottles, add a sprig of the appropriate herb for decoration and cap tightly. One cupful of herbal vinegar per bath should be adequate.

Bath bags

Bath bags are simple to make, provide an instant infusion and are re-usable. Cut a piece of cheesecloth or muslin 20cm/8in square. Fill the centre with one or more herbs selected from the recommended list. Take up the corners of the cheesecloth and tie together firmly with ribbon or string. Either attach the bag to the tap so that it is hit by the hot running water, or simply place it in the bath and pour very hot or boiling water over it. Fill up the bath and use the bag to scrub yourself with. When the herbs have been exhausted, untie the bag and discard them. Rinse out the cheesecloth and refill with fresh herbs.

A few sprigs of fresh or dried soapwort added to the bath bag will give the water a gentle cleansing effect.

Below Sunflower oil is highly recommended as a base for bath oils. Try adding herb such as mint for an especially invigorating bath. Bottom Rose petals strewn in the bath may look very attractive but the romance wears off when you try to remove them afterwards. A much simpler means of adding herbs to your bath water is to make a bath bag. A 20cm (8in) square of cheesecloth or muslin filled with herbs and then firmly tied with ribbon or string will provide an instant and simple means of infusion.

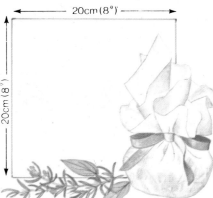

20cm (8″)

20cm (8″)

HERBS IN THE KITCHEN

For centuries herbs have played a vital role in the kitchen, helping to preserve food and making it more palatable and digestible. They were cultivated in the ancient civilizations of Assyria and Babylon, fed by the Egyptians to their slaves, and the Romans added them to practically everything they cooked. Nowadays the use of herbs is equally important to help counter the blandness of modern convenience food and to allow room for expression in terms of individuality and skill in preparing food.

Fresh or dried

It is, of course, preferable to use fresh herbs in cooking, but where this is impossible, dried or frozen ones can be substituted. Remember that the flavour of herbs tends to become more concentrated with drying (although not with freezing) so you need a much smaller amount of them, usually a third to half the amount you would use fresh is sufficient.

If you are forced to rely mainly on dried herbs, try at least to grow or buy fresh parsley. This invaluable fresh-tasting herb is a great help in bringing out the flavour of all dried herbs.

When to add

Some herbs should be added at the beginning of a recipe and others only at the last minute, as prolonged cooking destroys their flavour. Usually a good recipe will tell you when to add seasoning but a rough guide is to add herbs to meat loaves, stuffings, roasts, stocks, soups and casseroles at the beginning of cooking, and to cooked vegetables and sauces ten minutes before the end of cooking time. Uncooked sauces, such as salad dressings will benefit if the herbs are added and left for several hours before use.

It is interesting that flavourings cooked with a dish do tend to become more intense after freezing. So these dishes should either be eaten within two months of preparation, or the herbs omitted at the cooking stage and only added when reheating.

What goes with what

There are no hard and fast rules to this, and once you are used to cooking with herbs you may like to experiment. But for the inexperienced we have included a guide.

Foods/herbs to use with them

Soups
Basil, bay, chervil, chives, coriander, dill, lovage, marjoram, parsley, sage, savory, sweet cicely, tarragon, thyme.

Breads
Basil, coriander, dill, fennel, marjoram, parsley, savory, thyme.

Fish
Basil, bay, dill, lemon balm, lovage, marjoram, rosemary, sage, savory, tarragon, thyme.

Eggs
Basil, bay, chervil, chives, dill, fennel, garlic, marjoram, parsley, rosemary, savory, tarragon, thyme.

Shellfish
Basil, bay, dill, lemon balm, marjoram, savory, tarragon, thyme.

Poultry
Basil, bay, dill, lemon balm, lovage, marjoram, parsley, rosemary, sage, savory, tarragon, thyme.

Lamb
Basil, bay, dill, garlic, marjoram, mint, rosemary, sage, savory, thyme.

However tempting and attractive glass storage jars may look, they are not really suitable containers for herbs. In order to preserve their flavour for as long as possible herbs should be stored in air-tight containers, which do not expose them to the light, and kept in a cool place.

Beef
Basil, bay, chervil, dill, garlic, marjoram, parsley, rosemary, sage, savory, tarragon, thyme.
Pork
Basil, coriander, dill, fennel, marjoram, rosemary, sage, tarragon, thyme.
Vegetables
Basil, bay, chervil, coriander, dandelion, dill, lovage, marjoram, mint, parsley, rosemary, sage, savory, sweet cicely, salad burnet, thyme.
Desserts
Bay, coriander, marigold, thyme, sweet cicely, lemon verbena.

Bouquet garni

Bouquet garni is an essential ingredient in stocks and many soups and casseroles. The classic bouquet garni is made up of a sprig of fresh or dried thyme, a dried bay leaf and a few sprigs of fresh parsley. Tie them up with white thread or string and leave a long end coming out of the pan (tie it to the handle if you like as it often falls in). This enables you to extract the herbs easily before serving—otherwise an unsuspecting guest may get an unpleasant shock. If you are using dried herbs, use one teaspoon and one whole dried bay leaf. Try to avoid using dried parsley, as the flavour is much inferior to that of the fresh herb. These can then be crumbled into a 23cm (8in) circle of muslin or cheesecloth, tightly secured to form a little bag with a long piece of thread or string, and used in the same way as a fresh bouquet garni.

You can vary the herbs in a bouquet garni to suit the ingredients of the particular dish you are preparing. Do not be tempted to add too many different herbs or their flavours will simply cancel each other out. A sprig of rosemary is a good addition to mutton and lamb dishes, tarragon with chicken, marjoram and perhaps a few juniper berries with game, balm or lemon verbena with chicken or fish, and fennel with fish.

Fines herbes
Fines herbes is the French culinary term for a finely chopped fresh herb mixture, usually consisting of parsley, chervil, tarragon and chives. Fines herbes are used as a flavouring for soups, sauces, omelettes and grilled (broiled) meats. As neither chives nor chervil dry very well, try to use fresh or frozen herbs.

Used imaginatively and with discretion herbs can add a new dimension to your cooking. The recipes included in this book are here as a guideline, but with experience and confidence you will soon learn which herb and how much to add, to give your dishes flavour and character.

Top *Parsley has numerous culinary uses and may be added to almost all savoury dishes. Although it is easy to freeze parsley does not dry well. The best solution is to grow enough fresh parsley to last the whole year through.* Above *Balm leaves are chiefly used in tisanes but may also be added to fish or lamb dishes.* Left *A basic bouquet garni consists of a few sprigs of fresh parsley and thyme and a bay leaf tied together. If you are using dried herbs they can be tied up in a piece of cheesecloth.* Opposite page *Crushing garlic in a press is one of the most convenient ways of extracting its flavour.*

35

HERBS TO DRINK

Tisanes

A tisane, or tea, is simply an infusion made by adding boiling water to the leaves or flowers of herbs. In many parts of Europe, herbal teas have been an accepted part of the standard eating habits for years. Indeed, a cup of tisane taken after a rich meal is as common as coffee is in other parts of the world. Unlike tea and coffee, however, tisanes contain neither tannin nor caffeine, both strong stimulants, and are much more suitable for aiding the digestion or promoting sleep.

Prepared tisanes are available from herbal shops, homeopathic pharmacists (drugstores) and health food stores in either sachet form or loose. The ailments they are reputed to help are given here but the cures cannot be vouched for.

If you grow your own herbs, why not make your own tisanes? Tisanes may be made from fresh or dried herbs, and full instructions for drying herbs are given in the chapter on preserving herbs (see page 44). The actual preparation is much the same as making ordinary tea, and like ordinary tea it may be drunk on its own or with the addition of milk, a slice of lemon, honey or sugar.

Method If you are making the tisane in individual tea cups, allow one level tablespoon of fresh herbs per cup or one level teaspoon of dried herbs. Pour on boiling water, cover the cup and leave to infuse for three to five minutes. If you are making it in a teapot, allow however many table- or teaspoons required for each cup, plus one for the pot. Leave to infuse for about five minutes and pour through a strainer into the cups.

For teas made from seeds, these should first be pounded in a mortar, and then follow the same process as for dried herbs.

The most common herbs, together with any generally recognized properties they may have, are listed below:

Herb	Part used	Effect
Angelica	Leaves	Helps headaches and exhaustion.
Balm (*Melissa*)	Leaves	Taken hot or cold, this tea is soothing and relaxing.
Basil	Leaves	Taken hot or cold, this tea helps gastric upsets and colds.
Bergamot	Leaves	Drink alone or mixed with China (non-fermented) tea. Relaxing and sleep-inducing.
Borage	Leaves	Hot or cold, borage tea is an exhilarating tonic and helps catarrh.
Catnip	Leaves	A tonic which lessens fever and headaches.
Chamomile	Flowers	Digestive and soothing, particularly useful for sore throats when it may be also used as a gargle.
Coltsfoot	Flowers or leaves	Used for catarrh and chest complaints. Contains vitamin C.
Comfrey	Leaves and dried roots	Soothing and a digestive, helps chest complaints
Dandelion	Leaves	Beneficial to liver, helps rheumatism and acts as a general tonic and blood purifier.
	Roots, dried, roasted and ground	Used as a substitute for coffee, and as a diuretic.

Opposite page A *tisane is a herbal tea made by pouring boiling water over the leaves or flowers of selected herbs. Unlike tea or coffee, tisanes do not contain harmful stimulants, like tannin or caffeine, and may have properties which are beneficial to the body.* Below A *tisane made from the leaves of the angelica plant is said to relieve headaches and exhaustion.*

Elder	Flowers	Delicious, sleep-inducing and good for throat infections and colds.
Horehound	Leaves	Coughs and colds.
Hyssop	Leaves	Taken hot or cold helps coughs and colds.
Juniper	Berries	Antiseptic and stimulant, good for chest complaints, indigestion and nerves.
Lady's mantle	Leaves	Premenstrual and menstrual tension.
Lime	Flowers	Delicious, sleep-inducing, soothing drink, good for colds and indigestion.
Lovage	Leaves	More like a broth, add salt for a cleansing and refreshing drink.
Melilot	Whole plant	Wind and general tonic.
Mint (*especially peppermint and spearmint*)	Leaves	Taken for colds, headaches, diarrhea, heartburn, nausea and stomachache.
Nettle	Leaves	General tonic and blood purifier.
Parsley	Leaves	General tonic and diuretic. Helps rheumatism.
Rosemary	Leaves	Headaches and insomnia.
Sage	Leaves	General tonic.
Thyme	Leaves	Good for coughs and sinus ailments.
Vervain (*verbena*)	Leaves and dried roots	Slightly bitter tisane, acts as a sedative and digestive.
Yarrow	Leaves	Taken for fevers, coughs, colds and as a general tonic.

Above The flowers of the elder are used to make a tisane which tastes slightly of muscatel. As well as having an attractive taste, an elderflower tea promotes sleep and helps alleviate sore throats. *Opposite page* Long before the hop, a wild herb which can also be cultivated, was used in brewing, beer tended to be cereal-based. Some beers still rely on barley as a principal ingredient. Beer was commonly drunk up until the introduction of tea, and every housewife would have had to brew a regular supply for her family.

Tisanes may also be made from the seeds of fennel and caraway and the leaves of tansy, costmary and St. John's wort.

Do not expect instant results from drinking a tisane, their benefits are cumulative.

Herbal beer and wine

Wine and beer have been made in the home since time immemorial and, as commercial wines become more and more expensive, interest in this ancient domestic art is reviving. Almost any fruit, vegetable or herb can be used for wine making and brewing beer—even the dregs of tea.

A number of shops sell very adequate wine making kits and equipment. Once the initial outlay has been made it is only necessary to purchase the ingredients for subsequent batches as the equipment can be used over and over again.

Herb beer

Herbal beer is a term usually applied to beers made with herbs other than hops. The hop is, however, a wild herb as well as being widely cultivated for beer making.

After the initial investment in equipment, the cost of making beer, especially from herbs like the common nettle, is relatively small.

Equipment
Large pan (sufficient to contain all the weeds collected)
4.5 litre/1 gallon (10 pint) polythene or plastic fermenting vessel with a lid (a polythene or plastic bucket will suffice)
Strainer or remnant of terylene net curtain
Wooden spoons

Bucket or other larger container
Beer bottles (cleaned and sterilized) and stoppers
The equipment should always be used spotlessly clean and if possible sterilised. (Kits for sterilising babies' bottles are useful for this.)

Nettle beer

Using rubber gloves and scissors gather fresh, young green stinging nettle shoots. Take only the top two or three pairs of leaves. The quantity is not vital, but the shoots, not pressed down, should just about fill the brewing bucket. This will make approximately 4.5 litres/1 gallon (10 pints).

Crystal malt, hops and ale yeast (for quantity follow the manufacturer's instructions) are obtainable from home wine and beer kit suppliers. One teaspoon of citric acid may be substituted for the juice of half a lemon.

	Metric/U.K.	U.S.
Nettles		
Crystal malt (broken)	125g/4oz	4oz
Malt extract	1kg/2lb	2lb
Sugar	250g/8oz	1 cup
1 handful of dried hops		
Juice of ½ lemon		
Salt	¼ tsp	¼ tsp
Yeast		

Simmer the washed nettles and crystal malt in a large pan for about 40 minutes.

Put malt extract, sugar, lemon juice and salt into the fermenting vessel fitted with a good lid and strain contents on to the washed nettles and crystal malt. A remnant of terylene net curtain is preferable to an open strainer. The nettle shoots should be squeezed by gloved hands, to extract the full flavour. Stir the mixture thoroughly.

Make the quantity up to 4.5 litres/1 gallon (10 pints) with tap water.

When cool (between 18°-20°C or 65°-70°F), stir in yeast according to the manufacturer's instructions. Maintain this temperature, and keep the vessel covered.

Allow to ferment for four to seven days. Remove the yeast from the top at intervals if necessary. When fermentation has finished the liquid looks clear and bubbles cease to rise. Siphon beer into another clean container.

Dissolve 50g/2oz (¼ cup) sugar in a small quantity of hot water. Add to the beer. Siphon into clean beer bottles and stopper down well. Store in a warm room for two days.

Transfer to a cool place and store for at least a month before drinking.

Herb wine

Herbal wines are made from an infusion of the chosen herb often referred to as herb tea or tisane. The spent herbs must be strained out of the infusion. A remnant of net curtain or muslin can be made into a bag and and the herbs placed in this. The bag is then pressed to extract the full flavour.

The most welcome modern adjunct to home wine making is concentrated pure grape juice. Old recipes for herbal wines usually add dried grapes, often picturesquely described as 'raisins of the sun'. Grape concentrate is a trouble free substitute and gives excellent vinosity. The variety available is enormous.

The mixture of liquids to be fermented is called the must.

Yeast Fermentation is caused by the addition of yeast to the must. If you have been browsing through old books you will be familiar with the recommendation to float brewer's yeast on toast in the liquid—this should be avoided at all costs. A vigorous fermentation can be obtained using

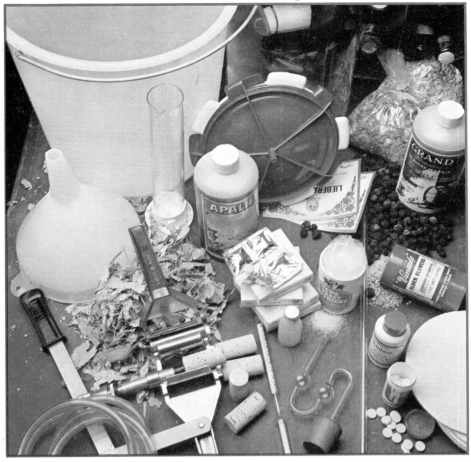

Ingredients and equipment, including a corking-tool, used for wine making. Many of these items will already be in the home while the others are inexpensive to buy and will quickly repay the small initial outlay.

dried baker's yeast, but it is preferable to use a true wine yeast (available from home wine kit suppliers). There are several quick-acting, general purpose yeasts which produce reliable results. To work effectively, the yeast needs sustaining by the addition of certain salts. These are bought ready mixed as yeast nutrient (available from home wine kit suppliers). Use more or less nutrient in relation to the quantity of fruit juice you use. Follow the manufacturer's instructions as these will vary.

Yeast works best in an acid medium. Herb infusions may be low in acid. By adding the juice of lemons or oranges or crystals of citric acid this can be remedied.

Sweetener Honey was the traditional sweetener of the herbal wine maker. In wines made with bitter herbs the dual taste of the sharp leaf or flower and the soft sweetness of honey is a gastronomic delight. Whenever you can—use honey in place of sugar to sweeten your wine. The wine is then called a melomel.

Equipment The basic equipment needed for home wine making is extremely simple and costs very little. Some of the items may already be in the home.

9 litre/2 gallon (20 pint) boiling container
9 litre/2 gallon (20 pint) plastic pail with a lid
4.5 litre/1 gallon (10 pint) fermentation and storage jars
Airlock for each fermentation jar
Plain bungs to fit the fermentation jars for storage
A siphon tube at least 1.2m/4ft long
Wine bottles
Corks
Corking tool
Nylon strainer—at least 15cm/6in in diameter
Funnel—at least 15cm/6in diameter

airlock ↓

bung ←

Top *Two pieces of equipment used in making wine: a fermentation jar and an air-lock with bung. Above Dandelion wine has an attractive and interesting flavour. Pick the dandelions on a sunny day, shake out any insects and twist off the calyx and stems as these impart a bitter flavour.*

— calyx

Do not use any equipment made of iron, steel, copper and brass as these will spoil your wine. In all wine making it is essential to keep equipment clean and sterile. The method for all the recipes given here is basically the same.

Dandelion wine

Pick the dandelion flowers on a warm, sunny morning. Shake out any small insects. Then holding the yellow petals with one hand, twist off the calyx and stem. These are too bitter for wine and should be discarded.

	Metric/U.K.	U.S.
Dandelion petals	1.2L/2pt	5 cups
*Commerical grape concentrate	½ can	½ can
Lemon	1	1
Orange	1	1
Citric acid	1 tsp	1 tsp
Infused tea or	175ml/6floz	¾ cup
grape tannin	¼ tsp	¼ tsp
Sugar or clear honey	700g/1½lb	3 cups
Wine yeast and nutrient		
Campden tablets		

*Can grape concentrate refers to the size sold to make 4½L/1 gallon (10 pints) of wine.

Place everything except the dandelions and the yeast into a bucket. Make an infusion of the dandelion flowers and allow to stand for about half an hour. Strain the infusion into the bucket and stir thoroughly until all is dissolved. Allow to cool to 24°C (75°F) and add yeast.

Fermentation The bucket should be placed in a warm room for the first fermentation which should last from three to six days. This is the aerobic (in the presence of air) fermentation, nevertheless the bucket must have a lid or be fitted with a clean cloth held in place by a firm band.

As the yeast starts to work considerable bubbling and frothing cocurs. The must will change to a milky colour as the yeast grows.

Once the fermentation gets under way the must should be transferred to a fermentation jar. This should be topped up with water and a fermentation or air lock fixed.

Keep an eye on the fermentation lock for the first few days to make sure there is always water present to maintain the trap. Evaporation may necessitate topping up daily. The temperature should be maintained at about 21°C (70°F).

Fermentation will gradually decrease and after about four or five weeks the line of bubbles around the top of the container will have died completely away—if not wait another few days to make sure no gas is being given off.

Storage Dead yeast and perhaps other solid matter (the lees) will by now have settled at the bottom of the fermentation jar. If left there unpleasant flavour may be imparted to the wine, so they should be removed.

To do this the wine has to be siphoned into a second sterilized container with a siphon tube. Stand the wine container on a table and set the second container on the floor. This process is called racking the wine and must be done several times.

The lower container should be topped up with cooled boiled water if necessary as it is preferable to have the minimum of air space remaining.

Crush one campden tablet per 4.5 litre/1 gallon (10 pints) of wine and add before sealing the container with a solid bung or safety lock—these tablets act as a preservative and help to stop further fermentation. Store in a cool dry place.

Above Wine can be made from many flowers other than those of the dandelion. Rose petals in particular make a delightfully fragant wine. Left A selection of home-made wines will enrich and enlarge your wine cellar.

Rack off the wine into a clean container every eight weeks or so, to remove sediment till the wine becomes clearer.

Bottling When the wine is clear, then only is it ready to be bottled. For each 4.5 litres/1 gallon (10 pints) wine you will need six sterilized bottles and corks. Always label your bottles. The wine should then be stored from three to six months although, like herb beer, it will improve for keeping a month or so longer if possible.

Many flowers can be used instead of dandelions. Broom, clover, coltsfoot, cowslip and roses all make delightful wine.

Some flowers such as the carnation, elderflower, chamomile and wall-flower have a more pungent taste and should be used sparingly. No more than 0.5 litre/1 pint (2½ cups) flowers should be infused for each 4.5 litres/ 1 gallon (10 pints) wine.

Any herb which makes a herb tea or tisane can be used as a basis for wine. Lemon balm, sage, rosemary, raspberry leaves, borage and comfrey are recommended. Young blackberry shoots also make a light wine. There is always lots of room for experimentation.

HERBS TO PRESERVE

There is nothing quite like the flavour and aroma of fresh herbs, but as many are annuals and not available throughout the whole year, the answer is to preserve them in the way most appropriate to their use.

Harvesting

The art of harvesting and preserving herbs to retain as much of their essential qualities as possible, is one that is acquired with practice. There are, however, a few simple rules, which if followed should produce successful results:

Always gather herbs in the early morning, after the dew has had time to dry and before the sun has drawn out and dispersed their volatile oils.

Do not pick herbs when they are damp after rain.

Cut them with a sharp knife, except for chives which should be cut with scissors.

Place the cut herbs in one layer in a tray or shallow box.

Never collect more than you can deal with immediately. Herbs left lying around quickly deteriorate and lose their essential oils.

Keep different herbs separate from one another, to avoid cross-flavouring.

Handle as little as possible to avoid bruising.

Leaves Pick in the summer time, just before flowering when their volatile oils are at their peak. Leave the leaves attached to the stem. Discard any leaves which are not perfect.

Flowers Pick as soon as they are fully open, and only select those which are absolutely unblemished. Lavender, wormwood, southernwood, roses, hyssop, chamomile and bergamot are all suitable.

Berries Gather when they are fully ripe, glossy and well coloured but before they darken or stiffen.

Seeds Cut the stems with seed heads on of lovage, dill, fennel and coriander for example, as soon as the seeds are ready to fall and the seed heads have turned brown.

Roots Gather in the autumn, except for horseradish which may be harvested at any time.

After harvesting, there are several ways to concentrate the oils and aromatic properties of herbs so that you can use them for cooking, making cosmetics and pot-pourri throughout the year.

Drying

All herbs should be dried in an airy, shady place where there is no danger of condensation. There are several methods of drying, choose the one that is most appropriate to your circumstances.

Herbs contain approximately 80% of water. The object of drying them is to remove this water without losing any of their valuable properties. About 3.6kg/8lb of fresh herbs are needed to produce ½kg/1lb of dried herbs.

Your aim is to dry the herbs quite quickly with an even, low warmth—not less than 21°C (70°F) or more than 38°C (100°F). A good, even ventilation is just as important as the heat to carry away the humidity of the drying plants. Too much heat or too sunny or light a place will brown the leaves, or at least, dissipate the aromatic properties you are trying to conserve. So you want a dark place with little or no dust, but warmth and plenty of air.

Possible drying places are an airing cupboard or a clothes drying cupboard; a plate-warming compartment of an oven; a darkened, warm,

Those herbs which do not grow all the year round may be preserved for use when out of season by drying or freezing. One of the oldest methods is by air drying, where bunches of herbs are hung upside down in a dry, airy place until all the superfluous moisture has evaporated.

well-ventilated room, passage or cupboard where you could set up a small fan heater; an attic, garage or darkened green-house, a dry, well-aired cellar, perhaps near a boiler.

The shelves must be well separated so that air can pass freely between them. You could use muslin tacked to a wooden framework, hessian or any open weave cloth stretched over dowels or framing, or the flat bottoms of cardboard boxes which have been perforated to let air through, but do not use wire mesh.

If you can alter and regulate the heat, one method is to begin drying with a temperature of about 32°C (90°F) for one day and then reduce the heat to 21°C (70°F) until the drying process is finished.

The drying space should only faintly smell of herbs; a strong smell means there is too much heat and escaping aromas. Don't add a fresh batch of herbs until the first batch is dry or you will add more humidity to the air. Turn the herbs as they are drying from time to time.

Air drying Tying a bunch of herbs and flowers and hanging them upside down in a dry, airy space is an old method of drying herbs, and more satisfactory in a dry climate than in a humid one. Air drying is likely to retain less colour and scent but needs no special arrangements.

Experiment with drying until you get the fullest colour and smell in the herbs. It takes from four to fourteen days or more to dry herbs and flowers. Some flowers, such as rosemary flowers, are better dried slowly at a lower temperature than herbs.

Leaves are dry when they are brittle but will not shatter. Flower petals should feel dry and slightly crisp. Roots should dry right through with no soft centre. The dried roots should then be ground like coffee beans. Seeds should be dried for a few hours in the sun after they have been removed from the seed heads.

Storing Strip leaves from their stems, crumble them—but not too finely or they will quickly lose their flavour—and put them into clean, air-tight containers and store in a cool, dark place. Some herbs, such as sage, thyme and rosemary can be left on the stalk. (This makes them easier to put into casseroles and stews and remove afterwards when the cooking is completed.) Dried bay leaves should be kept whole. Seeds and flower heads should be put straight into an air-tight container.

If moisture starts to form on the inside of the container, the herbs have not been dried correctly. Put them on to paper and allow a further drying time.

Dried herbs in general last a year at the most, and the more finely powdered they are the sooner they lost their taste. It is a good idea to date your containers so that you know exactly how long you have had the herbs. Lemon balm, parsley, summer savory and tarragon only last nine months to a year when dried. Basil, lovage, mint and marjoram last a year or more. And rosemary, sage and thyme can last longer still—but it is a good idea to replace them yearly if you can.

Freezing

Freezing is one of the best methods of preserving herbs for culinary use as the flavour, appearance, texture and nutritional value remain virtually unchanged. It is particularly suitable for soft-leaved herbs which do not dry quite so well, such as mint, chives, parsley, balm, fennel, basil, dill and sorrel. Always freeze herbs in small quantities and remember that while they are perfectly good for cooking, they are not suitable for garnishes.

Having harvested your herbs, wash them if they are not clean and shake dry. If you intend to use them within two months they can be frozen as they are. For longer storage tie them in bunches, dip each bunch first in boiling water and then in chilled water to blanch them. Either leave the herbs whole but separate them into small bunches, or chop them up

Below Thyme, *including lemon thyme illustrated here, responds well to drying and will last for a year or more without losing its flavour. Bottom* Balm *also dries well but should not really be used dried after about nine months. It is a good idea to replace dried herbs annually if you can.*

Tarragon makes a particularly good salad oil and enables you to enjoy the flavour of this herb throughout the year.

finely with a sharp knife or a pair of scissors. Whole herbs, or bouquets garnis, may be packed in foil or plastic bags, sealed and frozen. Chopped herbs should be packed tightly into an ice-cube tray and topped up with water and frozen. When the cubes are solid turn them out into a plastic bag. In both cases make sure the wrapping has been previously labelled. Bouquet garni and whole sprigs may be used straight from the freezer. If you wish to chop whole leaves, this can be done by simply crumbling the leaf while it is still frozen. Chopped herbs in cubes may also be added to dishes straight from the freezer, or if you prefer, the cubes of chopped leaves may be left to thaw in a fine strainer.

Herbs have a freezer life of about six months.

Herbal oils

Herbal oils are a boon in the kitchen if you want to marinate, brown meats and braise, baste, make fried rice, cook in oil and make salad dressings. They can also be used, made in a slightly different way, in beauty preparations.

Herbs that make good culinary oils are basil, savory, fennel, thyme, rosemary and tarragon. The taste of basil goes well with tomatoes, so cook ratatouille in basil oil; fennel goes well with fish and in salads; tarragon suits fish, poultry or meats; thyme is excellent with vegetables.

If possible make your herb oils in summer as strong sunlight is needed for the aromatic oils to be extracted from the herbs.

Method Crush the freshly cut herbs in a pestle and mortar, or put them through a blender. Put two tablespoons of the pounded herbs in a 300ml/ $\frac{1}{2}$ pint ($1\frac{1}{4}$ cups) crock or wide-necked, screw-top bottle. Fill three-quarters full with sunflower, corn, vegetable or olive oil. Add one tablespoon of wine vinegar and three or four black peppercorns. Seal the bottle tightly and put it somewhere where it will receive hot sunlight. Leave it for two to three weeks, shaking the bottle once or twice a day. After this time, strain off the oil, pressing all the oil out of the crushed herbs and discard the herbs.

Repeat the process with freshly cut herbs for another three weeks. Then test to see if the oil is sufficiently saturated. A little oil on the back of the hand should really smell of the herb.

If there is not enough sunshine to bring out the flavour of the herb then you can put the crock or bottle, securely fastened of course, into a double boiler and warm it below boiling point for a few hours each day. The oil should be strong enough after seven or eight days of this treatment.

When the oil is ready, pour it through a strainer set over a funnel into a dry clean bottle. Add a sprig of the fresh herbs for decoration, tightly cork the bottle and store for use as required.

Herbal vinegars

Vinegar, like alcohol, is another good medium for absorbing the flavour and aromatic qualities of herbs. They will improve any salad dressing or marinade, particularly in winter when many fresh herbs are unobtainable. Like herbal oils they may be used as a bath additive.

Excellent vinegars can be made using the leaves of one or more of the following herbs: lemon balm, basil, borage, salad burnet, dill, fennel, marjoram, summer savory, mint, tarragon (tarragon vinegar can also be bought) and thyme. Or try mixing some of them—such as summer savory, marjoram, chives and tarragon.

Use only fresh herbs gathered according to the harvesting instructions at the beginning of this chapter. You will need about 125g/4oz (2 cups) of leaves to 1.2 litre/1 quart (5 cups) of vinegar.

You can use red or white wine vinegar, cider vinegar or malt vinegar. White wine vinegar goes well with tarragon, basil and salad burnet; cider vinegar suits mint, and red wine vinegar goes well with garlic.

Herbs add their own special flavours to cooking and salad oils and vinegar. They can be made simply by steeping the herb in oil. From left to right: thyme oil, rosemary oil and dill vinegar.

Wash and dry the leaves and pack loosely into a wide-mouthed glass jar. Pour over the vinegar and add two or three black peppercorns. Cover the jar tightly and put it where you will remember to shake it, or stir the contents with a wooden spoon, every other day.

After ten days taste it. If it is not herby enough strain out the herb leaves and discard them. Add fresh leaves and start all over again. Leave for another ten days and check again.

When the vinegar is flavoured enough, strain it into bottles through a funnel. Push in a sprig of fresh herb for decoration and cork or cap tightly.

Vinegar from seeds Herbal vinegars from coriander or dill seeds have a spicy flavour—dill tastes mildly of caraway. Bruise the seeds with a pestle and mortar. Allow two tablespoons of seeds to every 1.2 litre/1 quart (5 cups) of vinegar. Put them into a jar and pour over warmed vinegar. Cork or cover the jar tightly and put in a warm place for two weeks, shaking it from time to time. When the vinegar is ready. strain it into clean dry bottles through a funnel lined with filter paper, muslin or cheesecloth and cork tightly.

Garlic vinegar Put garlic cloves into vinegar. Leave for twenty-four hours and then remove them.

HERBS FOR EVER

The fragrance of sweet smelling herbs, spices and flowers can be captured all the year round in pot-pourri and sachets. Rooms, closets, household and personal linen can be kept fragrant and fresh with aromatic plants. You can give each drawer, closet or cupboard a distinctive scent—sweet, spicy, delicate or intoxicating—making it both a special pleasure to open it and the contents delightful to wear or use.

Herbs and flowers grow everywhere. They can be gathered and dried at home (as explained on page 44) or bought already dried at herb shops and mixed at home with essential oils and fixatives to make their scents last. It is in the subtle blending of these fragrances, and in the use of colour, that the art of making pot-pourri and herb mixtures for sachets lies.

Pot pourri

The making of pot-pourri is an old but still popular method of presenting dried flowers and leaves so that their perfume may continue to be enjoyed. Indeed, they can be made from all scented plants—flowers, fruits, herbs, barks, spices—and it is the combination of these that produces the dimly fragrant, sometimes mysterious aromas.

Each pot-pourri should have a main scent, or base, usually of rose petals to which the other ingredients are added. Obviously it is best to choose a rose which is highly scented, such as a damask rose. The dried petals should be placed in an air-tight container, and for every large handful of rose petals, a small handful of salt should be added.

Leave the salted petals for about a week, shaking or stirring them once or twice a day. Once you have a base scent, the other leaves and flowers may be added. Choose from dried flowers such as pinks, carnations, honeysuckle, orange blossom, jasmine, lavender, sweet peas, chamomile, elder, marigolds, nasturtiums, mignonette, heliotrope, lime flowers, violets, wallflowers, jonquils, lily of the valley, acacia, oleander and gardenias. Other flowers which may be added for visual effect, although they do not retain their scent, are borage and pansies.

Leaves could include those of angelica, bergamot, verbena, lovage, lavender, southernwood, bay, myrtle, sage, sweet cicely, tarragon, eucalyptus, basil, sweet marjoram, lemon and orange thyme, balm, mint and rosemary, while spices, such as cloves, nutmeg, coriander, cinnamon, mace, vanilla pod, woodruff, sandalwood and cedar also make attractive additions. Thinly pared orange and lemon peel which has been dried in a cool oven, warming drawer or any closed dry space, and then pounded in a mortar or ground, add scent and colour.

To whatever combination of ingredients you choose you can then add a few drops of essential oils, bought from a herb shop, to reinforce a particular fragrance. Finally a fixative, such as powdered orris root, is needed to hold the perfume longer than the flowers would naturally.

Fixative

	Metric/U.K.	U.S.
Oil of lavender	30ml/1floz	2 Tbs
Orris root	125g/4oz	4oz
Ground mace	25g/1oz	2 Tbs
Cloves	25g/1oz	2 Tbs
Coriander seed	25g/1oz	2 Tbs

Mix the oil into the ground orris root, and when they are thoroughly combined, add the remaining ingredients. Stir the mixture into the rose petals, cover and leave for a month, stirring occasionally. If the mixture is too dry and powdery, add more flower petals. If the mixture is too moist,

Opposite page *Making a pot-pourri enables you to capture the sweet fresh scents of summer all the year. Simple to prepare they also make marvellous presents. Numerous recipes for pot-pourri have been handed down to successive generations, but why not experiment with your own mixtures? Below Once you have made your selections of flowers and leaves for pot-pourri, you need a fixative to hold the perfume. The seed of the coriander plant is one of the ingredients in the fixative recipe given in this chapter.*

add more orris root. Finally pour the pot-pourri into a suitable container and it is ready for use.

The combinations of colour and scent are endless but there are a few recipes you may like to try. The fluid measurement refers to the amount of space the petals take up in a measuring jug or cup.

Floral pot-pourri

	Metric/U.K.	U.S.
Rose petals	1L/2pt	5 cups
Rose geranium leaves	½L/1pt	2½ cups
Lavender flowers	½L/1pt	2½ cups
Rosemary leaves	225ml/8floz	1 cup
FIXATIVE		
Ground cloves	2 Tbs	2 Tbs
Ground cinnamon	2 Tbs	2 Tbs
Grated nutmeg	2 Tbs	2 Tbs
Ground orris root	3 Tbs	3 Tbs
Ground gum benzoin	3 Tbs	3 Tbs
Oil of rose	20 drops	20 drops
Oil of sandalwood	5 drops	5 drops

Jasmine pot-pourri

	Metric/U.K.	U.S.
Jasmine flowers	½L/1pt	2½ cups
Orange blossoms	125ml/4floz	½ cup
Gardenias	125ml/4floz	½ cup
Lemon- and rose-scented geranium leaves	225ml/8floz	1 cup
FIXATIVE		
Cassia	50g/2oz	4 Tbs
Ground gum benzoin	50g/2oz	4 Tbs
Oil of vanilla	20 drops	20 drops

Containers If you are making a beautifully scented pot-pourri, the presentation is also important. Choose an attractive apothecary jar, cermic pot, china or porcelain, box or urn, and add flowers for colour rather than scent, such as borage. Pot-pourris are not only lovely to have in your own home, they make delightful and welcome presents.

Pomanders

Pomanders were originally mixtures of aromatic herbs and spices carried around in perforated boxes or spheres of gold, silver or ivory to ward off infection and the unpleasant smells that were prevalent before the days of barns and sewerage.

The word pomander is derived from the old French *pomme d'ambre*, or apple of amber. Amber probably refers to ambergris which was used as a perfume base, although it was also the name for a medieval alloy of four parts gold to one part silver.

By the late Middle Ages, the containers were elaborately chased and decorated and hung from lovely chains. It was thought in medieval and Tudor times that plague was in the air and carried on the prevailing wind— so it made sense to sniff your own private disinfectant mixture.

China pomanders Perforated china pomanders are now available in large stores and gift shops. Some of the ingredients in old pomander mixtures included cassia, cinnamon, cloves, benzoin, betel nuts, musk, frankincense and bay leaves. You can try these too and also use many other herbs and flowers (or essential oils of flowers), woods or citrus fruits to make your own old-fashioned pomander.

Pomanders can be used to scent closets, cupboards and drawers and make very attractive presents. You can make your own pomander, simply and inexpensively, by following the instructions on the opposite page.

Another version of a pomander was a scooped out orange shell filled with spices, or an orange stuck with cloves and rolled in spices. Old orange and clove pomanders still in existence are shrunk to tiny proportions and iron-hard—for the fruit dries out and shrivels but doesn't rot. You can make your own pomander, simply and inexpensively, to scent closets, cupboards and drawers, and act as a moth deterrent or to give as delightful and unusual presents. Try hanging a few on your Christmas tree, they not only look pretty, but the mixture of scents—orange, cinnamon and pine—is delicious.

Method 1

	Metric/U.K.	U.S.
Large, fresh, thin-skinned orange	1	1
One jar of whole cloves		
Ground cinnamon	2 tsp	2 tsp
Orris root powder	2 tsp	2 tsp

Make a ring of holes around the middle of the orange with a toothpick, wooden skewer, or cocktail stick; and press a whole clove into each hole, or work directly, simply pressing in cloves working in circles towards each end. The cloves should be so close together that the entire orange skin is covered.

Mix together the cinnamon and orris root powder. Roll the clove-studded orange thoroughly in the mixture so that as much of it is taken up as possible. Wrap in tissue paper and put in a dark, dry drawer for three to five weeks. During this time the orange will dry through completely and shrink slightly.

Take the orange out and shake off any surplus powder. The pomander is now ready for use.

Orris root Orris root powder is the ground, dried root of a variety of iris *Iris florentina*. The powder does have a delicate perfume but its chief purpose is as a fixative for the other scents. It is available from herb shops but can be omitted without ill effect.

To make a be-ribboned pomander
It is possible simply to tie ribbon around the orange leaving a loop at the top for hanging, or to insert a loop of ribbon through a staple pressed into the top of the orange. For a smoother effect, however, leave two channels in the orange, wide enough to lay a ribbon in, when you are sticking in the cloves. This way the cloved pomander will be dried into four sections, as shown in fig. 1a.

When you have completed studding the orange and left it to dry out, cut one piece of ribbon long enough to go around the circumference of the orange, and pin the ends together at the top with dressmaking pins. Cut a second piece of ribbon, that measures the circumference of the orange plus enough to make a bow or a loop with which to hang up the pomander (fig. 1b) and tie it to the pomander, fitting the ribbon around the remaining channel.

Use velvet ribbon in old-fashioned shades of soft pink, crimson, or braid two or three ribbons together.

Floral pomander In addition to cloves, you can also use fresh flowers to decorate the pomander, such as rosebuds, jasmine or sprigs of lavender.

It is reassuring to note that the orange will not rot but become petrified and shrink slightly. The fragrance lasts for several years, and although we cannot pretend that it will protect you from infections, we are sure that it will give you pleasure.

Fig 1a: *To make a be-ribboned pomander, two channels, wide enough to lay a ribbon in, should be left when you are sticking in the cloves. Fig 1b. When the orange is completely studded, cut one piece of ribbon the same length as the circumference of the orange, attach and fasten with pins. Cut a second length long enough to make a bow or loop with which to hang it, and tie it around the remaining channel.*

Fig 1a

Fig 1b

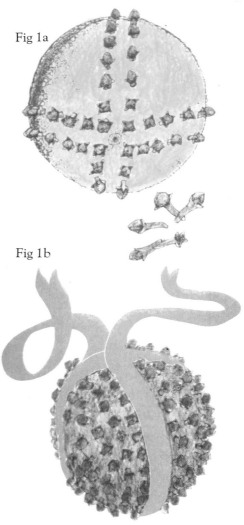

Presentation is part of the delight of herbs. While the delicate colouring of pot-pourri should be visible, the fragrance of herbal pillows is emphasized by floral printed casing, and a bit of lace adds freshness to sachets.

Herb pillows

For dreams of summer why not slip a herb pillow into your pillowcase? Herb pillows have been used since Victorian days to soothe the nerves and to induce a refreshing sleep. Indeed, the clean, fresh scent of a little lavender cushion tucked behind the head was held to be an excellent cure for the vapours.

The simplest way to provide yourself with a herb pillow is to make a bag of whatever size you require out of cotton, linen, cheesecloth or muslin, to hold the herbs. Then make a cover for it that can be laundered in sprigged cotton, or white embroidery on white cotton, or perhaps in gay, bold stripes or other patterns. Then fill the inside bag with soporific and sweet-smelling *dried* herbs from the following collection of mixtures.

Mixture 1 Use equal quantities of lavender, lemon verbena and peppermint for an aromatic base. In addition, for sleep-inducing properties, add small quantities of any of the following herbs—all of which are pleasantly scented and will blend well together: angelica, bergamot, dill, hops, balm, marjoram, rosemary, sage or thyme.

Mixture 2 Mix together equal parts of rosemary blossoms, rosemary leaves, pine needles, rose geranium leaves and balm.

Mixture 3 Mix together equal parts of rose petals and lavender, and add small amounts of woodruff, chamomile, dill, sage, bergamot and tarragon.

Mixture 4 Use hops only. Many people feel a hops pillow is best for insomnia.

Herb sachets

Smaller bags, enclosing the same herbs as those used in herbal pillows, not only scent cupboards and drawers but also act as moth deterrents. The addition of a dried stalk or two of southernwood or wormwood is particularly good for repelling moths as well as giving a subtle aromatic scent. It is interesting to note that the French name for southernwood is *garderobe*.

Sachets can be made of small squares of silk, printed cotton or organdie, and treated as miniature pillows, or they can be gathered across the top and secured with a ribbon. This method means that they can be refilled later on. Fill either with mixtures of herbs as suggested for pillows, or simply one herb, such as lemon verbena or lavender, or try some of the following mixtures.

Mixture 1 Equal quantities of tansy, rosemary and southernwood or wormwood plus 15g/½oz of ground cloves. This is both sweet-scented and moth repelling.

Mixture 2 Equal quantities of santolina (cotton lavender, or santonica), wormwood, mint and tansy plus a crushed cinnamon stick. Mix well and add a little dried lemon or orange peel. This mixture also acts as an insect repellent.

Mixture 3 Equal quantities of southernwood or wormwood and balm, with twice the amount of rose petals, and twice as much again of lavender. A few crushed coriander seeds, cloves or cinnamon can be added.

Lavender bags

This pretty selection of lavender cushions has a general theme in terms of colour but variety is achieved with the use of different, lightweight fabrics.

Each completed cushion measures about 7cm (3in) square, except for the gathered-up sachets, which are rectangular in shape. (If you choose a fabric with an open weave you will also need lining fabric.) Cut out a back and front from the fabric, with a small seam allowance on each side. Embroider fabric with cross stitch, satin stitch, leaf or running stitch in contrasting threads. Alternatively, sew on trimmings such as lace or rickrack.

With right sides facing, sew the two pieces together leaving one side open. Turn sachet right side out and fill with lavender. Whip stitch open side seams together.

Note that the gathered-up sachets have been back stitched; in one example a frayed edge has been introduced.

For further finishing touches add bows or fabric flowers, as appropriate.

Lavender bags provide an attractive way of scenting your clothes and linen. Small pieces of fabric left over from making dresses and furnishings are ideal for this purpose.

HERBS FOR GARDENS & POTS

Herbs are pretty, aromatic, useful and above all fun to grow. Nearly all herbs grow best in the open ground, with a few exceptions they also do well in containers and tubs, and most can be grown successfully indoors as well.

Herbs in the garden

There is room in every garden to grow a few herbs. If you do not have enough room to devote one specific area to herbs, they are quite happy to grow among vegetables, fruit and flowers. If you do have more space then a herb garden is a delight. They need not be large, but they should be enclosed, by a wall or hedging, or in a sheltered position and the plants spaced out. Herb gardens are very pleasant to sit in or walk through, occasionally picking a leaf and crushing it to release its perfume. On hot days, the aromatic scent of the herbs will permeate the whole garden.

The idea that herb gardens need be near the kitchen may be ignored. Choose the most suitable place and if you have to change your footwear to pick them this isn't really very serious. It is more important that your garden should look neat and that you are able to reach each plant to pick it with ease. This can be achieved by dividing the garden into squares, in a checkerboard design and separating one herb from the next with squares of stone or brick. Or you may choose to arrange them in the traditional wheel pattern, in which case the spokes could be defined in gravel paths. (A sundial or rose or bay tree in the centre looks very attractive.) Paths of chamomile, creeping thyme or pennyroyal are also attractive and produce a delicious scent when walked on. The design may be bold or formal so long as it is functional as well as decorative.

Divisions between herbs also prevent plants getting mixed up, so if you do not like the idea of stones or bricks you could cultivate small, low-growing hedges of rosemary or lavender. These, however, need regular clipping to keep them neat.

Planning a herb garden Any herb garden, whether it is a simple border or based on the more complicated Elizabethan designs, needs careful thought. You must know about the heights and growing habits of the plants, otherwise your tall subjects may be planted in the front of the bed, or near to and smothering the short or creeping herbs. Similarly, different herbs have different requirements in terms of liking sun or shade, heavy or light soil. All these details are specified individually in the growing section of this book, so only general requirements will be referred to here.

Situation and soil Most herbs come originally from the Mediterranean countries, where they grow in dry, poor and sometimes rocky soil. So unless your climate and soil are similar, choose a sheltered spot facing the sun for your herb garden and make sure that the soil is well-drained. Herbs will usually grow in most soils except for heavy clay. If possible it is a good idea to have the ground sloping slightly towards the south as this helps with drainage. Then herbs that need sun can be planted at the top of the slope, and those that prefer a damper, shadier spot can be put in the bottom.

Which herbs to grow This is, of course, a question of personal taste and the size of the proposed herb garden. Also you may wish to grow them for a specific use, either for cooking, cosmetics, for their scent or for their medicinal use, but a small selection of the better known herbs, both annuals and perennials, will give you a useful stock for cooking. If you wish to attract bees, butterflies and other pollen-collecting insects, then

Opposite page *The John Blair Herb Garden in Williamsburg, USA, was designed in 1937 as part of the colonial restoration of this village, which is why it has the simple formality reminiscent of much older, traditional gardens.* Below *Although rue is now grown principally for its decorative qualities, it was once regarded as being both beneficial to the eyesight and as a protection from plague and jail fever. Sprigs of rue were always included in the small bouquets of flowers, called tussie-mussies, carried by judges in the law courts. Its inclusion was in no way due to its perfume, however, which, to say the least, is unpleasant.*

Below Used as a garnish and flavouring throughout the world, parsley is in constant demand by cooks everywhere. It will grow successfully both indoors and outside and is an attractive as well as a useful herb.
Centre Angelica growing in a pretty and informal setting
Bottom A traditional herb garden where the plants are decoratively separated by low-growing hedges and brick paths.

grow flowering herbs such as lavender, thyme, savory, hyssop and bergamot. All such features are mentioned under the individual growing specifications of each herb.

Preparing the soil The better prepared the bed is the better the garden will be. The soil, of whatever type, should be well dug, a certain amount of compost worked in, given a final raking and firmed. Do all this in the early autumn and then give the bed a final dig in the spring prior to planting.

Growing from seed Some herbs, the annuals and those which will self-seed but for the purposes of cultivation are treated as annuals, are freshly grown from seed each spring.

Sow the seeds as soon as the danger of frost is over. (Most seed packets from reputable seed companies have good directions on them.) Water the soil. Sow the seeds thinly—otherwise the seedlings will choke each other as they try to grow—and then press the soil down lightly with a board.

The seeds can be sown where the plants are to grow—*Anthriscus cerefolium* (chervil), for example, hates being moved—and then thinned out to the required distance apart when the seedlings are 5-8cm (2-3in) high. Alternatively, sow them in seed mixture in a seed box, and plant the seedlings out when they are large enough to handle.

If you have a greenhouse or frame you can sow many of the annuals a month early so as to be ready for planting outside when there is no longer any danger of frost.

In dry periods the seedlings need almost constant attention, and careful watering with a fine rose on the watering can. Hand weeding between the tiny plants is important, too.

Many of the annual herbs only take from two to three months to flower, and if planted out at the beginning of the summer, will be ready to harvest at the end of it. *Borago officinalis* (borage) and *Satureia hortensis* (savory) ripen particularly quickly (and borage will seed itself happily all over the garden).

If you feel growing from seed entails too much time and trouble, do not despair, many of these annual herbs, like the perennials, can be bought as plants. Indeed, in temperate climes you may have no alternative to buying small plants for such herbs as French tarragon.

Growing plants and cuttings The perennial herbs, and the annuals, too, if you prefer, are bought as plants or cuttings and put directly into the bed during the summer. Dig a hole with a trowel and if it is dry, fill the whole with water. Put in the plant and firm the soil back down around it so that it is well anchored in case of rain or gale. For the first two weeks protect the young plants from sun and wind and water them carefully every evening.

Care Weeding is even more important in a herb garden than in a flower garden. Each plant, clump, or row must stand alone. They need to be kept neat with no weeds or grass growing near. Label any perennial plants which are going to die down in the winter—or you may forget where they are. Water according to the plants' needs but remember that in very hot weather succulent herbs like mint and chives will need watering three times a day, although normally they would only require watering twice a week; and herbs like sage will need watering every other day in dry weather. In cooler climates, delicate perennials will need mulching to protect them from severe frost.

Growing herbs in containers Position the container in the sun or shade according to the preference of the herb you intend to grow in it. Make sure there are plenty of drainage holes and place a layer of broken clay flower pots or shards in the bottom. Fill to within 2.5cm (1in) with a mixture of five parts garden soil, two parts compost and one and a half parts each of peat and sand. Topdress once a month with organic fertiliser and make sure the plants have plenty of root room. Water according to the plants' needs—overwatering can kill them.

Growing herbs indoors

For those people without a garden, it is perfectly possible to grow most herbs in pots or window boxes. Growing herbs indoors has the added advantage of enabling some herbs to grow all year round which, in cooler climates, would only flourish outdoors in the summer. Although the individual requirements of each herb regarding position, soil type, watering and feeding are given later in the book, here is some general advice.

Which herbs to grow Low-growing herbs are most suitable for pots and window boxes. These could include the following: thyme, tarragon, basil, rosemary, geraniums, chives, mint, parsley, marjoram, oregano and pennyroyal. Larger herbs, such as sage, fennel and borage will tend to become dwarfed naturally if grown in a restricted area. Herbs with a wandering root, such as mint, lemon balm and tarragon need to be grown in individual pots, which can then be placed in a window box.

Position Herbs should be placed in a south- or west-facing window that gets plenty of sun and light. If you turn them around 45° every day they shouldn't become too tall and weedy, or deformed in shape through growing constantly towards the light.

The temperature of the room should not fall below 10°C (50°F) or exceed 16°C (60°F) at night. Herbs do not like sudden changes of temperature, and therefore they should not really be grown in a kitchen.

If your rooms receive little light, this can be achieved with the aid of overhead mercury fluorescent lamps, but natural light is preferable.

Herbs also need plenty of air. Ventilation is particularly necessary if you have gas central heating, but remember that they do not like draughts. If you have a roof, balcony or patio, try to put them outside whenever it is warm. Before balancing pots on window sills, however, check that it is not too windy. A potted plant falling from a great height can be a lethal missile.

Soil The soil for herbs in pots or window boxes is very important. Get a special bag of potting mixture from a nursery or gardening shop, stating what you want it for. A good potting mixture for herbs is one made up of equal parts of sand, leaf mould and soil, although a bay tree is happier in a pot of rich soil. Fill pots or boxes up to 1cm (½in) of the top to leave room for water.

Planting You can now buy ready-to-germinate herbs in small peat pots which make herb gardening even simpler. If these are unobtainable then they may be grown from seed or cuttings according to the instructions in the section on growing herbs outside. Buying small plants, although slightly more expensive, does, of course, produce quicker results. Ordinary clay pots are perfectly suitable so long as you remember to put some broken pots or shards in the bottom to provide good drainage.

Care Apart from ensuring that the temperature is reasonably even and that they are well ventilated the other important points are watering and feeding. Each plant has its individual requirements but watering should also take into account the season and the indoor temperature. Never leave your plants permanently wet and soggy, and allow the soil almost to dry out between waterings. Feed regularly with liquid organic fertiliser, following the manufacturer's instructions carefully. As soon as the roots begin to protrude through the drainage holes, transfer the herb to a larger pot.

Harvesting Never remove more than a fifth of the leaves from one plant at a time and make sure that new leaf growth has begun to form before cutting again.

This rule does not, however, apply to chives, of which all the leaves may be cut at once, so it is a good idea to grow more than one pot.

Finally, although some care and attention is obviously required to grow herbs indoors, the results are extremely rewarding. Healthy herbs look superb and provide you with attractive, aromatic houseplants—as well as being extremely useful.

Herbs grown indoors should be placed in a window which receives as much natural light as possible. Try to remember to turn the plants around completely every day as all plants grow towards the light. If you have access to a patio or balcony, your herbs will benefit from being set outside on warm, sunny days. When harvesting herbs in pots, never remove more than one fifth of the total number of leaves, and wait for new leaf growth to appear before you cut them again.

WILD HERBS

'Anything green that grows out of the mould
Was an excellent herb to our fathers of old.'

Rudyard Kipling

Almost any piece of uncultivated land, whether it is a wood or a building site, will yield wild plants which contain both nutritional and healing properties. Alas, when they appear on cultivated land, such as in the garden, we tend to destroy them on the pretext that they are weeds. These properties, and the knowledge of how to use them, were well known to our ancestors, but it is only in recent years that, as research laboratories confirm scientifically what was once learnt through experience and inherited knowledge, we have also been able to make use of the same information. Indeed, many previously 'wild' herbs are now being cultivated for the drug market and are also available in herbalist stores.

However tempting the idea may be of gathering your own herbs from the veritable medicine chest in hedgerows, meadows and fields do be careful. It is important to distinguish between those plants which are good for us and those which are not (if not actively poisonous), and to avoid selecting those plants which have been made harmful by pollution from cars and factories, and from the poisonous chemicals that may have been sprayed on them. Always arm yourself with a good illustrated reference book, and do not risk picking herbs where crop spraying has been going on. If in any doubt about a plant, leave it. A good herbalist will stock many dried wild herbs and should also be able to supply you with the relevant information on how to use them.

However, as collecting wild fruits and berries is becoming an increasingly popular activity, here is a list of the easiest to come by and recognise.

Achilla millefolium
YARROW

Yarrow is one of the most useful of wild herbs as it is an all round remedy, strengthener and antiseptic. It has feathery leaves on tough, ribbed stems and dense, flat clusters of small white, or occasionally pink, flowers. It will grow almost anywhere and assists other plants nearby as it helps them to resist disease. Yarrow grows to a height of 45-60cm (18-24in). The leaves may be used fresh or dried to make tea which helps rheumatism and the circulation. Fresh, young yarrow leaves may be chopped and added to salads and sandwiches. Warmed, and made into a poultice, the leaves were also used to staunch wounds.

Agrimonia eupatoria
AGRIMONY

A common, perennial weed, found in Europe, Asia and Africa, agrimony was used in the past to treat and heal wounds. It grows 60cm (2ft) tall with hairy, pinnate leaves and small yellow flowers in spikes. The infused leaves are a tonic and said to be good for coughs and to purify the blood.

From the time of the ancient Greeks, agrimony (also known as church' steeples) has been valued for its medicinal properties, and Culpeper admired its sweet and fruity scent.

Alchemilla vulgaris
LADY'S MANTLE

This pretty, little, low perennial grows in clumps and is found in Europe, Asia and North America. It was a wound herb. The leaves are kidney-shaped and downy, and the small flowers are yellowish green.

The leaves are used and cut when the plant is flowering to be dried and used as a tisane. It is recommended to be taken during the mentrual cycle and pregnancy, and it is also a general tonic. As a skin tonic it is effective against freckles and acne, and the mixture is 1-2 teaspoons of the dried or fresh leaves to a cup of water steeped for ten minutes.

It is easily grown from seed and when established will spread itself readily.

Artemisia vulgaris
MUGWORT

An aromatic plant with dark green, finely cut, downy leaves, dark red stems and small greyish flowers. Mugwort grows to a height of 90-120cm (3-4ft) and is found in fields and hedgerows. The leaves are used, fresh or dried, both cooked with fatty foods like goose and eel and to make a tea which is taken for rheumatism and female complaints. A strong infusion dabbed on the skin is said to repel insects.

Betonica officinalis
BETONY

Betony is a perennial plant found growing wild in woods and hedgerows.

Top and centre Lady's mantle was once known as the 'alchemist's herb' and considered to have almost magical healing properties. Reaching a height of 15-45cm (6-18in) it has yellow-green flowers and is found growing in soil which is moist but well-drained. Above Mugwort grows to a height of about 90cm (3ft). The flower shoots are cut from mid to late summer and the buds used as a seasoning.

It has hairy, toothed leaves and crimson flowers. The tea made from it is aromatic and astringent.

Centaurea cyanus
CORNFLOWER

These familiar, blue-flowered plants may be seen growing wild in corn fields, or cultivated in gardens as pretty summer annuals. The flowers have no scent but are used dried to give colour to *pot-pourri* and also to make an infusion with which to bathe the eyes.

Euphrasia officinalis
EYEBRIGHT

Found growing on dry heaths, pastures, and other poor-soiled open areas of land, eyebright is a small, annual plant about 15cm (6in) high. The tiny flowers are white or lilac, and it needs to grow amongst grass or other plants as it depends on their roots for nourishment. Its use is medicinal. The whole plant is pressed and the juice extracted and used to make an eye lotion.

Hypericum perforatum
ST. JOHN'S WORT

Also known as ragwort, this herbaceous perennial has bright golden, fringed flowers and toothed leaves and grows to 90cm (3ft) high. In the past St. John's wort was thought to keep away evil. St. John himself was also patron saint of horses, and an infusion of leaves was used as a remedy for equine diseases. Nowadays the oil is used to help heal rheumatism, strains, insect bites and bruises, while a tea made from the leaves is said to alleviate fever, depression and insomnia.

Meliotus officinalis
MELILOT

A tall annual with leaves in groups of three and spikes of small, yellow flowers, melilot is found growing in hedgerows and fields all over Europe and Asia. The leaves have a scent reminiscent of newly mown hay, which becomes more intense when dried. Consequently, the dried leaves are sometimes added to *pot-pourri* as well as for making tisanes. The leaves may also be used to give flavour to marinades and dishes made with rabbit or cheese.

Menyanthes trifoliata
BUCK BEAN

Also called bog bean and water or marsh trefoil, this is an aquatic plant found growing on the muddy fringes of pools and ponds and in marshy places. It has clusters of pink, lily-shaped flowers and grows wild in North

America, and in the cooler parts of Asia and Europe. The leaves may be made into a tisane or the roots cooked as a vegetable. It is mainly of medicinal value and used to be recommended as a cure for scurvy.

Plantago major
PLANTAIN

A common, perennial weed in lawns, plantain produces flat rosettes of leaves and spikes of pinky-purple flowers. Both the seeds and leaves are eaten for their medicinal value. The leaves may be applied direct to wounds and stings, and also made into a tea which acts as a diuretic.

Sambucus nigra
ELDER

The elder bush or tree varies in height between 3-10m (9-30ft) and is found growing along hedges and in fields. It is an elegant plant, with cork-like bark, delicate leaves and flat clusters of sweet-smelling, lacy, cream flowers from which develop the rich, dark red berries in the autumn. All parts of the elder are rich in vitamins and capable of utilization. The flowers are used for wine and tea, for cosmetics and lotions; the berries for wine, sauces, jellies and puddings, where they can be used as a substitute for currants, and to cure neuralgia; the roots can be made into an infusion and used as a laxative; and a juice can be extracted from the bark and leaves to use as a dye.

Sedum acre
STONECROP

Stonecrop is a succulent which is found growing wild in rocky and stony places throughout the world but may also be cultivated as a house-plant. It is a low-growing perennial with tiny, yellow flowers. The fresh leaves are too bitter to use, but dried they make an excellent substitute for pepper.

Smyrnium oluestratum
ALEXANDER

A biennial of medium height with yellow-green umbels and small, black, ripe seeds, stonecrop can be found growing on wasteland, particularly near the sea, in most countries. The young shoots and leaf stems have a celery-like taste and may be cooked as a vegetable. At one time it was widely cultivated as a pot herb and is a useful addition to soups and stews.

Spiraea ulmaria
MEADOW SWEET

A common, perennial plant with serrated leaves, clusters of small, creamy, sweet-smelling flowers and red stems, meadow sweet can be found growing wild in marshy fields and along river banks in Asia, Europe and America. In the Middle Ages it was a popular strewing herb, but nowadays the

Top *There are about 260 varieties of plantain, mainly small plants under 15cm(6in) high with tiny, insignificant flowers. Once prized as a herb with healing properties, plantain is now, alas, almost universally regarded as a weed.* Above *Elder berries are picked in early autumn and used for wine-making and in jams and tarts with apple.*

Top and above *Dandelions are very nutritious and, with their distinctive flowers, are easily recognizable. The flowers may be used for making wine, and the leaves used fresh in salads or fresh or dried for tisanes, while the ground, roasted roots are used as a substitute for coffee.*

leaves are generally made into a tisane which acts as a diuretic and is reputedly good for colds.

Stellaria media
CHICKWEED

A ubiquitous annual found growing all over the temperate world, chickweed is generally regarded as a weed. It is a low, sprawling plant with white flowers which seeds itself and flowers again so quickly that it is about virtually throughout the year. Full of nutrients, the whole plant may be chopped and added to salads and sandwiches. It has a salty, fresh flavour and may also be cooked and served as a vegetable. Chickweed acts as a diuretic and made into an ointment is said to cure chilblains.

Taraxacum officinale
DANDELION

A distinctive plant about 25cm (10in) high with green serrated leaves and spiky yellow flowers, the dandelion is easily recognized. It is very nutritious and contains vitamins, proteins and minerals, so it is fortunate that dandelion is a perennial and found growing almost everywhere. The leaves may be used raw in salads or cooked as a vegetable, and to make dandelion and burdock wine. The roots are toasted and used as a substitute for coffee. The creamy white liquid exuded by the whole plant can be made into a tisane, which like the teas made from the leaves, is good for digestive upsets and for rheumatism.

Tussilago farfara
COLTSFOOT

One of the prettiest of weeds, coltsfoot is a hardy perennial found growing on wasteland in towns, banks and ditches—in fact, anywhere. It has fringed, yellow, daisy flowers on scaly stalks which appear in spring and fragrant leaves which do not appear until after the flowers have died. Coltsfoot is rich in vitamin C (but was used as a medicinal herb long before people understood nutritional values). Both the leaves and the flowers may be dried and used in wine or to make tisanes. The Latin name for coltsfoot means 'cough' and an infusion of the leaves of this plant is one of the oldest remedies for catarrh, coughs and other similar chest complaints.

Urtica dioica
NETTLE

One of the commonest and easily recognized of weeds throughout the temperate regions of the world, the nettle has many medicinal and nutritional properties. The plants are about 1-1.5m (3-5ft) high, perennial and have dark green leaves covered with stinging hairs. They thrive almost anywhere but particularly where the soil is rich in nitrogen. The young leaves have a salty flavour and may be added to salads after blanching, or boiled as a vegetable. Fresh or dried the leaves make an excellent tisane which acts as a blood purifier and, because they contain vitamin C, as a preventative against colds.

A CONCISE HERBAL

Allium sativum

GARLIC

Garlic is not a herb in the botanical sense of the word, being a member of the onion group and therefore a vegetable. However, because of its use in cooking and medicine it is treated as such. The plant has long, flat leaves and a bunch of small, white, star-shaped flowers at the top of each flower stem. The bulb is a collection of 'cloves' held together by the outer skin. A garlic plant reaches a height of about 30cm (12in).

Soil Well-drained, rich.

Position Full sun.

Planting and cultivation Split a garlic bulb into cloves and plant each clove, pointed end up, 5cm (2in) deep and 20cm (8in) apart. Leave 30cm (12in) between each row. Weed well by hand.

Harvesting In later summer, when the stems and leaves have lost their greenness and have toppled over, lift the garlic bulbs with a fork and spread them out in a warm, dry, sunny place to dry and ripen off. Don't try to pull them out, as any damage done to the stems tends to cause the bulbs to rot. After several days, store the garlic bulbs in string bags and use as required.

Propagation From cloves saved from previous year's crop.

Pot growth Not suitable.

Uses Medicinally garlic is reputed to aid the digestion, reduce high blood pressure, expel catarrh from the chest and act as an antiseptic. Except when boiled, garlic is strong so use with discretion in cooking. It is used crushed in salad dressings and crushed or whole in meat, fish, poultry dishes, soups, stews and vegetable dishes. The mainstay of much Italian cooking and also French, it is particularly used in combination with parsley, with which it has a great affinity.

The attractive pinky-purple flowers of the chive plant are normally cut off in order to promote the growth of new leaves.

Allium schoenoprasum

CHIVES

Like garlic, the chive is a member of the onion group but again is treated as a herb. This hardy perennial is native to the temperate climes of Europe and North America. It has thin, hollow, grass-like leaves, reaching about 25cm (10in) in height, and pretty, pinky-purple flowers. The leaves have the most delicate flavour of any member of the onion family. The clumps grow from clusters of tiny, flat bulbs.

Soil Rich, moist alkaline soils.

Position Semi-shade.

Planting and cultivation Easily grown from seeds sown in spring or early summer in drills 1cm ($\frac{1}{2}$in) deep and 30cm (12in) apart. Thin seedlings to 15cm (6in) apart. Do not allow the plant to flower if you want a continual source of fresh leaves. Water well and give a little organic fertilizer from time to time.

Harvesting Cut the leaves with scissors as and when they are needed to about 3cm (1in) above soil level. Cut clumps in succession to ensure a constant supply. Chives do not dry well but freeze successfully.

Propagation Multiplies rapidly underground. Every three to four years divide during the autumn into clumps of about six bulblets and replant.

Pot growth Grows well in pots, needing one with an ultimate diameter of 18cm (7in).

Uses In cooking, wherever a mild oniony taste is required; in salads, cheese or egg dishes, over soups and cooked vegetables, especially new and jacket potatoes and even on bread and butter. Use generously with any except the most delicate of vegetables.

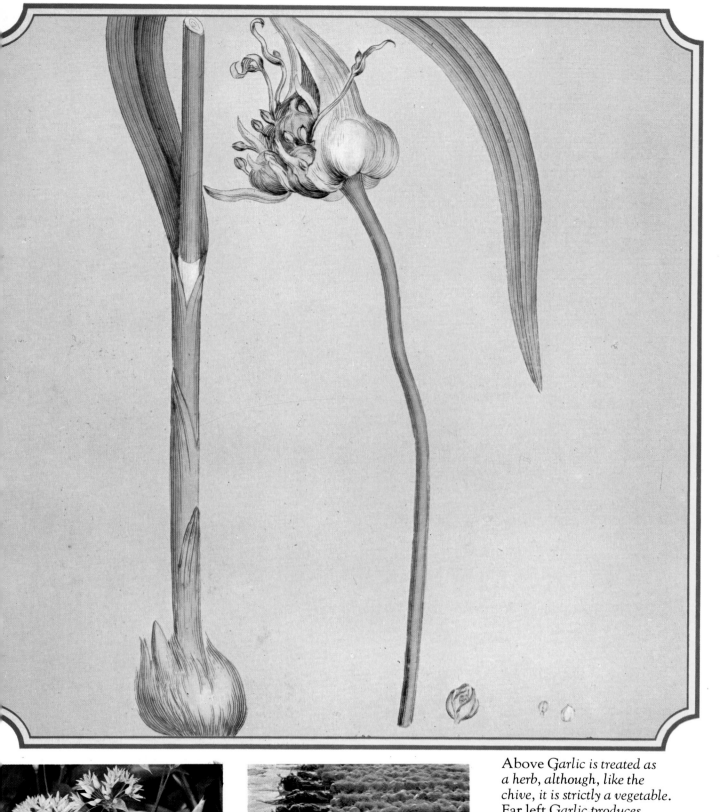

Above Garlic is treated as a herb, although, like the chive, it is strictly a vegetable. Far left Garlic produces bunches of small white flowers at the top of each flower stem. Left To harvest garlic, the whole plant should be carefully lifted with a fork and spread out in a warm, sunny place to dry and ripen off.

Plate 496.

The angelica plant is one of the tallest of herbs, reaching a height of about 2m (6ft). It has large serrated leaves with an attractive scent and strong, ridged stems. Towards the end of summer, it produces beautiful umbels of flowers which are particularly unusual in that they are yellow-green in colour.

Angelica archangelica

ANGELICA

One of the tallest and most decorative of herbs, angelica is a biennial that becomes almost a perennial if the seeds are allowed to sow themselves. It grows to about 2m (6ft) high and has large indented leaves with a strong fragrance and strong, ridged stems. Beautiful umbels of green flowers appear in late summer.

Soil A rich, moist soil.

Position Semi-shady and open. Angelica withstands moderate frosts.

66

The leaves of the angelica plant can be made into a tisane and either drunk or applied to the face as a skin tonic. The stems are candied and used for decoration and flavouring and should be cut before the plant flowers.

Planting and cultivation Seeds sown in late summer will produce stalks for candying by the following summer when fresh seeds may be sown. Plants which are allowed to flower and seed themselves will soon produce seedlings to plant out the following spring. Angelica plants should be watered regularly and the soil dressed with compost. If the stems need to develop further before they are ready for harvesting, then the flowers should be removed, as once the plant has flowered it dies.

Harvesting Cut leaves as required during the early summer. The stems should be harvested before the plant flowers.

Propagation By root division and sowing seeds.

Uses The leaves, fresh or dried, may be infused in boiling water for a tisane or as a basis for a skin tonic. The dried leaves also make an attractive and fragrant addition to *pot-pourris*. The stems may be candied and then used both for cake decoration and to flavour food, such as jam. Infusions of angelica were also reputed to be a protection against the plague and dog bites.

Anthriscus cerefolium
CHERVIL

Although an annual, by successional sowing, fresh chervil may be harvested for most of the year. Similar in appearance to parsley but more delicate, it

Chervil is similar in appearance to parsley but is more delicate and fern-like. The fresh, green leaves, with their slight flavour of aniseed, may be substituted for parsley or chives and sprinkled over salads and soups. It is one of the principal ingredients of fines herbes and is used with egg, cheese and fish dishes and in liqueurs.

has pale green, fern-like leaves and small white flowers, and reaches a height of about 60cm (2ft). The leaves have a slightly sweet flavour of aniseed and it is a particulatrly popular herb in France. It dislikes hot, dry climates.

Soil Most soils that are light and moist but well drained.

Position Chervil prefers semi-shade in the heat of the summer and full sun in the spring and autumn.

Planting and cultivation Sow a little seed from early spring onwards at regular intervals. The plants take about four weeks to mature. Press the seed gently into the ground in drills about 30cm (12in) apart. Thin the seedlings to 20cm (5in) apart. Always keep slightly moist. To prevent chervil running to seed too quickly, try to pick off any flowers as they appear.

Harvesting The leaves are ready to pick about six weeks after sowing; pick before the flowers bloom. Not suitable for drying.

Propagation By seed.

Pot growth Grows well in pots or window boxes, provided it is kept moist.

Uses Use the leaves generously in cooking wherever you would use parsley. Chervil is best added to food at the last moment. It is an important constituent of *fines herbes* and sometimes of *bouquet garni*. It is particularly good in salads, soups, dressings and in fish and egg dishes.

Finely chopped and warmed, and then applied as a poultice to bruises and sprained joints, chervil leaves are said to relieve pain.

Artemisia abrotanum
SOUTHERNWOOD

Southernwood is a perennial shrub with beautiful, silvery-grey foliage. The dried leaves and stems not only smell lovely but also repel insects such as moths. Consequently, these are often put in sachets and used to protect and scent clothes and linen.

Also known as lad's love, this small perennial shrub can reach a height of 90cm (3ft). It is a native of southern France where it can be found growing wild. It has a woody stem and feathery, grey-green leaves covered with down. The flowers, which rarely appear in temperate climes, are yellow. The leaves of southernwood have a highly attractive aroma and a bitter lemon taste. Southernwood was traditionally grown in herb gardens to keep witches out but nowadays is grown mostly for its appearance.

Soil Sandy, light and well drained.

Position Sunny.

Planting and cultivation Plant in late autumn or early spring and leave 38cm (15in) between each plant. Each spring the plant should be pruned to within two buds from the ground.

Harvesting Cut branches at the end of summer and dry them.

Propagation Take 25cm (10in) cuttings in spring.

Pot growth Will grow well in tubs and is suitable for towns as it is not adversely affected by fumes.

Uses Southernwood is rarely used in cooking although the shoots are occasionally added to cakes. The dried stems are, however, put in bags and used in clothes' cupboards to repel moths or as an ingredient of *pot-pourri*. Infused in boiling water, southernwood makes a refreshing tisane which acts as a tonic and is reputed to cure worms. The leaves of this plant should never be eaten as they are very poisonous.

Artemisia dracunculus
TARRAGON

Both varieties of tarragon, French (*A. dracunculus*) and Russian (*A. dracunculoides*) are shrubby perennials which become larger each year. French tarragon is slightly more difficult to grow but has a far superior taste to that of Russian and so is the only one worth growing. French tarragon comes from the Middle East and grows to a height of about 1m (3ft). The French variety has widely spaced leaves on the stems from which the clusters of whitish flowers also grow. The leaves are smoother, darker and shinier than those of Russian tarragon.

Soil Light and well drained.

Position Full sun.

Planting and cultivation French tarragon can almost never be grown from seed but only from root divisions or cuttings. Plant these in the spring, when there is no danger of frost, about 45-60cm (18-24in) apart. The root system becomes quite large so the plants need a lot of room. Protect plants from frost in winter. French tarragon deteriorates after about four years so plants should be divided and replanted, or replaced by new plants, after this time.

Harvesting Use fresh leaves as required in the summer and autumn. Cut stems for drying in mid-summer.

Propagation By root division or cuttings.

Pot growth Can be grown successfully indoors in pots with an ultimate diameter of 30cm (12in). Care must be taken, however, to ensure good drainage. Tarragon will not tolerate wet roots.

Uses The leaves are one of the main ingredients in Béarnaise, Hollandaise and Tartare sauces. They are also excellent cooked or raw with chicken, fish, some salads, tomato soup and some meats and vegetables. Tarragon leaves are, of course, used in tarragon vinegar, and also in several stuffings, in *fines herbes*, marinades and with egg dishes. Excessive use of dried tarragon can produce a slightly bitter flavour.

Asperula odorata
WOODRUFF

A low, carpeting perennial with ruff-like leaves in whorls and white, star-shaped flowers. It grows 15-30cm (6-12in) high in shady woodland. Woodruff has shiny leaves and a scent like that of freshly mown hay.

Soil Damp and full of humus—like that found in a wood.

Position Shady, under trees and bushes.

Planting and cultivation As the seeds can take as long as a year to germinate, it is more satisfactory to plant rootstock or young plants in spring with 20cm (8in) spaces between them. Once established it will form a carpet and as it is self-seeding will not need replacing.

Harvesting The plants develop their full scent when first picked and beginning to dry. Sprigs should be picked in spring before or during flowering and dried at a low temperature so that they stay green. Use fresh leaves as required.

Propagation By seed and root division.

Pot growth Quite suitable if the plant is kept moist and shaded.

Uses Woodruff leaves are added to summer drinks, such as fruit cups, white wine and apple juice. It is also made into tisanes and is supposed to lift the spirits. Like southernwood, woodruff can be strewn amongst linen both for its attractive fragrance and for its power to repel insects.

The fresh leaves of the borage plant, with their faint cucumber like flavour, are added to cold, summer drinks, especially Pimms, and to salads.

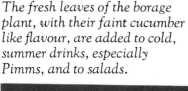

Borago officinalis
BORAGE

The name is derived from the latin *burra*, meaning rough hair. This refers to the rough hairs on the stems and large, grey-green leaves of the plant. Borage, a sturdy annual, originates from the Mediterranean, and grows to a height of about 60-90cm (2-3ft) tall. It has vivid blue flowers which grow in drooping clusters and is very attractive to bees. Both the flowers and the leaves are edible, the leaves having a faint cucumber-like flavour.

Soil Most soils, but preferably chalky or sandy.

Position Sunny.

Planting and cultivation The seeds should be grown at 45cm (18in) intervals in spring and covered well with soil. They germinate quickly and reach maturity within five to six weeks. Once the plants are established they sow themselves so there is no need to replace plants. Borage plants continue to bloom throughout the year in mild climates and until the first

frost elsewhere.

Harvesting Use fresh leaves and flowers as required. It does not respond well to drying.

Propagation By seed and root division.

Pot growth Not recommended for pots but will grow in large window boxes.

Uses The flowers may be candied and used for cake decoration. The leaves are used in drinks, especially wine cups, such as Pimms, with apple juice, in salads and cooked with cabbage. Borage makes a refreshing tisane, iced or hot, which is reputed to have a wonderful effect on both the mind and body and dispels depression.

With its vivid blue, star-shaped flowers, which grow in drooping clusters, and its large, furry, grey-green leaves, borage is a particularly enchanting herb. The flowers, which are very attractive to bees, are added to pot-pourri to give colour and have always been a popular motif in embroidery. They may be candied like violets.

71

Marigolds have been cultivated in herb gardens from ancient times and are one of the easiest and most rewarding of flowers to grow. Their glorious bright orange flowers are a colourful addition to any garden and if the dead flowers are picked off regularly the plants will bloom throughout the summer and into the autumn.

Calendula officinalis
MARIGOLD

An annual with familiar, bright, daisy flowers with petals ranging in colour from pale yellow to a deep, rich orange. Marigold can reach a height of about 50cm (20in) depending on the variety. The plant is thought to have originated in India and may be seen today growing wild in the fields and vineyards of southern Europe.

Commercially available marigold plants tend to be double-flowered and are easy to grow in beds or window boxes and pots.

Soil Any kind of soil but preferably loam.
Position Full sun.
Planting and cultivation Sow seeds in spring and thin seedlings to 45cm (18in) apart. Marigold plants will re-seed themselves but tend to revert to single heads if allowed to do so.
Harvesting Only the petals are used and these may be fresh or dried. To dry, place in thin layers at a low temperature in a dark, airy place so that they retain their colour.
Propagation By seed.
Pot growth Seeds or young plants will grow well in pots and windows boxes.
Uses In cooking, marigold petals can be substituted for saffron, for instance in saffron rice. They produce the same colour effect but not the same flavour. They are a colourful addition to salads and are also used in omelettes and stews. Soaked in oil, they are reputed to aid the complexion if rubbed on the skin, and heal wounds. Made into a tisane, they are said to remedy digestive problems and improve the complexion.

Carum carvi
CARAWAY

Although the caraway plant is a herb, its seeds are generally treated as a spice. It is a biennial with delicate, ferny leaves and white umbels of flowers. The ripe fruits of these flowers split into two seeds. The caraway plant grows to a height of about 60cm (2ft) and is widely grown in Russia, Europe, Scandinavia, India and North America.
Soil Most soils if they are dry and well-drained.
Position Sunny.
Planting and cultivation Sow seeds in spring and thin to 23cm (9in) apart. Prune plants in the autumn. They need little care other than weeding and ensuring that they have water in very dry weather. Plants will flower and go to seed in the summer of the following year. The roots are delicate and so the seed should be sown *in situ* to avoid transplanting. Once established caraway will seed itself.
Harvesting When the seeds are ripe, cut off the plants at ground level and hang up in sheaves in a dry, airy place. When the seeds have dried they can be shaken off on to paper and stored in airtight jars.
Propagation By seed.
Pot growth Not recommended.
Uses The seeds are delicious cooked in seed cakes, with fatty meats such as goose and pork, and particularly with cabbage dishes, carrots and cheese. It is an important ingredient of Kümmel and other liqueurs. The roots may be boiled and eaten as a vegetable, while the tender young leaves add a refreshing taste to salads and soup. Made into a tisane, caraway is said to aid the digestion.

Chrysanthemum balsamita or Tanacetum balsamita
COSTMARY or ALECOST

A medium-sized perennial, dying down each winter and coming up again each spring. The leaves are long and thin and have a scent of mint and a flavour of lemon. The leaves are grey-green in colour while the flowers are white with yellow centres and grow in clusters. The name alecost dates from the time when it was used in the preparation of home-brewed ale.
Soil Any well-drained soil.
Position Sunny.

Top *The petals of marigolds are used in cooking both for their colour and their flavour. They may be used in salads and omelettes and as a cheaper alternative to saffron.* Centre *The caraway plant with its ferny leaves and white flowers should be grown in situ as it reacts badly to transplanting. Both the leaves and seeds are used in cooking.* Above *Caraway seeds are treated as a spice and used to flavour both food and liqueurs.*

Top *Horseradish will grow easily in most rich soils. The leaves cannot be eaten but the roots, as well as having antibiotic qualities, have a delicious flavour and can be made into a sauce which tastes particularly good with beef.* Above *The pungent, aromatic seeds of coriander can be included in soups, ground over meat and used to flavour vinegars and vegetable dishes.*

Planting and cultivation Buy a small plant and plant in spring. Costmary originates from the East and will not grow from seed in temperate climes. Take care that its extensive root system does not damage those of more delicate plants, and chop the roots back regularly.

Harvesting Pick leaves as required and dry or use fresh.

Propagation By root division.

Pot growth Not recommended.

Uses The fresh leaves may be used in brewing beer, in stuffings and to make tisanes. The dried leaves are occasionally added to *pot-pourri*.

Cochlearia armoracia
HORSERADISH

Horseradish is a hardy perennial member of the mustard family. Originating from eastern Europe, it was for many years regarded as a medicine rather than as a condiment. The leaves and stems contain a poisonous substance but the white, fleshy root is safe to eat and high in vitamin C. Horseradish is extremely easy to grow and reaches a height of about 60cm (2ft).

Soil Rich, deep, moist soil, preferably with plenty of manure worked in.

Position Sunny or semi-shade.

Planting and cultivation Plant horseradish crowns in the spring leaving 30cm (12in) between them. Keep the bed weed free to allow the roots to develop and pick off flower buds as they appear. Horseradish spreads rapidly so it is advisable to dig up the whole bed when harvesting and replant the following spring.

Harvesting Lift all roots in the autumn when they are about 25cm (10in) long. Store smaller, thinner thongs in sand to plant next spring.

Propagation By root division as the seed pods rarely mature.

Pot growth Not suitable.

Uses It is used principally raw and grated to make the condiment horseradish sauce which is excellent with beef. It does, however, have strong antibiotic properties and is reputed to prevent scurvy.

Coriandrum sativum
CORIANDER

This hardy annual herb is grown both for its small round seeds, which are used as a spice, and for its glossy, dark green, feathery leaves. Coriander grows to a height of about 60cm (2ft) and bears pale pinky-mauve flowers. The leaves and unripe seeds have an unpleasant smell which fortunately disappears as ripeness sets in.

Soil Fertile and well drained; and preferably manured the year prior to planting. Do not plant in recently manured soil.

Position Sunny.

Planting and cultivation Sow seeds in early spring for mature plants by the summer. Self-sown seedlings often appear in later summer. Thin seedlings to 10cm (4in) apart.

Harvesting Do not harvest until you are sure the seeds are fully ripe, that is when the fruits have turned from green to grey. Cut the plants and leave for a day or two on the ground to complete ripening. Shake out the seeds of the plants and store.

Propagation By seed.

Uses The seeds are used whole and grown to flavour confectionery, liqueurs, curry powders, sauces, pickles, desserts and breads. The fresh, young leaves are chopped like parsley and used to garnish and flavour,

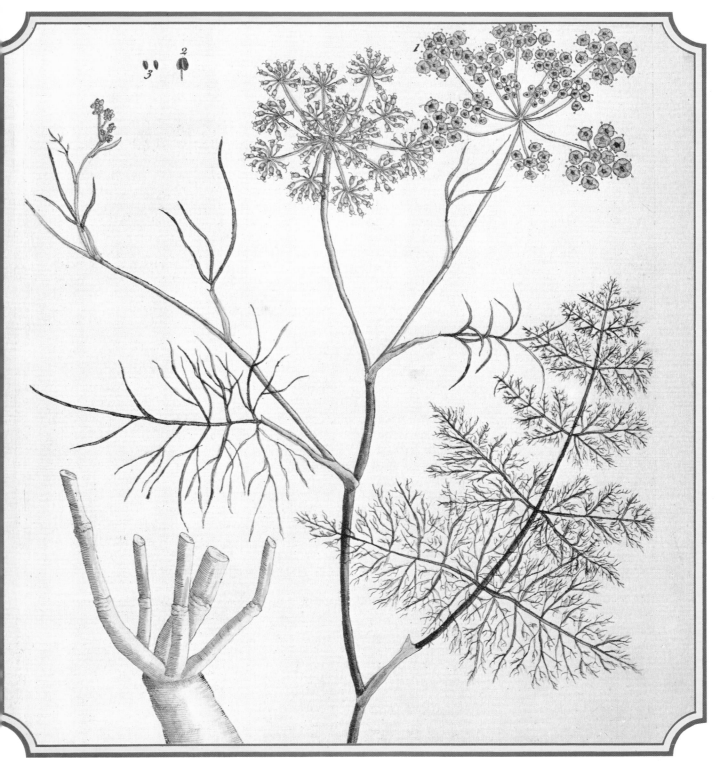

soups, salads, curries, stews and cooked meats and vegetables, especially in India, Greece and Mexico.

Foeniculum vulgare
FENNEL

Fennel is native to southern Europe, and although a perennial normally it may need to be treated as an annual in temperature climes. Tall, sometimes, reaching 1.5m (5ft) or more, it has beautiful, yellow-green, feathery leaves

Fennel, with its feathery foliage and yellow umbels of flowers, is a tall, decorative plant. An infusion made from the seeds makes a soothing lotion for the eyes, but it is for its culinary use that it is generally grown. Resembling dill in flavour, fennel leaves are used fresh, but the stems and seeds are dried and used to make gripewater.

and umbels of flowers of the same colour. Although similar to dill in appearance it has a more distinct flavour of aniseed.

Soil Most well drained soils.

Position Sunny.

Planting and cultivation Sow seeds in shallow drills in early spring 5cm (2in) deep and thin seedlings to 40cm (16in) apart. They may need some support against the wind as they become larger. Pinch out all flower buds as they develop. Do not plant near dill as cross pollination may occur. In the autumn cut plants down to 10cm (4in) above the ground. Transplant clumps to pots and bring indoors to prolong harvesting.

Harvesting Pick fresh leaves as required, gather flower heads for seeds in the autumn before they are completely ripe and dry slowly on paper to complete ripening. Shake off the seeds when ripe and store.

Propagation Propagate by lifting pieces of root in spring when they first begin to shoot and replant 30cm (12in) away.

Pot growth Grows well in tubs, window boxes and large pots.

Uses Particularly good with fish, and in marinades, soups, sauces and salads. The seeds are also used in cooking.

Hyssopus officinalis
HYSSOP

Hyssop is a hardy perennial, herbaceous shrub which is partially evergreen. The whole plant is very aromatic and it grows to a height of about 60cm (2ft) making it very attractive as a low hedge. Hyssop has dark green, slim, pointed leaves and deep blue flowers. This highly decorative plant is attractive to bees.

Soil Well-drained ordinary garden soil.

Position Sunny.

Planting and cultivation Sow seeds in spring, or put in plants in the spring or autumn. Transplant seedlings to their final position as soon as they are large enogh to handle. If you are cultivating a hedge, trim it into shape in the autumn.

Harvesting Harvest just as the flowers begin to bloom.

Propagation By cuttings and root division which must be made in the spring or autumn, and by seed.

Pot growth Suitable for growing in a tub or a 25cm (10in) diameter pot.

Uses Hyssop has a strong flavour so use sparingly. Add the tender young growths and flowers to salads. soups and meat, particularly pork. It is an ingredient of Chartreuse and the shoots and leaves make a fragrant tisane which was used as an expectorant and for use in chest complaints.

Juniperus communis
JUNIPER

Juniper is a hardy, perennial shrub which occasionally grows to the size of a small tree and may be found growing wild in Europe, North America and Asia. It has reddish stems and needle-like leaves and the whole plant is highly aromatic.

Soil Any well-drained chalk or limey soil.

Position Juniper favours hill-sides and does not like deep shade.

Planting and cultivation Sow seed or set out small plants in spring, 1.2m (4ft) apart. It is necessary to have two plants as it is very rare to find male and female flowers growing on the same bush. The male flowers resemble green catkins, while the female flowers are cone-like. Although juniper will thrive in extremely barren conditions it responds well to moderate doses

Hyssop, with its bright blue or sometimes pink or even white, flowers, is ideal for borders in the herb garden. It grows to a height of about 60cm (2ft) and is happy in most locations although it prefers a sunny place in light soil. The leaves have a slightly bitter, minty flavour and should be used sparingly in cooking. Regular consumption of a tisane made from the leaves is said to relieve coughs and chest complaints.

of organic fertiliser which will promote growth.

Harvesting The berries should be picked in the autumn when they have turned black. They begin by being green in colour and may take two to three years to mature fully. Use fresh or dry.

Propagation By cuttings or by seed, three of which are contained in each berry. The seeds are slow to germinate.

Pot growth Suitable if grown in a large pot or tub.

Uses To flavour spirits, particularly gin, and food. Good in marinades and with pork, beet, venison and poultry. Medicinally it is reputed to be an effective diurectic and may be taken for this purpose either raw or infused with hot water to make a tisane.

Juniper is a shrub which occasionally grows to the size of a tree. The whole plant is aromatic, from the reddish stems to the needle-like leaves and spicy berries which grow on them. The berries are used to flavour gin, to make tisanes and to flavour marinades for pork, beef, venison and poultry dishes and to make beer.

77

The bay tree is sacred to Apollo and the leaves have been a symbol of honour for poets, soldiers and athletes alike. A mature tree may grow to 4.75m (12ft) tall or more over twenty years. It has small, yellow flowers in spring, followed by purplish berries, but it is the aromatic leaves which are important for their use in cooking.

Laurus nobilis
SWEET BAY

The sweet bay is an evergreen, shrub-like tree with shiny leathery pointed leaves. A native of Mediterranean lands, it was used particularly by the Romans for making garlands to honour poets, soldiers and atheletes. It has unsignificant flowers which are followed immediately by little black round fruits; but it is the aromatic leaves which are important.

Soil Most soils that are well-drained and dryish.

Position Semi-shade though will withstand full sun.

Planting and cultivation Plant small established plants and try not to move them from their original positions. Young plants should be protected from frost with sacking. Many people train young bushes into various shapes, such as pyramids or balls. This is done by wiring branches into the appropriate position and pinching out unwanted new shoots.

Harvesting Pick fresh leaves as required. When drying leaves, do so in darkness to ensure that they retain their colour.

Pot growth An ideal herb for tubs and large pots. Use a 38-45cm (15-18in) pot with ordinary potting mixture. In temperature climes bring the pot or tub indoors during the winter.

Uses Apart from being reputed to ward off evil its principal use is culinary. A bay leaf is one of the principal ingredients of *bouquet garni*, and it is also used in marinades, pâtés, meat and fish stocks, and soups and stews.

Lavandula spica (syn. *L. officinalis*)
LAVENDER

The word lavender is derived from the latin *lavo*, to wash, since the Romans and the Greeks used lavender to scent their bath water. This perennial shrub has tiny flowers, in shades of blue and purple, clustered on spikes which stand up above the grey-green, narrow-leaved foliage. Lavender bushes are frequently used to make low-growing hedges which smell and look beautiful and attract bees.

Soil Well-drained, limey soil.

Position Open and sunny.

Planting and cultivation Although lavender can be grown from seed it takes a long time. So it is better to buy young plants and plant them in the spring or autumn. Set the plants about 30cm (12in) apart and do not give them too much water. Do not let the flowers go to seed as this encourages them to straggle. After flowering, the bushes should be clipped and shaped, taking care not to cut into the old wood. Trim gently in spring to encourage growth at the base of the plant.

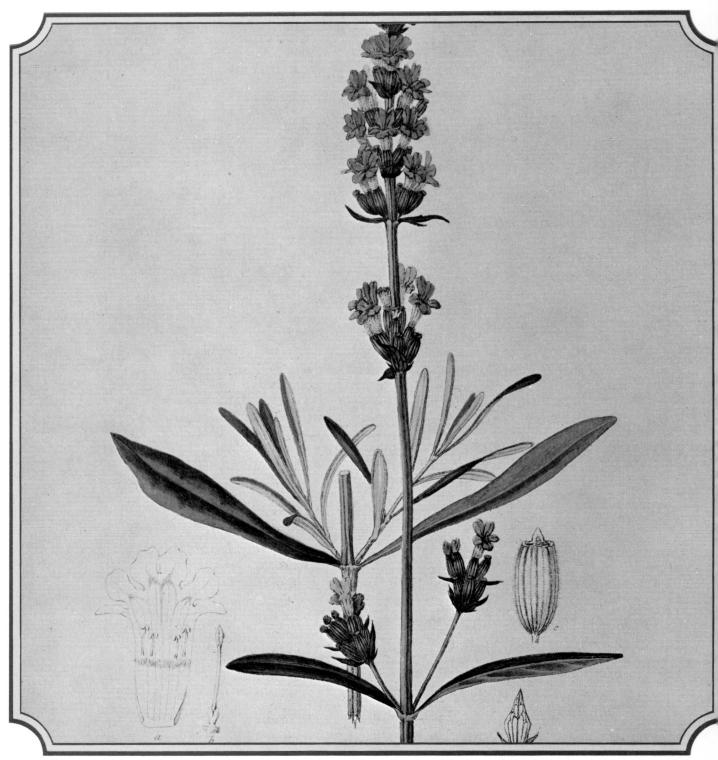

There are many varieties of lavender, but all of them have the same delightful perfumed flowers and leaves. The flowers vary in colour from white, pink, deep blue to pale purple, the most traditional form. The blooms may be used as cut flowers or dried and used in lavender bags or in a pot-pourri both for scent and colour.

Harvesting Gather flower spikes as they come into flower and dry in a warm, 26-38°C (80-100°F), dark place, so that their colour does not fade.

Propagation From cuttings 10-15cm (4-6in) long, taken with a heel in the autumn. Root in a sandy soil mix and plant out the following spring.

Pot growth It is quite possible to grow lavender in large pots and boxes in a suitably sandy, alkaline, soil mix. Protect such plants from frost in winter.

Uses Lavender is not a culinary herb, but its beautiful scent has meant that the essential oil yield from the flowers is used for scent and the dried flower spikes are found in *pot pourri* or made into lavender bags to scent clothes and linen and placed in drawers and closets.

Ligusticum scoticum (syn. *L. officinalis*)
LOVAGE

Lovage is a tall perennial, growing to a height of 2m (6ft), with large, dark, shiny leaves and yellow flowers. It is similar in appearance and scale to angelica.

Soil Deep, rich, wet and preferably organically fertilized.
Position Sunny or semi-shaded.
Planting and cultivation The seed germinates best in darkness and should be sown as soon as it ripens as it quickly loses its germinating power.

Lovage is an extremely vigorous herb, reaching a height of up to 2m (6ft) when in flower. However, unless you want the plant to flower in order to produce seed, it is better to cut off the flower stalks as soon as they have been thrown up from the base as this promotes further leaf production. One plant is sufficient per household.

Right The large, deeply lobed leaves of lovage taste like spicy celery and are delicious added to salads. Use with discretion as the flavour is strong. *Far right* Lemon verbena is a highly aromatic plant with an exquisite lemony taste. A few leaves added to an ordinary pot of tea will give it an extra special flavour.

Either sow the seed in spring, in a box or *in situ*, or buy small plants. If you have a greenhouse or frame you can sow a month early so as to be ready for planting outside when there is no danger of frost.

Transplant seedlings, or thin them, to 45cm (18in) apart as soon as they are large enough to handle. Water well. Lovage takes about four years to reach full size and one plant will normally be sufficient per household. Unless you want more seed, cut off to flower stalks to encourage the growth of leaves.

Harvesting Use fresh leaves as required. Drying the thick leaves is difficult but possible and takes about four to five days. Gather seeds as they ripen.

Propagation By seed, or by root division in spring.

Pot growth Not recommended because the roots are so large.

Uses Both the seeds and leaves are used to enrich soups, stews, sauces and salads. The flavour is strong, resembling a cross between celery and yeast, and should be used with discretion. Infused to make a tisane, the leaves are supposed to aid the digestion.

Lippia citriodora
LEMON VERBENA

A deciduous shrub from Chile, lemon verbena is a tender perennial. It should not be confused with verbena or vervain, which although related has little in common. Lemon verbena has lance-shaped leaves and spikes of pale mauve flowers. When any part of the plant is bruised it gives off a delicious lemon scent.

Soil Poor, dry soil to which humus has been added.

Position Sunny and sheltered.

Planting and cultivation Although originating from South America, lemon verbena will grow in temperate climes if protected from frost. Buy small plants, put in the ground in spring and water freely except in winter, when the plant is dormant. Pinch out the lead shoots as it grows to stop it straggling. A severe pruning in early spring will help production of leaves. Pot up and move indoors if there is any danger of frost.

Harvesting Collect the leaves as the plant sheds them in the autumn.

Propagation From cuttings of half ripened wood which take easily in spring or summer under glass.

Pot growth A very successful houseplant. Use a standard loam potting mixture.

Uses An essential oil is distilled from its leaves which is used in the preparation of some scents and soaps. A few leaves added to the tea pot will transform ordinary tea, although it also makes a refreshing tisane either alone or with mint. When dried it can be added to *pot pourri*, while fresh it is delightful when cooking if added to lemon sauces, salads, fruit drinks and fruit dishes such as compôtes.

Matricaria chamomilla (Anthemis nobilis)
CHAMOMILE

There are two plants called chamomile which look very similar. True chamomile, *Matricaria chamomilla* is an annual and the one used for tisanes and cosmetics, while Roman chamomile, *Anthemis nobilis*, is a perennial and used to make sweet-smelling lawns.

Soil Ordinary, dryish soils.

Position Full sun.

Planting and cultivation Sow the seeds of true chamomile in rows at

Although a tisane made from chamomile has a somewhat bitter flavour, it is a very good carminative. A hot infusion of the flowers is also an excellent steam bath for the face, and used as a hair rinse after a shampoo is said to lighten fair hair as well as conditioning it. Chamomile is readily grown from seed.

83

Right *The tiny white flowers of balm, or lemon balm as it is also known, are particularly attractive to bees, which makes it an ideal plant to grow if you have fruit trees that need cross-pollinating. It is only necessary to grow one balm plant as, like mint, balm has an invasive root system and will spread rapidly once established.*

23cm (9in) intervals. Roman chamomile should be sown as for grass seed to make a lawn. Neither type needs any particular after care.

Harvesting It is only worth picking the pretty blue flowers of true chamomile as they come into bloom. Dry them in an airing cupboard or warm oven and store in a dark place.

Propagation By seed.

Pot growth In window boxes or tubs which allow for lateral spreading.

Uses It is from the flowers of true chamomile that the deep blue oil is extracted which is so good to drink or to use cosmetically. A tisane, made from chamomile will help cure stomach ache and relieve indigestion. An infusion of flowers makes a good conditioning rinse for fair hair, or a steam bath to cleanse the face.

Melissa officinalis
BALM

This hardy, perennial herb, better known as lemon balm, originates from southern Europe and Asia. It derives its name from the Greek word *melissa* meaning a honey bee and does indeed attract these valuable insects by the delightful fragrance of its lemon-scented leaves. Balm has pale green, heart-shaped leaves and small, whitish flowers and forms a shrubby bush about 60-90cm (2-3ft) in height.

Soil Ordinary garden soil.

Position Sunny and sheltered. Leave enough space for the leaves to develop.

Planting and cultivation Either sow seeds or plant cuttings in spring. Balm has an extensive root system so either contain the roots in bottomless buckets submerged in the open ground, or grow in large tubs. Do not allow the plant to flower if you want the leaves for cooking but pinch out the buds as they appear. Weed regularly. In winter cut the plants low and protect from frost where necessary with leaf mould.

Harvesting Pick fresh leaves as required. To dry balm, wait until the end of summer and cut the stems. Tie them in small bunches and hang in an airy place to dry.

Propagation By root division in spring or autumn, or allow it to seed itself.

Uses In cooking, its attractive lemon flavour complements stewed fruit, fish and poultry dishes, stuffings sauces and marinades. It makes a good tisane and is reputed to cure insomnia, soothe the nerves and dispel melancholy. Balm is also used in perfumes, liqueurs and furniture polish, and by bee keepers who rub it on the insides of hives to attract bees.

Mentha
MINT

Mint is a hardy perennial herb remarkable for its aromatic leaves. There are many varieties of mint found widely distributed throughout the world. But the most commonly grown varieties, and the most useful, are as follows; M.*spicata*: spearmint, M.*rotundifolia*: apple or Bowles mint and M.*piperita*: peppermint. All have square stems and white or mauve flowers in spikes and spread rapidly wherever they are planted. Mint originated from the East via North Africa although it is named after the

Mentha piperata (*peppermint*) *is one of the most commonly used herbs. The essential oil is used as an ingredient in toothpaste, confectionery, indigestion tablets and the liqueur* crème de menthe. *A peppermint tisane is said to aid the digestion. It is one of the few varieties of mint which can be grown from seed and will quickly establish itself.*

Above *Bergamot is one of the most decorative of scented herbs. It produces an abundance of aromatic foliage and scarlet flowers.* Right *Similar in appearance to peppermint but having little or no leaf stalks, spearmint has lilac pink flowers and narrow, thin leaves.*

nymph, Minthe, who is reputed to have been turned into this plant. M.*spicata* grows 30-45cm (12-18in) high and has thin, pointed leaves. M.*rotundifolia* has a broader, fleshier and slightly hairy leaf and can grow to 60-120cm (2-4ft) high. M.*piperita* is thinner and is pale green to red in colour. With the exception of M.*rotundifolia*, all mints are prone to rust disease.

Soil Very moist and well dug.

Position Sun or partial shade.

Planting and cultivation Plant roots of all varieties in spring or autumn. Control spreading by restricting roots in a clay pot or old bucket sunk in the ground. Pinch out flower buds on appearance to maintain maximum leaf growth. Renew beds every three to four years by pulling up roots, dividing them and replanting. Keep free from weeds. If rust disease occurs, destroy the bed and start a fresh one.

Harvesting Pick fresh leaves as required and cut for drying when the flowers are in bud. Dry on or off the stems in a dark, well ventilated room at a temperature of about 23°C (73°F).

Propagation By root division in spring or autumn.

Pot growth Will grow in large pots or window boxes in good moist soil. Keep plants pinched down to about 15cm (6in).

Uses Used particularly by the British to make mint sauce or jelly for roast lamb. Also good with boiled vegetables such as potatoes and carrots, and chopped raw into salads and fruit drinks. The dried leaves can be added to *pot-pourri*, and tisanes made from mint, especially peppermint, taste excellent and aid the digestion.

Monarda didyma
BERGAMOT

Originating from North America, this perennial herb is both decorative and fragrant. Bergamot grows to a height of about 60-90cm (2-3ft) and has serrated leaves and spiky flowers whose colours range from white, pink and mauve through to red. Like balm, it is particularly attractive to bees.

Soil Rich and moist.

Position Sun or partial shade.

Planting and cultivation Plant small plants in spring or autumn and top dress the soil, or sow seed out of doors in a semi-shaded position. Seeds germinate easily but discard any drab coloured plants which result. Dig up, divide the roots and replant every two to three years. Water well.

Harvesting The flowers and leaves may be used fresh or dried. Drying should be done in darkness to preserve colour.

Propagation By root division in spring, cuttings in autumn or by seed.

Pot growth Possible with young plants, but will need an enormous tub as they get larger and lots of water.

Uses Both the leaves and flowers can be chopped and added with advantage to salads and pork dishes. The flowers make beautiful table decorations and last for about a week. The commonest use is as tea, either on its own (as drunk by the Oswego Indians) or added to Indian tea.

Myrrhis odorata
SWEET CICELY

A pretty perennial herb, Sweet Cicely takes several years to reach its full height of 150cm (5ft). It is the first herb to appear in spring and the last to die down in the autumn, and so can be used fresh for nearly the whole year. It has large, feathery leaves and umbels of white flowers. The sweet smell and taste of this herb is reminiscent of aniseed.

Soil Any well drained and nourished soil.

Position Partial shade.

Planting and cultivation Either buy and plant small plants or sow seed in spring. Only lightly cover the seed and keep weed free. Leave 45cm (18in) between each plant and pinch out flower buds as they appear to stimulate leaf growth. If allowed to flower this herb will quickly seed itself.

Harvesting Pick fresh leaves as required and leaves for drying in the spring.

Propagation By seed, or by root division in the spring or autumn.

Pot growth Not really suitable, but could be grown outside in a tub as it has large roots.

Uses The roots can be cooked and used as a vegetable. Chopped fresh leaves can be added to salads or stewed with fruit. As it is very sweet, this herb will reduce the amount of sugar normally added to stewed fruit. The leaves may also be added to perfume bath water.

Ocimum basilicum
BASIL

Originating from India, basil is a delicate plant extremely sensitive to frosts and is safer grown indoors in cooler climates where it should be treated as an annual. There are two basic varieties, sweet basil and bush basil. Sweet basil is larger, more aromatic and subtler in flavour than bush basil, and produces white flowers. The scent of sweet basil is said to drive away flies.

Soil Rich and well drained.

Position Sunny and sheltered.

Planting and cultivation Sow sees in early spring, under glass in areas which do not have tropical climates. Grow in sterilized soil as they are prone to 'damping off' disease. Keep seedlings warm and protected. Plant out in early summer in a sheltered border. Remove flowers as they appear to prolong the growth of fresh leaves.

Propagation By seed.

Harvesting Cut leaves for use as needed. It changes flavour when dried.

Pot growth Choose dwarf varieties and keep transplanting to large pots as they grow.

Uses Usually associated in cooking with tomatoes, both raw and cooked, particularly in the form of salads and soups. Equally good with egg dishes, on pizzas and in other Italian dishes.

As dried basil does not retain the same delicate, yet peppery, flavour of the fresh herb, it really is worth growing some in a pot or garden. A few chopped leaves added to some sliced tomatoes and left to marinate for an hour or so before serving is one of the most delicious salads.

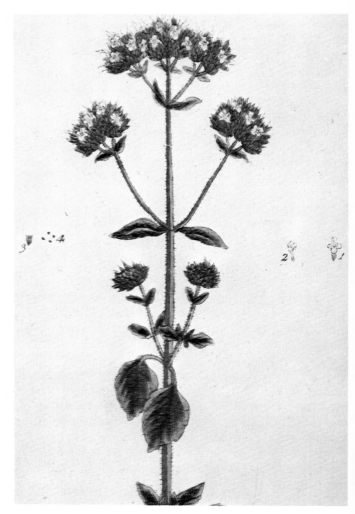

Left *Sweet marjoram has reddish stems, small leaves and pinky-white flowers. It may be substituted for oregano in recipes. The leaves are at their best just before the plant flowers. Right Oregano, like all members of this family, is easily grown from seed and responds well to drying.*

Origanum

MARJORAM and OREGANO

There are many different varieties of *Origanum*, each with the same characteristic scent and flavour. The most popular are *O. vulgare*, oregano, *O. onites*, pot marjoram and *O. marjorana*, sweet marjoram. Although all three are perennials *O. marjorana* should be regarded as an annual in cooler climates.

Soil Light, well drained and slightly acidic.

Position Full sun.

Planting and cultivation All varieties can be grown from seed sown in spring in boxes or buy small plants. Do not plant outside in temperate climes until all danger of frost is over. Thin seedlings to 23cm (9in) apart. Water well and protect perennial varieties from frost in winter. Cut regularly to encourage growth.

Harvesting Pick fresh leaves and flowers as required. All varieties dry well as their scent and flavour become more intense. Dry in the dark at a temperature of not more than 23°C (73°F).

Propagation By cuttings, root division in spring or autumn and seed.

Pot growth Grows well in pots or window boxes if enough room is allowed for roots. Water well.

Uses To add flavour to meat dishes, sausages, most Italian dishes but particularly pizzas, salads, egg and vegetable dishes. Sweet marjoram has the most subtle taste. The dried leaves are often added to *pot-pourri*.

Petroselinum crispum
PARSLEY

Perhaps the best known and most frequently used of herbs, parsley is a biennial usually grown as an annual. Most varieties have dark green, curly leaves but some have flatter, broader leaves. Hamburg parsley (*Petroselinum sativum*) is grown for its roots. Parsley is native to the Mediterranean regions and therefore needs protection in winter in cooler climes. It is not surprising that it has been in use for over 300 years as not only does parsley improve the taste and appearance of most savoury

Don't be put off by the story that parsley will only grow for a household where a woman is the dominant partner. Given the right attention it will flourish anywhere and provide you with an instant garnish and flavouring for almost any savoury dish. Container grown plants may be brought indoors over winter.

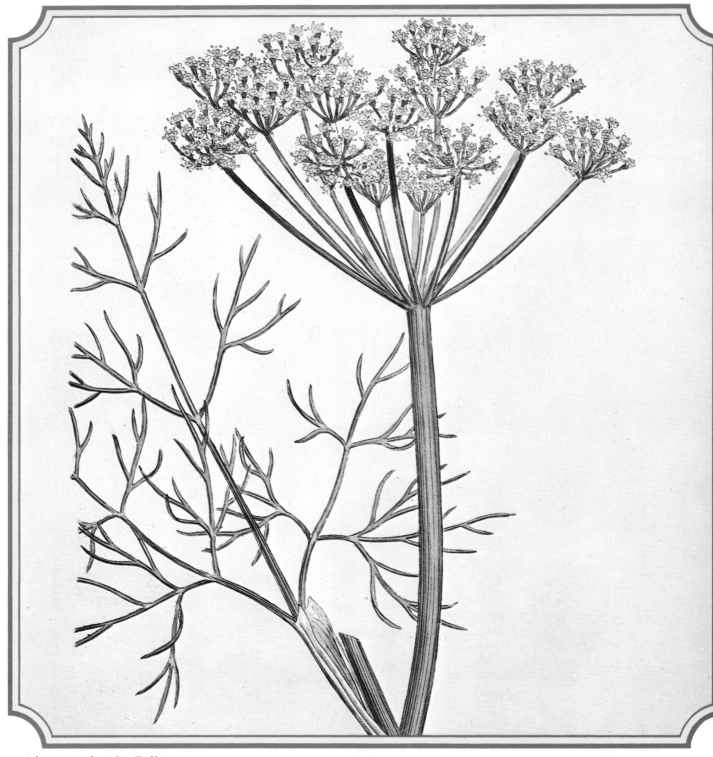

Above and right *Dill is a large, decorative herb, reaching a height of about 90cm (3ft). It has feathery leaves, similar to those of fennel, and yellow flowers. Both the leaves and the seeds are used in cooking, particularly to flavour vinegar. The leaves can be added to salads and vegetable and fish dishes.*

dishes, but is also an important source of iron, vitamin C and iodine and eaten regularly it will improve your health.

Soil Moist but well-drained with natural or added lime.

Position Semi-shade.

Planting and cultivation Sow seeds in spring and in succession throughout the summer, watering the seedlings well. The seeds are slow to germinate, taking about five to eight weeks, although an initial soaking may help speed the process. Thin seedlings to 8cm (3in) apart and then to 20cm (8in) apart as, ideally, parsley plants should not touch each other. Weed regularly and protect from winter frosts. Flower stalks should be cut off as soon as they appear in the second year to delay the plant going to seed.

Harvesting Pick fresh as required. Parsley does not respond well to drying.

Pot growth Will grow well in pots, if they are deep enough to contain the long root. Or grow in tubs, containers or special parsley pots in a yard or patio.

Uses To make parsley sauce and butter, and chopped and sprinkled over almost every savoury dish you can think of, as well as being part of *bouquet garni*. Chewed after eating garlic, parsley will remove the smell. Made into a tisane, parsley tea acts as a diuretic.

Peucedanum graveolens (syn. *Anethum graveolens*)
DILL

Similar in appearance to fennel, dill is an annual, originally from around the Mediterranean, grown for its aromatic seeds and leaves. It has delicate, feathery, blue-green leaves, yellow flowers and grows to a height of about 90cm (3ft). It is found growing wild in the warmer parts of Europe.

Soil Well drained and of fine tilth for the seeds.

Position Sunny, but not near fennel as they might cross-pollinate one another.

Planting and cultivation Sow seeds shallowly in the spring and then successfully throughout the summer. Sow *in situ* as dill does not like being transplanted. Thin seedlings to 23cm (9in) apart and keep free from weeds.

Harvesting Pick fresh leaves as required from six weeks after sowing. Leaves for drying are best picked just before the flowers come out when the leaves are at their best. To obtain seeds, let the plant flower and allow the seeds to ripen on the plant. Shake out and store.

Propagation By seed.

Pot growth Will grow in pots and window boxes if they are deep enough.

Uses Both the leaves and seeds are used to flavour vinegar, pickles (especially cucumber), soups, fish dishes and sauces and vegetables such as cabbage and courgettes (zucchini). Use with restraint as the flavour is quite strong. The seeds contain an essential oil with carminative and stimulant properties, which is particularly associated with dill water used by mothers to wind their babies.

Pimpinella anisum
ANISE

A medium tall annual with serrated leaves and clusters of white flowers. The aromatic fruits containing the oil-bearing seed are called aniseed, and it is principally for these that anise is grown. It is native to the Middle East but is also grown in quantity in India, Greece, Spain and Egypt.

Soil Light, dry and limy.

Position Sunny and sheltered.

Although anise is native to the Mediterranean regions, it will grow in cooler climates. The seeds, known as aniseed, were once popular as flavourings for confectionery and cakes but are now more frequently used to flavour curries, liqueurs and spirits, such as ouzo and pernod, and to make tisanes which are said to aid the digestion.

Planting and cultivation Sow seeds in spring to allow them to produce seed to be ripened during the summer.

Harvesting The fruits will only ripen if it has been a really hot summer, when the fruit will turn greyish-green in colour. Cut the whole flower stems and hang them upside down in an airy place to continue ripening. Shake out the seeds and store them.

Propagation By seed.

Pot growth Not recommended.

Uses The seeds are used for flavouring drinks, such as Pernod, Ouzo and Anisette, biscuits (cookies), bread and cakes. Aniseed tea is reputed to be a remedy for diarrhoea and to soothe indigestion.

Portulaca oleracea
PURSLANE

Purslane is a half-hardy annual with a low-spreading habit. It grows principally in tropical and sub-tropical regions but will survive quite happily in cool temperate climes if planting is delayed until after the last frost. The roots of purslane are fibrous and the leaves small, ovate and fleshy. It grows to a height of about 15cm (6in) and has yellow flowers. Purslane is rich in vitamins and minerals and may be found growing wild in hot, dry climates but is also quite easy to cultivate.

Purslane is a sprawling plant with rosettes of fleshy leaves. Combined with sorrel, the leaves are an important ingredient of the French soup bonne femme. Young leaves may be used raw for salads while older, tougher leaves should be cooked in the same way as spinach or pickled in vinegar for winter use.

Top *Purslane seed, sown in early spring, should produce a good crop, although it does require more water than other herbs. Above Rosemary is an evergreen shrub which can grow to a height of 2m (6ft) or more. It is more commonly grown from rooted cuttings or bought plants rather than seed and will thrive in the garden or indoors. Rosemary is strong and aromatic, so use it sparingly in cooking. Add it to meat, game, fish, egg and poultry dishes. It can be used to make excellent tisane.*

Soil Sandy and well drained.
Position Sunny.
Planting and cultivation Either sow seed or set out small plants in spring and sow in succession until the end of summer. Purslane plants should be thinned out to allow about 15cm (6in) between them.
Harvesting The leaves may be picked, for use fresh or to be dried, about six weeks after sowing. Pick whole shoots when they are about 8cm (3in) long.
Propagation By seed, cuttings or root division.
Pot growth Not suitable.
Uses The young leaves may be used in salads, but as they become older and more fibrous, use them in the same way as those of spinach, in soups and as a vegetable. The shoots may also be cooked and eaten as a vegetable while the leaves make a pleasant herbal tisane.

Rosmarinus officinalis
ROSEMARY

A beautiful, evergreen shrub with aromatic leaves, rosemary makes a useful small hedge. It originates from the Mediterranean region and its Latin name means 'dew of the sea'. The leaves of rosemary are leathery, needle-like in shape and grey-green in colour while the flowers are pale blue. This perennial shrub reaches a height of about 90cm (3ft) and is very attractive to bees.
Soil Sandy and well drained, it will not tolerate wet roots.
Position Sheltered and sunny, preferably against a warm wall.
Planting and cultivation It can be grown from seed but germination is so slow that it is more satisfactory to grow from rooted cuttings or bought plants. Put these out in late spring or early summer 38in (15in) apart. Prune new shoots after flowering each year. Protect young plants from frost in winter in areas where this is necessary.
Harvesting Pick fresh leaves and flowers as required, and cut shoots for drying in the summer.
Propagation Easily propagated from cuttings taken from new growth in spring or by root division. Overwinter cuttings in a greenhouse and plant out the following spring.
Pot growth Rosemary makes a good pot plant which should be brought indoors during the winter in cooler climates and clipped into a neat shape.
Uses With roast meats, particularly lamb, veal and chicken. In stuffings, marinades and egg dishes, and with fish, shellfish and vegetables. It is also good with sweeter things such as jellies and fruit drinks. It makes a good tea and the fragrant oil extracted from the leaves is used in perfumes, shampoos and other cosmetics.

Rumex acetosa
SORREL

Rumex acetosa is the most common form of sorrel, although there is another variety *R. scutatus* which is particularly prized for soup-making. Both are members of the dock family and border between being a herb and a leaf vegetable. Sorrel is a hardy perennial, with hastate leaves rich in vitamin C. Cosmopolitan in its distribution, the sorrel plant grows to a height of about 60cm (2ft).
Soil Most light, well-drained soils, preferably acidic.
Position Sunny but will tolerate partial shade.
Planting and cultivation It can be raised from seed sown in spring or from

root divisions. Plant in spring or autumn. Leave 30cm (12in) between plants. Cut off the flowering stems to encourage leaf growth and prevent it going to seed. Replant bed every four years.

Harvesting Leaves may be used fresh about three months after sowing, and if sorrel plants are protected in winter, may be picked throughout the year.

Propagation By seed and root division in spring or autumn.

Pot growth Not suitable.

Uses The taste is bitter and lemony so use with discretion in cooking. Young, tender leaves may be eaten raw in salad but later treat like spinach leaves and use in soups as a puréed vegetable. A tea made from the leaves is a sharp-tasting tonic and is said to purify the blood.

There are in fact two varieties of sorrel, garden sorrel, illustrated above, and French sorrel. Both are members of the dock family and have a high vitamin C content. The leaves are used raw in salads, cooked to make a delicious soup (which has become a speciality of France) and as a vegetable dish similar to spinach.

Right Rue is a hardy, evergreen shrub with lovely, blue-green leaves and soft, yellow flowers in summer. It is now grown almost entirely for its decorative qualities and because of its long historical association with the herb garden. Far right Sage is traditionally used with all rich and fatty meats, as its strong taste counteracts greasiness.

Ruta graveolens
RUE

Rue is a highly aromatic and decorative evergreen shrub. It has lacy, blue-green leaves, small yellow flowers and grows to a height of about 60-90cm (2-3ft). Although it is native to the Mediterranean, this perennial herb will tolerate cooler climates and is an attractive hedging plant grown almost entirely for its decorative qualities.

Soil Well drained with natural or added lime.
Position Full sun.
Planting and cultivation Either sow seeds or set out plants in early spring. Prune to shape and pinch out the flower buds.
Harvesting Use leaves as required.
Propagation By seed, root division or cuttings 10-14cm (4-6in) long, taken from ripened side shoots in late summer and rooted in a cold frame to plant out the following autumn or spring.
Uses Rue is grown principally as a decorative plant. Its leaves are bitter but may be used in very small quantities to flavour salad dressings. Many centuries ago it was taken medicinally as a tisane and thought to preserve good health.

Salvia officinalis
SAGE

This fast-spreading, perennial shrub has had a reputation for centuries as a cure for all ills and an aid to longevity. There are numerous varieties of sage but the one most commonly grown in nurseries for culinary purposes does not flower in cooler climates and so cannot be raised from seed. The common or garden variety has small mauve flowers and nearly all varieties have hairy, grey-green, deeply-veined leaves. There is one particularly individual variety called pineapple sage (*Salvia rutilans*) whose leaves smell of pineapple. It has red flowers and is of no culinary use. Sage grows well around the Mediterranean and in areas with temperate climates and reaches a height of about 60cm (2ft).

Soil Dry and well drained. Sage hates wet soil.
Position Full sun.
Planting and cultivation Sow seeds, where possible, in spring and do not plant out in cooler climates until after the last frost. Otherwise set out small plants 40cm (16in) apart in well hoed and weeded soil. Prune to

shape regularly and renew bed every four years.

Harvesting Pick leaves as required, but they are at their best just before flowering, where this occurs. Dry very slowly at a low temperature.

Propagation For layers, peg down peripheral stems, and when they have grown independent roots, cut away and transplant or take cuttings.

Pot growth Grows well in large pots, tubs and window sills. Shape regularly.

Uses Most famous in sage and onion stuffing. Particularly used with rich, fatty meats such as pork, eel and duck, but tastes equally good with veal, liver, sausages, cheese and tomato dishes. As a tisane it has been taken medicinally for centuries and also used as a mouthwash.

Sage is a small shrub which grows to a height of about 60cm (2ft). There are many different varieties of sage but the most frequently grown garden sage has narrow, grey-green leaves and blue to purple flowers. All varieties, however, have a tendency to straggle and need to be trimmed regularly to give them shape.

97

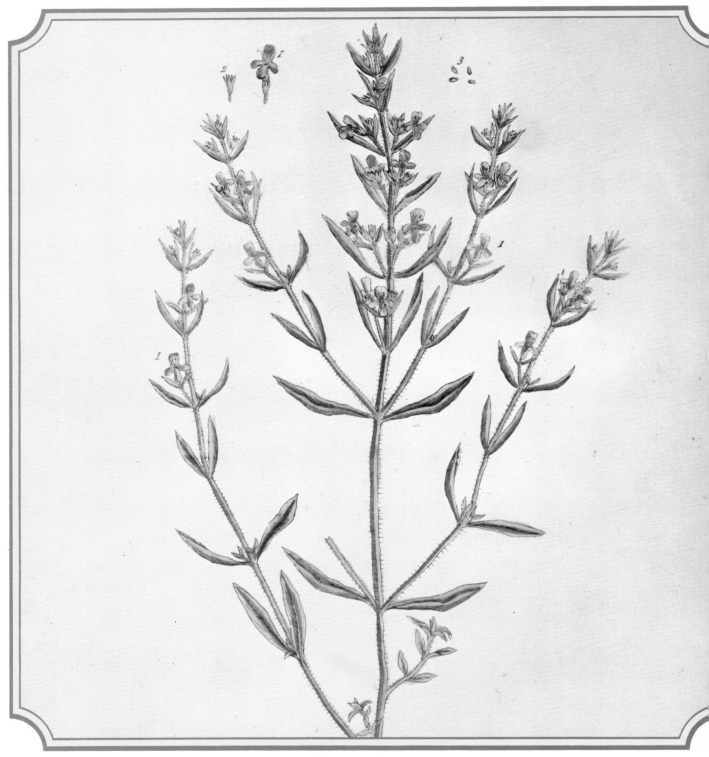

Savory is an aromatic herb of which there are two different types: summer and winter savory. Summer savory is an annual and grows to a height of about 30cm (1ft). Winter savory is a perennial plant which grows rapidly into a bushy shrub. Both types of savory have a similar spicy flavour resembling that of thyme.

Satureia hortensis

SUMMER SAVORY

Satureia montana

WINTER SAVORY

Both varieties have a similar spicy taste, although that of summer savory is subtler and more highly valued by cooks. *S. hortensis* is an annual, 30cm (12in) high with sparse, dark green, narrow leaves and white or lavender flowers. *S. montana* is a low growing, hardy perennial, 15-30cm (6-12in) high with aromatic leaves and white or blue flowers. Both savories are of Mediterranean origin and collectively are known as the 'bean herb'.

Soil Good, well drained soils.

Aspect Sunny.

Planting and cultivation Sow seeds in spring, or buy and set out small plants for quicker results. Set 15cm (6in) apart. Winter savory may need protection from frost in winter.

Harvesting Cut summer savory sprigs before the plant begins to flower and use fresh or dried. Winter savory is an evergreen and may be picked sparingly throughout the winter as well as the summer.

Pot growth Both savories grow well in pots, tubs and boxes, although it is advisable to bring winter savory indoors during the winter in cooler climates.

Uses Traditionally used in all bean dishes to increase the flavour and make them more digestible. Good in stuffings and casseroles, and, chopped fresh, can be added to salads and soups. Also served with trout and pork dishes.

Symphytum officinale
COMFREY

Native to the temperature regions of Europe and Asia, comfrey has been used for centuries as a healing herb of great virtue. It is a hardy perennial, about 90cm (3ft) high, with hairy leaves and stem. The bell-shaped flowers may be coloured blue, purple, pink or cream.

Soil Damp.

Position Shady.

Planting and cultivation Sow seeds in spring but nip off flower buds as it is self-seeding and spreads quickly.

Harvesting Pick leaves during the summer and dig up roots, if required in the autumn.

Propagation By seed or root division during the autumn.

Pot growth Not suitable.

Uses Mainly medicinal; as a tisane, ointment or root poultice it is used as a cough medicine and to staunch bleeding and heal wounds. The leaves may be cooked like spinach and are good with eggs, or fresh chopped leaves can be added to salads. It is also used to make wine.

Tanacetum vulgare
TANSY

A particularly beautiful, perennial herb introduced into the garden with discretion as it spreads quickly. Tansy may also be found growing wild throughout Europe and parts of America. It grows to 60-90cm (2-3ft) tall and has aromatic, dark green, ferny leaves which can be 25cm (10in) long

Below, left Tansy is a wild herb which can be successfully cultivated. It has small, yellow flowers whcih contrast pleasingly with the intensely green leaves. The name is derived from the Greek word for immortality, although this may refer to its persistence as a plant rather than to any therapeutic quality. Below, centre Comfrey is particularly renowned for its use in medicine through which it acquired its other common name of 'knit-bone'. It was believed to mend broken bones and to heal sprains, swellings and backache. Below, right Winter savory is a hardy dwarf evergreen which is extremely useful as a flavouring in winter when most other herbs are not available. It has a rather strong flavour which goes particularly well with broad or runner (lima) beans and is frequently added to bean and pea soups.

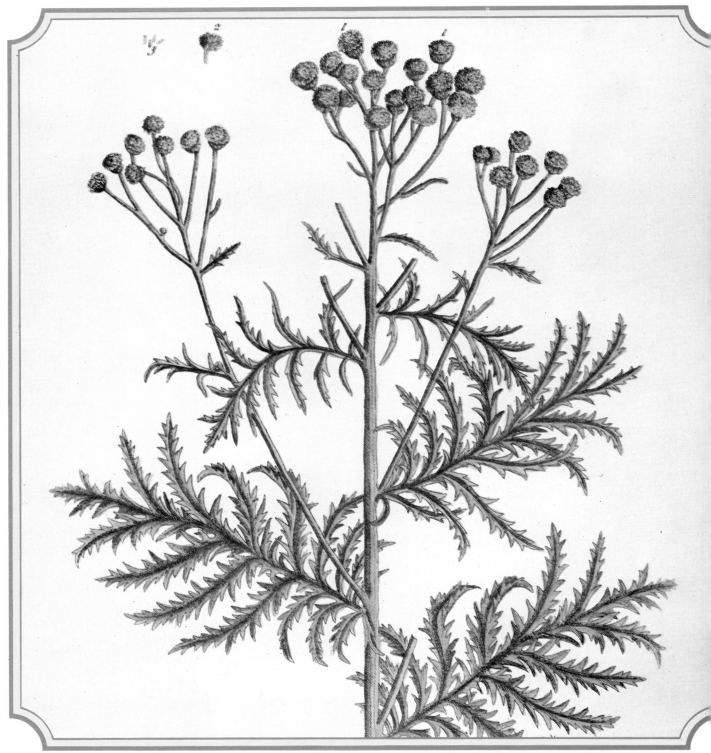

Tansy has bitter, aromatic leaves which are used in cooking to give a surprisingly pleasant flavour to desserts or savoury dishes. At one time the leaves were an important ingredient of the traditional British tansy, a confection of sugar, tansy, mint and currants enclosed in pastry and baked and eaten at Easter.

and clusters of yellow 'button' flowers.

Soil Ordinary.

Position Sunny.

Planting and cultivation Sow seed in the open in spring.

Harvesting The leaves may be harvested as required.

Propagation By seed or root division in spring or autumn.

Pot growth Not suitable.

Uses The leaves used to form an important ingredient in tansy cakes, traditionally served at Easter. The leaves were mixed with mint, sugar and currants, wrapped in pastry and baked. Tansy tea is hot and peppery and should only be taken occasionally in small quantities.

Thymus
THYME

There are numerous varieties of thyme of which the common (*T. vulgaris*) and lemon (*T. citriodorus*) are the main culinary species, although orange thyme (*T. fragantissimus*) also has a very attractive flavour. Thyme plants are perennial, grow to about 25cm (10in) tall, and are beautifully scented. Common thyme grows in the shape of a bush and has tiny, very dark leaves. Lemon thyme, along with several other varieties, is a shorter, creeping growth which spreads quickly and looks very attractive among

There are many different varieties of thyme of which the two most frequently used in cooking are common thyme and lemon thyme. Thyme is one of the three herbs that make up a bouquet garni and is particularly good in stuffings and meatball mixtures. It has a strong flavour and should be used with caution.

101

A nasturtium plant will add colour to your garden and flavour to your cooking. The young leaves are rich in vitamin C and give a peppery, sharp flavour to salads and cheese dishes, but use them in moderation. The flowers are lovely in salads and the green buds when pickled make a good substitute for capers.

paving stones in pathways and terraces. Thyme attracts bees.

Soil Light and well drained.

Position Full sun.

Planting and cultivation Sow seed or plant young stock in spring. Trim tops after flowering to keep plants compact. Replant every three to four years. Protect from frost in winter.

Harvesting Pick as required up to and during its flowering stage. Thyme responds well to drying.

Propagation Root division, seed or cuttings taken with a heel from the old stem. Or peg down peripheral branches and sever and transplant when independent roots have formed.

Pot growth Thyme grows well indoors in pots or in window boxes and outdoor containers.

Uses Stuffing made with a combination of common and lemon thyme is particularly good. Thyme forms part of a *bouquet garni*, and adds flavour to stews, poultry, sausages and game. Lemon thyme is good with fish or fruit dishes, and may be used dry in a *pot-pourri*. As a tisane, thyme is recommended as a cough mixture and for its digestive qualities.

Trigonella foenum graecum
FENUGREEK

A native of southern Europe and northern Africa, fenugreek should be treated as a hardy annual in temperate climates. The leaves, like those of clover, are divided into three segments and in summer the scented cream flowers produce the large pods of seeds for which the herb is grown.

Soil Well drained.

Position Sunny.

Planting and cultivation Sow seeds in spring.

Harvesting The plant is mature after about four months when it should be lifted whole and dried and the seeds shaken out.

Propagation By seed.

Pot growth Not suitable.

Uses The seeds are used in curry powders, pickles, chutneys and in the sweetmeat *halva*. Shoots from seed can be used in salad. Tisanes made from fenugreek seeds are good for the digestion. Scientists are also trying to utilise a substance found in the seed to act as an oral contraceptive.

Tropaeolum majus
NASTURTIUM

A decorative, creeping or climbing annual with bright green leaves like inverted umbrellas and brilliant flowers of yellow, orange or red. This plant originates from Peru and is rich in vitamin C.

Soil Any soil, preferably poor.

Position Sunny.

Planting and cultivation Sow seeds in spring *in situ*.

Harvesting Pick leaves and flowers as required.

Propagation By seed.

Pot growth Suitable for tubs, hanging baskets and window boxes.

Uses Apart from its purely decorative value, nasturtium buds are eaten pickled and can be substituted for capers, while the flowers and leaves can be chopped and used fresh in salads. The leaves have a hot, peppery taste so use with discretion. The roots also exude a substance which repels undesirable insects in the soil.

Verbena officinalis
VERVAIN

Also called 'verbena', this hardy perennial herb should not be confused with lemon verbena (*Lippa citriodora*). It has serrated, grey leaves and spikes of unscented lilac flowers in summer. Vervain was grown in herb gardens mainly because of its magical associations – it was said to ward off evil powers – although it does make a good tea.

Top Common, or black, thyme is one of the most frequently used of culinary herbs and is consequently the one most commonly grown. It is from this plant that thymol is extracted to be used in antiseptic gargles and mouthwashes. *Above* Although the nasturtium is native to Peru, it is extremely easy to cultivate in temperate climates as well. The beautiful, exotic flowers vary in shade from pale apricot to deep red and the leaves are excellent for ground cover. Many varieties can be trained to climb or trail up or down walls and trellises.

Verbena officinalis

Vervain is grown in herb gardens mainly because of its ancient magical associations—it was used to ward off evil powers—although vervain tisane is still popular, particularly in France. It was also reputed to have medicinal properties and was frequently added to hair tonics and eye wash preparations.

Soil Rich and well drained.
Position Sunny.
Planting and cultivation Sow seeds in early spring.
Harvesting Cut sprigs in summer to use fresh, or dry before the flowers open.
Propagation Seed, cuttings and root division.
Uses A tisane made with the leaves and sweetened with honey is particularly good as a mild sedative and a remedy for digestive problems. It used to be considered as a general panacea. An infusion of the leaves used for compresses in cases of tired eyes or for inflammation of the eyelids has a cleansing and strengthening effect.

COOKING WITH HERBS

SOUPS & STARTERS
FISH & SHELLFISH
POULTRY & GAME
VEGETABLES & SALADS
MEAT & MAIN COURSES
SAUCES, STUFFINGS & STOCKS
PUDDINGS & DESSERT
BREADS & CAKES

SOUPS & STARTERS

Lovage soup

	Metric/UK	US
Butter	25g/1oz	2 Tbs
Medium onions, sliced	2	2
Garlic clove, crushed	1	1
Flour	25g/1oz	¼ cup
Chicken stock	1¼l/2 pints	5 cups
Chopped fresh lovage	2 Tbs	2 Tbs
Large potatoes, sliced	4	4
Salt and pepper		
Milk	300ml/10floz	1¼ cups
Chopped fresh parsley	1 Tbs	1 Tbs

Melt the butter in a large saucepan. Add the onions and garlic and fry until they are soft. Remove from the heat and stir in the flour to form a smooth paste. Gradually stir in the stock and return to the heat. Bring to the boil, stirring constantly. Add the lovage, potatoes and seasoning to taste. Reduce the heat to low, cover the pan and simmer for 30 to 40 minutes, or until the potatoes are tender. Stir in the milk and bring to the boil.

Purée the soup in a blender until smooth, or rub through a strainer. Return the purée to the rinsed-out pan and reheat gently until it is hot but not boiling.

Sprinkle over the parsley and serve at once.

6 Servings

Cucumber and mint soup

	Metric/UK	US
Chicken stock	900ml/ 1½ pints	3¾ cups
Small onion, chopped	1	1
Cucumber, thinly sliced	1	1
Mint sprigs	3	3
Cornflour (cornstarch), blended with 1½ Tbs water	½ Tbs	½ Tbs
Salt and pepper		

Bring the stock to the boil in a large saucepan. Reduce the heat to low and add the onion. Simmer for 10 minutes, or until it is soft. Reserve a little cucumber for garnish and add the remainder to the stock, with one mint sprig. Simmer the soup for a further 7 minutes.

Purée the mixture in a blender until smooth, or rub through a strainer. Return the purée to the rinsed-out pan

Refreshing and cooling, Cucumber and Mint Soup is ideal for serving on a hot summer's day.

and stir in the cornflour (cornstarch) mixture. Stirring constantly bring the soup to the boil, then cook for 2 to 3 minutes, or until the soup thickens and is smooth. Season to taste. Remove from the heat and set aside to cool.

Pour the soup into a large serving bowl and chill in the refrigerator until very cold. Garnish with the remaining mint sprig and reserved cucumber and serve at once.

4 Servings

Cauliflower soup

	Metric/UK	US
Large cauliflower, trimmed	1	1
Chicken stock	900ml/ 1½ pints	3¾ cups
Salt	¼ tsp	¼ tsp
Butter	50g/2oz	4 Tbs
Flour	40g/1½oz	⅓ cup
Milk	300ml/ 10floz	1¼ cups
White pepper	½ tsp	½ tsp
Ground mace	¼ tsp	¼ tsp
Chopped fresh chervil	1½ tsp	1½ tsp
Egg yolk	1	1
Single (light) cream	2 Tbs	2 Tbs
Lemon juice	1 tsp	1 tsp

Break the cauliflower into small flowerets. Rinse in cold water and reserve about 10 of them. Chop the remaining flowerets.

Put the stock and salt into a saucepan and bring to the boil. Add the whole flowerets and cook for about 10 minutes, or until they are tender but firm. Using a slotted spoon, transfer the flowerets to a plate. Reserve the stock.

Melt the butter in a large saucepan. Remove from the heat and stir in the flour to form a smooth paste. Gradually add the reserved stock and the milk and return to the heat. Bring to the boil, stirring constantly and cook for 2 to 3 minutes, or until the mixture thickens and is smooth. Add the chopped cauliflower, pepper, mace and chervil, and half-cover. Simmer for 15 minutes, or until the cauliflower is soft enough to be mashed. Remove the pan from the heat and rub the mixture through a strainer set over a

saucepan. (Do not use a blender – the purée will be too smooth.)

Beat the egg yolk and cream together until they are lightly blended. Gradually add about 4 tablespoons of the soup purée, beating constantly. Pour the mixture very slowly into the pan, stirring constantly.

Add the reserved cauliflower flowerets to the soup and simmer gently until the soup is hot but not boiling. Do not let it come to the boil or it will curdle.

Stir in the lemon juice and serve at once.

4-6 Servings

Marigold fish and oyster soup

	Metric/UK	US
White fish, cleaned with the heads and tails left on	½kg/1lb	1lb
Onion, thinly sliced	1	1
Large carrot, thinly sliced	1	1
Bay leaf	1	1
Chopped fresh thyme	1 tsp	1 tsp
Black peppercorns, crushed	3	3
Salt	1 tsp	1 tsp
Water	1¼l/2 pints	5 cups
Beurre manié (two parts flour and one part butter blended to a paste)	50g/2oz	4 Tbs
Medium potatoes, diced	6	6
Milk	900ml/1½ pints	3¾ cups
Dried marigold petals	2 Tbs	2 Tbs
Fresh oysters, shelled, or canned oysters, drained	18	18

Put the fish in a large saucepan and add the vegetables, herbs, peppercorns and salt. Pour over the water and bring to the boil. Reduce the heat to low and simmer for 30 minutes, or until the fish flakes easily. Remove the pan from the heat. Pour the mixture through a fine strainer set over a bowl. Remove and discard all the bones, heads and tails from the fish and the bay leaf. Add the remaining fish flesh and vegetables to the strained stock in the bowl.

Put the stock into a blender and blend until the mixture forms a purée. Return the liquid to the rinsed-out pan and bring to the boil. Add the beurre manié, a little at a time, and cook for 2 to 3 minutes, stirring constantly, until the soup is thick and smooth.

Reduce the heat to low and add the potatoes and milk. Cook for 20 minutes, or until the potatoes are tender. Add half the marigold petals and the oysters and simmer for 2 to 4 minutes, or until the colour from the petals has infused into the soup.

Remove the pan from the heat and transfer the soup to a warmed tureen. Sprinkle with the remaining marigold petals and serve at once.

8 Servings

Chervil and leek soup

	Metric/UK	US
Butter	75g/3oz	6 Tbs
Large leeks, washed and chopped	3	3
Medium carrot, chopped	1	1
Medium potatoes, diced	3	3
Chicken stock	1¼l/2 pints	5 cups
Salt and pepper		
Chopped fresh chervil	1 bunch	1 bunch
Single (light) cream	125ml/4floz	½ cup

Melt 50g/2oz (4 tablespoons) of butter in a large saucepan. Add the vegetables and fry for 10 minutes, stirring occasionally. Pour in the stock, then add the seasoning and chervil and bring to the boil. Reduce the heat to low, cover the pan and simmer for 40 minutes.

Purée the soup in a blender until smooth, or rub through a strainer. Return the purée to the rinsed-out pan and bring to the boil. Simmer for 5 minutes, then add the cream and remaining butter. Simmer until the butter melts. Serve at once.

6 Servings

Split pea soup with mint and tomatoes

	Metric/UK	US
Butter	25g/1oz	2 Tbs
Medium onion, chopped	1	1
Medium tomatoes, blanched, skinned, seeded and chopped	4	4
Split peas, soaked overnight and drained	225g/8oz	1 cup
Beef stock	300ml/10floz	1¼ cups
Water	300ml/10floz	1¼ cups
Salt and pepper		
Chopped fresh mint	2 Tbs	2 Tbs
Chopped fresh basil	1 tsp	1 tsp
GARNISH		
Large tomato, blanched, skinned, seeded and cut into strips	1	1
Chopped fresh mint	1 tsp	2 tsp

Melt the butter in a large saucepan. Add the onion and fry until it is soft. Add the tomatoes and peas and stir until they are well coated with the butter. Pour in the stock and water add

the seasoning, mint and basil. Bring to the boil. Reduce the heat to low, cover the pan and simmer the soup for 1½ hours, or until the peas are very soft.

Purée the mixture in a blender until smooth, or rub through a strainer. Return the purée to the rinsed-out pan and bring to the boil, stirring constantly. Garnish with the tomato strips and mint, and serve at once.

4 Servings

Celery with red caviar

An elegant and simple appetizer, Celery with Red Caviar takes only minutes to prepare. It can be accompanied, in a separate dish, by black olives.

	Metric/UK	US
Celery	2 small heads	2 small heads
Full-fat cream cheese	225g/8oz	1 cup
Chopped fresh chives	2 Tbs	2 Tbs
Chopped fresh parsley	2 Tbs	2 Tbs
Jar red caviar	90g/3½oz	3½oz
White pepper	½ tsp	½ tsp

Clean the celery and cut each stalk into three, crosswise.

Combine the cream cheese, chives, parsley, caviar and pepper until they are thoroughly blended.

Spread a little of the caviar mixture on to each celery piece and chill in the refrigerator for 30 minutes before serving.

4-6 Servings

Tarragon liver pâté

	Metric/UK	US
Butter	25g/1oz	2 Tbs
Onion, finely chopped	1	1
Lean belly of pork, minced (ground)	175g/6oz	6oz
Chicken livers, cleaned and finely chopped	½kg/1lb	1lb
Chopped fresh tarragon	2 Tbs	2 Tbs
Eggs, lightly beaten	2	2
Double (heavy) cream	2 Tbs	2 Tbs
Salt and pepper		
Ground cinnamon	½ tsp	½ tsp

Preheat the oven to cool 150°C (Gas Mark 2, 300°F).

Melt the butter in a frying-pan. Add the onion and fry until it is soft. Add the pork and fry until it is lightly browned. Add the chicken livers and fry for 5 minutes, or until they are almost cooked through. Stir in the tarragon and remove from the heat.

Rub the mixture through a strainer into a bowl, discarding any pulp

The addition of oysters and marigold petals makes Marigold Fish and Oyster Soup a colourful and luxurious first course with a delicate flavour.

Fresh mackerel cooked in wine, herbs and spices, Soused Mackerel makes an ideal supper dish for the family.

remaining in the strainer. Alternatively, purée the mixture in a blender until smooth. then add the seasoning and cinnamon.

Spoon the mixture into a lightly greased terrine or deep ovenproof dish and smooth down the top. Cover terrine or dish and place it in a deep roasting tin. Pour in enough hot water to come half way up the sides of the terrine. Put the tin into the oven and bake for 1¼ hours, or until the pâté is lightly browned and has shrunk away from the sides of the terrine. Set aside to cool completely, then chill in the refrigerator for at least 2 hours before serving. Either serve in the tin or invert over a serving plate.

4-6 Servings

Soused mackerel

	Metric/UK	US
Mackerel, filleted and rolled with the skin on the outside	8	8
Dry white wine	1l/1¾ pints	4½ cups
Carrots, sliced	2	2
Medium onions, thinly sliced	2	2
Chopped fresh marjoram	4 tsp	4 tsp
Cloves	2	2
Bay leaves	4	4
Black peppercorns	1 tsp	1 tsp
Allspice berries	1 tsp	1 tsp
Salt	1 tsp	1 tsp
Lemon, sliced	1	1
Salt	1 tsp	1 tsp
Lemon, sliced	1	1

Preheat the oven to cool 150°C (Gas Mark 2, 300°F). Place the mackerel in

110

a large ovenproof dish and set aside.

Put the wine, carrots and onions in a saucepan and bring to the boil. Reduce the heat to low and simmer for 10 minutes. Strain the mixture over the fish, then sprinkle over the marjoram, cloves, bay leaves, peppercorns, allspice and salt. Arrange the lemon slices around the sides of the dish.

Put the dish into the oven and bake for 1½ to 2 hours, or until the fish flakes easily. Remove from the oven and set aside to cool completely before serving.

8 Servings

Nasturtium spread
This spread can be served on crispbread or toast as a canapé or snack, or with raw vegetables as a dip. Serve as soon as it is prepared since it will discolour if set aside for any length of time.

	Metric/UK	US
Cream cheese	125g/4oz	½ cup
Finely chopped nasturtium leaves	2 tsp	2 tsp
Paprika	½ tsp	½ tsp
Nasturtium flowers	3	3

Put all the ingredients, except the flowers, into a bowl and beat with a wooden spoon until they are well blended.

Transfer to a serving dish and garnish with the nasturtium flowers. Serve at once.

4 Servings

FISH & SHELLFISH

Bream (porgy) with fennel and white wine

	Metric/UK	US
Bream (porgy), cleaned and gutted	1x1kg/2lb	1x2lb
Fennel sprigs	2	2
Thyme sprigs	2	2
Butter	25g/1oz	2 Tbs
Salt and pepper		
Dry white wine	150ml/5floz	$\frac{2}{3}$ cup
Olive oil	1 Tbs	1 Tbs
Fennel, sliced	1 bulb	1 bulb
Tomatoes, sliced	2	2
Lemon, thinly sliced	1	1

Preheat the oven to moderate 180°C (Gas Mark 4, 350°F).

Make two deep incisions along the back of the fish. Insert the fennel sprigs into the incisions. Divide the thyme sprigs and butter and place inside the fish, then rub them all over with salt and pepper. Arrange the fish on a rack in a large roasting pan. Pour over the wine and oil and arrange the fennel, tomato and lemon slices on top.

Put the pan into the oven and bake for about 30 minutes, or until the fish flakes easily. Baste the fish occasionally during the cooking time.

Carefully transfer the fish to a warmed serving dish and serve at once.

4 Servings

Mullet baked with rock salt

	Metric/UK	US
Rock salt	350g/12oz	2 cups
Grey mullet, cleaned but with the head left on	1x2kg/4lb	1x4lb
Chopped fresh chives	1 tsp	1 tsp
Chopped fresh tarragon	1 tsp	1 tsp
Rosemary sprig	1	1
Juice of 1 lemon		

Preheat the oven to warm 170°C (Gas Mark 3, 325°F).

Cover the bottom of a large, deep ovenproof dish with approximately one-third of the rock salt. Place the fish on the salt. Sprinkle over the chives and tarragon and arrange the rosemary sprig on top. Sprinkle over the lemon juice. Pour in the remaining rock salt to surround and cover the fish completely. With the back of a wooden spoon, pat down the salt.

Put the dish into the oven and bake the fish for 50 minutes. Remove from the oven. Using a rolling pin or pestle, break the hardened crust of the salt. Prise off with a sharp knife and discard.

Serve the fish at once, from the dish.

4 Servings

Grilled (broiled) salmon with herb butter

	Metric/UK	US
HERB BUTTER		
Chopped fresh chervil	1 Tbs	1 Tbs
Chopped fresh tarragon	1 Tbs	1 Tbs
Chopped fresh parsley	1 Tbs	1 Tbs
Chopped spinach	1 Tbs	1 Tbs
Chopped watercress	1 Tbs	1 Tbs
Anchovy fillets	8	8
Capers	2 Tbs	2 Tbs
Small gherkins	4	4
Hard-boiled egg yolks	4	4
Butter	125g/4oz	8 Tbs
Olive oil	50ml/2floz	4 Tbs
Tarragon vinegar	4 Tbs	4 Tbs
Salt and pepper		
SALMON		
Thick salmon steaks	4	4
Butter, melted	75g/3oz	6 Tbs
Salt and pepper		
Lemon, sliced	1	1
Parsley sprigs (to garnish)		

To make the butter, half-fill a saucepan with water and bring to the boil. Add the herbs, spinach and watercress and boil for 1 minutes. Drain, then pat dry on paper towels. Put into a large mortar, with the anchovy fillets, capers, gherkins and egg yolks. Pound together for 5 minutes.

Beat the butter with a wooden spoon until it is soft and creamy. Blend in the herb mixture. Put the mixture into a strainer set over a bowl and press through with the back of a wooden spoon. Gradually add the olive oil, stirring constantly. Stir in the vinegar and season to taste. Alternatively, put all the ingredients except the butter in a blender and blend until completely smooth. Transfer to a bowl and beat in the butter. Spoon the herb butter into a sauceboat and set aside.

Preheat the grill (broiler) to high.

Dry the salmon steaks with paper towels and arrange them on a rack in a lined grill (broiler) pan. Brush the melted butter over both sides of the steaks. Grill (broil) for 3 minutes on each side. Baste with any remaining melted butter and sprinkle with salt and pepper to taste. Grill (broil) for a further 3 minutes on one side, then turn over and grill (broil) them for 5 minutes more, basting once with the melted butter. If the steaks look as if they are drying out, reduce the grill (broiler) to moderate.

Transfer the salmon steaks to a warmed serving dish and garnish with lemon slices and parsley sprigs. Serve at once, with the herb butter.

4 Servings

Perch with oregano

	Metric/UK	US
Perch, filleted	1kg/2lb	2lb
Butter	25g/1oz	2 Tbs
Chopped fresh oregano	1 Tbs	1 Tbs
Salt	1 tsp	1 tsp
Red pepper flakes	¼ tsp	¼ tsp
Chopped fresh parsley	2 Tbs	2 Tbs
Lemon slices	4	4

Preheat the grill (broiler) to high.

Lay the fillets in a lined grill (broiler) pan. Melt the butter in a small saucepan. Stir in the oregano, salt and pepper flakes and remove from the heat. Pour the mixture over the fillets and grill (broil) the fillets for 5 minutes. Turn over and cook for a further 5

Simple and quick to prepare, Perch with Oregano tastes quite delicious.

minutes, or until the fish flakes easily. Remove from the heat.

Transfer the fillets to a warmed serving dish. Pour the cooking liquid over the fillets, sprinkle over the parsley and garnish with the lemon slices. Serve at once.

6 Servings

Provençal scallops

	Metric/UK	US
Scallops, cut into 1cm/½in pieces	700g/1½lb	1½lb
Juice of ½ lemon		
Salt and pepper		
Flour	50g/2oz	½ cup
Vegetable oil	75ml/3floz	⅓ cup
Shallots, finely chopped	3	3
Garlic cloves, crushed	3	3
Finely chopped fresh basil	1 tsp	1 tsp
Butter	25g/1oz	2 Tbs
Chopped fresh parsley	1 Tbs	1 Tbs

Gently rub the scallops with the lemon juice and salt and pepper to taste. Coat the scallops in the flour, shaking off any excess.

Heat half the oil in a large frying-pan. (The oil should cover the bottom of the pan in a thin layer so if necessary add the rest.) Add the scallops and cook for 5 minutes, or until they are evenly browned. Add the shallots, garlic and basil and cook for 2 minutes, stirring frequently. Remove from the heat and stir in the butter and parsley until the butter melts.

Serve at once.

4 Servings

Eels in herb sauce

	Metric/UK	US
Butter	75g/3oz	6 Tbs
Spinach, chopped	225g/8oz	2 cups
Chopped fresh tarragon	1 tsp	1 tsp
Chopped fresh parsley	3 Tbs	3 Tbs
Chopped fresh sage	1 tsp	1 tsp
Eels, skinned, cleaned and cut into 8cm/3in pieces	1kg/2lb	2lb

Provencal Scallops is a superb dish of scallops sautéed with garlic, basil and parsley.

	Metric/UK	US
Salt and pepper		
Dry white wine	300ml/ 10floz	1¼ cups
Egg yolks, lightly beaten	3	3
Lemon juice	1 Tbs	1 Tbs

Melt the butter in a large, deep frying-pan. Add the spinach and herbs and fry for 2 minutes, stirring constantly. Add the eel pieces and seasoning, then pour over the wine. Bring to the boil, reduce the heat to low and cover the pan. Simmer for 15 minutes, or until the eel is cooked through and tender. Remove the pan from the heat.

Gradually add about 4 tablespoons of the pan liquid to the egg yolks, beating constantly. Pour the egg mixture very slowly into the frying-pan, stirring constantly. Add the lemon juice and adjust the seasoning. Set aside until cool, transfer the eels to a serving dish, then chill in the refrigerator until very cold.

6 Servings

Trout with rosemary

	Metric/UK	US
Trout, cleaned	4	4
Salt and pepper		
Garlic cloves, halved	2	2
Rosemary sprigs	4	4
Olive oil	3 Tbs	3 Tbs
Lemon, cut into 8	1	1

Preheat the grill (broiler) to moderate.

Rub the fish all over with salt and pepper. Put half a garlic clove and a rosemary sprig into the cavity of each fish. Make three shallow incisions along each side of each fish and arrange them in the grill (broiler) pan.

Lightly coat the trout with the oil, then grill (broil) for 5 minutes. Turn the fish over, brush with the remaining oil and grill (broil) for a further 5 to 6 minutes, or until the fish flakes easily.

Transfer the fish to a warmed serving dish. Remove and discard the garlic and rosemary and garnish with the lemon wedges. Serve at once.

4 Servings

Eels in Herbs Sauce is a Flemish dish of eels simmered in wine and green herbs. Although it is occasionally eaten hot, it is preferable to serve this dish when it is cold. Fresh herbs should be used whenever possible and such herbs as sorrel and chervil can be included, when available, and fresh, tender nettles substituted for the spinach.

Moules mariniéres

(Mussels with White Wine Sauce)

Serve Moules Mariniéres in deep soup bowls with a fork to eat the mussels and a soup spoon for the juices.

	Metric/UK	US
Mussels	3½l/3 quarts	4 quarts
Butter	50g/2oz	4 Tbs
Small onion, finely chopped	1	1
Garlic clove, crushed	1	1
Bouquet garni	1	1
Dry white wine	450ml/15floz	2 cups
Salt and pepper		
Chopped fresh parsley	2 Tbs	2 Tbs

Wash the mussels in cold water and scrub to remove any mud and tufts. Discard any that are not tightly shut or do not close when sharply tapped. Put the mussels into a bowl of cold water and soak for 1 hour. Drain and set aside.

Melt the butter in a large saucepan. Add the onion and garlic and fry until they are soft. Add the bouquet garni, wine and seasoning and bring to the boil. Reduce the heat to low and add the mussels. Simmer, shaking the pan occasionally, for 6 to 10 minutes, or until the shells open. Using a slotted spoon, transfer the mussels to a warmed serving dish. Set aside and keep hot.

Strain the cooking liquid into a bowl, then return to the rinsed pan. Bring to the boil and boil briskly for 2 minutes. Pour over the mussels, sprinkle over the parsley and serve at once.

4 Servings

Parsley and fish pie

	Metric/UK	US
Puff pastry, chilled	350g/12oz	3 cups
Egg yolk	1	1
FILLING		
Milk	300ml/10floz	1¼ cups
Shallot, sliced	1	1
Chopped fresh marjoram	1 tsp	1 tsp
Chopped fresh dill	1 tsp	1 tsp
Bay leaf	1	1
Salt and pepper		
Butter	25g/1oz	2 Tbs
Flour	25g/1oz	¼ cup
Cod fillets, cooked, skinned and flaked	½kg/1lb	1lb
Chopped fresh parsley	8 Tbs	8 Tbs
Lemon juice	1 tsp	1 tsp

Preheat the oven to fairly hot 190°C (Gas Mark 5, 375°F).

To make the filling, put the milk, shallot, herbs and seasoning into a saucepan and set over low heat. Infuse the milk for 10 minutes. Remove from the heat and strain into a bowl. Discard the contents of the strainer.

Melt the butter in a saucepan. Remove the pan from the heat and stir in the flour to form a smooth paste. Gradually stir in the strained milk and return the pan to the heat. Cook, stirring constantly, for 2 to 3 minutes, or until the sauce is thick and smooth. Remove from the heat and stir in the fish, parsley and lemon juice. Set aside while you roll out the pastry.

Roll out the pastry dough on a lightly floured surface to a square approximately ½cm/¼in thick. Trim the edges to straighten if necessary, then moisten the edges with a little cold water. Carefully arrange the square over a well-greased baking sheet. Spoon the fish filling into the centre of the dough. Lift each of the four corners of the dough up and over the filling until they meet in the centre. Pinch the points of the corners together to seal.

Brush the top of the pie with the egg yolk and put the sheet into the oven. Bake for 30 to 40 minutes, or until the pastry is golden brown. Remove from the oven, transfer the pie to a warmed serving dish, and serve at once.

4 Servings

Above Cod fillets folded into a creamy sauce flavoured with parsley and enveloped in a light puff pastry, Parsley and Fish Pie makes an excellent supper dish for the family. Opposite page Moules Marinière is generally served in a soup bowl, with a soup spoon for the juices, although the mussels themselves are eaten with the fingers. A good idea is to provide each person with a plate on which to put discarded shells and a bowl of water in which to rinse the fingers after eating.

POULTRY & GAME

Roast chicken with tarragon

	Metric/UK	US
Butter, softened	125g/4oz	8 Tbs
Salt and pepper		
Tarragon sprigs, finely chopped	6	6
Chicken	1x2½kg/5lb	1x5lb

Preheat the oven to fairly hot 190°C (Gas Mark 5, 375°F).

Beat half the butter with a wooden spoon until it is soft and creamy. Beat in salt and pepper to taste and the tarragon until thoroughly blended. Stuff the mixture into the cavity of the chicken.

Rub half the remaining butter over the breast of the chicken and place the bird, on its side, in a roasting pan. Put the pan into the oven and roast for 30 minutes. Turn the chicken on to its other side and add the remaining butter. Roast for a further 30 minutes, Reduce the oven temperature to moderate 180°C (Gas Mark 4, 350°F).

Turn the chicken on to its back and baste well with the melted butter in the pan. Roast for a final 30 minutes, basting once more, or until the chicken is cooked through and tender.

Remove from the oven and serve at once, with the pan juices.

6 Servings

Chicken with basil

	Metric/UK	US
Chicken breasts	2	2
Salt and pepper		
Butter	5g/2oz	4 Tbs
Dry white wine	125ml/4floz	½ cup
Chicken stock	125ml/4floz	½ cup
Chopped fresh basil	2 tsp	2 tsp
Beurre manié (two parts flour and one part butter blended to a paste)	2 tsp	2 tsp

Rub the chicken breasts all over with salt and pepper.

Chicken with Basil is a simple and economical dish. Serve with stuffed tomatoes and new potatoes for an appetizing lunch or dinner.

Melt the butter in a large saucepan. Add the chicken breasts and fry for about 10 minutes, or until they are evenly browned on both sides. Reduce the heat to low, cover the pan and cook for 20 to 25 minutes, or until the breasts are cooked through and tender. Using tongs, transfer the chicken to a warmed serving dish. Keep hot while you finish the sauce.

Skim any fat from the surface of the pan liquid. Add the wine, stock and basil and bring to the boil. Boil for about 10 minutes, or until the liquid has reduced by about half. Add the beurre manié, a little at a time, and cook until the sauce thickens and is smooth.

Pour the sauce over the chicken and serve at once.

2 Servings

Chicken casserole

	Metric/UK	US
Chicken pieces	4	4
Carrots, chopped	2	2
Garlic cloves, crushed	2	2
Chopped fresh parsley	2 tsp	2 tsp
Chopped fresh savory	2 tsp	2 tsp
Salt	1½ tsp	1½ tsp
Water	900ml/1½ pints	3¾ cups
SAUCE		
Butter	25g/1oz	2 Tbs
Mushrooms, sliced	125g/4oz	1 cup
Chopped fresh savory	1 tsp	1 tsp
Chopped fresh parsley	½ tsp	½ tsp
Flour	25g/1oz	¼ cup
Dry white wine	125ml/4floz	½ cup
Sour cream	2 Tbs	2 Tbs

Put the chicken pieces, carrots, garlic, herbs, salt and water into a large saucepan and bring to the boil. Reduce the heat to low, cover the pan and simmer for 40 to 45 minutes, or until the chicken is cooked through and tender. Using tongs, remove the chicken from the pan. Strain and reserve the stock. When the chicken is cool enough to handle, remove and discard the skin and bones and set the meat aside.

Meanwhile, to make the sauce, melt the butter in a deep frying-pan. Add the mushrooms and herbs and fry for 3 minutes, stirring constantly. Remove the pan from the heat and stir in the flour to form a smooth paste. Gradually stir in the reserved stock and wine and return to the heat. Bring to the boil, then cook for 2 to 3 minutes, stirring constantly, or until the sauce thickens and is smooth.

Return the chicken pieces to the pan and baste well with the sauce. Simmer for a further 2 minutes to reheat the chicken, then remove from the heat. Stir in the sour cream and transfer the mixture to a warmed serving dish. Serve at once.

4 Servings

Chicken with rosemary

	Metric/UK	US
Large chicken quarters	4	4
Salt and pepper		
Butter	75g/3oz	6 Tbs
Large onions, thinly sliced	2	2
Orange juice	450ml/15floz	2 cups
Chopped fresh rosemary	1 Tbs	1 Tbs
Grated orange rind	1 Tbs	1 Tbs
Cornflour (cornstarch), blended with 1 Tbs water	1½ Tbs	1½ Tbs

Rub the chicken pieces all over with salt and pepper.

Melt two-thirds of the butter in a large saucepan. Add the chicken pieces and fry until they are deeply and evenly browned. Using tongs, transfer them to a plate. Melt the remaining butter in the pan. Add the onions and fry until they are soft. Pour over the orange juice and bring to the boil, stirring occasionally. Stir in the rosemary and orange rind.

Reduce the heat to low and return the chicken pieces to the pan. Baste well with the juice. Cover and simmer for 40 minutes, or until the chicken is cooked through and tender. Using tongs, transfer the chicken to a warmed serving dish. Keep hot while you finish the sauce.

Bring the pan liquid to the boil and boil briskly for 3 minutes, or until it has reduced slightly. Reduce the heat to low and stir in the conrflour (cornstarch) mixture. Cook for 2 to 3 minutes, stirring constantly, or until the sauce is thick and smooth. Pour over the chicken and serve at once.

4 Servings

Rosemary is an evergreen shrub of Mediterranean origin whose leaves are used to flavour meat, especially lamb, and breads as well as poultry.

Marinated overnight in a mixture of yogurt, herbs and spices, Indian Chicken Kebabs are delicious served with naan bread, salad and a variety of chutneys.

Chicken Kiev

	Metric/UK	US
Butter	125g/4oz	8 Tbs
Chopped fresh parsley	1 Tbs	1 Tbs
Chopped fresh chives	1 Tbs	1 Tbs
Garlic cloves, crushed	2	2
Salt and pepper to taste		
Chicken breasts, skinned and boned	8	8
Flour	50g/2oz	½ cup
Eggs, lightly beaten	2	2
Dry breadcrumbs	175g/6oz	2 cups
Sufficient vegetable oil for deep-frying		

Beat the butter with a wooden spoon until it is soft and creamy. Beat in the parsley, chives, garlic and season to taste with salt and pepper. Divide the butter mixture into eight pieces, then shape them into small cigar shapes. Chill the shapes in the refrigerator until they are firm.

Place each chicken breast between two sheets of greaseproof or waxed paper and pound until it is thin. Remove the greaseproof or waxed paper and wrap each breast around a piece of the butter mixture, envelope fashion, so that the butter is completely enclosed.

Dip the chicken parcels, first in the flour, then in the eggs and finally in the breadcrumbs, coating them completely and shaking off any excess. Chill the pieces in the refrigerator for 1 hour.

Heat the oil in a deep-frying pan until it reaches 185°C (360°F) on a deep-fat thermometer, or until a small cube of stale bread dropped into the oil turns golden in 55 seconds. Carefully arrange the breasts, two or three at a time, in a deep-frying basket and lower them into the oil. Fry for 5 to 6 minutes, or until they are golden brown and crisp. Remove from the oil, drain on paper towels and keep warm while you fry the remaining pieces.

Serve hot.

4 Servings

Indian chicken kebabs

	Metric/UK	US
Yogurt	150ml/5floz	$\frac{2}{3}$ cup
Garlic cloves, crushed	4	4
Fresh root ginger, peeled and chopped	4cm/1$\frac{1}{2}$in piece	1$\frac{1}{2}$in piece
Small onion, grated	1	1
Hot chilli powder	1$\frac{1}{2}$ tsp	1$\frac{1}{2}$ tsp
Ground coriander	1 Tbs	1 Tbs
Salt	1 tsp	1 tsp
Chicken breasts, skinned and boned	4	4
GARNISH		
Large onion, thinly sliced into rings	1	1
Large tomatoes, thinly sliced	2	2
Chopped fresh coriander leaves	2 Tbs	2 Tbs

Put the yogurt, garlic, ginger, onion, chilli powder, coriander and salt into a bowl and beat well to blend. Set aside.

Cut the chicken meat into 2$\frac{1}{2}$cm/1in cubes and add to the yogurt mixture, basting thoroughly. Cover the bowl and put into the refrigerator. Leave for at least 6 hours, or overnight.

Preheat the grill (broiler) to high.

Thread the chicken cubes on to skewers and arrange on a rack in a lined grill (broiler) pan. Cook for 5 to 6 minutes, turning occasionally, or until the cubes are cooked through and tender.

Remove the skewers from the heat and slide the kebabs on to a warmed serving dish. Garnish with the onion rings, tomato slices and chopped coriander leaves. Serve at once.

4 Servings

Matzo chicken with dill

	Metric/UK	US
Eggs, lightly beaten	8	8
Medium onion, finely chopped	1	1
Chopped fresh dill	6 Tbs	6 Tbs
Chopped fresh parsley	4 Tbs	4 Tbs
Salt	2 tsp	2 tsp
Black pepper	1 tsp	1 tsp
Ground mace	$\frac{1}{2}$ tsp	$\frac{1}{2}$ tsp
Cooked chicken meat, cut into strips	$\frac{1}{2}$kg/1lb	1lb
Mushrooms, finely chopped	225g/8oz	2 cups
Butter	50g/2oz	4 Tbs
Matzos	5	5
Chicken stock	450ml/ 15floz	2 cups

Preheat the oven to fairly hot 190°C (Gas Mark 5, 375°F).

Beat the eggs, onion, dill, 3 tablespoons of parsley, seasoning and mace until they are light and frothy. Add the chicken and mushrooms and mix well. Set aside.

Melt the butter in a small saucepan. Remove the pan from the heat and pour about $\frac{1}{2}$ tablespoon of the melted butter into a 23cm/9in square baking tin or dish. Tip and rotate the dish to cover evenly. Reserve the remaining butter.

Soak the matzos in the chicken stock for 1 minutes. Remove from the dish and set aside. Discard the stock.

Put one matzo on the bottom of the prepared dish and cover with about a quarter of the chicken mixture. Top with another matzo. Repeat these layers until the ingredients are used up, ending with a layer of matzo. Pour over the reserved butter and remaining parsley.

Put the dish into the oven and bake for 30 minutes, or until the top is browned. Remove from the oven and serve at once.

4-6 Servings

Duck with sauerkraut

	Metric/UK	US
Duck	1x2$\frac{3}{4}$kg/6lb	1x6lb
Salt and pepper		
Butter	75g/3oz	6 Tbs
Canned sauerkraut, drained and rinsed	1kg/2lb	2lb
Salt pork, diced	50g/2oz	$\frac{1}{3}$ cup
Vegetable oil	50ml/2floz	$\frac{1}{4}$ cup
Medium onions, thinly sliced	2	2
Medium carrots, thinly sliced	2	2
Cooking apple, peeled, cored and chopped	1	1
Dry white wine	250ml/8floz	1 cup
Chicken stock	175ml/6floz	$\frac{3}{4}$ cup
Garlic clove	1	1
Peppercorns	6	6
Parsley sprigs	4	4
Bay leaf	1	1
Juniper berries	10	10

Preheat the oven to warm 170°C (Gas Mark 3, 325°F).

Prepare the duck by clipping the wing ends and neck and trussing so that the wings and legs are close to the body. Prick the skin around the thighs, back and lower breast. Rub salt and pepper into the cavity, then close with a skewer.

Melt the butter in a large flameproof casserole. Add the duck and fry until it

Opposite page, above, *Crisp, golden pastry enclosing a creamy herb-flavoured filling, Turkey and Walnut Pie is a delectable way of using up leftover cooked turkey. Opposite page, below Stuffed Roast Goose filled with a juicy and aromatic combination of parsley, thyme and apples is the ideal dish for a large dinner party.*

is evenly browned. Cover the casserole and put into the oven. Braise for 2 hours, or until the duck is cooked through and tender.

After the duck has been cooking for about 1 hour, prepare the sauerkraut. Blanch the salt pork in water for about 5 minutes to remove the excess salt. Drain and dry thoroughly on paper towels.

Heat the oil in a large, deep frying-pan. Add the salt pork and fry until it resembles small croûtons and has rendered most of its fat. Add the onions and carrots and fry until they are soft. Add the apple and sauerkraut and stir well. Pour in the wine and stock and bring to the boil. Tie all the remaining ingredients together in a small cheesecloth bag and put into the middle of the sauerkraut mixture. Reduce the heat to low, cover the pan and simmer the sauerkraut for 30 to 40 minutes. Remove the cheesecloth bag at the end of the period. Remove the juniper berries from the bag and return them to the sauerkraut. Discard the remaining contents of the bag. Season to taste.

When the duck is cooked, transfer it to a warmed serving dish. Untruss. Surround the duck with the sauerkraut mixture and serve at once.

4 Servings

Stuffed roast goose

	Metric/UK	US
Oven-ready goose	1x3½kg/8lb	1x8lb
Lemon, quartered	1	1
Salt and pepper		
STUFFING		
Fresh white breadcrumbs	350g/12oz	6 cups
Finely grated rind and juice of 3 lemons		
Finely chopped fresh parsley	10 Tbs	10 Tbs
Finely chopped fresh lemon thyme	1½ tsp	1½ tsp
Salt and pepper		
Cooking apples, peeled, cored and grated	2	2
Eggs, lightly beaten	3	3
Butter, melted	40g/1½oz	3 Tbs
Cider	300ml/10floz	1¼ cups

Preheat the oven to very hot 230°C (Gas Mark 8, 450°F).

Prick the goose all over with a fork. Rub the skin with three of the lemon quarters. Squeeze the juice of the remaining quarter into the cavity. Rub the skin all over with salt and pepper and set the goose aside.

To make the stuffing, beat the breadcrumbs, lemon rind and juice, herbs, seasoning and apples together. Then add the eggs, melted butter and cider until the mixture is smooth and thick. Spoon the stuffing into the cavity of the goose and secure the opening with a skewer or a trussing needle and thread.

Arrange the goose, on its breast, on a rack in a roasting pan. Place the pan in the oven and roast for 15 minutes. Reduce the oven temperature to moderate 180°C (Gas Mark 4, 350°F) and roast for a further 2½ to 3 hours, or until the bird is cooked through and tender, removing the fat frequently from the pan. Turn the goose on to its back halfway through the cooking period.

Remove the goose from the oven and remove and discard the skewer or trussing thread. Serve at once.

8 Servings

Turkey and walnut pie

	Metric/UK	US
Butter	25g/1oz	2 Tbs
Mushrooms, sliced	225g/8oz	2 cups
Flour	25g/1oz	¼ cup
Salt and pepper		
Double (heavy) cream	300ml/10floz	1¼ cups
Sour cream	150ml/5floz	⅔ cup
Chopped fresh thyme	1 tsp	1 tsp
Chopped fresh sage	1 tsp	1 tsp
Bay leaf	1	1
Cooked turkey, cubed	700g/1½lb	1½lb
Walnuts, chopped	125g/4oz	⅔ cup
Puff pastry, chilled	375g/12oz	3 cups
Egg yolk	1	1

Preheat the oven to hot 220°C (Gas Mark 7, 425°F).

Melt the butter in a saucepan and add the mushrooms. Cook, stirring frequently, for 3 minutes.

Remove the pan from the heat and transfer the mushrooms to a plate. Stir the flour, salt and pepper into the pan juices to make a smooth paste. Gradually add the double (heavy) cream and sour cream, stirring constantly. Stir in the thyme, sage and bay leaf.

Return the pan to the heat and cook, stirring constantly, for 10 minutes. Remove and discard the bay leaf. Return the mushrooms to the pan and add the turkey and walnuts. Spoon the mixture into a deep pie dish and set aside.

Roll out the dough to about ½cm/¼in thick. Cut off a strip of dough about 1cm/½in wide, long enough to fit the rim of the pie dish. Moisten the rim

with a little water and press down the dough strip. Moisten the strip with water.

Lift the remaining dough on to the rolling pin, and lay it over the pie dish. Trim and crimp the edges to seal. Make a small slit in the centre of the dough. Brush the top with the egg yolk.

Place the pie in the oven and bake for 50 minutes. Reduce the temperature to fairly hot 190°C (Gas Mark 5, 375°F) and continue baking for 35 minutes or until the pastry is golden brown. Remove the pie from the oven and serve immediately.

4-6 Servings

Partridge pot roast

	Metric/UK	US
Butter	50g/2oz	4 Tbs
Medium onions, chopped	2	2
Carrots, sliced	2	2
Streaky (fatty) bacon slices, chopped	6	6
Mushrooms, sliced	125g/4oz	1 cup
Partridges, trussed and larded	4	4
Salt and pepper		
Bouquet garni	1	1
Beef stock	900ml/1½pts	3¾ cups
Red wine	125ml/4floz	½ cup
Chopped fresh parsley	2 Tbs	2 Tbs

Melt the butter in a large frying-pan. Add the onions and carrots and fry until the onions are soft. Transfer the vegetables to a large flameproof casserole. Add the bacon and mushrooms to the pan and fry until the bacon is crisp and has rendered most of its fat. Transfer the bacon mixture to the casserole.

Place the partridges in the pan and cook, turning them occasionally, for 8 to 10 minutes or until they are lightly and evenly browned. Add the partridges to the casserole along with the salt, pepper and bouquet garni. Pour over the stock and wine. Place the casserole over high heat and bring the liquid to the boil. Reduce the heat to low, cover and cook, stirring occasionally, for 1 hour or until the partridges are tender and cooked through.

Remove the partridges from the casserole, cut each one into 4 pieces and keep hot while you make the sauce.

Strain the cooking liquid and set the vegetables aside to keep warm. Remove and discard the bouquet garni.

Return the cooking liquid to the casserole. Bring to the boil and keep at the boil for about 8 minutes or until

the liquid has reduced by about 1 third. Return the partridges and vegetables to the casserole and stir in the parsley. Simmer for a few minutes until the partridges are heated through. Serve immediately.

4 Servings

Venison pie

	Metric/UK	US
Boned lean venison, cubed	700g/1½lb	1½lb
Lambs' kidneys, skinned, cored and chopped	225g/8oz	8oz
Salt and pepper		
Mixed spice or ground allspice	1 tsp	1 tsp
Ground mace	¼ tsp	¼ tsp
Large onion, finely chopped	1	1
Chopped fresh parsley	2 Tbs	2 Tbs
Beef stock	250ml/8floz	1 cup
Puff pastry, chilled	175g/6oz	1½ cups
Red wine	50ml/2floz	¼ cup
Red wine vinegar	1 Tbs	1 Tbs
Olive oil	2 Tbs	2 Tbs
Egg yolk, lightly beaten	1	1

Put the meats, seasoning, spices, onion and parsley into a large saucepan and pour over the stock. Bring to the boil. Reduce the heat to low, cover the pan and simmer for 2 hours. Remove the pan from the heat and set aside to cool completely. When the mixture is cold, skim any fat from the surface.

Preheat the oven to very hot 230°C (Gas Mark 8, 450°F).

Roll out the pastry dough on a lightly floured surface to a 25cm/10in diameter circle. Cut a strip from outside the circle, about 2½cm/1in wide.

Using a slotted spoon, transfer the venison and kidneys to a 23cm/9in pie dish and pour in 75ml/3floz (⅓ cup) of the cooking liquid, the wine, vinegar and oil. Discard the remaining cooking liquid. Put a pie funnel in the middle of the dish. Press the thin dough strip around the rim of the pie dish and moisten with water. Lift the dough circle on to the pie dish and press the edges together to seal. Brush the dough with the beaten egg yolk.

Put the dish into the oven and bake for 10 minutes. Reduce the oven temperature to moderate 180°C (Gas Mark 4, 350°F) and bake for a further 20 to 25 minutes, or until the pastry is golden brown.

Remove from the oven and serve at once.

6 Servings

A traditional British dish, Venison Pie tastes delicious. The meat is first simmered in stock, and then enclosed in puff pastry. Serve with new potatoes boiled with mint for a delicious and nourishing meal.

MEAT & MAIN COURSES

Marinated beef and pot roast

	Metric/UK	US
Rump steak, rolled and tied	1x2¾kg/6lb	1x6lb
Dry red wine	600ml/1 pint	2½ cups
Medium onion, thinly sliced into rings	1	1
Garlic cloves	4	4
Finely chopped fresh basil	2 tsp	2 tsp
Finely chopped fresh oregano	1 tsp	1 tsp
Butter	25g/1oz	2 Tbs
Olive oil	50ml/2floz	¼ cup
Salt and pepper		
Canned peeled tomatoes, drained	425g/14oz	14oz
Black olives, stoned (pitted)	50g/2oz	½ cup
Beurre manié (two parts flour and one part butter blended to a paste)	1 Tbs	1 Tbs
Chopped fresh parsley	1 Tbs	1 Tbs

Put the meat into a large bowl. Add the wine, onion, garlic, basil and oregano, and stir well. Set aside at room temperature for 6 hours, basting occasionally.

Preheat the oven to moderate 180°C (Gas Mark 4, 350°F).

Remove the meat from the marinade and dry on paper towels. Reserve the marinade.

Melt the butter with the oil in a large flameproof casserole. Add the meat and fry until it is evenly browned. Add the reserved marinade and season to taste. Bring to the boil. Remove the casserole from the heat and transfer it to the oven. Braise for 1½ hours. Add the tomatoes and braise for a further 1 hour, or until the meat is cooked through and tender.

Remove the casserole from the oven. Using two large forks, transfer the meat to a carving board. Cut into thick slices, arrange them on a warmed serving dish and keep hot while you finish the sauce.

Skim off any fat from the surface of the cooking liquid, then strain into a bowl, pressing down on the vegetables with the back of a wooden spoon to extract all the liquid. Return the strained liquid to the casserole. Set the casserole over high heat and bring to the boil. Add the olives. Reduce the heat to low and add the beurre manié, a little at a time, and cook until the liquid thickens and is smooth.

Pour the sauce over the meat slices, sprinkle over the parsley and serve.

10 Servings

Beef and bean casserole

	Metric/UK	US
Dried black-eyed beans, soaked in cold water over night	450g/1lb	2⅔ cups
Cold water	1½l/2½ pints	6¼ cups
Salt and pepper		
Pork sausages	½kg/1lb	1lb
Cooking oil	1 Tbs	1 Tbs
Large onions, chopped	2	2
Garlic cloves, crushed	2	2
Stewing beef (beef chuck), cubed	1kg/2lb	2lb
Chopped fresh savory	1 tsp	1 tsp
Bay leaf	1	1
Chopped fresh marjoram	½ tsp	½ tsp
Large tomatoes, blanched, skinned and sliced	4	4
Beef stock or red wine	175ml/6floz	¾ cup

Drain the beans and transfer them to a large saucepan. Pour over the water and add salt and pepper to taste. Bring to the boil, reduce the heat to low and simmer for 1½ hours, or until the beans are cooked through and tender. Drain and reserve about 350ml/12floz (1½ cups) of the cooking liquid.

Preheat the oven to cool 150°C (Gas Mark 2, 300°F).

Slice the sausages into 2½cm/1in lengths. Heat the oil in a large frying-pan. Add the sausages and fry until they are evenly browned. Using a slotted spoon, transfer the sausages to drain on paper towels.

Pour off all but 3 tablespoons of the oil in the pan. Add the onions and garlic and fry until they are soft. Add the beef cubes and fry until they are evenly browned. Transfer the pan mixture to a large ovenproof casserole, and stir in the savory, bay leaf, marjoram, tomatoes and stock or wine. Season to taste, cover and put the casserole into the oven. Cook for 2 hours.

Remove the casserole from the oven and stir in the beans, sausage pieces

Beef and Bean Casserole is a hearty, filling dish, ideal for a family lunch on a cold winter's day.

and the reserved bean cooking liquid. Return to the oven and cook for a further 1 hour, stirring occasionally, or until the beef is cooked through and tender.

Remove from the oven and serve at once.

8 Servings

Marjoram beef ring

	Metric/UK	US
Minced (ground) beef	1kg/2lb	2lb
Fresh breadcrumbs	50g/2oz	1 cup
Salt and pepper		
Finely chopped fresh marjoram	2 Tbs	2 Tbs
Chopped fresh parsley	2 Tbs	2 Tbs
Small eggs, lightly beaten	2	2
Butter	25g/1oz	2 Tbs
Onion, finely chopped	1	1
SAUCE		
Vegetable oil	3 Tbs	3 Tbs
Small onion, finely chopped	1	1
Carrot, finely chopped	1	1
Small celery stalk, finely chopped	1	1
Flour	1 Tbs	1 Tbs
Beef stock	600ml/ 1 pint	2½ cups
Tomato purée (paste)	2 tsp	2 tsp
Bouquet garni	1	1
Madeira	75ml/3floz	⅜ cup

Preheat the oven to moderate 180°C (Gas Mark 4, 350°F). Lightly oil a large ring and set aside.

Put the beef, breadcrumbs, seasoning, herbs and eggs into a large bowl and beat until they are thoroughly mixed.

Melt the butter in a frying-pan. Add the onion and fry until it is soft, then stir into the beef mixture. Spoon the mixture into the prepared mould and put the mould into a deep roasting tin. Pour in enough hot water to come halfway up the sides of the mould. Place the tin in the oven and bake for 2 hours or until the beef mixture is lightly browned and comes away slightly from the side of the dish.

Meanwhile, to prepare the sauce, heat the oil in a small saucepan. Add the vegetables and fry until they are soft. Remove the pan from the heat and stir in the flour to form a smooth paste. Gradually add the stock, tomato purée (paste) and bouquet garni, return to the heat and bring to the boil, stirring constantly. Cook for 2 to 3 minutes, stirring constantly, or until the sauce thickens. Simmer for 20 minutes, stirring occasionally.

Strain the sauce into a bowl, pressing down on the vegetables with the back of a wooden spoon to extract all the liquid. Return the strained sauce to the saucepan, and bring to the boil. Stir in the Madeira, remove from the heat and keep warm.

When the meat loaf is cooked, remove from the oven and set aside in the mould for 5 minutes. Run a knife around the edge of the mould and turn the beef ring out on to a warmed serving dish. Serve at once, with the sauce.

6-8 Servings

NOTE: You can fill the centre of the ring with fresh minted peas, or sautéed mushrooms for a special effect.

Flank steak stew with herbs

	Metric/UK	US
Flank steak, cubed	1½kg/3lb	3lb
Seasoned flour (flour with salt and pepper to taste)	50g/2oz	½ cup
Butter	75g/3oz	6 Tbs
Vegetable oil	2 Tbs	2 Tbs
Medium onions, thinly sliced	3	3
Garlic cloves, crushed	3	3
Large green pepper, pith and seeds removed and chopped	1	1
Walnuts, finely chopped	50g/2oz	⅓ cup
Chopped fresh parsley	2 Tbs	2 Tbs
Chopped fresh oregano	1 tsp	1 tsp
Chopped fresh thyme	1 tsp	1 tsp
Bay leaves	2	2
Salt	1 tsp	1 tsp
Beef stock	450ml/ 15floz	2 cups
Tomato purée (paste)	2 Tbs	2 Tbs
Beurre manié (two parts flour and one part butter blended to a paste)	25g/1oz	2 Tbs

Coat the meat cubes in the seasoned flour, shaking off any excess.

Melt 50g/2oz (4 tablespoons) of the butter with the oil in a large saucepan. Add the meat cubes and fry until they are evenly browned. Using a slotted spoon, transfer the cubes to a plate. Add the remaining butter to the pan and add the onions, garlic and pepper. Fry until they are soft. Stir in the walnuts, herbs and salt and cook the mixture for 3 minutes, stirring occasionally. Add the stock and tomato purée (paste) and bring to the boil, stirring occasionally.

Return the meat cubes to the pan, reduce the heat to low and cover. Simmer for 2 hours, or until the meat is cooked through and tender. Add the beurre manié, a little at a time, and cook uncovered until the mixture

thickens and is smooth. Simmer for 5 minutes, stirring occasionally. Serve at once.

8 Servings

Beef with parsley dumplings

	Metric/UK	US
Stewing beef (beef chuck), cubed	1kg/2lb	2lb
Seasoned flour (flour with salt and pepper to taste)	40g/1½oz	⅓ cup
Butter	25g/1oz	2 Tbs
Cooking oil	1 Tbs	1 Tbs
Large onion, chopped	1	1
Bay leaf	1	1
Beef stock, hot	1¼l/2 pints	5 cups
Mushrooms, quartered	175g/6oz	1½ cups
Sour cream	150ml/5floz	⅔ cup
DUMPLINGS		
Fresh breadcrumbs	225g/8oz	4 cups
Water	50ml/2floz	¼ cup
Eggs, lightly beaten	3	3
Salt and pepper		
Chopped fresh parsley	1½ Tbs	1½ Tbs
Onion, finely chopped	1	1
Ground mace	½ tsp	½ tsp

Preheat the oven to warm 170°C (Gas Mark 3, 325°F).

Coat the beef cubes in the seasoned flour, shaking off any excess.

Melt the butter with the oil in a frying-pan. Add the onion and fry until it is soft. Add the beef cubes and fry until they are evenly browned. Using a slotted spoon, transfer the beef and onion to an ovenproof casserole. Add the bay leaf and hot stock, cover and put the casserole into the oven. Cook for 2 hours.

Meanwhile, to make the dumplings, put the breadcrumbs in a large bowl. Gradually stir in sufficient of the water so that the breadcrumbs are moist but not soggy. Gently beat in the remaining ingredients until the mixture is thoroughly blended. Using floured hands, shape the mixture into walnut-sized balls. Add the dumplings to the casserole, with the mushrooms, re-cover and cook for a further 30 minutes.

Remove from the oven and pour over the sour cream before serving.

6 Servings

Beef with Parsley Dumplings, mushrooms and sour cream is a substantial and satisfying main dish.

Lamb stew with dill

	Metric/UK	US
Butter	125g/4oz	8 Tbs
Lean lamb, cubed	1kg/2lb	2lb
Salt and pepper		
Garlic clove, crushed	1	1
Medium onion, finely chopped	1	1
Chopped fresh dill	3 Tbs	3 Tbs
Flour	50g/2oz	½ cup
Grated nutmeg	¼ tsp	¼ tsp
Chicken stock	600ml/1 pint	2½ cups
Large carrots, thinly sliced	2	2
Leeks, washed and thinly sliced	2	2
Double (heavy) cream	250ml/8floz	1 cup

Preheat the oven to moderate 180°C (Gas Mark 4, 350F).

Melt half the butter in a flameproof casserole. Add the meat and fry until the cubes are evenly browned. Stir in the seasoning, garlic, onion and dill. Cook until the onion is soft. Remove the casserole from the heat and stir in the flour to form a paste. Gradually stir in the nutmeg and stock. Return to the heat and bring to the boil, stirring constantly. Cover the casserole and put into the oven. Cook for 1 to 1¼ hours, or until the meat is cooked through and tender.

Meanwhile, melt the remaining butter in a frying-pan. Add the vegetables and fry for 5 minutes, stirring occasionally. Remove from the heat. Remove the casserole from the oven and stir in the cream, then stir in about half the vegetable mixture. Transfer the stew to a warmed serving dish and garnish with the remaining vegetable mixture. Serve at once.

4-6 Servings

Lamb chops with thyme

	Metric/UK	US
Olive oil	50ml/2floz	¼ cup
Lemon juice	2 Tbs	2 Tbs
Salt and pepper		
Chopped fresh thyme	1 Tbs	1 Tbs
Garlic clove, crushed	1	1
Thick lamb chops	4	4

Put the oil, lemon juice, seasoning, thyme and garlic into a shallow bowl and mix well. Add the lamb chops and baste well. Set aside in a cool place for 2 hours, basting frequently.

Preheat the grill (broiler) to high.

Arrange the chops on a rack in a lined grill (broiler) pan and cook for 2 minutes on each side. Reduce the heat to moderately low and cook the chops for a further 8 minutes on each side, basting them frequently with the marinade, or until they are cooked through and tender.

Transfer the chops to a warmed serving plate and spoon over the marinade. Serve at once.

4 Servings

Leg of lamb with rosemary

	Metric/UK	US
Leg of lamb	1x2kg/4lb	1x4lb
Garlic cloves, cut into 4 slices lengthways	2	2
Salt and pepper		
Dried rosemary	2 tsp	2 tsp
Butter	50g/2oz	4 Tbs
Beef stock	225ml/8floz	1 cup

Preheat the oven to fairly hot 200°C (Gas Mark 6, 400°F).

Lay the meat on a work surface and make eight deep incisions in it. Insert one garlic slice into each incision. Rub the meat all over with the salt, pepper and rosemary and set aside.

Melt the butter in a large roasting tin set over moderate heat. Add the meat and fry, turning frequently, for about 10 minutes or until it is lightly browned all over. Pour over the stock.

Transfer the roasting tin to the oven and roast the meat for 15 minutes. Reduce the heat to moderate 180°C (Gas Mark 4, 350°F) and roast the meat for a further 1½ hours or until the lamb is cooked through and tender. Transfer the meat to a warmed serving dish. Skim off any fat from the surface of the cooking juices, pour over the meat and serve immediately.

4 Servings

Saddle of lamb with rosemary

	Metric/UK	US
Saddle of lamb	1x2¾kg/6lb	1x6lb
Salt and pepper		
Garlic cloves, cut into 8 slices	2	2
Rosemary sprigs	8	8
Flour, blended with 2 Tbs beef stock to a smooth paste	1 Tbs	1 Tbs
Beef stock	150ml/5floz	⅔ cup
MARINADE		
Red wine vinegar	50ml/2floz	¼ cup
Olive oil	50ml/2floz	¼ cup
Tomato purée (paste)	1 Tbs	1 Tbs
Fresh root ginger, peeled and finely grated	2½cm/1in piece	1in piece

Rub the meat all over with the salt and pepper. To make the marinade, put all the ingredients into a large, shallow dish and mix well. Add the meat to the marinade and set aside at room

The addition of rosemary and garlic to this dish gives Leg of Lamb with Rosemary a taste and aroma to tempt the most jaded palate. Serve with parsley potatoes and sauteed courgettes (zucchini) for a special family lunch or dinner party.

temperature for 3 hours, basting occasionally.

Preheat the oven to moderate 180°C (Gas Mark 4, 350°F).

Remove the lamb from the marinade and discard the marinade. Put the meat on a flat surface. Make eight deep incisions at intervals in the meat and insert one garlic slice and one rosemary sprig into each incision. Arrange the saddle on a rack in a deep roasting pan and put the pan into the oven. Roast for 1 hour. Reduce the oven temperature to cool 150°C (Gas Mark 2, 300°F) and roast for a further 1 to 1¼ hours, or until the lamb is cooked through and tender. Remove from the oven and transfer the lamb to a carving board. Carve into thick slices and transfer them to a warmed serving dish. Keep hot while you finish the sauce.

Remove the rack from the roasting pan and skim off any fat from the surface of the pan juices. Strain the juices into a small saucepan and stir in the flour mixture and stock. Set the pan over moderate heat and cook, stirring constantly, for 3 minutes, or until the sauce is smooth and has thickened. Pour into a warmed sauceboat and serve at once, with the meat.

8 Servings

Lamb and cashew nut curry

	Metric/UK	US
Fresh root ginger, peeled and chopped	4cm/1½in piece	1½in piece
Garlic cloves	3	3
Green chillis	2	2
Unsalted cashew nuts	50g/2oz	⅓ cup
Water	50-75ml/ 2-3floz	¼-⅓ cup
Cloves	4	4
Cardamom seeds	¼ tsp	¼ tsp
Coriander seeds	1 Tbs	1 Tbs
White poppy seeds	1 Tbs	1 Tbs
Butter	50g/2oz	4 Tbs
Onions, finely chopped	2	2
Lean lamb, cubed	1kg/2lb	2lb
Yogurt	300ml/10floz	1¼ cups
Saffron threads, soaked in 2 Tbs boiling water	¼ tsp	¼ tsp
Salt	1 tsp	1 tsp
Juice of ¼ lemon		
Chopped coriander leaves	1 Tbs	1 Tbs
Lemon, sliced	1	1

Put the ginger, garlic, chillis, nuts and half the water into a blender. Blend until it forms a purée. Add the cloves, cardamom, coriander and poppy seeds and blend with enough of the remaining water to make a smooth purée. Transfer the purée to a bowl.

Melt the butter in a large saucepan. Add the onions and fry until they are golden. Stir in the spice purée and reduce the heat to moderately low. Fry for 3 minutes, stirring frequently. Add the lamb cubes and fry until they are evenly browned.

Beat the yogurt, saffron and salt together, then pour the mixture into the saucepan. When the mixture begins to bubble, reduce the heat to low and simmer the curry for 1 hour, stirring occasionally.

Stir in the lemon juice and sprinkle over the coriander leaves. Cover the pan and cook for a further 20 minutes, or until the lamb is cooked through and tender.

Garnish with the lemon slices and serve at once.

4-6 Servings

Sage pork fillets

	Metric/UK	US
Pork fillet (tenderloin)	1kg/2lb	2lb
Salt and pepper		
Butter	50g/2oz	4 Tbs
Chopped fresh sage	2 Tbs	2 Tbs
Emmenthal (Swiss) cheese, cut into 12 slices	225g/8oz	8oz
French mustard	2 Tbs	2 Tbs
Single (light) cream	175ml/6floz	¾ cup

Rub the fillet all over with salt and pepper.

Melt the butter in a large saucepan. Add the fillet and sprinkle over the sage. Fry until the meat is deeply and evenly browned. Reduce the heat to low, cover the pan and simmer for 40 minutes, turning the meat occasionally. Remove from the heat. Using a slotted spoon, transfer the fillet to a chopping board. Make 12 deep incisions along the meat. Spread the cheese slices with three-quarters of the mustard and put one slice into each incision.

Carefully return the pork to the pan and set the pan over moderate heat. Cook for a further 5 to 10 minutes, or until the pork is cooked through and tender and the cheese has melted. Transfer the meat to a warmed serving dish. Carve into serving pieces and keep hot while you finish making the sauce.

Stir the remaining mustard into the pan juices. Pour in the cream and cook for a further 1 minute, stirring constantly, until the sauce is hot but not boiling. Pour the sauce into a warmed sauceboat and serve at once, with the meat.

6 Servings

French pork pie

	Metric/UK	US
Puff pastry, chilled	350g/12oz	3 cups
Egg yolk, lightly beaten	1	1
FILLING		
Lean pork, minced (ground)	1kg/2lb	2lb
Brandy	50ml/2floz	¼ cup
Butter	1 Tbs	1 Tbs
Vegetable oil	2 Tbs	2 Tbs
Shallots, finely chopped	2	2
Garlic clove, crushed	1	1
Finely chopped fresh sage	1 Tbs	1 Tbs
Finely chopped fresh parsley	1 Tbs	1 Tbs
Finely chopped fresh chervil	1 Tbs	1 Tbs
Salt and pepper		
Cornflour (cornstarch) mixed to a paste with 1 Tbs water	1 Tbs	1 Tbs

First prepare the filling. Place the pork in a large shallow dish. Pour over the brandy and set aside to marinate for at least 1 hour.

Meanwhile, melt the butter with the oil in a large frying-pan. Add the shallots and garlic until the shallots are soft. Add the pork and brandy to the pan and fry, stirring frequently, until the pork is lightly browned. Add the herbs and salt and pepper to taste. Cook, stirring occasionally, for a further 15 minutes.

Remove the pan from the heat and stir in the cornflour (cornstarch) mixture. Set aside.

Preheat the oven to hot 220°C (Gas Mark 7, 425°F).

Divide the dough in half. Roll out one half into a circle large enough to line a greased 23cm/9in pie plate. Lift the dough on to one plate and press gently into position. Trim off any excess dough and add the filling, doming it up in the centre. Moisten the edges of the dough with a little water.

Roll out the remaining dough in the

Lamb and Cashew Nut Curry is a delicately flavoured dish which may be served with rice and chappatis for an authentic Indian meal.

same way and lift it on to the filling. Trim the edges and crimp them together. Cut a fairly large cross in the middle of the dough. Roll out the trimmings and make decorative shapes. Press the shapes on to the dough and brush with the beaten egg yolk.

Place the plate in the oven and bake for 5 minutes. Reduce the heat to moderate 180°C (Gas Mark 4, 350°F) and continue baking for a further 30 minutes or until the pastry is a deep golden brown.

Remove the plate from the oven and serve either hot or cold.

6 Servings

Pork with peaches

	Metric/UK	US
Leg of pork	1x2¾kg/6lb	1x6lb
Salt		
White wine vinegar	225ml/8floz	1 cup
White wine	225ml/8floz	1 cup
Ground allspice	1 tsp	1 tsp
Ground cinnamon	½ tsp	½ tsp
Canned peach halves, drained	12	12
Cornflour (cornstarch) mixed to a paste with 1 Tbs peach can juice	1 Tbs	1 Tbs
MARINADE		
Olive oil	125ml/4floz	½ cup
Garlic cloves, crushed	2	2
Salt and pepper		
Prepared French mustard	1 tsp	1 tsp
Finely chopped fresh thyme	1 tsp	1 tsp

First make the marinade. Combine all the ingredients in a large shallow dish. Add the pork and leave to marinate for 2 hours, basting occasionally.

Preheat the oven to fairly hot 190°C (Gas Mark 5, 375°F).

Remove the pork from the marinade and place it on a working surface. Discard the marinade. Make small incisions in the thickest part of the flesh, then rub salt in the skin.

Put the pork on a rack in a roasting tin and roast for 2½ to 3 hours or until the meat is cooked through and tender. Test by inserting the sharp point of a knife into the thickest part of the flesh. If the juices run clear then the meat is cooked.

Meanwhile, pour the vinegar and white wine into a small saucepan and place over low heat. Stir in the allspice and cinnamon. Simmer for 30 minutes, then remove the pan from the heat.

Place the peach halves in a large shallow dish and pour the vinegar and wine mixture over them. Set aside.

When the pork is cooked, transfer it to a large warmed serving dish. Remove the peach halves from the vinegar and wine mixture and arrange them around the pork. Reserve the vinegar and wine mixture. Keep the pork hot while you make the sauce.

Skim the excess fat from the top of the cooking juices in the roasting tin, then pour the juices into a saucepan and place over moderate heat. Add the reserved vinegar and wine mixture and bring to the boil. Reduce the heat to low, add the cornflour (cornstarch) mixture and cook, stirring constantly, for 2 to 3 minutes or until the sauce has thickened. Pour the sauce into warmed sauceboat.

Serve the pork immediately with the sauce.

6-8 Servings

Juniper pork chops

	Metric/UK	US
Large pork chops	4	4
Garlic cloves, halved	2	2
Salt and pepper		
Juniper berries, crushed	20	20
Olive oil	4 Tbs	4 Tbs

Preheat the grill (broiler) to high.

Rub each chop all over with half a garlic clove, then with salt and pepper to taste. Gently press the juniper berries into both sides of the meat.

Arrange the chops on a rack in a lined grill (broiler) pan and brush with oil. Reduce the heat to moderate and grill (broil) the chops for about 10 minutes on each side, or until the meat is cooked through and tender.

Transfer the chops to a warmed serving dish and serve at once.

4 Servings

Stuffed loin of pork

	Metric/UK	US
Loin of pork, boned	1x2kg/4lb	1x4lb
Liver pâté	175g/6oz	6oz
Chopped fresh sage	2 tsp	2 tsp
Garlic cloves, crushed	2	2
Salt and pepper		
Fresh white breadcrumbs	50g 2oz	1 cup
Egg, lightly beaten	1	1
Mushrooms, thinly sliced	125g/4oz	4oz
Vegetable oil	1 Tbs	1 Tbs

Preheat the oven to fairly hot 190°C (Gas Mark 5, 375°F).

Place the pork, skin side up, on a working surface and score the skin into thin parallel slices ½cm/¼-inch apart. Turn the pork over.

In a bowl, mix together the pâté, sage, garlic, salt and pepper to taste, breadcrumbs and egg. Spread the mixture over the meat to within 3cm/1in of the edges. Top with the sliced mushrooms, roll up Swiss (jelly) roll style and tie with string.

Rub more salt into the scored skin and brush with the vegetable oil. Put the meat on a rack in a roasting tin and roast for 2½ hours, or until the meat is cooked through and tender. To test, insert the sharp point of a knife into the flesh. If the juices run clear then the meat is cooked.

Increase the heat to hot, 220°C (Gas Mark 7, 425°F), and roast for a further 20 minutes or until the skin is crisp. Remove and discard the string, transfer to a warmed serving dish and serve immediately.

8 Servings

Loin of veal with herb stuffing

	Metric/UK	US
Boned loin of veal, trimmed of excess fat	1x2¾kg/6lb	1x6lb
Salt	2 tsp	2 tsp
Black pepper	1 tsp	1 tsp
Egg yolks	2	2
Double (heavy) cream	3 Tbs	3 Tbs
Fresh white breadcrumbs	75g/3oz	1½ cups
Onion, grated	1	1
Finely chopped fresh chives	1 Tbs	1 Tbs
Finely chopped fresh parsley	1 Tbs	1 Tbs
Finely chopped fresh sage	1 Tbs	1 Tbs
Finely chopped fresh marjoram	½ Tbs	½ Tbs
Finely grated rind and juice of 2 oranges		
Butter	50g/2oz	4 Tbs
Streaky (fatty) bacon	8 slices	8 slices
Beurre manié (two parts flour to one part butter, blended to a paste)	1 Tbs	1 Tbs
Orange, thinly sliced	1	1
Watercress sprigs to garnish		

Preheat the oven to fairly hot 190°C (Gas Mark 5, 375°F).

Rub the veal all over with half the salt and the pepper. Place it, fat side down, on a flat surface.

Beat the egg yolks, cream, breadcrumbs and remaining salt and pepper together until the mixture forms a smooth paste. Stir in the onion, herbs and orange rind. Spoon the mixture on to the veal and spread to within about 2½cm/1in of the edges of the meat. Roll the meat up and tie securely with string at 2½cm/1in intervals. Set aside.

Melt the butter in a large flameproof casserole. Add the veal roll and fry until it is evenly browned. Lay the bacon slices over the top of the roll, cover the casserole and put into the centre of the oven. Braise for 2½ to 3 hours, or until the veal is cooked through and tender. Remove from the oven and, using two large forks, transfer the meat to a carving board. Remove the string and bacon and carve the meat into thick slices. Arrange on a warmed serving dish and keep the meat hot while you make the sauce.

Skim off any fat from the surface of the casserole juices. Set the casserole over moderate heat and stir in the orange juice. Add the beurre manié, a little at a time, and cook until the sauce has thickened. Strain the sauce into a sauceboat and serve at once. Garnish the meat with the orange slices and watercress sprigs and serve at once, with the sauce.

10-12 Servings

Veal escalopes with tarragon sauce

	Metric/UK	US
Veal escalopes, pounded thin	4	4
Seasoned flour (flour with salt and pepper to taste)	40g/1½oz	⅓ cup
Butter	75g/3oz	6 Tbs
Tomatoes, blanched, skinned and sliced	2	2
Button mushrooms, sliced	125g/4oz	1 cup
Chopped fresh tarragon	1 Tbs	1 Tbs
Salt and pepper		

Coat the escalopes in the seasoned flour, shaking off any excess.

Melt two-thirds of the butter in a large frying-pan. Add the escalopes and fry for 4 to 6 minutes on each side, or until they are cooked through and tender. Transfer them to a plate and keep the chops warm while you cook the vegetables.

Melt the remaining butter in the pan. Add the tomatoes and mushrooms, and fry until they are soft. Stir in the tarragon and seasoning and simmer for 3 minutes.

Return the escalopes to the pan and baste with the vegetable mixture. Simmer for 5 minutes.

Serve at once.

4 Servings

A superb dish of veal stuffed with herbs and orange rind and then braised slowly in the oven, Loin of Veal with Herb Stuffing makes a stunning dinner party dish.

Sweetbreads with cheese

	Metric/UK	US
Sweetbreads, soaked in cold water for 3 hours, drained, skinned and trimmed	½kg/1lb	1lb
Onion, sliced	1	1
Chopped fresh tarragon	2 tsp	2 tsp
Chopped fresh chervil	2 tsp	2 tsp
Chopped fresh parsley	1 Tbs	1 Tbs
Bay leaf	1	1
Salt and pepper		
Dry white wine	300ml/10floz	1¼ cups
Butter	50g/2oz	4 Tbs
Flour	25g/1oz	¼ cup
Cheddar cheese, grated	175g/6oz	1½ cups

Place the sweetbreads in a large saucepan and cover with water. Bring the water to the boil, remove the pan from the heat and set aside for 10 minutes.

Remove the sweetbreads and drain on paper towels. Discard the water. Cut the sweetbreads into 1cm/½in slices.

Place the sweetbreads, onion, herbs, salt and pepper in a bowl. Pour over the wine and leave to marinate for 30 minutes.

Using a slotted spoon, remove the sweetbreads from the marinade and drain on paper towels. Strain the marinade into a bowl and discard the contents of the strainer.

Melt half the butter in a frying-pan. Add the sweetbreads and fry, turning occasionally, for 10 to 15 minutes or until they are lightly browned.

Transfer the sweetbreads to a shallow flame-proof dish and keep them hot while you make the sauce.

Preheat the grill (broiler) to high.

Melt the remaining butter in a small saucepan. Remove the pan from the heat and stir in the flour to make a smooth paste. Gradually stir in the marinade. Return the pan to the heat and bring the sauce to the boil, stirring constantly. Cook the sauce for 2 to 3 minutes or until the sauce is thick and smooth.

Add half of the cheese and stir constantly until it has melted. Pour the sauce over the sweetbreads and sprinkle over the remaining cheese.

Place the dish under the grill (broiler) for 5 minutes or until the cheese has melted and is golden brown. Serve at once.

3 Servings

An exceptionally tasty dish, Liver and Sausage Kebabs consists of bite-sized pieces of liver, chipolata sausages, mushrooms, tomatoes and bay leaves threaded on skewers and quickly grilled (broiled). Serve the kebabs on a bed of rice and accompany with a mixed green salad.

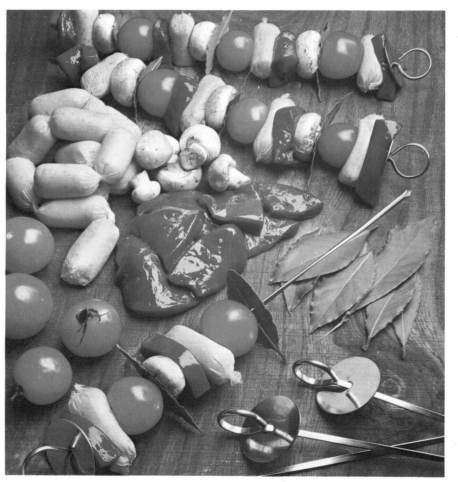

Liver and sausage kebabs

	Metric/UK	US
Calf's liver	½kg/1lb	1lb
Small chipolata (skinless) sausages	½kg/1lb	1lb
Butter, melted	175g/6oz	12 Tbs
Black pepper		
Button mushrooms	225g/8oz	2 cups
Bay leaves	24	24
Large tomatoes, quartered, or 24 tiny (cherry) tomatoes	6	6

Preheat the grill (broiler) to moderate.

Cut the liver into 2½cm/1in cubes. Leave the sausages whole if they are very small, otherwise halve them.

Pour half the melted butter into a shallow bowl and roll the liver cubes in it, then season with pepper to taste.

Thread the liver, sausages, mushrooms, bay leaves and tomatoes or tomato quarters on to skewers, in alternating order. Brush with half the remaining melted butter.

Arrange the skewers on a rack in a lined grill (broiler) pan and cook for 6 to 8 minutes on each side, or until the meat is cooked through and tender, brushing occasionally with the remaining melted butter.

Transfer the skewers to a warmed serving dish and serve at once.

4 Servings

Kidneys, Dijon-style

	Metric/UK	US
Butter	15g/½oz	1 Tbs
Vegetable oil	1 Tbs	1 Tbs
Lambs' kidneys, skinned, cored and cut into large pieces	675g/1½lb	1½lb
Flour	2 Tbs	2 Tbs
Milk	300ml/10floz	1¼ cups
French mustard	2-3 Tbs	2-3 Tbs
Salt and pepper		
Chopped fresh parsley	4 Tbs	4 Tbs

Melt the butter with the oil in a large deep frying-pan. Add the kidney pieces and fry until they are deeply and evenly browned. Using a slotted spoon, transfer them to a plate.

Stir the flour into the liquid in the pan to form a smooth paste. Gradually add the milk and bring to the boil, stirring constantly. Stir in the mustard, seasoning and all but 1 tablespoon of the parsley and simmer gently for 5 minutes.

Return the kidney pieces to the pan and baste well with the sauce. Simmer for 2 to 3 minutes, or until they are cooked through and tender. Sprinkle over the remaining parsley and serve at once.

4 Servings

Tomato tripe casserole

	Metric/UK	US
Tripe, blanched	1kg/2lb	2lb
Large onions, quartered	2	2
Carrots, thickly sliced	2	2
Bouquet garni	1	1
Salt and pepper		
Chicken stock	900ml/1½ pints	3¾ cups
Vegetable oil	2 Tbs	2 Tbs
Canned peeled tomatoes	700g/1½lb	1½lb
Tomato purée (paste)	2 Tbs	2 Tbs
Sugar	2 tsp	2 tsp
Garlic cloves, crushed	2	2
Chopped fresh basil	1 Tbs	1 Tbs
Chopped fresh parsley	3 Tbs	3 Tbs
Squeeze of lemon juice		
Grated cheese	3 Tbs	3 Tbs
Dry white breadcrumbs	2 Tbs	2 Tbs
Butter	15g/½oz	1 Tbs

Preheat the oven to warm 170°C (Gas Mark 3, 325°F).

Cut the tripe into 5cm/2in squares and lay them in a flameproof casserole. Add the onions, carrots and bouquet garni, and sprinkle over salt and pepper to taste. Pour over the stock, cover and bake in the oven for 1 hour.

Meanwhile, heat the oil in a saucepan and add the tomatoes and can juice. Stir in the tomato purée (paste),

sugar, garlic and herbs. Cook over moderate heat for about 10 minutes, stirring occasionally, or until the liquid has thickened. Taste and flavour with lemon juice and adjust the seasoning. Set aside.

Strain the tripe, discard the carrots and bouquet garni and reserve the cooking liquid. Chop the onions and add them to the tomato sauce with the tripe.

Return the tripe and tomato mixture to the casserole and bring to the boil. Cover, return to the oven and bake for a further 1 hour, or until the tripe is tender.

Increase the heat to 190°C (Gas Mark 5, 375°F). Uncover the casserole and sprinkle with the cheese and breadcrumbs and dot with the butter, cut into small dice. Return to the oven and bake until the cheese is golden and bubbling. Serve immediately.

4 Servings

Tripe, much praised by Samuel Pepys and the people of Caen, is one of the cheapest foods you can buy and can be mouth-wateringly delicious. Tomato Tripe Casserole is a particularly good dish which consists of a combination of cheese, tomatoes, herbs and tripe.

VEGETABLES & SALADS

Broad beans with savory

	Metric/UK	US
Vegetable oil	2 Tbs	2 Tbs
Onion, finely chopped	1	1
Garlic clove, crushed	1	1
Chopped fresh parsley	1 Tbs	1 Tbs
Chopped fresh savory	1 tsp	1 tsp
Chopped fresh lovage	½ tsp	½ tsp
Broad (lima or fava) beans, soaked overnight in cold water and drained	1kg/2lb	5 cups
Chicken stock	600ml/1 pint	2½ cups
Salt and pepper		
Grated nutmeg	½ tsp	½ tsp
Sour cream	250ml/8floz	1 cup

Heat the oil in a large saucepan. Add the onion and garlic and fry until they are soft. Add the herbs and beans and cook for 2 minutes. Add the stock, seasoning to taste and nutmeg and bring to the boil. Reduce the heat to low, cover the pan and simmer for 1 to 1½ hours, or until the beans are tender.

Drain off any excess liquid and stir in the sour cream. Serve at once.

6-8 Servings

Baked potatoes with sour cream and chives

	Metric/UK	US
Large potatoes, scrubbed	4	4
Salt and pepper		
Butter	50g/2oz	4 Tbs
Sour cream	250ml/8floz	1 cup
Chopped fresh chives	2-3 Tbs	2-3 Tbs

Preheat the oven to fairly hot 200°C (Gas Mark 6, 400°F).

Prick the potatoes with a fork and then arrange them on a baking sheet, or wrap them in aluminium foil. Put them into the oven and bake for 1 to 1¼ hours, depending on the size of the potatoes (the tops should be soft to the touch when the potatoes are cooked.)

Remove the potatoes from the heat and arrange them in a serving dish. Make a deep incision across the tops of the potatoes and scoop out a little of the potato flesh from each one. Transfer the flesh to a bowl. Season the potatoes, salt and pepper to taste and add a dollop of butter. Set aside.

Beat the sour cream and chives into the bowl with the potato flesh until they are well blended. Spoon the sour cream mixture back into the baked potatoes and serve at once.

4 Servings

Potato salad

	Metric/UK	US
Potatoes, cooked and sliced	½kg/1lb	1lb
Mayonnaise	125ml/4floz	½ cup
Lemon juice	1 Tbs	1 Tbs
Olive oil	1 Tbs	1 Tbs
Salt and pepper		
Chopped fresh chives	2 Tbs	2 Tbs
Chopped leeks	4 Tbs	4 Tbs

Put three-quarters of the potatoes into a bowl. Add the mayonnaise, lemon juice, oil, seasoning and half the chives. Using two large spoons, carefully toss until the potatoes are thoroughly coated.

Spoon the mixture into a serving bowl. Arrange the remaining potato slices over the top of the salad and sprinkle with the remaining chives. Scatter the leeks around the edge of the bowl.

Cover the bowl and put into the refrigerator to chill for 30 minutes before serving.

4 Servings

Artichoke hearts with herbs

	Metric/UK	US
Water	900ml/1½pts	3¾ cups
Lemon juice	2 Tbs	2 Tbs
Salt	1 tsp	1 tsp
Fresh artichoke hearts	12	12
Butter	40g/1½oz	3 Tbs
Chopped fresh chervil	1 tsp	1 tsp
Chopped fresh parsley	½ tsp	½ tsp

Bring the water to the boil in a saucepan. Add the lemon juice and salt and reduce the heat to moderately low. Carefully arrange the artichoke hearts in the water and simmer for 10 minutes. Remove from the heat, transfer the hearts to a plate and leave until they are cool enough to handle. Cut them into thin slices.

Melt the butter in a frying-pan. Add the artichoke hearts and fry gently for

This simple Potato Salad with mayonnaise dressing may be served with cold meats or as one of a selection of salads. Use the green part of the leeks for this recipe and save the white parts for future use.

Quick and easy to prepare, Aniseed Carrots is an unusual and delicately flavoured vegetable dish.

about 1 minute, turning them at least once. Transfer the slices and any remaining butter to a warmed serving dish and sprinkle over the chervil and parsley.

Serve at once.

4 Servings

Salsify sautéed with butter and herbs

	Metric/UK	US
Butter	25g/1oz	2 Tbs
Garlic clove, crushed	1	1
Salsify, trimmed, boiled, drained and peeled	½kg/1lb	1lb
Chopped fresh chervil	1 tsp	1 tsp
Finely chopped fresh parsley	2 Tbs	2 Tbs
Salt and pepper		
Lemon juice	1 tsp	1 tsp

Melt the butter in a frying-pan. Add the garlic and fry for 1 minute, stirring constantly. Add the chervil, parsley, salt and pepper and cook, stirring constantly, for 6 to 8 minutes, or until the salsify is lightly browned. Pour over the lemon juice. Transfer the salsify to a warmed serving dish and serve immediately.

4 Servings

Aniseed carrots

	Metric/UK	US
Soft brown sugar	1 Tbs	1 Tbs
Butter	50g/2oz	4 Tbs
Aniseed	1½ tsp	1½ tsp
Salt and pepper		
Carrots, quartered if large, whole if small	700g/1½lb	1½/lb

Put the sugar, butter, aniseed and seasoning into a large saucepan. When the butter and sugar have melted, add the carrots. Stir well, reduce the heat to low and cover the pan. Simmer for 15 minutes, or until the carrots are tender.

Transfer the mixture to a warmed serving dish and serve at once.

4 Servings

Chervil and avocado salad

	Metric/UK	US
Ripe avocados, peeled and stoned (pitted)	4	4
Lemon juice	125ml/4floz	½ cup
Salt and pepper		
Chopped fresh chervil	1 Tbs	1 Tbs

Cut the avocados, lengthways, into long, thin slices and arrange them in a shallow glass dish. Pour over the lemon juice and season to taste. Cover and marinade the avocado in the

A beautiful way to cook a delicate vegetable, Salsify Sautéed with Butter and Herbs is an ideal side dish for a dinner party

refrigerator for 1 hour.

Remove from the refrigerator and, using a slotted spoon, transfer the avocado slices to a chilled serving dish. Discard the lemon juice. Sprinkle over the chervil.

Serve at once.

4 Servings

Salsify with tarragon sauce

	Metric/UK	US
Salsify, cleaned	½kg/1lb	1lb
Toasted breadcrumbs	1 Tbs	1 Tbs
SAUCE		
Butter	25g/1oz	2 Tbs
Flour	2 Tbs	2 Tbs
Milk	125ml/4floz	½ cup
Chicken stock	125ml/4floz	½ cup
Single (light) cream	125ml/4floz	½ cup
Salt and pepper		
Grated nutmeg	½ tsp	½ tsp
Finely chopped fresh tarragon	2 tsp	2 tsp

Cut the salsify into 8cm/3in lengths and put them into a bowl of cold water with a little vinegar added (they will turn brown otherwise). Half-fill a large saucepan with water and bring to the boil. Add the salsify and cook over moderate heat for 20 minutes, or until it is tender. Drain and keep hot while you make the sauce.

Melt the butter in a saucepan.

Remove from the heat and stir in the flour to form a smooth paste. Gradually add the milk, stock and cream and return the pan to the heat. Cook, stirring constantly, for 2 to 3 minutes, or until the sauce is smooth and has thickened and is hot but not boiling. Stir in the seasoning, nutmeg and tarragon and simmer for a further 3 minutes.

Arrange the salsify in a warmed, deep serving dish. Pour over the sauce and sprinkle over the breadcrumbs. Serve at once.

4 Servings

Baked tomatoes with basil

	Metric/UK	US
Butter	75g/3oz	6 Tbs
Large onions, thinly sliced into rings	2	2
Large tomatoes, blanched, skinned and thinly sliced	10	10
Chopped fresh basil	2 Tbs	2 Tbs
Salt and pepper		
Sugar	1 tsp	1 tsp
Fresh breadcrumbs	75g/3oz	1½ cups

Preheat the oven to fairly hot 200°C (Gas Mark 6, 400°F).

Melt a third of the butter in a frying-pan. Add the onion rings and fry until they are soft. Remove the pan from the heat.

Arrange a layer of onion rings over the bottom of a well-greased medium baking dish. Cover with a layer of tomato slices, generously sprinkled with basil, seasoning and sugar. Cut about 1 tablespoon of the remaining butter into dice and scatter over. Repeat the layers until all the ingredients are used up.

Top with the breadcrumbs. Cut the remaining butter into dice and scatter over the breadcrumbs.

Put the dish into the oven and bake for 30 minutes, or until the top is browned and bubbling slightly. Serve at once.

4-6 Servings

Pizza Margherita
(Pizza with Basil, Tomatoes and Cheese)

This pizza is positively patriotic—the three main colours of the filling (green, red and white), are intended to represent the colours of the Italian flag.

	Metric/UK	US
Fresh yeast	15g/½oz	½oz
Sugar	¼ tsp	¼ tsp
Lukewarm water	125ml/4floz plus 3 tsp	½ cup plus 3 tsp
Flour	225g/8oz	2 cups
Salt	1 tsp	1 tsp
FILLING		
Tomatoes, thinly sliced	6	6
Mozzarella cheese, sliced	175g/6oz	6oz
Chopped fresh basil	2 Tbs	2 Tbs
Salt and pepper		
Olive oil	2 tsp	2 tsp

Crumble the yeast into a small bowl and mash in the sugar. Add the 3 teaspoons of water and cream the mixture. Set aside in a warm, draught-free place for 15 to 20 minutes, or until the mixture is puffed up and frothy.

Sift the flour and salt into a large, warmed bowl. Make a well in the centre and pour in the yeast mixture and the remaining lukewarm water. Using a spatula, gradually draw the flour into the liquid until it is all incorporated and the dough comes away from the sides of the bowl.

Turn the dough out on to a floured surface and knead for about 10 minutes. The dough should be elastic and smooth.

Rinse, dry and lightly grease the bowl. Shape the dough into a ball and return it to the bowl. Cover and set aside in a warm, draught-free place for 45 minutes to 1 hour, or until the dough has risen and almost doubled in bulk.

Preheat the oven to very hot 230°C (Gas Mark 8, 450°F).

Turn the dough out on to the floured surface and knead for 3 minutes. Cut the dough in half and roll out each piece into a circle, about ½cm/¼in thick. Arrange the circles, well spaced apart, on a well-greased baking sheet. Arrange the tomato slices in decorative lines over each circle, and separate them with overlapping Mozzarella slices. Sprinkle the basil generously over the top and season to taste. Dribble over the oil.

Put the sheet into the oven and bake for 15 to 20 minutes, or until the dough is cooked through and the cheese has melted. Serve at once.

2 Servings

Ratatouille
(Mixed Vegetable Casserole)

	Metric/UK	US
Butter	25g/1oz	2 Tbs
Olive oil	50ml/2floz	¼ cup
Large onions, thinly sliced	2	2
Garlic cloves, crushed	2	2
Medium aubergines (eggplants), thinly sliced and dégorged	3	3
Large green pepper, pith and seeds removed and chopped	1	1
Large red pepper, pith and seeds removed and chopped	1	1
Medium courgettes (zucchini), sliced	5	5
Canned peeled tomatoes	425g/14oz	14oz
Chopped fresh basil	2 tsp	2 tsp
Chopped fresh rosemary	2 tsp	2 tsp
Salt and pepper		
Chopped fresh parsley	2 Tbs	2 Tbs

Melt the butter with the oil in a large saucepan. Add the onions and garlic and fry until they are soft. Add the aubergine (eggplant) slices, peppers and courgette (zucchini) slices, and fry for 5 minutes, shaking the pan frequently. Add the tomatoes and can juice, herbs, salt and pepper and sprinkle over the parsley. Bring to the boil. Reduce the heat to low, cover the pan and simmer for 40 to 45 minutes, or until the vegetables are tender but still firm.

Serve hot or cold.

6 Servings

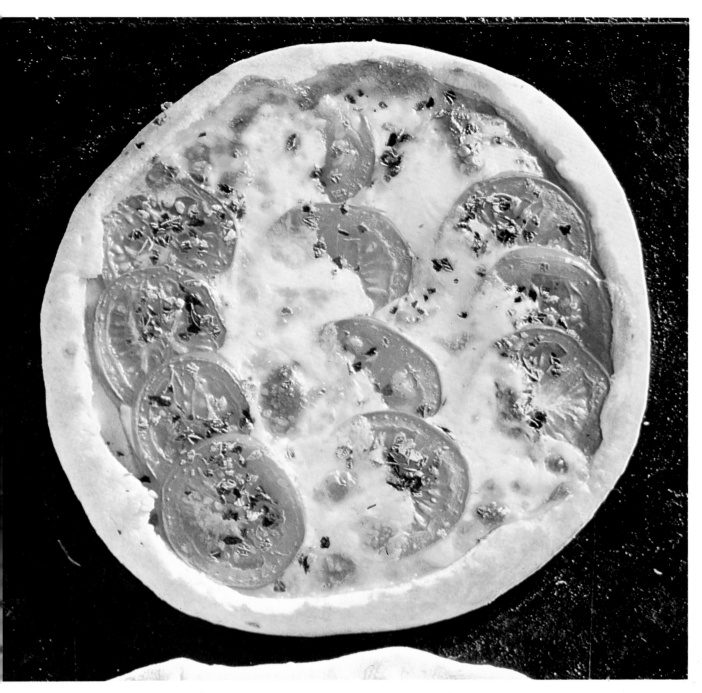

Vegetable rissoles

	Metric/UK	US
Red lentils, soaked in cold water overnight, cooked and drained	125g/4oz	½ cup
Large onion, finely chopped	1	1
Celery stalk, finely chopped	1	1
Small carrots, grated	2	2
Green beans, cooked and finely chopped	50g/2oz	⅓ cup
Fresh white breadcrumbs	50g/2oz	1 cup
Eggs	3	3
Salt and pepper		
Chopped fresh mixed herbs	1 Tbs	1 TPs
Vegetable oil	50ml/2floz	¼ cup

Put the lentils, vegetables, fresh bread-crumbs, 2 of the eggs, the seasoning and mixed herbs into a bowl and beat until thoroughly blended. Set aside at room temperature for 30 minutes.

Using your hands, shape the mixture into eight equal-sized balls, then flatten to make small cakes. Set aside.

Beat the remaining egg in a shallow dish, and put the dry breadcrumbs on a plate. Dip each rissole first in the eggs, then the breadcrumbs, coating them completely and shaking off any excess.

Heat the vegetable oil in a large frying-pan. Add the rissoles and fry for 10 minutes on each side, or until they

Pizza Margherita is extremely patriotic as the colours of the filling ingredients, basil, tomatoes and Mozzarella cheese, echo those of the Italian flag: green, red and white.

are golden brown. Remove from the pan and drain on paper towels. Serve at once.

4 Servings

Tomato salad with chives and basil

	Metric/UK	US
Firm tomatoes, thinly sliced	½kg/1lb	1lb
Finely chopped fresh chives	1 Tbs	1 Tbs
Finely chopped fresh basil	2 tsp	2 tsp
DRESSING		
Olive oil	3 Tbs	3 Tbs
White wine vinegar	1 Tbs	1 Tbs
Lemon juice	½ tsp	½ tsp
French mustard	¼ tsp	¼ tsp
Salt and pepper		
Chopped fresh basil	½ tsp	½ tsp

Arrange the tomato slices decoratively on a salad plate and sprinkle over the chives. Set aside.

To make the dressing, put all the ingredients into a screw-top jar, cover and shake well. Dribble the dressing over the tomato slices.

Sprinkle over the basil and serve at once.

4 Servings

Coleslaw with caraway

	Metric/UK	US
Large white cabbage, cored and shredded	1	1
Medium onion, finely chopped	1	1
Green pepper, pith and seeds removed and Finely chopped	2	2
Lemon juice	½ tsp	½ tsp
Caraway seeds	1 Tbs	1 Tbs
DRESSING		
Double (heavy) cream	175ml/6floz	¾ cup
Sour cream	75ml/3floz	⅓ cup
French mustard	1 Tbs	1 Tbs
Lemon juice	3 Tbs	3 Tbs
Sugar	1 Tbs	1 Tbs
Salt and pepper		

Arrange the cabbage in a large serving dish and sprinkle with the onion, pepper and lemon juice. Set aside.

To make the dressing, beat all the ingredients together until they are thoroughly mixed. Pour the dressing over the cabbage mixture and add the caraway seeds. Using two large spoons, gently toss the mixture until the cabbage is thoroughly coated. Put the bowl into the refrigerator to chill for at least 1 hour before serving.

8 Servings

Walnut and rice salad

	Metric/UK	US
Large firm tomatoes	6	6
Walnuts, halved	175g/6oz	1⅓ cups
Cooked long-grain rice	215g/7½oz	3 cups
Cooked ham, diced	350g/12oz	12oz
Green beans, cooked and drained	225g/8oz	1⅓ cups
Sultanas or seedless raisins	125g/4oz	⅔ cup
Canned sweetcorn, drained	425g/14oz	14oz
Chopped fresh basil	2 tsp	2 tsp
Chopped fresh sage	1 tsp	1 tsp
French dressing	50ml/2floz	¼ cup
GARNISH		
Walnut halves	12	12
Chopped fresh parsley	1 Tbs	1 Tbs

Put the tomatoes on a board and cut off the tops. Discard the tops, then scoop out and discard the seeds, taking care not to pierce the skins. Set the tomato shells aside.

Put all the remaining ingredients, except the garnish, into a bowl and mix together until they are thoroughly combined. Using two large spoons, toss the salad until all the ingredients are well coated.

Fill the tomatoes with the rice mixture and arrange them around the edge of a serving dish. Spoon the remaining rice mixture into the centre. Garnish with the walnut halves and parsley and serve at once.

6 Servings

Herb and spinach flan

	Metric/UK	US
Shortcrust pastry	175g/6oz	1½ cups
FILLING		
Butter	50g/2oz	4 Tbs
Small onion, thinly sliced into rings	1	1
Lean bacon slices, chopped	3	3
Spinach, trimmed and cooked	½kg/1lb	1lb
Eggs, lightly beaten	2	2
Double (heavy) cream	150ml/5floz	⅝ cup
Salt and pepper		
Chopped fresh thyme	2 tsp	2 tsp
Chopped fresh basil	1 tsp	1 tsp
Chopped fresh parsley	1 Tbs	1 Tbs
Cheddar cheese, grated	50g/2oz	½ cup

Preheat the oven to fairly hot 200°C (Gas Mark 6, 400°F).

Roll out the pastry dough on a flat surface to about ½cm/¼in thick, then use to line a 23cm/9in flan ring. Put the flan ring on to a baking sheet and set aside.

To make the filling, melt the butter in a large frying-pan. Add the onion and fry until it is soft. Add the bacon and fry for 5 minutes, or until it is crisp. Stir in the spinach and cook until the spinach is heated through. Remove the pan from the heat and spoon the mixture into the prepared pastry shell.

Beat the eggs, cream, seasoning and herbs together until they are thoroughly blended. Stir in the cheese and mix well. Pour the mixture over the spinach and put the baking sheet into the oven. Bake for 30 minutes, or until the filling is set and the top has browned.

Serve hot or cold.

4-6 Servings

Garlic potatoes

The number of garlic cloves given below is NOT a mistake—nor will you be fearsome to be near for hours after eating this delicious dish! Once the cloves have been boiled they lose their strength, but retain a pleasant taste.

	Metric/UK	US
Potatoes, quartered	1½kg/3lb	3lb
Salt	1½ tsp	1½ tsp
Garlic cloves, peeled	25	25
Butter	25g/1oz	2 Tbs
Flour	1 Tbs	1 Tbs
Double (heavy) cream	250ml/8floz	1 cup
Black pepper		
Finely chopped fresh chives	1 Tbs	1 Tbs

Put the potatoes into a large saucepan and sprinkle with 1 teaspoon of salt. Cover with water and set the pan over moderate heat. Bring to the boil and cook for 20 minutes, or until the potatoes are tender.

Meanwhile, put the garlic cloves in a saucepan and cover with water. Bring to the boil and boil briskly for 3 minutes. Remove from the heat and drain the garlic. Grind the cloves or blend them to a smooth purée.

Melt the butter in a saucepan. Add the garlic and cook for 5 minutes, stirring frequently. Remove from the heat and stir in the flour to form a smooth paste. Gradually add the cream and return the pan to the heat. Cook for 2 minutes, stirring constantly, or until the sauce is thick and smooth and hot but not boiling. Stir in the remaining salt, pepper to taste and the chives. Set aside.

Drain the potatoes, then mash them well. Rub them through a strainer and return the puréed potatoes to the saucepan. Gradually beat in the garlic and cream sauce. Set the pan over moderate heat and cook, stirring constantly, for 2 to 3 minutes, or until the mixture is reheated.

Serve at once.

10 Servings

Coleslaw with Caraway is a crunchy combination of shredded cabbage, onion and green pepper topped with a sour cream, mustard, lemon juice and caraway seed dressing.

SAUCES, STUFFINGS & STOCKS

Below
1 *For Béarnaise Sauce, strain the simmered vinegar mixture into a small bowl, cream the butter until it is soft and beat the egg yolks in a third ovenproof bowl.*
2 *Place the bowl of egg yolks over a pan filled with warm water, or use a double boiler, and add the butter mixture in small pieces, stirring constantly.*
3 *Having stirred in the vinegar, remove the bowl from the pan and add the pepper, tarragon and chervil.*

Opposite page *The use of home-made Beef Stock will add a touch of distinction to soups and casseroles.*

Béarnaise sauce

	Metric/UK	US
Wine vinegar	5 Tbs	5 Tbs
Shallot or small onion, quartered	1	1
Bay leaf	1	1
Tarragon sprig	1	1
Chervil sprig	1	1
Peppercorns	4	4
Butter	125g/4oz	8 Tbs
Large egg yolks	2	2
Salt and pepper		
Chopped fresh mixed tarragon and chervil	1 tsp	1 tsp

Put the vinegar, shallot or onion, herbs and peppercorns into a small saucepan. Simmer until the vinegar is reduced to about 1 tablespoon. Strain and set aside. Discard the contents of the strainer.

Beat the butter until it is soft. Beat the egg yolks in a second, ovenproof bowl until they are thoroughly blended. Add a heaped teaspoon of the butter and salt to the egg yolks and cream thoroughly. Stir in the vinegar.

Put the bowl in a saucepan containing warm water and set the pan over low heat. (The water should heat gradually but should not be allowed to boil.) Add the remaining butter in small pieces, stirring constantly. When all the butter has been added and the sauce is the consistency of whipped cream, add the pepper, chopped tarragon and chervil. Taste and adjust seasoning if necessary.

About 150ml/5floz ($\frac{5}{8}$ cup)

Béchamel sauce

	Metric/UK	US
Milk	450ml/ 15floz	2 cups
Bay leaf	1	1
Peppercorns	6	6
Pinch of grated nutmeg		
Butter	2 Tbs	2 Tbs
Flour	25g/1oz	$\frac{1}{4}$ cup
Salt and white pepper		

Put the milk, bay leaf, peppercorns and nutmeg into a saucepan. Simmer for 10 minutes, taking care not to let the milk come to the boil. Strain the milk into a bowl and set aside.

Melt the butter in a saucepan.

Remove the pan from the heat and stir in the flour to form a smooth paste. Gradually add the infused milk: Return the pan to the heat and season to taste. Bring to the boil, then cook for 2 to 3 minutes, stirring constantly, or until the sauce thickens and is smooth.

About 450ml/15floz (2 cups)

Bergamot sauce

	Metric/UK	US
Butter	25g/1oz	2 Tbs
Shallots, finely chopped	2	2
Flour	1 Tbs	1 Tbs
Dry white wine	125ml/4floz	$\frac{1}{2}$ cup
Juice of $\frac{1}{2}$ lemon		
Chopped fresh bergamot	1 Tbs	1 Tbs
Salt and white pepper		

Melt the butter in a small saucepan. Add the shallots and fry until they are soft. Stir in the flour to form a smooth paste. Gradually add the wine and lemon juice, stirring constantly, and cook for 2 to 3 minutes, or until the sauce thickens and is smooth. Stir in the bergamot and seasoning and simmer for a further 2 minutes, stirring constantly.

Pour into a warmed sauceboat and serve hot.

About 125ml/4floz ($\frac{1}{2}$ cup)

Mint sauce
This is the classic British accompaniment to roast leg of lamb.

	Metric/UK	US
Finely chopped fresh mint	12 Tbs	12 Tbs
Sugar	1$\frac{1}{2}$ Tbs	1$\frac{1}{2}$ Tbs
Malt or distilled white vinegar	75ml/3floz	6 Tbs
Hot water	1 Tbs	1 Tbs

Pound the mint and sugar together in a mortar with a pestle, or mix them in a bowl with a wooden spoon. Add the vinegar and hot water and stir until the sugar has dissolved.

Set aside for 1 hour before serving.

About 175ml/6floz ($\frac{3}{4}$ cup)

Tomato sauce with herbs

	Metric/UK	US
Tomatoes, blanched, skinned, seeded and chopped	½kg/1lb	1lb
Olive oil	1 Tbs	1 Tbs
Onion, finely chopped	1	1
Garlic clove, crushed	1	1
Bouquet garni	1	1
Chopped fresh marjoram	2 tsp	2 tsp
Sugar	1 tsp	1 tsp
Salt and pepper		

Put all the ingredients into a saucepan and bring to the boil. Reduce the heat to low and simmer for 25 to 30 minutes, or until the liquid has reduced a little and the sauce thickened.

Remove from the heat and remove and discard the bouquet garni. Strain the sauce into a warmed sauceboat or jug and adjust the seasoning if necessary. Serve at once.

About 150ml/5floz (¾ cup)

Pesto sauce

This classic sauce is made from fresh sweet basil and pine nuts and is usually served over spaghetti. Noodles, however, could be substituted if you prefer them.

	Metric/UK	US
Garlic cloves, crushed	2	2
Finely chopped fresh basil	50g/2oz	½ cup
Finely chopped pine nuts	3 Tbs	3 Tbs
Salt	½ tsp	½ tsp
Pepper to taste		
Olive oil	250ml/8floz	1 cup
Grated Parmesan cheese	50g/2oz	½ cup

Crush the garlic, basil, pine nuts and seasoning in a mortar until the mixture forms a smooth paste. Gradually pound in the oil, then the cheese, until the sauce is thick and smooth.

Pour the sauce over spaghetti or noodles and toss until the pasta is thoroughly coated. Serve at once.

4-6 Servings

Tarragon butter

	Metric/UK	US
Butter	125g/4oz	8 Tbs
Lemon juice	1 Tbs	1 Tbs
Chopped fresh tarragon	2-3 Tbs	2-3 Tbs
Salt and white pepper		

Beat the butter with a wooden spoon until it is soft and creamy. Drop by drop, beat the lemon juice into the butter, then beat in tarragon and salt and pepper to taste.

Chill until firm.

Fines herbes vinaigrette
(Herb Salad Dressing)

	Metric/UK	US
Finely chopped fresh chervil	½ tsp	½ tsp
Finely chopped fresh chives	1 tsp	1 tsp
Finely chopped fresh parsley	1 Tbs	1 Tbs
French mustard	1 tsp	1 tsp
Salt and pepper		
Garlic clove, crushed	1	1
Olive oil	175ml/6floz	¾ cup
Tarragon vinegar	50ml/2floz	¼ cup
Lemon juice	2 tsp	2 tsp

Put the herbs, mustard, seasoning and garlic into a small bowl and beat well. Gradually stir in the oil. Pour the mixture into a screw-top jar and add the remaining ingredients. Cover and shake well. The vinaigrette is now ready to be used.

About 250ml/8floz (1 cup)

French dressing

The ingredients for French dressing and the proportion of vinegar to oil are very largely a matter of personal taste, but this is a good basic recipe which will give enough dressing to toss a salad for four people. Try using a herb-flavoured oil or vinegar (see page 46) for a variation in flavour, or add a clove of crushed garlic. French dressing can be stored for a month in a cool place and it is a good idea to make up a large quantity so that you always have some on hand.

	Metric/UK	US
Mustard, dry	¼ tsp	¼ tsp
Salt and black pepper		
Sugar	¼ tsp	¼ tsp
Wine vinegar	1 Tbs	1 Tbs
Olive oil	2 Tbs	2 Tbs

Put the mustard, seasoning to taste, sugar and vinegar into a bowl and

Below Pesto is a classic Genoese sauce which is marvellous with all pasta dishes and as a flavouring for soups. Bottom left To make Tarragon Butter, having creamed the butter first, gradually add the lemon juice, seasoning and tarragon. Beat until there are no droplets of lemon juice visible on the surface. Bottom right Fines Herbes Vinaigrette is a piquant salad dressing flavoured with fresh herbs and mustard. Stir well to emulsify.

beat well. Stir in the oil. Alternatively, put all the ingredients into a screw-top jar and shake well. The dressing is now ready to be used.

50ml/2floz (¼ cup)

Ravigote butter

This classic butter is traditionally used to garnish steaks, or any other grilled (broiled) meats, but it also makes a flavouring for sauces and casseroles.

	Metric/UK	US
Butter	50g/2oz	4 Tbs
Finely chopped fresh chives	1 Tbs	1 Tbs
Finely chopped fresh parsley	1 Tbs	1 Tbs
Finely chopped fresh chervil	1 Tbs	1 Tbs
Finely chopped fresh tarragon	1 Tbs	1 Tbs
Garlic clove, crushed	1	1

Beat the butter with a wooden spoon until it is soft and creamy. Beat in the herbs and garlic until the mixture is well blended.

Cover and chill in the refrigerator for 1 hour, or until firm.

Herb and orange stuffing

This stuffing can be used to stuff lamb duck or goose, but it is especially good with chicken. The quantity given below is enough to fill a 2½kg/5lb chicken.

	Metric/UK	US
Butter	25g/1oz	2 Tbs
Large onion, very finely chopped	1	1
Lean veal, minced (ground)	½kg/1lb	1lb
Fresh white breadcrumbs	175g/6oz	3 cups
Salt and pepper		
Finely grated rind of 1 orange		
Chopped fresh marjoram	2 tsp	2 tsp
Chopped fresh thyme	1 tsp	1 tsp
Finely chopped fresh chives	1 Tbs	1 Tbs
Double (heavy) cream	2 Tbs	2 Tbs
Orange juice	50ml/2floz	¼ cup

Melt the butter in a saucepan. Add the onion and fry until it is soft. Add the veal and fry until it loses its pinkness. Stir in the breadcrumbs, seasoning, orange rind and herbs and cook the mixture for 5 minutes, stirring constantly.

Stir in the cream and orange juice until the mixture is thoroughly combined. The stuffing is now ready.

About 575g/1¼lb

Sage and onion stuffing

This traditional stuffing is excellent with poultry, or even pork. The quantity given below is enough to fill a 1½kg/3lb chicken.

	Metric/UK	US
Large onions, finely chopped	2	2
Chopped fresh sage leaves	12	12
Fresh white breadcrumbs	125g/4oz	2 cups
Salt and pepper		
Melted butter	1 Tbs	1 Tbs
Egg yolk	1	1

Half-fill a saucepan with water and set over high heat. When the water boils, add the onions. Reduce the heat to low, cover the pan and simmer for 10 minutes, or until the onions are tender. Remove from the heat and strain the mixture. Discard the water.

Put the onions into a small bowl. Stir in the sage, breadcrumbs and seasoning, and mix well. Stir in the melted butter and egg yolk until the stuffing is thoroughly combined. The stuffing is now ready to be used.

About 225g/8oz

Note: If you do not wish to use the stuffing immediately, cover and store in the refrigerator and do not add the butter and egg yolk until just before the stuffing is required.

Thyme stuffing

This stuffing is excellent with poultry, veal or even fish. The quantity given below is enough to fill a 1½kg/3lb chicken, or fish.

	Metric/UK	US
Fresh white breadcrumbs	125g/4oz	2 cups
Eating apples, peeled, cored and finely chopped	2	2
Medium onion, finely chopped	1	1
Sultanas or seedless raisins	75g/3oz	½ cup
Finely chopped fresh thyme	2 tsp	2 tsp
Finely chopped fresh lemon thyme	2 tsp	2 tsp
Salt and pepper		
Egg, lightly beaten	1	1

Put all the ingredients into a bowl and stir until the stuffing is thoroughly combined. If the mixture is still slightly crumbly, add a little water or lemon juice. The stuffing is now ready to be used.

About 225g/8oz

Rosemary Jelly is an apple and vinegar based condiment flavoured with sprigs of fresh rosemary. It is the ideal accompaniment to roast meats, especially lamb and veal.

Rosemary jelly

This savoury jelly is usually served with meat, particularly lamb and veal dishes. You will need about 450g/1lb (2 cups) of granulated sugar per 600ml/1 pint (2½ cups) of strained apple juice.

	Metric/UK	US
Cooking apples, sliced	2½kg/5lb	5lb
Water	600ml/	
	1 pint	2½ cups
Fresh rosemary leaves	4 Tbs	4 Tbs
Malt vinegar	250ml/8floz	1 cup
Granulated or preserving sugar		
Green food colouring	6 drops	6 drops

Scald a jelly bag or cheesecloth by pouring boiling water through it into a large bowl. Hang the bag or cheesecloth on a frame or tie the ends to the legs of an upturned chair or stool and place a large bowl underneath.

Put the apples and water in a large saucepan and stir in half of the rosemary. Bring to the boil, reduce the heat to low and simmer the fruit for 40 to 50 minutes, or until it is soft and pulpy. Add the vinegar and boil for 5 minutes.

Pour the mixture into the bag or cloth and leave to drain through for at least 12 hours. Do not squeeze the bag to hurry the process as this will make the jelly cloudy. When the juice has completely drained through, discard the pulp remaining in the bag or cheesecloth.

Measure the juice before returning it to the rinsed-out pan. Add 450g/1lb (2 cups) of sugar to each 600ml/1 pint (2½ cups) of liquid. Set the pan over low heat and stir until the sugar has dissolved. Increase the heat to high and bring to the boil. Boil briskly, without stirring, for about 10 minutes, or until the jelly has reached setting point. (To test, remove the pan from the heat and spoon a little jelly on to a cold saucer. Cool quickly. If the surface is set and wrinkles when pushed with your finger, it is set; if setting point has not been reached return to the heat and continue boiling, testing frequently.)

Skim the foam from the surface of the jelly with a metal spoon. Sprinkle the remaining rosemary and food colouring over the jelly and stir well.

Ladle the jelly into hot, clean, dry jam jars, leaving 1cm/½in space at the top. Wipe with a damp cloth, cover and secure the covers with rubber bands. Label the jars and store in a cool, dry place until ready to use.

About 2kg/4lb

Beef stock

	Metric/UK	US
Beef shin bone, cut into pieces	1kg/2lb	2lb
Marrow bone	1	1
Water	3½l/6 pints	7 pints
Large onion, halved	1	1
Carrots, chopped	2	2
Large leek, washed thoroughly and halved	1	1
Celery stalk, halved	1	1
Peppercorns	8	8
Cloves	4	4
Bouquet garni	1	1
Salt	1 Tbs	1 Tbs

Put the bones into a large saucepan. Add the water and bring slowly to the boil, skimming any scum from the surface. Continue to remove the scum until it stops rising.

When the scum stops rising, add the remaining ingredients and cover the pan. Simmer gently for 4 hours, or until the liquid has reduced by about half.

Strain the stock through a strainer lined with two layers of cheesecloth. If you are going to use the stock immediately, cool it and remove the fat. If you are storing it, leave the fat intact.

About 1¾l/3 pints (7½ cups)

Chicken stock

	Metric/UK	US
Carcass, bones and giblets (excluding the liver) of a cooked or raw chicken	1	1
Carrot, sliced	1	1
Celery stalks, sliced	4	4
Onion, stuck with 2 cloves	1	1
Bouquet garni	1	
Grated rind of ½ lemon		
Salt	1 tsp	1 tsp
Peppercorns	10	10
Water	1¾l/3pints	7½ cups

Put the carcass, bones and giblets (if available) into a large saucepan. Add the vegetables, bouquet garni, lemon rind, salt, peppercorns and water and bring to the boil, skimming any scum from the surface as it rises. Half-cover the pan, reduce the heat to low and simmer for 2 hours.

Remove the pan from the heat and strain the stock into a bowl. If you are going to use the stock immediately, cool it and remove the fat. If you are storing it, leave the fat intact.

About 1½l/2½ pints (6¼ cups)

The use of home-made stocks in soups and casseroles can make an enormous difference to their flavour. Simple and cheap to make, they will keep for several days in a refrigerator and months in a freezer.
1 Put the chicken carcass, giblets and vegetables into a large saucepan.
2 Add water, lemon rind and seasoning, and, to give it a special flavour, a bouquet garni. Tying the bouquet garni to the handle will facilitate its easy removal.
3 After the stock has cooked, strain into a bowl and discard the contents of the strainer. If you are going to use the stock immediately, cool it and remove the fat.

PUDDINGS & DESSERTS

Pineapple upside down cake

	Metric/UK	US
Butter	150g/5oz	10 Tbs
Soft brown sugar	2 Tbs	2 Tbs
Medium fresh pineapple, peeled, cored and cut into 9 rings, or 425g/14oz canned pineapple rings, drained	1	1
Glace (candied) cherries	9	9
Sugar	125g/4oz	½ cup
Eggs	2	2
Self-raising flour, sifted	175g/6oz	1½ cups
Milk	3 Tbs	3 Tbs
Angelica, cut into 18 leaves	5cm/2in piece	2in piece

Preheat the oven to moderate 180°C (Gas Mark 4, 350°F). Lightly grease a 20cm/8in square cake tin. Cut 25g/1oz (2 tablespoons) of the butter into small pieces and dot them over the base of the tin. Sprinkle the brown sugar over the top. Arrange the pineapple slices decoratively on top of the sugar and put a cherry in the centre of each ring. Set aside.

Beat the remaining butter with a wooden spoon until it is soft and creamy. Add the sugar and beat until the mixture is light and fluffy. Add the eggs, one at a time, beating well until they are thoroughly blended. Fold in the flour. Stir in enough of the milk to give the batter a dropping consistency.

Spoon the batter into the baking tin, being careful not to dislodge the cherries. Put the tin into the oven and bake for 50 minutes to 1 hour, or until a skewer inserted into the centre of the cake comes out clean. Remove the tin from the oven and set aside to cool for 5 minutes. Run a knife around the sides of the cake and invert on to a serving dish. Decorate each cherry with two angelica leaves.

Serve the cake warm, or set aside to cool completely before serving.

9 Servings

Crystallized angelica

Crystallized angelica is expensive to buy because the process of crystallizing is time consuming. If you do the crystallizing yourself you can afford to use angelica more liberally. It is difficult to estimate the quantity that this recipe will make as the amount will vary according to the thickness of the stalks used. As well as adding crystallized angelica to cakes, it is an attractive way of adding flavour and colour to home-made candies and hot milk.

	Metric/UK	US
Angelica, stalks and leaves removed, cut into 15cm/6in lengths	225g/8oz	8oz
Sugar	450g/1lb	2 cups
Water	600ml/1pint	2½ cups
Icing (confectioners') sugar		

Cook the stalks in boiling water until they give slightly when pressed with the fingers.

Plunge the stalks in icy water to refresh and, as soon as they are cold, drain and thinly peel away any stringy fibres.

Stir the sugar into the water over low heat until dissolved. Bring to the boil. Lay the angelica stalks in a shallow heatproof dish and pour over the boiling sugar syrup. Cover and leave to soak for 24 hours.

Drain the syrup off the angelica and reheat to 110°C (225°F), then pour it over the angelica again. Cover and set aside for a further 24 hours. Repeat this process for two further consecutive days.

On the fourth day, heat the syrup to 120°C (245°F) and add the angelica. Bring to the boil three or four times. This is to stop the syrup bubbling over and to allow the angelica to absorb it. Set aside until cool. Lift the pieces of angelica out of the syrup onto a wire rack and set aside until the surface is dry.

Preheat the oven to very cool 110°C (Gas Mark 1, 275°F).

Roll the dry pieces of angelica in icing (confectioners') sugar. Place on a baking sheet and put in the oven until dried through. (The amount of time this takes varies according to the thickness of the angelica stalks.) The surface should not be sticky to the touch when the angelica is thoroughly dried.

Wrap in greaseproof or waxed paper and store in bottles in a cool dark place until needed.

Opposite page Pineapple Upside-down cake is a popular American cake which makes a splendid and filling dessert. The fruit and the angelica, which gives the cake colour as well as taste, are arranged in the bottom of the cake tin and the batter poured over the top. When the cake is baked, it is turned out, upside-down, to display the fruit. Below The addition of Crystallized Angelica to desserts and cakes adds both to their appearance and taste. As it is expensive to buy we have included this recipe so that you can make it yourself from the angelica plants in your own garden to ensure a constant and cheap supply throughout the year.

Suédoise
(Fruit Jelly [Gelatine] Mould)

	Metric/UK	US
Large eating apple, peeled, cored and thinly sliced	1	1
Lemon juice, blended with 2 Tbs water	2 tsp	2 tsp
Maraschino cherries	6	6
Blanched almonds	6	6
Angelica leaves	12	12
Fresh apricots, halved, stoned (pitted) and poached	½kg/1lb	1lb
Fresh plums, halved, stoned (pitted) and poached	½kg/1lb	1lb
JELLY (GELATIN)		
Boiling water	900ml/ 1½ pints	3¾ cups
Sugar	225g/8oz	1 cup
Gelatine, dissolved in 4 Tbs boiling water	25g/1oz	1oz
Orange-flavoured liqueur	125ml/4floz	½ cup

First make the jelly (gelatin). Pour the water into a large bowl. Add the sugar and stir until it has dissolved. Stir in the gelatine mixture and liqueur. Set aside to cool. Chill the mixture in the refrigerator until the jelly (gelatin) is on the point of setting.

Meanwhile, combine the apple slices and lemon juice mixture and set aside.

Rinse a straight-sided 1½l/2½ pint (1½ quart) mould with water. Pour enough of the jelly (gelatin) mixture into the mould to make a ½cm/¼in layer on the bottom. Arrange the cherries, almonds and angelica leaves decoratively over it, remembering that the pattern will be the other way up when the dish is served. Spoon a little jelly (gelatin) over the pattern and place the mould in the refrigerator for 15 minutes, or until it has set. Remove from the refrigerator.

Arrange half the apricots over the jelly (gelatin) and spoon enough jelly (gelatin) to cover them completely. Chill the mould in the refrigerator for a further 30 minutes, or until it is set. Continue making layers in this way, using up the remaining apricots, the plums and apple slices, until all the ingredients are used up. Chill in the refrigerator for a final 2 hours, or until the mould has completely set.

Remove from the refrigerator and quickly dip the bottom into hot water. Place a chilled serving dish over the mould and invert the two, giving a sharp shake. The jelly (gelatin) should slide out easily.

4-6 Servings

A pretty French dessert, Suédoise is made with alternating layers of fresh fruit, nuts and angelica set in liqueur-flavoured jelly (gelatin). Serve with whipped cream.

156

Coriander fruit crumble

	Metric/UK	US
Cooking apples, peeled, cored and thinly sliced	700g/1½lb	1½lb
Blackberries	225g/8oz	8oz
Brown sugar	2 Tbs	2 Tbs
Ground cinnamon	1 tsp	1 tsp
TOPPING		
Flour	175g/6oz	1½ cups
Sugar	175g/6oz	¾ cup
Butter	175g/6oz	¾ cup
Ground coriander	2 tsp	2 tsp

Preheat the oven to moderate 180°C (Gas Mark 4, 350°F).

Put the apples and blackberries into a medium baking dish and sprinkle over the sugar and cinnamon.

To make the topping, put the flour and sugar into a bowl. Add the butter, cut into small dice, and rub the butter into the flour until the mixture resembles breadcrumbs. Mix in the coriander.

Sprinkle the topping mixture over the fruit, to cover it completely. Put the dish into the oven and bake for 45 minutes. Serve at once.

6 Servings

Verbena and apricot sherbet

	Metric/UK	US
Apricots, halved and stoned (pitted)	700g/1½lb	1½lb
Dried or fresh verbena leaves	8	8
Water	450ml/15floz	2 cups
Sugar	225g/8oz	1 cup
Gelatine, dissolved in 2 Tbs boiling water	15g/½oz	½oz
Double (heavy) cream	125ml/4floz	½ cup
Egg whites, stiffly beaten	2	2

Set the thermostat of the refrigerator to its coldest setting.

Put the apricots, verbena leaves water and sugar into a saucepan. Cover and bring to the boil. Reduce the heat to low and simmer the mixture until the apricots are tender and soft. Remove from the heat and set aside to cool.

Using a slotted spoon, transfer the apricots to a blender and blend until they form a smooth purée. Transfer the purée to a bowl. Add the apricot syrup and gelatine to the bowl and,

The inclusion of ground coriander in the crunchy topping of Coriander Fruit Crumble gives this dessert an attractive aroma and flavour.

A traditional British dessert, *Tansy Apples is quick to make and delightful to eat — especially when served with sugar and cream.*

using a wire whisk or rotary beater, whisk the mixture for 2 to 3 minutes, or until it is well blended. Cover and put into the refrigerator to chill for 1 hour.

When the mixture is cold, spoon it into a cold freezing tray and put it into the frozen food storage compartment of the refrigerator for 1 hour.

Meanwhile, beat the cream until it is thick but not stiff. Fold in the egg whites.

Remove the tray from the refrigerator and scrape the sherbet into a large bowl. Fold in the cream and egg white mixture. Beat the sherbet until it is smooth, then spoon back into the tray. Return the tray to the freezing compartment and freeze for 6 hours, or until the sherbet is firm to the touch.

Remove from the freezing compart-

ment. Dip a serving spoon into hot water, then spoon the sherbet into individual glasses. Serve at once.

6 Servings

Gooseberry cream with elderflowers

	Metric/UK	US
Gooseberries, trimmed	½kg/1lb	1lb
Dried elderflowers	1 Tbs	1 Tbs
Water	300ml/	
	10floz	1¼ cups
Dry white wine	125ml/4floz	½ cup
Grated rind of 1 lemon		
Sugar	125g/4oz	½ cup
Eggs, separated	3	3

Put the gooseberries, elderflowers, water, wine and lemon rind into a saucepan and bring to the boil. Reduce

158

Tansy apples

	Metric/UK	US
Butter	25g/1oz	2 Tbs
Eating apples, peeled, cored and sliced	2	2
Eggs, lightly beaten	2	2
Double (heavy) cream	150ml/5floz	$\frac{2}{3}$ cup
Chopped fresh tansy	2 tsp	2 tsp
Grated lemon rind	$\frac{1}{2}$ tsp	$\frac{1}{2}$ tsp
Grated nutmeg	$\frac{1}{4}$ tsp	$\frac{1}{4}$ tsp
Fresh white breadcrumbs	2 Tbs	2 Tbs

The addition of elderflowers to this dessert, with their pleasant, sweet and distinctive flavour, makes Gooseberry Cream with Elderflowers a delicious end to any meal.

the heat to low and simmer, stirring occasionally, for 20 minutes, or until the gooseberries are soft. Remove the pan from the heat. Rub the mixture through a strainer into a bowl, discarding any pulp in the strainer. Rinse and dry the saucepan.

Return the purée to the saucepan and add the sugar. Set the pan over low heat and stir the mixture until the sugar has dissolved. Remove from the heat. Beat the egg yolks into the mixture, then set aside to cool to lukewarm.

Beat the egg whites until they form stiff peaks. Fold the egg whites into the mixture, then transfer it to a large bowl or individual serving glasses. Set aside in a cool place for 1 hour, or until the cream has set. Serve at once.

4 Servings

Melt the butter in a large frying-pan. Add the apple slices and fry, turning and stirring occasionally, until they are tender.

Meanwhile, beat the eggs, cream, tansy, lemon rind, nutmeg and breadcrumbs until they are well mixed.

Preheat the grill (broiler) to high.

Pour the egg mixture into the frying-pan, reduce the heat to low and cook the mixture for 10 minutes, or until it is almost firm to the touch. Do not stir. Remove from the heat and put under the grill (broiler) for 3 minutes or until the mixture is golden brown. Remove from the heat.

Cut into wedges and serve at once.

4-6 Servings

BREADS & CAKES

Rosemary bread

	Metric/UK	US
Fresh yeast	15g/½oz	½oz
Sugar	½ tsp	½ tsp
Lukewarm water	300ml/10floz	1¼ cups
Flour	350g/12oz	3 cups
Salt	1 tsp	1 tsp
Wholemeal (wholewheat) flour	125g/4oz	1 cup
Finely chopped fresh rosemary	3 Tbs	3 Tbs
Dried rosemary	1 tsp	1 tsp

Crumble the yeast into a small bowl and mash in the sugar. Add a tablespoon of the water and cream to the mixture. Set aside in a warm, draught-free place for 15 to 20 minutes, or until the mixture is puffed up and frothy.

Sift the flour and salt into a large warmed bowl. Stir in the wholemeal (wholewheat) flour and the fresh rosemary. Make a well in the centre and pour in the yeast mixture and remaining water. Using a spatula, gradually draw the flours into the liquid until they are all incorporated and the dough comes away from the sides of the bowl.

Turn the dough out on to a floured surface and knead it for about 5 minutes. The dough should be elastic and smooth.

Rinse, dry and lightly grease the bowl. Shape the dough into a ball and return it to the bowl. Cover and set aside in a warm, draught-free place for 1 to 1½ hours, or until the dough has risen and almost doubled in bulk.

Turn the dough out on to the floured surface and knead for about 3 minutes. Shape into a loaf and arrange in a well-greased ½kg/1lb loaf

An unusual accompaniment to cheese or soup, Rosemary Bread is particularly good served warm from the oven and spread with butter.

tin. Return to the warm, draught-free place for 30 to 45 minutes, or until the dough has risen to the top of the tin.

Preheat the oven to very hot 240°C (Gas Mark 9, 475°F).

Sprinkle the top of the bread with the dried rosemary and put the tin into the oven. Bake for 15 minutes. Reduce the oven temperature to fairly hot 190°C (Gas Mark 5, 375°F) and bake for a further 25 minutes, or until the bread is baked. (If the bread sounds hollow when you rap the undersides, then it is cooked; if not, return to an oven preheated to warm 170°C (Gas Mark 3, 325°F) and bake for a further 10 minutes.)

Cool the loaf before serving.

½kg/1lb Loaf

Aniseed and sesame biscuits (cookies)

	Metric/UK	US
Vegetable oil	350ml/12floz	1½ cups
Thinly pared rind of ½ lemon		
Aniseed	1 Tbs	1 Tbs
Sesame seeds	1 Tbs	1 Tbs
Dry white wine	125ml/4floz	½ cup
Fnely grated lemon rind	2 tsp	2 tsp
Finely grated orange rind	2 tsp	2 tsp
Sugar	125g/4oz	½ cup
Flour	575g/1¼lb	5 cups
Ground cinnamon	1 tsp	1 tsp
Ground cloves	1 tsp	1 tsp
Ground ginger	1 tsp	1 tsp
Blanched slivered almonds	25g/1oz	2 Tbs

Heat the oil in a saucepan. When it is hot, add the pared lemon rind, aniseed and sesame seeds and remove the pan from the heat. Set aside to cool. Remove and discard the lemon rind. Pour the oil mixture into a bowl and add the wine, lemon and orange rind and sugar, stirring until the sugar has dissolved.

Sift the flour and spices into a bowl. Gradually add the flour mixture to the oil, beating constantly until all the flour has been added and a stiff dough formed. Using your hands, lightly knead the dough until it is smooth. Form into a ball, wrap in greaseproof or waxed paper and set aside at room temperature for 30 minutes.

Preheat the oven to fairly hot 200°C (Gas Mark 6, 400°F). Line two large baking sheets with non-stick silicone paper and set aside.

Remove the paper from the dough and divide it into 24 equal pieces. Roll each piece into a small ball using the palms of your hands, then flatten them into flat, round biscuits (cookies), about 1cm/½in thick. Arrange the biscuits (cookies) on the baking sheets and press a few slivered almonds into each one.

Put the sheets into the oven and bake for 15 to 20 minutes, or until the biscuits (cookies) are firm to the touch and golden around the edges. Transfer the biscuits (cookies) to a wire rack to cool. Cool completely before serving.

24 biscuits (cookies)

Aniseed and Sesame Biscuits have a delightful flavour and will keep for up to two weeks if stored in an airtight tin.

SPICES

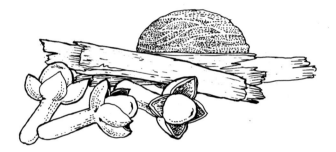

INTRODUCTION

Spices have played a vital part in every civilization since the beginning of time. As our knowledge of the past increases, we realize that they were indispensable to people who lived long before history was recorded. Excavations of tombs, temples and cities that have been buried and hidden for thousands of years are constantly offering fresh evidence of the importance of spices in religious ceremonies and the embalming of the dead, in medicine and folk lore, in the preservation and cooking of food, in skin and hair care and cosmetics, and as dyes for food and fibres.

Some spices are ground to a powder at their places of origin (usually tropical), others exported whole and milled when they reach their destination. It is convenient to have a range of ground spices to add instant flavour to any dish you are cooking, but it is well worth the extra time it takes to grind spices.

We tend to put most emphasis on their use as flavourings and condiments, since spices are no longer essential to the preservation of food. We can freeze meat, fish and vegetables, or buy freeze-dried packaged foods, without having to rely on salt and other spices to keep food safe to eat.

However, now that so many people are seeking to discover alternatives to the processed, pre-packaged foods we have grown accustomed to, spices seem set for a welcome come-back. We can use them to make delicious preserves—chutneys, pickles and flavoured oils and vinegars— and can experiment with salting and curing meat and fish.

Doubt about the advisability of relying on drugs every time we experience an ache or pain has led many people to look again at the natural medicines that were used to treat the sick for thousands of years. Health food shops usually have a section devoted to natural medicinal and beauty-care products, and there are some we can make ourselves.

Looking back to nature brings us—naturally—to ancient and beautiful crafts such as making vegetable dyes to give soft and lovely colours to natural fibres. Saffron and turmeric, for example, have 'endored' (a term meaning 'to turn a golden colour') not only clothes but food for hundreds of years. Experimenting with natural dyes is a fascinating hobby.

Other spices, such as frankincense, myrrh and sandalwood, have a long and important history and, burned as incense, still have religious significance today. Incense was burned as a form of fumigation and purification, and as an offering to the gods. Making incense is simple, the ingredients easy to buy from church furnishers' or suppliers.

Although most spices thrive best in tropical climates, there are some you can grow in the garden in temperate zones, and even more if you have a heated greenhouse.

Now that so many of us want to enrich our lives with a great knowledge of the past and of natural products, spices will once more have a wider part to play. As they are used in more subtle or adventurous cooking, in home crafts and beauty products, maybe they will become as indispensable today as they were to our ancestors.

165

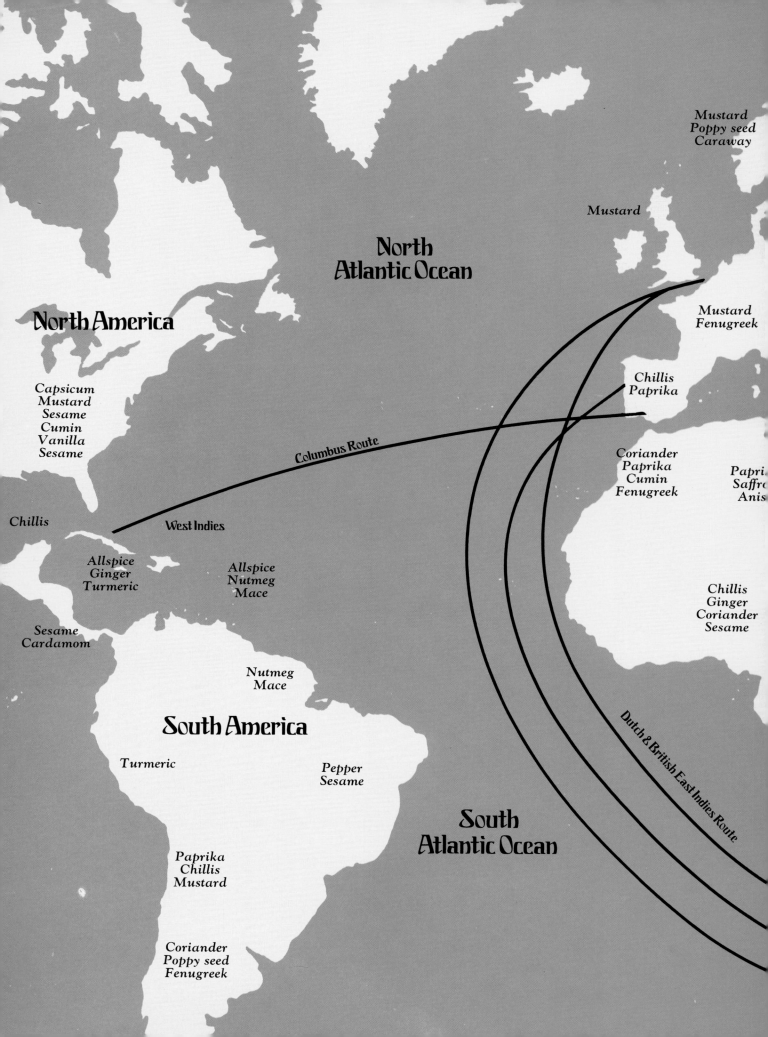

North
Atlantic Ocean

North America

Mustard
Poppy seed
Caraway

Mustard

Mustard
Fenugreek

Capsicum
Mustard
Sesame
Cumin
Vanilla
Sesame

Chillis
Paprika

Columbus Route

Chillis

West Indies

Coriander
Paprika
Cumin
Fenugreek

Papri
Saffr
Anis

Allspice
Ginger
Turmeric

Allspice
Nutmeg
Mace

Chillis
Ginger
Coriander
Sesame

Sesame
Cardamom

Nutmeg
Mace

South America

Turmeric

Pepper
Sesame

South
Atlantic Ocean

Dutch & British East Indies Route

Paprika
Chillis
Mustard

Coriander
Poppy seed
Fenugreek

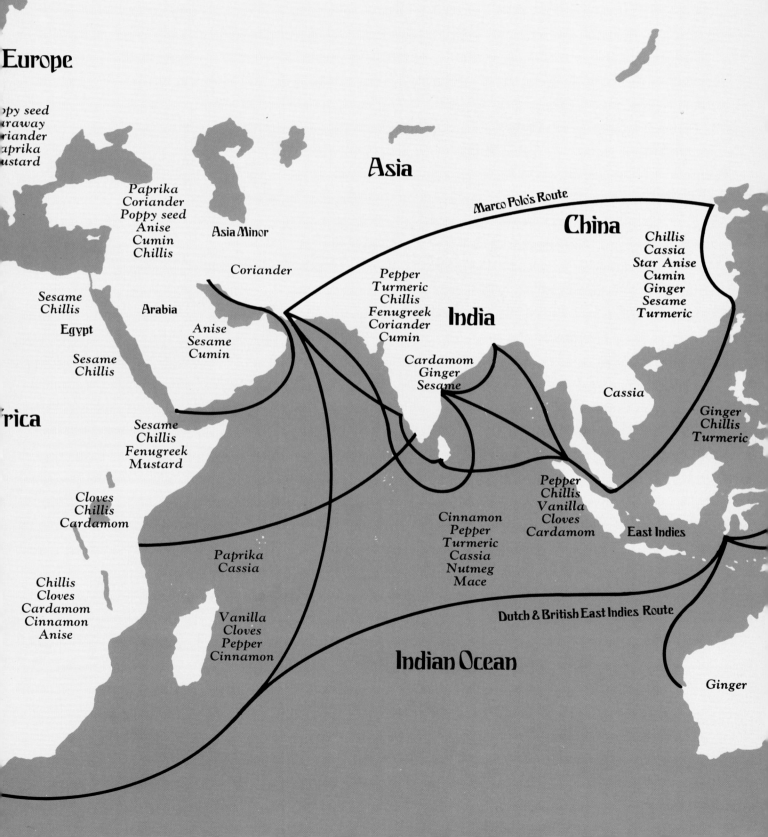

Ancient Trade Routes

Europe

Poppy seed
Caraway
Coriander
Paprika
Mustard

Paprika
Coriander
Poppy seed
Anise
Cumin
Chillis

Asia Minor

Asia

Coriander

Marco Polo's Route

China

Chillis
Cassia
Star Anise
Cumin
Ginger
Sesame
Turmeric

Sesame
Chillis

Arabia

Anise
Sesame
Cumin

Pepper
Turmeric
Chillis
Fenugreek
Coriander
Cumin

India

Egypt

Sesame
Chillis

Cardamom
Ginger
Sesame

Cassia

Ginger
Chillis
Turmeric

Africa

Sesame
Chillis
Fenugreek
Mustard

Cloves
Chillis
Cardamom

Paprika
Cassia

Cinnamon
Pepper
Turmeric
Cassia
Nutmeg
Mace

Pepper
Chillis
Vanilla
Cloves
Cardamom

East Indies

Chillis
Cloves
Cardamom
Cinnamon
Anise

Vanilla
Cloves
Pepper
Cinnamon

Dutch & British East Indies Route

Indian Ocean

Ginger

A COLOURFUL HISTORY

The colourful and romantic story of spices is woven into practically every branch of history. Reading about early religious rites and ceremonies one finds that spices, most precious of offerings, were used as an instrument in worship. The legends of the ancient world abound with stories of their magical powers. The foundation of medical knowledge is based on the healing properties of aromatic plants, which comprised the people's physic until comparatively recent times. And until modern methods of preserving and curing food were devised, spices, together with salt, played a vital part in the long-term storage of meat and fish, even before they were appreciated for their flavour.

Spices were such a highly-prized commodity, at times more precious even than gold, that their place of origin was the best-kept trade secret of all time. The search for spices not only caused a flotilla of seafaring explorations to set out on a wave of dangerous adventure, but resulted in the first drawing of the map of the globe. The first sponsored voyages were to find these Eastern riches: the first international trade agreements were to acquire them; and Britain became the first nation to draw up a minimum standard of quality for a trade that had become international.

As we use the spices we take so much for granted nowadays—a few cloves in an apple pie, perhaps, or crushed peppercorns on a steak—we might well wonder just how and why they commanded such a high price that men were prepared to pay for them with their lives. Part of the romance of their history lies in the fact that the very earliest use of spices is lost in the mists of antiquity; all we do know is that by the time the first records were kept, spices were already a treasured commodity.

Most spices are indigenous to the hot, damp tropical regions of the Orient, that is to say southern China, Indonesia, southern India, Sri Lanka and the Spice Islands of the East Indies, Java, Sumatra and the Moluccas. Some spices—notably allspice and chillis—were found when the New World was discovered in the fifteenth century and more have since been cultivated there, but very few will grow in the colder climates of Europe, especially Northern Europe. Full cultivation instructions for those spices you can grow at home are in the Dictionary of Spices later in the book.

Spices in ancient times

Not surprisingly, some of the earliest known records relating to spices come from the regions where the crops are indigenous. Among those that grow abundantly in China are ginger, cassia (a type of cinnamon), turmeric and anise, all greatly valued by the founder of Chinese medicine, Emperor Shen-Nung who lived around 2800 BC. He not only wrote a treatise on plant medicine, but held regular spice commodity markets and, practising what he preached, consumed vast quantities of ground spices every day to preserve his health and prolong his life. Legend goes further, claiming that Shen-Nung had the lining of his stomach surgically removed and replaced by a glass one, so that people could see the miracle powders at work.

Without going to quite those lengths, the Chinese have continued to put their faith in spices for medicinal purposes and for preserving and flavouring food. Confucius, about 550 BC, advised his followers not to eat any dish that lacked its proper seasoning, nor any that tasted or smelled bad. Ships plying to and from the Indian spice ports on the Malabar coast at that time carried pots planted with fresh ginger which was used to preserve the ships' stores and prevent scurvy among the mariners.

India was the natural home of pepper—always the world's most sought after spice—and also of chilli pepper, cardamom, ginger, turmeric, coriander, cumin and sesame, and the value of these and other aromatics, both in medicine and as food preservatives, was recognized in the earliest Sanskrit texts. Their use was 'authorized' in the *Ayurveda*, the treatise on the Hindu science of medicine, written in the fifth century BC.

One of the most primitive forms of Indian cooking, in a clay *tandoori* oven buried up to its neck in the soil, exemplifies the earliest use of spices to preserve, tenderize, flavour and colour food. The technique has been modified and is now so popular throughout the Western world that specialist restaurants enable us all to enjoy *tandoori* chicken sprinkled with salt and lime juice, marinated in yogurt and spices and coloured with hot chilli powder and paprika pepper.

Spices from China and India, with cinnamon from Sri Lanka and cloves, nutmeg and mace from the East Indies, comprised the precious cargo carried by hazardous land and sea routes to ports in the Eastern Mediterranean and Europe. The Arabs, geographically and temperamentally the natural middle men of this lucrative trade, maintained the monopoly for centuries and strengthened it by spreading fantastic tales of where and how the spices grew. For at least five thousand years caravans first of donkeys, then of camels plodded their way overland from Goa and Calicut (Calcutta), adding to their burden ivory and myrrh from East Africa and balm and frankincense from Arabia. Alternatively, the spices were carried by merchant ships through the Persian Gulf and along the Red Sea, to be taken overland from Egypt. Either way, the cargoes attracted tax, duties, tolls and colossal mark-ups at every handling point.

It was to one of these camel trains, travelling from Gilead, that Joseph, the favourite son of Rachel and Jacob, was sold by his jealous brothers for twenty pieces of silver, and resold by the merchants in Egypt.

Malacca, situated on the west coast of the Malay peninsula, controlled the European supply of spices in the later Middle Ages. At that time, it had a cosmopolitan merchant community with traders from China, South-east Asia, India, Persia and the Near East.

169

So great was the power of spices that they were used as symbols of homage and diplomacy. Rubens' painting of the Three Wise Men offering frankincense and myrrh to the Infant Jesus reflects this tendency and is also a reminder of the antiquity of the trade with the East for luxuries of all kinds.

The routes varied over the centuries according to which nation was in ascendancy, which tracks offered the least obstruction by bandits, and other factors. Tracing any one of the complicated network of routes with a finger on a map spells adventure even today—over the Khyber Pass, through Afghanistan, Iran, south to Babylon, on to the Euphrates and west to the Mediterranean—what mystery and magic a travel brochure could evoke from the journey, even one made in modern land-roving vehicles fully equipped with tents, radio, cooking facilities, canned and packaged foods and medical supplies.

The ancient Egyptians were good customers of the Arabian traders. They burned myrrh, frankincense, bdellium and balsam to banish evil spirits and appease the gods, and the upper classes used them as disinfectant to cleanse the air they breathed. Small drops of bdellium resin, in the form of 'pearls', were carried by ladies in their bags as a type of perfume. Spices played a very important part in the embalming process and cassia and cinnamon were imported particularly for this purpose. As long ago as 2500 BC the Egyptian Pharaoh Sahure received eighty thousand measures of myrrh from 'the land of Punt', a region of East Africa at the tip of the Red Sea.

From a later document; the Ebers scroll measuring 20m (65ft), it is clear that spices such as anise, caraway, coriander, fenugreek, poppy seed and saffron (some of which grew in the Middle East) were used not just as food preservatives but as flavourings and condiments, and some as cosmetics, too.

Whenever one ruler wished to create a good impression on another, spices were sure to be among the offerings taken or sent. The Queen of Sheba, who travelled to draw on King Solomon's wisdom, flattered him with camels laden with her most priceless possessions—gold, precious stones and spices. Then Phoenician sailors of King Solomon's empire, who were renowned for their seafaring ability, set sail for India and brought back wealth to the port of Tyre.

Spices were used as the currency of homage, too, as they were when the Three Wise Men chose frankincense and myrrh, together with gold, as an offering to the Infant Jesus.

Spices in classical civilizations

The Greeks and Romans made lavish use of spices and each civilization had its written authority on the subject. About 460 BC, Hippocrates, the Greek 'Father of Medicine', wrote a treatise documenting the importance of spices in both medicine and cooking. But the Greeks had no idea where the spices came from. Herodotus, the historian, believed that cassia grew in swamps effectively protected by ferocious bat-like animals which swooped over the forests uttering strange cries, and that curls of cinnamon were used by enormous birds to build their nests on high, inaccessible slopes. The story went that the spice could only be brought down by bribing the birds with chunks of meat so large that they sent the whole nests, complete with cinnamon sticks, crashing to the feet of waiting natives.

It was the Roman writer Pliny, the author of thirty-two books on natural history, who was the first to realize that the tales of spices growing in darkest African swamps and jungles were no more than a hoax. He estimated that by the time pepper and other spices reached Rome, the price demanded was one hundred times the original cost. At last, in 40 AD, a Greek merchant discovered the secret, long known to the Arabs, that the monsoons, the seasonal winds of the Indian Ocean, blow to the east in the summer and to the west in the winter. Now spices could be brought directly to Rome in record time, cutting out some of the greedy entrepreneurs. The wealth of first-century gold and silver Roman coins excavated on the Indian coast shows what a brisk trade developed.

There followed the greatest indulgence in the use of spices the world has ever known. The Romans used them to such excess that they can literally be said to have bathed in them. Men, even the legionaries, bathed themselves in the aromatic fragrances, spice-scented ointments and creams were popular as after-bath preparations and pillows filled with pungent, yellow saffron were used to induce sleep, or at least to lessen the effects of over-indulgence in the sweet, spiced wines. And, as expense was no object, Nero was said to have burned a whole year's supply of Rome's cinnamon at the funeral of his wife.

The extravagant use of spices was not confined to the bathroom and the boudoir. A cook book written by Apicius shows that if Rome had a motto for the kitchen, it must have been 'spices with everything'. It was quite out of the question to serve meat or fish unless it was heavily disguised, not to mention overpowered, by spices and spiced vinegars. Factory flavourings were introduced, in the form of sauce *liquamen*, a

On the strength of King Solomon's reputation, the Queen of Sheba, laden with gifts including a great wealth of spices, travelled far to test his wisdom. This illustration from a fifteenth century prayer book portrays the legend that she refused to cross a stream by the bridge because she recognized its timbers as those on which Christ would later be crucified.

171

A sixteenth century woodcut
depicts spice traders using camels to
transport goods to their ships.

seasoning made from dried fish, usually anchovies, and used in place of salt, and *garum*, made from blood and the entrails of tunny fish.

Spices were so indispensable to the Romans that they carried them everywhere their conquering armies went. Their gift to Britain consisted of some four hundred aromatic plants, mustard being one of them; mustard seeds, used for preserving, were excavated at a Roman site at Silchester. Although the British came to relish a taste for spices from this time, they had known them much earlier. Coriander seeds have been found on the floor of a late Bronze Age hut, and it is known that Britain traded raw materials for spices from Asia and wine and herbs from Mediterranean countries.

Just as spices figured in the glory that was Rome, so they featured in its downfall. When Alaric the Visigoth advanced on Rome in 408 AD one of the payments he demanded to raise the blockade was three thousand pounds of pepper, then worth its weight in silver. But two years later Rome fell anyway and, with the rise of Constantinople, the trading emphasis shifted.

The most famous spice trader of all was the prophet Mohammed, who started work as a camel driver and then went into partnership in a spice shop in Mecca. When, later, he married the widow of a spice merchant he carried on a dual mission, spreading the Islamic faith and trading in the lucrative spices at the same time. The Mohammedans were largely responsible for advancing the techniques of extracting and distilling scents and oils from aromatic plants.

The Medieval use of spices
As the cloud of the Dark Ages spread over Europe, the tapestry of the spice story, woven until then in such brilliant colours, was laid aside for hundreds of years, continuing in the Moslem East but with little documented contact with the Christian West. However, with the dawn of the twelfth century, the Crusades brought thousands of pilgrims to Syria and Palestine and an enormous two-way trade developed. Ships brought food, wool, clothing and metals to the crusading soldiers and returned to Italy

with spices, jewels and exotic fruit. Suddenly a way of life, which had passed into obscurity since Roman times, flourished again and the standard of living improved throughout Europe. Ports such as Venice and Genoa became rich as never before and here was the wealth on which the Italian Renaissance was founded.

Throughout the Middle Ages in Europe, one way in which wealth was demonstrated was in the vividly colourful presentation of the food. To tease noble palates dimmed by a surfeit of meat, game, fowl and fish, spices and herbs were used for their colour as well as their piquancy. Everything from roast peacock to spit-roasted minced meat balls was 'endored'— gilded with a saffron paste until it glittered like a gold crown; parsley provided a bright green colouring, sandalwood red and turnsole purple. Ginger, mustard and vinegar brought interest to meats and fish which had been dry salted or soused in brine, and ginger, cloves and other spices were infused in Hippocras, a mulled wine of the period.

English merchants travelled to the continental trade fairs to buy spices, and Venetian galleys sailed into British ports, but the British had to pay dearly for the Channel crossing. In the thirteenth century, pepper cost nearly twice as much in England as in France and peppercorns were so precious that they were counted singly and even accepted as currency in the payment of rent, taxes, tolls and dowry.

A set of household accounts for the year 1418–19 shows that Dame Alice de Bryene used five pounds of pepper, which she bought for 2s 1d per pound in London and 1s 11d at Stourbridge Fair, eighty-four pounds of mustard seed at less than a farthing a pound, three pounds of cinnamon, two-and-a-half pounds of ginger and three-quarters of a pound of saffron— used sparingly because it has always been the most costly spice of all. At this time a pound of saffron cost as much as a horse, a pound of ginger the same as a sheep, and two pounds of mace the same as a cow.

During the reign of Henry II, in 1180, a pepperer's guild of wholesale merchants was set up in London. This was later incorporated into a spicers' guild, and succeeded in 1429 by the present Grocers' Company, which was granted a Charter by Henry VI to sell goods in quantity—the term grocer deriving from the French *vendre en gros* (literally 'selling in bulk'). The Company was formed to manage the trade in spices, drugs and dyes—for many of the spices, saffron particularly, were commonly used to dye wool, linen and cloth as well as food—to select spices and medicinal products and to garble or cleanse them and ensure that they were of an acceptable standard quality.

The age of exploration

Against the background of continuing confusion and deliberate concealment about the origin of the spices, Marco Polo's journey from Venice to China was of tremendous significance. When he set out on foot at the beginning of the thirteenth century, many of the former trade links had been broken, and much of the knowledge of Roman times forgotten. And so, by the time he stood before the ruler, the Kublai Khan, he had crossed not only continents but centuries. When he returned home over twenty–five years later with tales of a market where one hundred and twenty thousand people brought their wares, of palaces, temples, silks, jewels and exotic fragrances, he was treated with scepticism. It was not until the Polo family put on a lavish feast, dressing themselves in luxurious silken robes and offering their guests a sumptuous menu spiced with Oriental delicacies that his account was accepted as fact rather than fiction. But it was not for another two centuries that the European nations finally tired of paying the exorbitant prices extracted by the middle men and decided to set out in earnest to search for the spice lands.

This determination heralded the age of exploration by sea, and throughout the fifteenth and sixteenth centuries nations entered into a race to finance voyages to discover and capture the riches. In a flurry of maritime activity, Portuguese ships discovered Madeira and the Spanish captured Mexico and Peru. Diaz, under the Portuguese flag, sailed to the Cape of Good Hope, and in 1497 Vasco da Gama rounded it, sailed on up the East Coast of Africa and, with the aid of a local marine pilot, reached the vital trading post of Calicut on the Malabar coast. The Indian ruler sent da Gama home with a message to King Manuel, 'A gentleman of your household came to my country, whereat I was much pleased. My country is rich in cinnamon, cloves, ginger, pepper and precious stones. That which I ask of you in exchange is gold, silver, corals, and scarlet cloth.' And so the Portuguese sent a merchant fleet to trade with the Zamorin—and took possession of Brazil in passing. They discovered the source of cinnamon in Sri Lanka and seized Malacca, one of the most important spice centres. By 1515, after the discovery of Madagascar, Borneo and Java, they had control of virtually the whole Far Eastern trade and brought back such quantities of bounty that Lisbon harbour had every appearance of an Eastern spice market.

The profits from this ever-increasing trade were ploughed back into exploration, enabling the king of Portugal to finance another great voyage, in which Magellan sailed almost round the world—he was actually killed by natives in the Philippines. And now the real charting of the seas could begin; the map of the world was drawn not on a flat sheet of paper, but on a globe.

Meanwhile, in 1492, Columbus persuaded the Spanish royalty to finance his voyage of discovery and with three ships he sailed West in search of India. Three months later when he stepped ashore, he found not glittering palaces but rambling, ramshackle huts and not pepper but chillis in Mexico and allspice—a berry with a flavour resembling a blend of cloves, cinnamon and nutmeg—in the West Indies. Later voyages returned with vanilla, the bean or pod of an orchid native to Central America.

The Dutch and the English began a simultaneous build-up of sea

A field of mustard in North Karnataka in India, an area which specialized in growing many of the spices that were so important to Western traders.

Vanilla became an important spice after Columbus's first voyage to America. It can now be grown in Northern hemispheres in greenhouses.

power. In 1579 the Netherlands declared their independence from Spain and began to trade direct with India. The rapid influx of wealth enabled them to establish the Dutch East India Company which took control of Malacca, the Malay Peninsula and northern Sumatra. In 1577 Sir Francis Drake sailed around the world to find a North-east passage to China, and brought back a large spice cargo. The English defeated the Spanish Armada, and Queen Elizabeth granted a charter to the East India Company to handle trade with the Eastern Hemisphere.

The growth of the modern spice trade

With so much profit at stake, rivalry developed to the point of warfare between the European maritime nations. By 1658 the Dutch had wrested from the Portuguese the cinnamon trade of Ceylon, and soon after that controlled the rich pepper ports of the Malabar coast, Java and Celibes. By 1690 the Dutch had the monopoly on cloves which they grew only on the island of Aboyna and, to keep the price up, had the trees on all the other islands burned. There are even stories of mountains of cloves being burned in the streets of Amsterdam. However, in 1749 a Frenchman smuggled some 'mother cloves' (the ripe fruit) out of the country and planted them in the French colonies.

With the growth of colonization most of the spice-producing areas came under British, French or Dutch influence and the three nations enjoyed a period of great prosperity. But the wheels of fortune turned again, and by the end of the eighteenth century, the Dutch company was bankrupted and England took over the Dutch ports in India and all the Dutch East Indian islands except Java.

Britain's reputation as a leading naval power was established, and London became the centre of the spice trade, with elegant headquarters at the Commercial Sale Rooms in Mincing Lane. With so many ships sailing to India, and so many British personnel in administrative posts there, curried dishes became almost a part of the national cuisine and a great many spiced fruit sauces and chutneys were imported to accompany them.

Across the Atlantic, the end of the American War of Independence had left fast and well-equipped ships available to ply for trade and the Yankee Clippers travelled to the East Indies, trading mainly for pepper and tea. Some of the first American fortunes were founded on the spice trade at this time, one being that of Elihu Yale, who founded Yale University.

Now the growth of independence for the spice-producing countries means that the spices contribute greatly to the economies of the new states. Nutmegs and mace, for example, are practically the sole export of the West Indian island of Grenada. Great industries still flourish from small beginnings for the bulk of the world's crop of cloves comes from those original smuggled plantings in Madagascar and Zanzibar.

SPICES IN MEDICINE

It was Hippocrates who, in the fifth century BC, wrote, 'Let food be your medicine'. This is what people the world over had been doing since the earliest times. They were dependent on the plants that grew locally for their food and, when they became unwell, for their medicine, too. The use of spices in remedies must have developed through trial and error. People suffering from flatulence would have noticed that a meal including, say, anise seed or cinnamon—both now recognized as carminatives—brought relief, or that those experiencing loss of appetite were persuaded back to normal eating habits when a dish spiced with black or cayenne pepper was put before them. And so a primitive but practical understanding of medicine grew and was handed down through the generations. Present-day chemical and botanical experiments have analyzed the spices and shown why many of the medicines self-prescribed almost by instinct were effective.

Medicinal spices through history

Each of the great civilizations of the ancient world had its authority on medicine, and each seems to have come independently to similar conclusions. Chinese folk medicine dates from primordial times, probably from 20,000 years ago, and as long ago as 3000 BC had been formulated into a recognizable pattern. It is based on the philosophy that each person is an individual with a delicately balanced system composed, on the one hand, of the power of darkness, the yin, and on the other, of the power of light, the yang. Medicinal remedies must restore and keep a balance of these two opposing facets and spices are categorized accordingly.

In India the *Ayurveda*, the Hindu science of medicine, in Egypt the *Ebers Papyrus*, in Greece the works of a physician, Dioscorides, in his herbal called *De Materia Medica*, all bear witness to the importance of spices in the treatment of illness and the preservation of health.

In Roman times, Pliny wrote a number of books on the subject, and the Roman soldiers took aromatics with them wherever they went. Under Roman occupation, the monasteries in Britain and France cultivated 'physic gardens' which were the beginning of a source of medical supplies

Opium was used in China as a sedative and a relaxant, and opium dens abounded in the last century as the drug raised the poor above the miseries and exigencies of their daily lives. Morphine, codeine and thebaine are extracted from opium for use in present-day medicine.

so important in later years to the hospitals built alongside the ecclesiastical communities.

Spices have played their part in world health not only as cures, but also as indirect killers. Ironically, the Black Death, which swept across Asia and North Africa in the fourteenth century before it killed one quarter of the population of Europe, is thought to have been carried there on the ships bringing spices from the East. In a desperate attempt to protect themselves from the devastating disease, people in Britain turned to spices for help, drinking juniper wine, saffron tea, garlic soup and bathing themselves with sponges soaked in extracts of cloves and cinnamon.

The work of Gerard and Culpeper

A number of erudite works showing the relationship between aromatic plants and medicine were written in Britain during the late Middle Ages. One of these, by William Turner, an admirer of Dioscorides' work, deals with the subject with the strictest caution, as perhaps befits a clergyman who became a Protestant and was also a doctor of medicine, a scientist and a botanist. Turner, who lived from 1508 to 1579, left, in his *Herbal*, a standard work of immense value.

Another man whose experience embraced both the laboratory and the garden was John Gerard, who was born in Cheshire, England, in 1545, and became an apothecary to James I. As superintendent to the gardens of one of Queen Elizabeth's ministers, Gerard wrote *A General History of Plants* with a colourful appreciation of the plants as they grew and made a unique collection culled from all over Europe.

In those days only rich and well-connected people could afford professional medical advice; others had to treat themselves with plants that were readily available. And it was for these people that, in 1649, Nicholas Culpeper wrote a book describing numerous plant remedies and advocating a branch of natural medicine called 'The Doctrine of Signatures'. Following this system, people would treat themselves on a 'like with like' principle taking, for example, yellow-coloured saffron or turmeric powder to treat yellow jaundice.

Homeopathic medicine

Homeopathic medicine can be said to be in sympathy both with the Chinese folk medicine, in that patients are treated as individuals with individually-prescribed remedies, and with the philosophy of treating like with like.

The basic philosophy of homeopathic medicine is attributed to an eighteenth-century physician, Samuel Hahnemann, who lived in Saxony (part of present-day West Germany). His aim was to find ways of curing patients with kindness and natural ingredients, rather than with some of the unnecessarily brutal methods he observed among his fellow doctors at that time. His first breakthrough was the observation that a minute dose of *Cinchona* bark, the tropical plant from which quinine is made, produced in a patient symptoms very similar to malaria, for which the drug quinine was usually prescribed. It seemed that quinine could not only combat malaria, but also induce symptoms very similar to those of malaria when given to a healthy person.

Working on this observation, Hahnemann carried out experiments with other plants, metals and minerals and came to the conclusion that 'what can cause can cure'. A drug would be effective by reinforcing the life forces in their struggle against the disease.

A feature of homeopathic medicine is that doses of any prescribed drug are extremely minute. First of all, a tincture is made from the raw material, such as the root or bark of a plant, and then diluted and 'successed'—violently shaken up—several times before being made into liquids, oils or tablets.

Turmeric, a yellow powder, was used in Elizabethan times to treat illnesses on a 'like with like' basis.

Aniseed and Star Anise have medicinal properties recognized by both conventional and homeopathic medicine. They are especially useful in aiding digestion.

Medical scientists have been making their discoveries, too, and progress has been rapid, if not alarming, in the field of drugs. With the ready availability of literally thousands of manufactured drugs in recent years, there has been a great swing away from natural cures, and bottles and packets quickly obtainable from doctors and pharmacists were our main weapon in the fight against illness. Now, however, when many people are concerned about the likely side effects of synthetic drugs, some impossible to identify until a drug has been in use for a number of years, there is a renewed interest in natural cures.

It is not always necessary to tramp the fields and hedgerows in search of cure-all plants, since reliable herbal remedies can be bought in health-food shops, or from professional homeopaths or herbalists. However, without delving deep into the realms of true medicine, it is possible to make some harmless and pleasantly soothing teas (tisanes), infusions and decoctions from the seeds and leaves of aromatic spice plants. These are quick and easy to do, consisting mainly of lightly crushing the seeds and infusing them for a few minutes in boiling water before straining the liquid and enjoying the refreshing aroma and taste. Specific quantities, and the conditions likely to be helped by the brews, are given under the name of each spice in the list that follows.

Other old-fashioned remedies are given, too, more from general interest than from a conviction that they will truly fulfil the claims made for them. Certainly if one could believe all one read about the power of such spices as sesame, saffron, liquorice root and sunflower seeds as sure-fire aphrodisiacs, none of us would waste our money on Valentine cards any more!

The medicinal spices

Anise *Pimpinella anisum* Anise seeds have for a long time held a place in folk lore and in magic, and are now recognized to have properties useful in the preparation of conventional and homeopathic medicines. In folk medicine, crushed anise seeds were mixed with oil of cloves into a paste and applied to the back of the neck, forehead and temples to relieve nervous headaches. The very thought of it somehow makes one feel at once more relaxed! The Aztecs chewed the seeds to relieve flatulence, and success has been claimed for an infusion of the seeds for complaints ranging from infantile catarrh, stimulation of the digestion—a theory held by Italian farmers—to tension and insomnia. Certainly anise tea would be a pleasanter remedy for sleeplessness than the old Eskimo cure—swallowing powdered animal bones washed down with melted snow!

To make Anise Tea

	Metric/U.K.	U.S.
Anise seeds	1 tsp	1 tsp
Water, boiling	300ml/½ pint	1¼ cups

Lightly crush the seeds, put them in a pot and pour on the boiling water. Allow to stand for at least 5 minutes then strain the tea into a stoppered bottle and leave it to cool. Take in frequent doses of 1 or 2 teaspoons. The tea will keep in the refrigerator for two to three days.

The Romans put their faith in anise seeds to send guests away from a feast in a not-too-serious state of discomfort, serving huge and heavily-spiced anise cakes at the end of a meal.

Gerard, in his *Herbal*, strengthened some of the earlier beliefs and recommended the seeds to relieve both hiccough and epilepsy; 'Aniseed helpeth the yeoxing or hicket and should be given to young children to eat, which are like to have the falling sickness or to such as have it by patrimony or succession'.

In conventional medicine, anise is an ingredient in linctus and lozenges given for the treatment of coughs. Essence of aniseed taken in hot water can help to relieve indigestion. Oil of aniseed is used in paregoric elixir, for its antiseptic properties in liquid dentifrices and as an insect repellent.

Star anise *Illicium verum*, known as Chinese anise, is highly valued in the East. The seeds are chewed after a meal to aid digestion, and the fruit is given to relieve colic and rheumatism. In Japan, the bark is ground to a powder and burnt as incense in the temples. In homeopathic medicine, a tincture is made from the seeds.

Caraway *Carum carvi* Gypsies seem to have detected a similarity in the properties of anise and caraway—it was an old Romany custom to chew caraway seeds to aid digestion. Caraway cake, eaten now solely for its pleasantly aromatic taste, was traditionally served to farm labourers to celebrate seedtime—when the last grain had been sown. The tradition of the Shakespearean era, when a dish of caraway was served with baked apples, is still carried on at Trinity College, Cambridge, while in Scotland, 'salt water jelly', a saucer of seeds, is set at the tea table and the buttered side of bread is dipped into it and then eaten.

An old-fashioned remedy for earache was a poultice of ground caraway seeds and breadcrumbs moistened with spirit, and to relieve the pain and discolouration of bruising, the ground seeds were mixed with vinegar.

Caraway julep was taken for the relief of nervous indigestion and flatulence, and sometimes given in cases of hysteria. It makes a pleasant tonic now and almost certainly helps to settle the stomach.

Cardamom was recommended as long ago as the fifth century B.C. for the relief of urinary diseases and headaches.

To make Caraway Julep

	Metric/U.K.	U.S.
Caraway seeds	25g/1oz	1oz
Water, boiling	600ml/1 pint	2½ cups

Lightly crush the seeds and put them in a teapot. Pour on the boiling water, put on the lid and stand overnight. Strain the mixture into a bottle, discarding the seeds. Take in doses of 1 tablespoon as needed.

Caraway is rarely used in medicinal preparations now, only to correct flavours and make other substances more palatable—to sugar the pill, in other words.

There is some evidence that oil of caraway—which gives the liqueur kümmel its characteristic 'burnt' flavour—stimulates the flow of bile, which is essential to the digestion. Dioscorides, the Greek physician, mentions the use of oil of caraway as a tonic for pale girls, and in India it is used in the manufacture of soap.

Cardamom *Elettaria cardamomum Maton* The *Ayurveda*, the Hindu science of medicine written in the fifth century BC, accepts cardamom as a cure for urinary complications, as a means of removing fat from the body and a cure for piles and jaundice. Other Brahmanic texts mention it in connection with halitosis, nausea, headache and fever, and as a soothing application in cases of eye disease.

Anything that might bring relief after the excesses of the table was welcome in Roman times and Apicius, who wrote and compiled the cook books that tell us so much about the Roman diet, recommended that cardamom be taken after any gastronomic indulgences—which, in those days, presumably meant frequently and often.

The Arabs also recognized cardamom seeds as an aid to digestion and put their faith in it, too, as a means of cooling the body and as an aphrodisiac.

Cardamom coffee, called *gahwa*, is given to visitors as a symbol of Arab hospitality and as an inducement to tranquil thoughts. It is a tradition that the ritual of the coffee is not disturbed by the discussion of business terms, and so negotiations are not entered into until the coffee has been sipped

Below A detail of the bark of Cinnamomum Cassia and Bottom Cinnamon sticks and powder. Both have similar properties and a mixture of cinnamon, hot milk and whisky or honey is recommended as a palliative for the common cold.

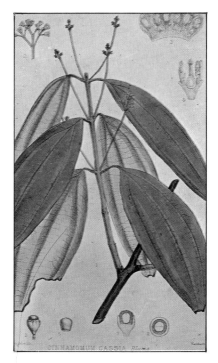

and enjoyed in peace. The perfect guest may accept up to three cups of the strong, pungent brew, which is poured from small brass pots in a ceremony verging on ritual. *Gahwa* is made from roasted green coffee beans, crushed with brass pestle and mortar and put into a small brass coffee maker with hot water, broken cardamom pods, cardamom seeds, sugar and a pinch of ground cloves. The coffee is then boiled for two to three minutes, strained and served 'black' in delicate little cups, and usually accompanied by small, sweet pastries.

Chillis Chilli peppers are the fruit of *Capsicum frutescens*, a perennial plant with red, orange or yellow pods up to about 10cm (4in) long which, when ground, are known as chilli or cayenne pepper. (They are not to be confused with capsicums, the fruit of *Capsicum annuum*, which are much larger and not, in spice terms, so 'hot'.) Chillis, whether whole, crushed or ground, are eaten in the tropics for the welcome effect they have of raising the body temperature and producing perspiration; welcome because this makes the surrounding air seem less oppressive, even cool. It is chilli powder which makes a hot curry 'hot'.

The Hindu *Ayurveda* strongly recommended chilli peppers as an aid to digestion and as a cure for paralysis. Chillis are known to stimulate the flow of saliva and gastric juices and may very well, therefore, aid weak digestion and help to overcome loss of appetite. If someone is 'off their food', they might be tempted to eat a dainty meal lightly spiced with cayenne.

The way appetite is tempted in the West Indies, one of the natural homes of chilli peppers, is with *mandram*, a dish that has at once both hot and cool flavours. It consists of chilled and thinly sliced unskinned cucumber sprinkled with lime or lemon juice, Madeira and cayenne pepper and mixed with chopped shallots and chives.

Cayenne pepper is sometimes used in tonics given to prevent disease, and herbalists use it in prescribed powders and pills. An old-fashioned remedy for chilblains, is to paint them with tincture of cayenne.

Cinnamon *Cinnamomum zelyanicum*, and **Cassia,** *Cinnamomum cassia,* are two of the oldest known spices. They have similar properties, though cinnamon has always been held to be the superior. In the fifteenth-century *Boke of Nurture*, John Russell wrote of 'Synamome for lordes, canell (cassia) for commyn people'. But no such distinction was made in the Biblical reference to the two spices, when the Lord asked Moses to anoint the tabernacle of the congregation of children of Israel with cinnamon, cassia and other spices.

Medieval magicians used both spices as ingredients in their sometimes harmless and often disappointing 'love potions'.

The Chinese took cinnamon as a remedy for excessive gases in the stomach, to normalize the temperature of the liver. Dioscorides who, according to legend, was the personal physician to Antony and Cleopatra, prescribed cinnamon bark in hot rum for colds, a practice which lingers even now in country cures. Ground cinnamon is added to hot milk, sometimes strengthened with whisky or sweetened with honey, or stirred into a mixture of lemon juice, honey and hot water, and taken at bedtime to lessen the miserable effects of the common cold.

In modern medicine, cinnamon is combined with other ingredients in medicines to relieve flatulence and arrest vomiting; with chalk and astringents it is a treatment for diarrhoea and internal haemorrhage.

Cloves *Syzygium aromaticum* The people of many early cultures discovered the soothing and healing powers of cloves. Early Brahmanic texts show that in India cloves and cardamom seeds were wrapped in betel-nut leaves and chewed to increase the flow of saliva and aid digestion. The *Ayurveda* recommends taking cloves for all manner of irregularities including fevers, dyspepsia and brain ailments, for toning up the heart and to relieve kidney, stomach, spleen and intestinal disorders.

In the third century BC courtiers seeking an audience with the Chinese emperor were required to sweeten their breath and make their presence more acceptable by chewing cloves, keeping the aromatics in their mouths for the duration of the interview. The Arabs tended to brush aside any medicinal claims made for the fruit and used them instead to offset the bitterness of mixtures prescribed in the treatment of fevers.

In the old folk medicine which verged on witchcraft, the buds, fruit and flowers of the tree, a member of the myrtle family, all had their part to play in bringing together would-be lovers, for they and the aromatic oil they produced were among the many ingredients used in 'love potions'.

For tension and headaches, country people found relief in the application of oil of cloves mixed to a paste with crushed anise seeds. Or they would inhale an infusion of cloves and hot, boiled vinegar. The same liquid was applied as a cold compress to the temples and neck. In Bolivia an infusion of a few cloves in a cup of boiling water was taken to relieve flatulence.

Cloves are now recognized to have the greatest stimulative and carminative powers of all spices and can assist the action of other medicines. Ground cloves or an infusion of cloves in water are prescribed for nausea, flatulence, weak digestion and dyspepsia. The volatile oil is a powerful antiseptic, and can be applied as a local anaesthetic in the manufacture of toothpaste and mouthwashes, as well as in the preparation of antiseptics and soap. It is often used in its concentrated state as a very effective relief for toothache.

Coriander *Coriandrum sativum* In early Hindu medicine coriander was mentioned as a treatment for constipation and insomnia, and an aid to child bearing. In medicine now, it is frequently used to mask the taste of other laxatives and to lessen the griping tendencies. Liberal use of the seeds is not recommended, because they can have a narcotic effect. In small quantities, both the seeds and leaves—highly pungent and much used in Indian cooking—can assist in the relief of flatulence. A few of the seeds mixed with a spoonful of honey and taken before meals, or infused in lemon juice and hot water, will be found helpful.

Cumin *Cuminum cyminum* The seeds, which are an essential ingredient in *garam masala* spice blends and curry powder, have long been appreciated by the Indians for their stimulative effects. Early Hindu medicine prescribed them for jaundice, piles and practically every organic complaint.

Herbalists in the Middle Ages wrote of the comforting, carminative properties of the seeds, and they were used to treat flatulence, weak digestion, colic and dyspeptic headaches. However, cumin seeds fell out of favour for individual use, because they were found less palatable than other spices with similar claims. For external application, where taste is of no account, they still have their uses. The bruised seeds are mixed to a paste and applied to relieve the pains in the side known as 'stitches' and, together with other drugs, form a stimulating linament. Apart from that, their medicinal use is now confined almost solely to veterinary practice. For example, an application of cumin seeds, bay salt and common salt is used to treat a condition known as scabby back and breast in pigeons.

Fenugreek *Trigonella foenum-graecum* The Latin name of this plant (also reflected in its common name), a native of western Asia, means Greek hay. It is sometimes mixed with hay to sweeten the fodder given to cattle and is prepared as a conditioning powder to make horses' coats shine.

However, it is as a treatment for almost countless human conditions that fenugreek merits attention here. In ancient times, in Asia and the Mediterranean countries to which the spice was indigenous, it was used to reduce fevers and soothe intestinal inflammation. Tribesmen mixed the crushed seeds to a paste and applied the poultice to battle wounds, boils and other 'open' disorders of the skin. Oriental physicians prescribed fenugreek for pregnant women in cases of difficult labour, and in Egypt it

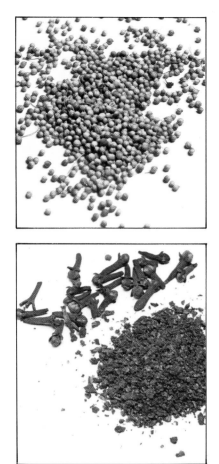

Top *Coriander seeds have a sweet flavour and are sometimes used in medicine to mask the bitter taste of other laxatives.*
Above *Cloves have powerful curative properties and the oil is sometimes used in the manufacture of toothpaste and mouthwashes.*

Top *Fenugreek was taken by Turkish women to guarantee a rounded plumpness and was also sometimes mixed with hay for fodder for cattle. It can be used as a conditioning powder to make horses' coats shine.*

Above *Juniper berries were used to stimulate the appetite and to cleanse the blood.*

was given to improve lactation. Ground fenugreek mixed with cotton seed was also given to increase lactation in cows.

Fenugreek had a heavy responsibility in Turkish family life, where it was used by the women to sweeten their breath and banish body odours. They took a mixture of the seeds and honey to improve their allure.

In the Middle Ages, a fenugreek preparation was recommended as a cure for baldness, and it is still used in Java as a hair tonic.

Culpeper was the first European herbalist to note its many medicinal properties and listed its efficacy as a diuretic, carminative and aphrodisiac.

One of the most important uses for fenugreek is in the breaking up of mucus in the body. In Albania, an infusion of the seeds is mixed with onion juice and lemon juice and taken to relieve inflammation of the mucous membranes, for head colds and sinusitis. A Bavarian medical practitioner described fenugreek as 'a liquid mucus solvent' and showed that it could remove collected mucus from the intestinal passages, organs and bloodstream, and help to dissolve fat in the kidneys. Any way of taking the seeds is said to be helpful in this connection—chewing them, particularly after a heavy meal, and drinking as a light infusion, or tisane.

To make Fenugreek Tea

	Metric/U.K.	U.S.
Fenugreek seeds	2 tsp	2 tsp
Water, boiling	200ml/⅓ pint	¾ cup
Honey (optional)	1 tsp	1 tsp
Lemon juice (optional)	½ tsp	½ tsp

Put the seeds in a cup, pour on the boiling water and allow to stand for 5 minutes, stirring occasionally. Strain the infusion, stir in the honey or lemon juice if used and drink while still hot.

This spice, which has figured in the self-help cures of so many cultures, and is still used by herbalists, is keeping pace with medical progress, for it is being used in experiments in the compilation of oral contraceptives, possessing as it does a steroidal substance, diosgenin.

Ginger *Zingiber officinale* Ginger has its roots in medical annals throughout the ages. In early Chinese medicine, it was recommended as a heart strengthener, and Dioscorides referred to its warming effect on the stomach and its properties as an aid to digestion and an antidote to poison. In early Hindu medicine, it was recommended for liver complaints, flatulence, anaemia, rheumatism, piles and jaundice. And, given the seal of Islamic approval, ginger was mentioned as a medicine in the Koran.

A pleasant way to enjoy the soothing powers of ginger is to make tea.

To make Ginger Tea

	Metric/U.K.	U.S.
Bruised root ginger, or powdered ginger	15g/½oz	½ oz
Water, boiling	600ml/1 pint	2½ cups

Put the bruised root or powdered ginger in a pot and pour on the boiling water. Leave for half an hour, then strain the liquid and leave it to cool. Take in doses of 1 fluid ounce (2 tablespoons) at a time.

American Indians drank a similar decoction of root ginger to relieve stomach upsets. Gypsies, whose culture has always been rich in remedies from the soil, have a cold 'cure' which is a blend of ginger, white horehound, hyssop and coltsfoot, and in Asia Minor for the same ailment, ginger, cinnamon, mustard seed and cayenne pepper are mixed to a paste with honey and spread on a piece of flannel to cover the chest.

Horseradish *Armoracia rusticana* Not strictly a spice, but a highly aromatic root, horseradish has been recommended as a stimulant since the Middle Ages. Because of its high Vitamin C content, it was effective in the prevention of scurvy. Horseradish syrup was taken as an expectorant medicine for coughs following bouts of influenza and an infusion, together with mustard seed, recommended for dropsy.

According to gypsy medical lore, horseradish leaves combat food poisoning and the ground root is effective against coughs, colds and bronchitis. To relieve neuralgic pain, a bag of scraped horseradish root was held against the source, and a compress of grated root with a little water used to alleviate tension pain in the back of the neck.

Juniper *Juniperus communis* Legends abound about the magical and holy powers of the juniper tree. A strong infusion of the berries in water was used as an antidote to poisonous bites, bee stings and insect bites—and if it worked, one can see how one of the tales of magic originated.

In Mongolia, strong belief is put in the power of juniper as a relaxant, and a decoction of juniper leaves and ground root is given to pregnant women at the onset of labour.

The berries are said to stimulate appetite and aid digestion, and thought to be cleansing for the blood. A strong decoction made from the stems of the plants was given as a remedy for piles and bleeding gums, and colicky babies were treated with a mild juniper berry tea, also found to be effective against cramp.

With their fragrantly sweet smell, juniper berries can be used as a disinfectant. In the nineteenth century they were burned and used to freshen the air in Swiss schools in the winter, when it was too cold to open the windows and allow air to circulate in the classrooms. The berries are still used sometimes for this purpose in invalids' rooms.

Folk lore has passed on belief in the efficacy of juniper berries in the treatment of dropsy; sometimes the berries were infused with either bruised ginger root or grated dandelion root.

Mustard There are three main types of mustard, Black mustard, *Brassica nigra*, Brown mustard, *Brassica juncea*, and White mustard, *Brassica alba* or *Brassica hirta*. All three are members of the cabbage family. Mustard seed is well documented as a virtual cure-all by the early Greeks, Romans and Egyptians. In 530 BC Pythagoras recommended it as an antidote to snake bites and scorpion stings, one of the most deadly killers, and over a century later Hippocrates documented the internal and external medicinal uses of the seeds. Roman soldiers had mustard as part of their diet, and it was used, in plaster form, to relieve rheumatism and arthritis.

Culpeper, in his *Herbal*, affirmed Pythagoras's theory about snake bites, and further recommended a paste of crushed mustard seed and honey to apply to bruises or pains in the neck.

Many a Victorian household was run on the assumption that a mustard bath or foot bath would keep colds at bay and relieve any symptoms already present. The theory was that the heat of the mustard drew the blood away from the congested area—the head or chest. Mustard bath powder is still sold commercially, the packet stating that the bath 'will be found pleasant, soothing and refreshing, especially after outdoor exercise and when feeling cold, tired or stiff'. The preparation is sprinkled on hot or cold water in the proportion of one half to one ounce per gallon of water. It is said to be relaxing and to tone up the skin. People take mustard baths, too, to relieve the pain of severe bruising and to draw out the bruise. Country people, especially farm workers and gardeners, put mustard leaves inside socks to promote circulation of the blood and thus keep the extremities warm in harsh wintry weather.

According to folk medicine, white mustard seeds were used as a laxative, and a strong infusion of the seeds in water was given in cases of chronic bronchitis. Mustard seed tea, a weaker infusion, was a refreshing gargle for a sore throat and a remedy for intestinal and digestive disorders.

Below *A traditional gypsy remedy advocated a concoction of mustard seeds, wholewheat flour and warm water for colds, congestion and kidney ailments.*

Top and Above One of India's most important spices, pepper has diverse properties and over the centuries has been used to treat a wide range of disorders from jaundice to arthritis.

Gypsies use chopped mustard leaves and the seeds to preserve and flavour food and, as a side effect, to aid digestion. An old gypsy remedy for constipation consists of chewing mustard leaves and sipping cold water at the same time—not an easy thing to do. For colds, congestion, bladder and kidney complaints, gypsy lore favours a plaster of one part of mustard seed mixed with four parts of wholewheat flour and warm water.

Nutmeg and **Mace** The large evergreen tree with the botanical name *Myristica fragrans* produces both nutmeg and mace—the mace grows around the thin shell surrounding the nut. Nutmeg has been prescribed in India for thousands of years as a cure for headaches, intestinal disorders, fevers and bad breath. Since the ninth century, Arab medical sources have claimed nutmeg to be a remedy for kidney ailments and stomach complaints, and acknowledged it as an aphrodisiac.

In the twelfth century the streets of Rome were fumigated with nutmeg before the coronation procession of Emperor Henry VI passed by. And sixteenth and seventeenth-century herbalists used nutmeg in many of their therapeutic cures. Grated nutmeg was mixed with lard and used as an ointment applied in the treatment of piles. Now, a relic of country lore, it is sometimes grated on top of malted or hot milk drinks to soothe head and chest colds.

Pepper *Piper nigrum*, the black pepper indigenous to India features in early Brahmanic texts where it is mentioned in the treatment of urinary complaints, disorders of the liver, piles, jaundice and as a means of removing fat. It has been used for centuries as a stimulant, carminative, to treat constipation, diarrhoea, cholera and arthritis, and as a digestive aid. It is hard to believe that a single spice could have such diverse properties.

Gerard, in his *Herbal*, showed that he was a follower of the Greek physician when he wrote that, 'All pepper heateth, provoketh, digesteth, draweth, disperseth and cleanseth the dimness of the sight, as Dioscorides noteth.' One can hardly have a better testimony than that!

Pepper is not greatly used in modern medicine, but is sometimes added to quinine.

Poppy seed *Papaver somniferum* Since ancient times, the red poppy has been the symbol of fallen warriors and now after two world wars, the Flanders poppy (*Papaver dubium*) has been adopted as the symbol of peace on Armistice Day, November 11th.

Since the Stone Age, poppy seed has been used to stimulate the appetite and at the time of the Olympic Games in Greece the competitors were given the tiny blue-black seeds mixed with wine and honey as part of their training diet, to encourage them to eat and grow strong! The drug opium, which can be obtained from the dried milky-white juice in nearly-ripe capsules, was known for its medicinal and narcotic properties to the Egyptians, Greeks and Romans. However, as the seed is not formed until after the capsule has lost this opium-forming matter, it has no narcotic effects.

Saffron *Crocus sativus* Because it has always been by far the most expensive of spices, the use of saffron has rarely been lavish, though in Greco-Roman times it was scattered on the floors to perfume theatres and public halls before a performance. According to Hetodt, a German medical practitioner in the seventeenth century, there was no sickness, from toothache to the plague, that saffron was not capable of eradicating. And at that time it was considered in other European countries to be an effective stimulant and antispasmodic and a remedy for measles, dysentery and jaundice—the latter an example of the 'like with like' cure, treating jaundice with a yellow-coloured spice.

In Ireland, country women dyed their sheets with saffron—even a very little produced a strong colour—believing that it strengthened the limbs of their children.

Saffron has also been used as a colourant in medicines. And in Arab countries, the combination of saffron, asparagus, egg yolks, milk and honey produced a delicious yellow-coloured concoction with allegedly irresistible results!

Salt The mineral sodium chloride, essential to human and animal life, makes salt one of the few raw materials of our diet which is basic to our needs. It has been used for centuries as a vital preservative for foods of all kinds and, effective in this important way, has contributed greatly to overall good health, especially in hot climates where food would normally deteriorate quickly.

In Roman times, a mixture of salt and spices was taken to settle the stomach. Old remedies involving salt include drinking heavily salted water to induce sickness in cases, for example, where something harmful has been eaten. And there is an old Cornish recipe for an eyebath to soothe eyes irritated by grit or smoke in the atmosphere. To make this, measure 600ml/1 pint (2½ cups) of water from the tap and leave it to stand uncovered overnight. This will draw off the chlorine in the water. Bring the water to the boil, add 1 tablespoon of sea salt and stir it until it has dissolved. Allow the salt water to cool a little, then pour it into a sterilized bottle or jar. Cover and use it in an eyebath or soaked on a pad of cotton wool (sterile cotton).

Sesame *Sesamum indicum* Probably the oldest crop grown for edible oil, sesame was mentioned as long ago as 1550 BC in the *Ebers Papyrus* and there are earlier records of its production in the Tigris and Euphrates Valleys.

The use of sesame goes back into the realms of mythology, when, according to Assyrian beliefs, the ancient gods drank sesame wine before they created the earth—presumably to give them the strength to undertake the mammoth task before them. The God of Death, Yama, pronounced sesame a purifier and symbol of immortality, to be used at funerals and ceremonies of expiation.

Sasruta the Elder, who is believed to have practised as a surgeon in India in about the fourth century BC, applied sesame poultices to wounds after an operation, and had the floors of his operating rooms and clinic strewn with the aromatic plants as fumigation.

Folk lore recommends sesame leaves steeped in boiling water to make an eyebath or compress for sore and tired eyes.

Throughout ancient times sesame was thought to have desirable properties as a sexual invigorator and aphrodisiac. In Arabia a mixture of sesame seed, liquorice root and stoned and chopped dates was simmered in water, sweetened with honey and taken three to four times a day—or as needed! And the women of ancient Babylon relied on a mixture of sesame seeds and honey, a delicious sweetmeat, to increase their sexual desire and fertility. Without making too many claims in the field of romance, sesame seeds may well help in improving lowered vitality—and their nutty flavour makes them pleasant to eat in any case.

Turmeric *Curcuma longa* This bright yellow spice is known in Europe as Indian saffron, because it has the same colouring qualities as real saffron.

In Malaysia, ground turmeric was mixed to a paste with water and smeared on the abdomen after childbirth, both for its believed healing properties and to ward off any lurking evil spirits.

In Asia, the spice is still used as a remedy for liver troubles and a tonic for ulcers, as well as externally for the treatment of skin disorders and as a depilatory. Country folk medicine recommends a recipe for turmeric boiled with sugar and milk as a remedy for the common cold.

Vanilla *Vanilla planifolia* In the sixteenth and seventeenth centuries, when it was first introduced into Europe, vanilla was considered to be a stimulant, stomachic and an antidote to poison. And, because of its pleasantly mild flavour, no doubt, was popular in sweet mixtures believed to be aphrodisiacs.

Below *The poppy plant and* Bottom *the poppy seeds. Opium is derived from the dried milky-white juice in nearly ripe capsules and has been in use for centuries. Poppy seeds were used to stimulate the appetite.*

185

SPICED DRINKS

Hot, fragrant, spicy wines—what a lovely, reassuring picture they conjure up! Carol singers stamping their way through the driven snow, and being rewarded with a steaming glass of mulled wine; a late-night drink around the log fire on Christmas Eve, with a glass of hot punch discreetly left near the glowing embers for Father Christmas, or a party to give friends the warmest welcome of all.

Few drinks—with the exception, perhaps, of champagne—allow guests to slip more readily into the party mood, or make them feel more instantly at home. Yet mulled wines need not be particularly alcoholic. Many of the recipes actually call for the wine to be diluted with fruit juice or even water. And they certainly need not be expensive, for no one on earth would recommend adding cloves, nutmeg, orange juice, lemon peel and honey to a fine vintage wine. If you want to give the drink a little more 'kick' you can mull a fortified wine such as sherry or port—many of the traditional recipes use these wines—or add a little brandy or liqueur to the punch. This depends entirely on your taste, your purse—and whether your guests have to drive home afterwards.

Spiced drinks of the past

Spiced wines were very popular in Roman times; so popular, it seems, that a whole range of other spices was called upon to restore calm to troubled heads and stomachs.

Throughout the Middle Ages, wines were commonly flavoured with sugar and spice, but this was simply to make them palatable. At that time, the art of winemaking and viticulture left a great deal to be desired. What was misleadingly termed 'wine of vintage' was simply the unfermented grape juice, the must, corked into the barrel the moment fermentation had started. Other casks, left to their own devices for a few months before being corked into the barrels, were sold at a considerably higher price as 'wine of rec'. But without a proper understanding of the treatment of casks, with no glass bottles, and scant regard for sterilization of equipment, the wine was harsh and bitter. If it was not drunk within a year of the grape harvest it turned to vinegar.

No wonder the favourite drink of the day was Hippocras, a spiced mull based on red or white wine, which was served at the table of the English King Richard II. A contemporary recipe gives instructions for infusing the wine with cinnamon sticks, powdered ginger, cardamom pods and cloves, each tied in a separate cheesecloth bag and suspended in the sweet wine as it heated over the fire. Such blends were called piments, and recommended —in moderate quantities—by apothecaries, as medicinal cures and aids to digestion—a case of a little of what you fancy doing you good!

Wine was even taken at breakfast in those days. A favourite morning tipple was 'soppes of wine', a bowl of spiced wine with chunks of bread crumbled into it. In poorer homes, this was substituted by 'milk mess', with the bread broken into a bowl of hot and sometimes spiced milk.

By the summer, when even the addition of sugar and spices left the wine pretty well undrinkable, ale came into its own. Brewed from corn, oats or barley, either individually or blended, it was probably not a bad drink in its own right, but mulled ale had an enthusiastic following. Tankards of the brew were heated by a hot iron from the fire plunged into the foaming liquid, and the spices were added to the quaffer's taste.

The adequate spicing of drinks took on such importance in Britain that a whole range of products was crafted to cater for the fashion. People who travelled about the country dared not trust the generosity of penny-pinching hotel- and inn-keepers, so they took their spices with them. Miniature nutmeg graters in the shape of acorns, barrels and mace (a play

Hot Toddy is a warming and welcoming drink to offer guests on cold, wintry evenings. The heavy, silver tureen and cups are eminently suitable for mulled wines.

187

A traditional Scandinavian punch, Glögg combines wine, spirit and fruit with ginger, cardamom, cinnamon and cloves to make a deceptively strong but delicious drink.

on words) and exquisitely fashioned from expensive hardwoods, silver, enamel and tortoiseshell are collectors' items today. Pocket-sized fruitwood boxes swivelled to reveal precious hoards of individual spices, and at home cinnamon casters and beautiful spice boxes and cabinets were standard equipment.

Where spiced drinks were concerned, quantity as well as quality must have been the order of the day, judging by an eighteenth-century description attributed to an innkeeper in *The Beaux Stratagem*. He spoke of a gigantic silver tankard, 'near upon as big as me; . . . and smells of nutmeg and toast like an East Indian ship'.

How to make mulled wines

You don't need any special equipment at all to serve mulled wines, or hot punches; you are not actually making the wines, only flavouring them. The choice of wine is important, of course; the wine you mull must not be so good that it will be offended by what you are going to do to it! Look in the wine shop or licensed retail store for inexpensive wines from California, Portugal, Spain, Italy or South America. If they are described on the label as fruity, full-bodied, 'stout' or 'round', so much the better. Mulled wines should taste (though need not actually be) strong. These days it is customary to make hot punches from red wine, and those long, cool summer fruit cups from white wine, but you can, if you wish, mull both white wine and cider.

You will probably already have all the spices you need in the kitchen. As you come to know the blends you enjoy and the degree of spiciness you like best, you can vary the recipes at will (you will find a selection of detailed recipes later in the book). Most recipes use two or three spices, usually ginger, cinnamon, cloves, mace, nutmeg and mixed spice, and you could experiment with cardamom, coriander, allspice and juniper berries. Unless you have a palate for the really unusual, avoid hot spices such as peppercorns and chillis. They not so much spice as fire the wine!

188

Vin Chaud uses the traditional spices for mulled wines: cloves, cinnamon and nutmeg. It is a festive drink and one that will warm guests as they arrive inside from the cold.

You can use spices whole or ground. Either way, you can tie them in cheesecloth or muslin and hang them in the wine—as you do with a *bouquet garni* of herbs in a casserole—then remove them when the wine has absorbed the aroma and is ready to serve. Or you can stir the whole or powdered spices into the wine with the honey or sugar. Although whole spices floating on top of the wine, mingling with thin slices of orange, lemon or apple, look decorative, a mouthful of cinnamon stick or root ginger is not always a pleasing experience, so it is best to strain them off before serving. Powdered spices, of course, form part of the brew, and are *there* when the wine is drunk. The flavour of the wine is stronger and slightly mustier, and the mull is more cloudy—it's a matter of preference.

The flavour of both oranges and lemons is a perfect complement to the sweet spiciness of punches—orange is a little more traditional. How you impart the orange flavour is a matter of choice, too, and always has been. One famous hot punch, called The Bishop, is based on non-vintage port

flavoured with orange. Dean Swift favoured using roasted oranges:

'. . . fine oranges
Well roasted with sugar and wine in a cup
They'll make a sweet Bishop when gentlefolks sup.'

Dr Johnson described the concoction as mulled port with Seville oranges, sugar and spices. Other authorities like to serve the mull with an orange pricked with cloves, like the prickles on a hedgehog's back—a very good way to tame the whole cloves when serving the wine—and others, perhaps with a little more patience at the preparation stage, prefer to rub the zest of the orange with lumps of sugar to sweeten the mull.

To add a sense of drama to an occasion, people sometimes add a little brandy to a bowl of steaming punch and set it alight, to be carried in triumphantly, blue flames leaping, like the Christmas pudding.

The Bishop, Sir Roger de Coverley and Negus, all evoking caricatures of portly gentlemen, are among the stronger mulls, based on port. The last one is said to have been invented in the eighteenth century by an East Anglian Member of Parliament, Colonel Francis Negus, who hit on the idea of diluting the port, and hopefully the tempers of his political contemporaries, at his dinner table. Sweet sherry and Madeira make heart-warming mulls, too, but most people settle for *vin ordinaire*, red wine of unremarkable quality, which can be strengthened with a small proportion of one of the fortified wines or with brandy, to give a feeling of largesse to the occasion. But there are many recipes which much more economically suggest diluting the wine with orange, grapefruit or pineapple juice, or with water—and these are probably the blends to go for when a party is to include a large number of young people. Even the most sophisticated drinkers have difficulty in detecting the strength of a drink when it is both spiced and sweetened—until, perhaps, it is too late.

Mulled wine must be heated gently, and never allowed to reach boiling point; this destroys both the flavour and the alcohol. Choose a large saucepan—enamel is ideal—but do not use aluminium. Pour in the wine, fruit juice, water or other liquor and stir in the sugar, honey and spices, or tie them into bags to dangle in the brew. Allow the wine to heat very slowly until it is just below simmering point. By this time it will have absorbed the sweet, pungent flavours. Taste it to be sure that it is neither too sweet nor too bitter. If it is, correct the balance by adding more fruit juice (lemon or lime juice is ideal if it is really over-sweet) or honey or sugar, stir and gently reheat. If you have used loose whole spices, strain the wine through fine muslin or cheesecloth.

The traditional way to serve the wine is in a large punch bowl, but not many of us have them. A large soup tureen or casserole dish does the job equally well, and you can use a ladle or small china or pottery jug for pouring. Or you can funnel the heated wine back into the bottles (heat them first) and stand them in a large pan of simmering water to keep a ready supply. Wrap a tea cloth round the bottles of heated wine and pour it with all the panache of a top wine waiter serving a vintage claret.

Do not be tempted to use your best glasses. The wine must be served

piping hot, and high temperatures and fine crystal do not really go together. Pottery goblets are ideal, or beer glasses which have handles. Warm the glasses first and move a silver spoon from one to the other as you pour in the wine.

Hot, fragrant, spicy wines—with these simple instructions you have all the makings of a friendly gathering. Make your hospitality generous, but not so generous that your guests go away with the telltale signs referred to in *The Knight of the Burning Pestle*,

'Nose, nose, jolly red nose,
And who gave thee this jolly red nose?'
'Nutmegs and ginger, cinnamon and cloves,
And they gave me this jolly red nose.'

For a hot drink with a difference, try Wassail Bowl which is made with beer, sherry, spices and apples.

PRESERVING FOOD

As we take a selection of out-of-season fruit and vegetables from the freezer, open a can of meat or fish, or choose a complete freeze-dried meal from the supermarket shelves, it is difficult to imagine what it was like to plan meals before these methods of food preservation were known.

Basic methods of preserving meat and fish, by drying in the wind, smoking, dry salting or pickling in brine (salted water) were known to most primitive peoples, and by the time the Romans invaded Britain much more sophisticated methods of preserving were commonplace. In the Roman cook book of Apicius there are recipes for pungent vinegars made aromatic by the lavish use of spices, and for pickling such humble vegetables as turnips.

Commercial refrigeration and food canning were unknown until about a century ago, and even then were not available to people in rural communities cut off from the march of progress by poor access roads, lack of communication or simply lack of money. There are still plenty of people who can remember and reminisce with pride about the days of frantic and anxious activity as each home-grown crop was harvested, or an animal was slaughtered in the autumn (fall). For where money was short, the barren winter months could prove too costly to keep a backyard animal. And so until very recently methods of food preservation had changed little. Salt was the staple preservative, spices were used in many of the pickling solutions and preserved food which had lost much of its original flavour in the processing was cooked in spiced broth to make it palatable again.

Another very recent innovation is the production of seeds which give a succession of vegetable crops which can be harvested over a period of several weeks or months. Before that, it was a short harvest and a frantic one while people worked long hours in the kitchen to cope with the glut.

The pantry shelves would fill up with dry salted beans, pickled red and white cabbage, sometimes spiced with cloves, chillis and peppercorns, picked cauliflower, marrow and ginger, mixed pickles and chutneys of every kind. For whereas the prime vegetables were needed for pickling in the various spiced vinegars, any slightly damaged 'windfall' vegetables could be used to make the glowing rich red, brown and amber chutneys which would give flavour to the cold meats.

Some fruits could be kept in storage throughout the winter. Apples and pears could be dried and hung like paper chains in a cool, airy place. Other fruits—plums, greengages, peaches and damsons, for example—would be bottled in spiced vinegar or syrup to emerge as tempting as the day they were harvested. We sometimes forget, too, that jams, jellies, fruit butter and cheeses and fruit and vegetable curd were not only ways of providing delicious tea-time confections, but also of preserving the crops.

Those were the days when the term self-sufficiency had real meaning, and could represent the difference between survival and, if not starvation, at least uncomfortable months of hunger and monotonous diet.

The most valuable food of all was the backyard animal, and cottagers, however small their plot, tried to keep at least one pig, top favourite for the kitchen because of the range of products that could be made from the meat. Sometimes within a community householders would agree to stagger the pig slaughtering so that each family could offer the others a piece of fresh meat; in that way they all saved some of the chore of processing the meat for storage. The remainder would be salted, pickled, cured—often by a recipe which was kept a closely-guarded secret within a family—gelatine would be made from the trotters or feet, brawn from the

This attractive array of preserves reflects how fulfilling preserving home-grown produce can be and is also a practical way of dealing with a glut of vegetables and fruit from the garden.

193

head, and sausages packed tightly into skins and smoked over the kitchen fire.

Fewer people had the opportunity to keep cattle, but when a bullock was killed the meat had to be preserved to last for many months. Joints for short-term keeping would be lightly salted, then steeped in a brine and vinegar pickle flavoured with mixed spices. In this way, the meat would keep for a few days in hot weather or a week or two in the winter. For longer-term preservation, the joints were dry salted, then steeped in brine or a 'sousing drink' for several days, then finally hung in a cloth to smoke over the kitchen or living-room fire. Many old farmhouses still have large S-shaped hooks hanging in the inglenooks to bear witness to this type of husbandry.

Fish has always been one of the most difficult foods to handle because it remains in peak condition for such a limited period. In the Middle Ages herrings already preserved by salting were imported from the Baltic and North Sea regions and the British were reported to be 'wonderfully fond' of them. The monasteries, castles and larger households had ponds and pools where pike and carp were cultivated—an early example of fish farming—and eels were bred in the ditches, so fresh fish was constantly available. Coastal communites preserved the catch by salting so that the fish could safely make the long, slow and tedious journeys to the urban areas. Fish was in great demand because in Medieval times all Fridays, some Wednesdays and Saturdays and the whole of Lent were proclaimed meatless days by the church.

Spices were in great demand, too, to flavour all the meat and fish that had lost so much of its original taste in the processing. In Roman Britain and, after the Dark Ages, again throughout the Middle Ages, food was considered barely fit for consumption unless it was completely masked by

Preserving fish is a most difficult process since fish does not keep in peak condition for very long. This photograph, taken in 1910, illustrates the popular 'Scotch cure' which consisted of brining the fish for a period of eight days. When the barrels were full of herrings, they were sealed with tight-fitting lids.

cooking in heavily spiced broths and served with overpoweringly pungent sauces.

The first European settlers in America took with them their knowledge of preserving food, and the spices they had become accustomed to using in the process. In the Pennsylvania Dutch community where even today the people, largely of German origin, farm the land without the aid of any form of mechanization, the preserved mixed pickles, known as chow chow, have endured as a regional speciality borne of necessity. Throughout America, salted meat and fish were sweetened with molasses, the locally grown sweetener, and this gave rise to the many regional recipes for curing ham with the characteristic blend of sweet spiciness.

The developments which have given us the convenience of modern ways of preserving food do not mean that earlier methods are entirely superceded and unnecessary. Just because we have electricity in our homes, it does not mean that we do not sometimes prefer the romance of candle-light or the gentle flicker of an oil lamp! And so as we harvest an abundant crop from our gardens, buy fresh food cheaply in bulk, or buy a whole animal from the butcher, it is useful to know the many tasty ways the food can be preserved with salt and spices.

Salting beans

If you have a good crop of beans and no freezer, there is no need to resort to distressing waste. You can salt the beans and store them for up to six months. Choose young, fresh runner (snap) or green beans, wash them under the cold tap and dry them on kitchen paper towels. Green beans can be preserved whole; all but the smallest runner (snap) beans should be sliced. Rinse and dry the beans thoroughly before salting. Use kitchen salt in the proportion of 450g (1lb) to every 1.50kg (3lb) of beans. Wash, rinse and dry the beans, and choose any non-metal container, such as the large glass jars that used to line confectionery shop shelves, or the kind of earthenware crocks you can buy cheaply in second-hand shops. Place a layer of salt in the bottom, then a layer of beans and fill the jar with alternate layers, pressing the beans down well as you go. Finish with a layer of salt and cover the vessel with heavy plastic tied with string or secured with a rubber band. You can also cover the crock with a lid if it has one. After two or three days when the beans have settled, top up the jar with more layers of salt and beans, then cover again.

To cook the beans, rinse them well under the cold tap, then soak them in warm water for 2 hours. Drain and cook them in boiling water for 20–30 minutes, until they are tender. Drain the beans and serve as usual.

Spiced sauerkraut

The German way of preserving finely-shredded cabbage spiced with caraway seeds or juniper berries is a very simple process and the sauerkraut, cooked with sausages, is a delightfully different way of serving the vegetable. Trim the stalk and tough outer leaves from a white càbbage and shred it finely. Allow 15g/½oz (2 Tbs) of salt to each 450g (1lb) of cabbage. Sprinkle a layer of the salt in a wooden tub or an earthenware crock, add a layer of cabbage and a few caraway seeds or juniper berries, and continue to the top, finishing with a layer of salt. Cover the container with a clean cloth then with a heavy weight and leave it to mature for three weeks in a warm temperature, such as in an airing cupboard, linen closet or kitchen with an all-night burning oven. For the necessary fermentation to take place, the temperature should be 20–25°C (70–80°F). As fermentation proceeds, a scum will rise to the top and this should be removed every few days. If the level of the brine falls, top it up to the original level with a solution of 50g/2oz (½ cup) of salt to 1 litre/2 pints (5 cups) of water.

Fresh sauerkraut should be cooked within 3 to 4 days—try it boiled with your favourite frankfurters or spiced sausages. To preserve the vegetable,

Pickling spice is a mixture of whole spices – mustard seeds, coriander seeds, allspice, dried chillis, mace, peppercorns and ginger root – and is used to spice the vinegar for chutneys and pickles. It can be bought ready-made but it is more fun to make your own with the spices mentioned above.

follow the normal bottling (canning) procedure. To do this, drain the liquor from the container, bring it to the boil in a pan, add the processed cabbage and simmer it. Pack the cabbage into warm, sterilized jars, top them up with some of the liquor and cover them with the caps. Process the jars in boiling water for 25 minutes, test the caps for a proper seal, then tighten the rings or fix the clips and store.

Pickling vegetables with spices

The time-honoured way of pickling vegetables in spiced vinegar has in no way been superceded by other methods of preserving. Nothing quite compares with a selection of crisp, colourful and lightly spiced vegetables to serve with cold meat, and particularly with the Christmas or Thanksgiving Day turkey.

All types of vegetables are suitable for preserving in this way. Large ones, such as cauliflower, cabbage and marrow (squash) are divided into florets, shredded or diced, according to type. Small ones such as pickling onions, mushrooms and baby carrots may be left whole. It is a matter of preference whether vegetables are pickled individually or combined. Usually the highly coloured ones, red cabbage and beetroot, are served alone, but most others are blended with at least one different vegetable to give variety of texture, shape and flavour.

Vegetables must be salted before pickling, to remove excess moisture—this helps to retain crispness—and prevent the formation of bacteria. Those with a high moisture content, such as courgettes (zucchini), marrows (squash) and cucumbers, should be put into a bowl with layers of block or sea salt in the proportion of about 1 tablespoon to each 450g (1lb) of vegetables. Others must be completely covered in brine solution made from 450g (1lb) of salt to each 5 litres/1 gallon (5 quarts) of water. This should be boiled to dissolve the salt, cooled and then strained. The vegetables are left to salt for up to two days, then thoroughly rinsed in cold water before being packed into clean jars. Jars must be of the type used for fruit preserving, or have screw-on lids and be lined with special vinegar-proof paper. The type of seal used for jams and marmalades is not suitable for this type of preserve.

Apples and pears, and stone fruits such as cherries, peaches, greengages, plums and damsons can be pickled, too, and are delicious accompaniments to meat dishes. To retain the plumpness and firmness of stone fruits, they should first be pricked all over with a needle. All fruits should be lightly cooked before being packed into jars.

You can use malt or cider vinegar or, for a lighter colour and more delicate flavour, particularly attractive with fruit pickles, wine vinegar. The spices you use will not only help in the preserving process but contribute significantly to the flavour of the individual pickles, so it is fun to experiment with different combinations. You can buy a mixture known as pickling spice, but this gives a uniformity to your preserves. Always use whole spices—ground ones would give cloudy results with less flavour. The basic recipe for spiced vinegar is 50mm (2in) cinnamon stick, 1 teaspoon whole cloves, 2 teaspoons allspice berries, 1 teaspoon whole black peppercorns, 1 teaspoon mustard seed and 2 to 3 bay leaves to each 1 litre/2 pints (5 cups) of vinegar. For a 'hotter' pickle, you can add dried whole chillis and for variety try cardamom, coriander or cumin seeds, and pieces of fresh root ginger.

To prepare the spiced vinegar, put the spices and vinegar into a pan, cover it and bring the vinegar just to the boil. Remove the pan from the heat and allow the spices to infuse for 2½ to 3 hours. The vinegar is poured cold on to vegetables which are to retain their crispness, but can be reheated and poured hot over fruit. In all cases make sure the vegetables or fruit are completely immersed in the spiced vinegar. Cover the jars with vinegar-proof paper, then with well-fitting metal lids.

Shelled, hard-boiled (hard-cooked) eggs can be preserved in spiced vinegar, too, and make a popular accompaniment to cold dishes. The spiced vinegar is poured cold over the eggs which should be stored for at least a month before serving.

Salting pork

If you buy pork in quantity for freezing, it is a good idea to pickle some joints and make what is called unsmoked or 'green' bacon to add variety to your bulk purchase. This is a very easy and quick process. Directions are also given to cure ham.

The best joints to choose for pickling are flank or belly (bacon). The meat must be of the best quality and fresh. Choose glass or stoneware crocks for the processing, and sterilize them before you begin. Make a brine from 2kg (4lb) of coarse salt, 60g/2½oz (¼ cup) of saltpetre and 6.5 litres/1½ gallons (7½ quarts) of water. Bring to the boil, simmer until the salt has dissolved and the liquid become clear, then skim. Cool the liquor. Place the pork in the sterilized vessel, cover it completely with the cooled brine and cover the crock. Leave it to steep at a temperature of 3–4°C (35–38°F)—in the refrigerator or a very cold larder or cellar—for 24 hours. Remove the pork, squeeze the excess moisture from it and dry it on kitchen paper towels. Store it in the refrigerator and use it within 1 week. It is good boiled in stock with vegetables, whole spices and herbs.

Curing ham

There are almost as many recipes for curing ham as there are regions where this means of preserving pork was carried out, the ingredients varying according to the products that were locally available. The principle is that the meat is first steeped for a short time in brine, then for several days in a spiced and sweetened liquor and finally hung in a cloth over a smoking fire or in a special smoke box.

One of the most popular 'cures' is the Wiltshire ham, which is given its characteristic flavour by the use of beer and black treacle or molasses. For a 4–5kg (8–10lb) boned ham, you will need a solution of 650g (1½lb) coarse

197

salt, 20g/¾oz (¼ cup) saltpetre, 1 litre/2 pints (5 cups) beer, 450g (1lb) treacle or molasses, 10 to 12 juniper berries and 15g (½oz) crushed black peppercorns. Boil these ingredients together, and leave them to cool. Meanwhile, soak the ham for 1 hour in the brine solution described for pickled pork. Remove the ham from the brine, rinse it well and place it in a sterilized glass or earthenware crock. Cover it with the cooled beer solution, cover the vessel and leave it at a temperature of 3°C (35°F) for two days for every 450g (1lb) weight of ham. Turn the ham in the vessel every other day and when the time is up, remove it from the solution, dry it with clean muslin or cheesecloth and place it in a strong cotton bag. Leave the ham in a cool place to dry for 24 hours, then hang it near a fire made of hardwood, or in a special smoke box and 'cool smoke' it at 25–30°C (75–85°F). If the smoking is continuous, 24 hours will be long enough, but intermittent smoking could mean leaving the ham to process for as much as a week. Store the smoked ham in a cool, dry larder with a free circulation of air. To serve the ham, remove the skin carefully, score the fat with a diamond pattern and stud each angle with a whole clove, then either roast or boil according to preference.

Salting beef

When buying beef in bulk for the freezer, you can add extra variety by salting some of the smaller joints. This is what the early American settlers did when they killed a beast—but they called it corned beef. To salt a joint weighing about 2.25kg (5lb), make a solution of 900g (2lb) salt, 1 tablespoon of saltpetre, 125g/4oz (½ cup) sugar and 3 litres/6 pints (5¾ quarts) of water. Bring the solution to the boil and pour it into a container. You can salt any joint of beef, but silverside, topside or brisket are traditional. Put the beef in the crock and make sure it is completely covered with the solution. Cover the container and leave it in the refrigerator or a cold place to steep for 4 to 5 days. Rinse the beef under cold, running water to remove the salt.

Spiced beef

This is a marvellous way to prepare beef to cook and serve cold for a buffet, or it can be pot-roasted with mixed root vegetables. Soak the beef in brine, as above, for 24 hours, remove it and pat the meat dry. Mix together 2 tablespoons each of sea salt, black pepper, crushed bay leaves, ground cloves and ground coriander. Rub this mixture thoroughly into the surface of the meat. Return the meat to the brine and soak for a further 4 to 5 days. Remove the beef from the liquid, pat it dry and rub 2 tablespoons of ground mixed spice well into the surface, before cooking.

Salting fish

Keen fishermen who want to preserve their catch to enjoy on later occasions, or people who can buy fish fresh and cheaply at the quayside might find it interesting to try this old method of salting. The prime requirement is that the fish should be perfectly fresh. Herrings are ideal for the process. Measure 3½ litres/6 pints (7½ pints) of hot water, 550g (1¼lb) salt and 125g/4oz (½ cup) of sugar. Put the salt and sugar into glass or earthenware bowls, pour on the hot water and stir until the salt and sugar have dissolved. Allow the mixture to cool before adding the fish. Each 800ml/1½ pints (3¾ cups) of the solution will be enough to preserve 6 to 8 herrings, depending on size, so you can process a large 'catch' in several crocks at the same time. Gut, bone and clean the fish, hold them under cold, running water, then put them into the cooled brine. Cover the vessels and put them in the refrigerator or a cold pantry. Leave them in the solution for 7 to 10 days, again depending on size. Eat the fish within two weeks at the most. To vary the flavour, you can add a few lightly crushed peppercorns, fennel seeds or bay leaves to the brine.

An attractive display of cured and smoked hams: (1) Bradenham hams (2 and 6) York ham, one of Britain's best known cooked hams (3) Suffolk ham (4) Parma ham, Italy's most famous raw ham (5) Boneless ham (6) See (2) (7) Westphalian ham, a German smoked ham served raw (8) Canned ham, pressed in jelly.

1

2

3

6

5

4

7

8

CASTING A BEAUTIFUL SPELL

For thousands of years, spices have been associated with beauty, purity, cleanliness and colour. Aromatic plants of various kinds have been entrusted with the beauty care of queens—kings, too. Their fragrances have been relied on to sweeten the body, mask unwelcome odours in the home and, in the form of incense, purify religious temples. The sometimes vibrant and often subtle colours have been extracted to dye wool, cotton and silks which were woven by traditional craftsmen into clothes, rugs and other furnishings of immense charm.

Of course, the earliest uses of spices in these many ways were a question of making a virtue out of necessity, when people were entirely dependent on the natural products that grew locally or could be imported through the old-established trading routes. Nowadays, when every aroma and colour can be reproduced with synthetic substances, we can preserve our complexions, waft about surrounded by sweet-smelling fragrances and drape ourselves and our homes in magnificently-coloured materials without the help of a single natural product—if we want to. But unless one is a scientist or a chemist at heart, beauty from a bottle does little to compare with the satisfaction of capturing an aroma or a colour from the natural products around us. If you have a love of nature, and a little more than average patience, a few simple experiments into making your own soap, incense and dyes can lead to lasting and rewarding hobbies.

As befits a lady's beauty secrets, the exact formulae of the first cosmetics and beauty products are veiled by the passage of time. But as more towns and cities of the ancient world are excavated and our knowledge of the past unfolds, so some of these secrets are at last being told. It is clear that cosmetic preparations in one form or another were known to all the ancient peoples. Sometimes the use of ointments and oils was largely to protect the skin and hair against the ravages of hot, dry climates; sometimes they had a religious significance—in ancient Egypt certain unguents could be made and distributed only by priests—and some had magical associations, as in the case of warriors who smeared their bodies with pungent oils before going into battle, relying on the mystical powers to ensure victory.

Fashion played its part, too, and in every society there was a pacesetter. Cleopatra fortified herself—and presumably weakened the political resolve of others—by appearing awe-inspiringly decorative at all times. She used face masks to soften and clarify her skin, rubbed fragrant oils on her body, painted her lips and cheeks with red ochre and accentuated her eyes with generous applications of kohl on the lids and lashes. Other tricks of the trade at the time were the use of butter and barley flour paste to eradicate skin blemishes (the Romans used white lead and chalk for the same purpose), ground pumice stone to polish the teeth, and henna, a safe, deep, reddish-brown vegetable dye, to colour the hair, nails, palms of the hands and soles of the feet.

Bathing for beauty

The Egyptians considered frequent baths essential to good health and purity, and always washed before and after meals. In Syria it was the custom for the king to join his subjects in mass bathing pools. Legend has it that on one occasion, in a fit of largesse, Antiochus poured his expensive bath oil over the heads of his admiring subjects—who presumably were loathe to wash it off for months afterwards. The Romans, too, liked to be seen to be clean, and in the public baths vied with each other to have the most fragrant of oils. The emperor Heliogabalus, renowned for his personal extravagance, took to bathing in saffron-scented water and emerging with a gentle golden, though impermanent, tan.

Perfumed baths became popular in England in the seventeenth century, when women gathered bath posies to scent the water, then rubbed themselves down with spiced vinegar. Recipes for these bath posies were as individual as the gardens where they grew. They would include some fragrant petals such as rose, thyme and lavender, possibly bay and mint leaves and dried lemon peel, sprinkled with a few drops of oil of spikenard and 'fixed' with musk or ambergris. These delightfully fragrant mixtures, similar to pot pourri blends which were placed in open bowls to scent the rooms, were tied into cheesecloth bags and trailed in the tepid bath water. This is a charming idea to copy, tying the mixture into disposable cheesecloth bags to hang under the tap. Lovely spicy mixtures to try include rose petals scattered with a few cloves, lightly crushed juniper berries stirred into young marigold leaves and fenugreek seeds blended with lemon balm leaves. Middle Eastern harem women preferred to eat their fenugreek seeds, though—they were thought to be the secret to rounded plumpness.

People who find that frequent baths have a drying effect on the skin—destroying the acid mantle which gives some protection from disease—can benefit from an ancient remedy, the addition of a little sesame oil to the water. Fragrant bath oils are very easy to make, and will last indefinitely in tightly-stopped bottles. You can make them with either a dispersing oil, which dissolves in water, or a floating one, which clings to your body when you get out—and makes your skin gleam. Dispersing oils have the advantage of not leaving a ring around the bath. Castor oil is an example of this type, but only in its treated form, known as Turkey Red oil. Mix together three parts of Turkey Red oil to one part of your favourite aromatic oil, bottle it and use 1 teaspoonful at a time in the bath water. For a floating oil, one that is lighter than water, you can use almond or avocado oil—full of Vitamin E which nourishes the skin—with aromatic oil in the same proportion. These bath oils, stored in pretty bottles with carefully hand-written labels, make delightful and highly personal gifts. You can surprise your friends with the elusive fragrance of oil of nutmeg or oil of cumin.

Mary Queen of Scots bathed in wine, but most of us would be content with cider vinegar which has the same effect and restores the acid mantle to the skin. Add two to three tablespoons to the water, or rub the cider vinegar diluted with six parts of water all over the skin before taking a bath. This treatment is especially good for dry skin. Salt added to the bath can remove dead cells and generally tone up the skin; for a real 'spa' treatment, mix together 225g/8oz (1 cup) of Epsom salts (Magnesium sulphate) and 450g (1lb) of Magnesium chloride with a few drops of oil of patchouli and dissolve in warm bath water.

Natural spice cosmetics

The first cosmetics must have been made from the natural vegetable oils and animal fats available. The first cleansing cream—a mixture of olive oil, wax and rose water—was blended by a Greek physician, Galen. Ladies all along the Mediterranean came to know the value of sesame oil as a dry skin food which penetrates and softens the skin. This polyunsaturated nut oil is a highly beneficial aid to sun-tanning because it absorbs most of the ultra-violet rays of the sun. Resistant to water, it is also ideal to use when swimming.

If you are buying myrrh to experiment with making incense—discussed later in this chapter—you might like to try the wrinkle preventative favoured by Athenian ladies. They burned a little myrrh powder on a stone and allowed the astringent resin fumes to penetrate and nourish the

Top Sesame produces a nourishing oil which when added to a bath keeps one's skin supple.

A detail of the leaves and flowers of the cinnamon tree. Cinnamon was one of the ingredients used to make up the chrism – a holy oil used to anoint the Tabernacle and its priests.

Making your own soap is a simple process and you can scent them according to taste as many essential spice oils produce a delightful fragrance.

skin in the form of a fragrant, cleansing steam facial.

Spicy soapmaking

It is thought that soap was first discovered by accident in Rome about 1000 BC when the fat from sacrificial animals was mixed with the ashes from the fire. Gradually spices were added to colour and perfume the soap and examples have been found in a soapmaker's shop in Pompeii.

The craft of soapmaking is one which we can easily practise in our kitchens and enjoy every day. Think how satisfying it is to lie in a bath wallowing in a natural fragrance you have blended yourself. The permutations of colour and scent are endless, you can use all kinds of disposable moulds to make the soap into attractive shapes, and even carve initials or little drawings as decorations.

At its simplest, soap is a combination of a fatty acid, normally tallow, and alkali, caustic soda (lye). The necessary chemical reaction takes place when the melted tallow and the caustic soda and water solution are mixed together at the same lukewarm temperature, so it is important to follow the instructions carefully.

Melt the tallow the day before you intend to make the soap—or earlier if it is more convenient. It will keep for several weeks in the refrigerator. Put the pieces of fat in a heavy pan, discarding any discoloured parts. Set it over a low heat until most of it has rendered, then strain it through two layers of cheesecloth or muslin lining a strainer. Leave it in a bowl to set. Each 250ml/8fl oz (1 cup) of melted tallow will be enough to make one large tablet of soap.

Before starting to make the soap, gather together all the kitchen utensils you will need, a wooden spoon, a hand whisk or electric mixer, a heavy saucepan and 2 mixing bowls. You will also need a standard measuring cup and a tablespoon. Protect all the surrounding kitchen surfaces with several layers of newspaper, and yourself with a large apron and a pair of rubber gloves.

To make one large tablet of soap

	Metric/U.K.	U.S.
Cold soft water (rain water, or tap water softened)	125ml/4fl oz	½ cup
Caustic soda (lye)	2 Tbs	2 Tbs
Tallow	250g/8oz	1 cup

Melt the tallow in the saucepan. Before measuring out the caustic soda (lye), read the manufacturers' instructions carefully. Caustic soda (lye), particularly in its dry form, can burn the skin. If you spill a speck on your hand, wash it off immediately under the cold tap and rub the skin with lemon juice or vinegar. *Never* leave the packet within reach of children.

Pour the water into a mixing bowl and add the caustic soda (lye). Stir the mixture with a wooden spoon until the soda dissolves as the mixture becomes hot. Allow both the matted tallow and the caustic soda (lye) solution to cool to lukewarm—test by putting your hand underneath the containers. Then pour the fat in a steady stream into the caustic soda (lye) solution, stirring slowly. Beat it with a whisk, watching carefully for the sudden transition from a shiny liquid to a thick, opaque mixture—soap. Pour it quickly into the mould and allow it to set overnight. Release the soap from the mould and place it in a warm, draught-free area such as an airing cupboard or linen cupboard to mature for at least two weeks.

If you like, you can carve the mature soap with the sharp point of a craft knife. Initialled soap tablets make a highly personal gift for friends. Collect the soap scrapings and use them in a metal soap saver.

To scent your soap

You can add essential spice oils to this basic recipe, making lovely fragrances of your own, and colour the soap with powdered spices or bottled food colouring. As soon as you have poured the melted tallow onto the caustic soda (lye) solution, add a few drops of oil of cloves, patchouli, nutmeg, caraway, or a few pinches of sandalwood powder. To colour the soap, add a pinch of turmeric or saffron powder for yellow or bottled food colouring. Stir the oils or colourants in thoroughly, otherwise they will form lumps or beads on the surface of the soap. To make honey spice soap which has a soft creamy colour, measure 1 tablespoon of olive oil, 1 tablespoon of sesame oil and 1 tablespoon of honey. Top up to the 250ml/8fl oz (1 cup) with melted tallow and, when the mixture is lukewarm, pour it on to the caustic soda (lye) solution.

Bottom right Food colouring can be added to soap to make it visually appealing.
Bottom left A mixture of tallow and caustic soda (lye) combine to make a thick, opaque mixture which, when set, makes a tablet of white soap.

The mystery of incense

Another way to scent your home with the sweet smell of spices is to make incense, which creates a lingering atmosphere evocative of the mystic East. It was, in fact, burned in Egypt, Babylon and China in magical and religious rites and introduced into the Christian church in the sixth century, where it was held to be a symbol of purity, virtue, and the ascent of prayer to God. Frankincense, the basis of church incense, produces phenol carbolic acid when it burns, so it was valued for its practical qualities as an antiseptic, too, and it was said that churches where incense was burned were never attacked by woodworm.

There are two basic types of incense; one is a simple blend of ground spices and fixatives which can be sprinkled on to charcoal glowing in a fire or a thurible, those beautifully decorative brass church ornaments. Or you can blend the spices with charcoal and gum and form them into cones or sticks to burn indoors.

You can buy the ingredients of traditional church incense, frankincense and myrrh, from church suppliers and sandalwood, the one so reminiscent of the East, from Indian stores. Much more cheaply, you can blend your own mixtures from your kitchen or garden spices. Although you can use ordinary charcoal for the shaped incense, there is a quick-lighting type which is chemically treated and ideal for the purpose. If it is to be burned indoors, charcoal should have a good draught—which is why church thuribles are swung backwards and forwards—and only be used in a well-ventilated room as the fumes can be harmful.

To make incense without charcoal

	Metric/U.K.	U.S.
Sandalwood powder	25g/1oz	1oz
Gum benzoin	25g/1oz	1oz
Cardamom seeds, ground	15g/½oz	½oz
Cloves, ground	15g/½oz	½oz
Cassia bark, ground	15g/½oz	½oz

For a basic incense mixture, blend these ingredients well together. Gum benzoin, which acts as a fixative, has an aura of well-cared-for antique furniture and you will find that the cassia chips are very reminiscent of cinnamon sticks.

For variety, you can add experimental ingredients of your own choice, such as grated dried orange or lemon peel, bay leaves, eucalyptus leaves and resin, dried lavender, crushed scented barks or one or two drops of cedarwood or nutmeg oil. For a more authentic church-like aroma, you can use a two-to-one mixture of frankincense and myrrh as the basis, adding sandalwood or the suggested barks or oils as variations.

To make incense shapes

	Metric/U.K.	U.S.
Charcoal, quick-lighting	175g/6oz	6oz
Gum benzoin, powdered	25g/1oz	1oz
Sandalwood, powdered	6g/¼oz	¼oz
Cassia, ground	6g/¼oz	¼oz
Mucilage of gum tragacanth, compound tragacanth powder or gum arabic		

Crush the first four ingredients together and mix them well. To bind the mixture into a pliable 'dough', use mucilage of gum tragacanth (which, because it has chloroform and alcohol in it, has to be made up by a pharmacist), compound tragacanth powder (a sucrose, starch and tragacanth mixture, also from pharmacists), or gum arabic. Your choice might very well be decided by local availability. The last two preparations have to

be mixed first with water, then stirred in to form a stiff paste.

To this basic mixture, you can add other aromatic ingredients of your choice (see the suggestions for making incense without charcoal) until you have a 50/50 mixture of charcoal and other ingredients. Once the mixture forms a stiff paste, mould it into cones or other shapes and leave them on a warm shelf for two or three days to dry. Wrap the shapes in plastic or aluminium foil so that they retain their scent in storage. To use the incense, stand the shapes on a non-inflammable base such as a tin plate or a brass bowl or dish.

The sweet smell of incense wafting through your house will evoke all the mysteries of the East, but always burn charcoal-based incense in a well-ventilated room as the fumes can be toxic.

205

Natural dyes extracted from plant material give clothes lovely hues.

Creating spicy colours

Before manufactured colourants were available, people used natural plant material to dye yarn and cloth. Saffron was used to dye the soft, flowing robes of the Buddhist monks—turmeric gives a similar effect—and powdered fenugreek seeds to give a paler shade. As a symbol of Chinese hospitality and welcome, saffron powder was sprinkled on the clothes of visitors; not always a welcome gesture, presumably.

The principle of plant dyeing is to make an extraction of the colour by simmering the plant material—flowers, leaves, berries, bark or powder—

in water. It is not an exact science and it takes a trained eye to see just when the infusion is strong enough and when the yarn has been simmered for long enough. The moisture content of the plant, the soil in which it was grown, the weather and the softness of the water are other factors which affect the final colour—and give the home craftsman some delightful surprises.

All natural fibres 'take' well, but wool is the most successful. White woollen garments can be given a new and brighter lease of life or the wool unpicked and rewound into skeins. Balls of wool need to be rewound into skeins, too, and lightly tied into a bundle. You can sometimes buy unbleached wool and, by dyeing it in batches with different plants, create your own fashion range of subtle and blending colours.

Apart from the plant material, you will usually need what is known as a mordant, a substance which enhances or deepens the colour and sets it fast. These are discussed later. As long as you are not using poisonous plants, you can use your kitchen utensils—pans and a strainer. You will also need rubber gloves, a stick for stirring each colour and rain water or softened tap water.

The amount of plant material you will need varies with each plant, but as a general guide, allow 125g (4oz) to each 25g (1oz) of wool. Powdered spices, flowers, petals and leaves might need as little as 20 minutes' simmering, but the tougher parts of the plant, such as bark and hard berries, can take up to 3 hours. Crushing tough plant material first helps to draw out the colour.

First of all you must weigh the wool to be dyed, then weigh the appropriate amount of plant material. Put it in a large pan, cover it with soft water and bring it slowly to simmering point. Top the pan up to the original level with more hot water as it evaporates. When the colour is the strength you want, strain the liquor through a strainer and discard the plant material. Allow the dye to cool to hand-heat to use it straight away. To store it for later use, let it cool completely before putting it in covered jars in the refrigerator.

Top *Wool is the easiest of natural fibres to dye and skeins of wool can be dipped into a pot of dye, but make sure the yarn is loosely tied. It can then be knitted or crocheted into a garment of your choice.*

Dyeing without a mordant

Some plants will give a lasting and satisfactory result by what is called the 'direct' dyeing method, that is to say without the addition of a mordant. These include ground turmeric (saffron is too expensive), the outside skins of onions, the tops and flowers of golden rod and of ragwort and the berries of white snowberries, which all give a yellow extract. Bilberries, blueberries and sloes give rose, pink and purple, depending on the length of time the plant material is simmered, and the whole plant of common grey wall lichen gives brown.

First, thoroughly soak the woollen garment or the yarn. Put the wet wool into the dyebath—a large saucepan or preserving pan—cover it with the dye and raise the temperature of the liquid very gradually to simmering point. Keep it simmering, stirring from time to time, until the wool is the colour you want. Lift it out on the end of a stick to gauge the colour, and remember that it will dry several shades lighter. Gently squeeze the wool to remove most of the excess liquid, then plunge it into warm, soft water and rinse it thoroughly.

Below *A crocheted skirt of beautiful, vivid colours, all of which have come from natural dyes.*

Dyeing with a mordant

Plant materials other than those mentioned above need 'fixing' with a chemical that has an affinity with both the fibre and the dyestuff. It takes experience to know in just what way a mordant will change a dye colour. Two of the best mordants to use are alum and iron, both obtainable from pharmacies. Alum generally speaking brightens natural dye colours; iron tends to darken most colours and can turn yellow dyes to green.

To mordant with alum (Potassium aluminium sulphate) use 25g (1oz) or

207

Top *The leaves of lily of the valley produce a lovely shade of green, besides being an attractive plant to have in your garden.*

Above *Blackcurrant fruit used with a mordant produces varying shades of rose, pink and purple.*

$1\frac{3}{4}$ teaspoons of alum for each 125g (4oz) of wool. The mordant is normally used before dyeing. Pour enough soft water to cover the wool into a pan, measure out the alum and stir it in thoroughly. Add the wet wool and heat the dye bath so slowly that it takes about an hour to reach simmering point. Keep it at this temperature—no more—for a further hour, gently stirring the wool occasionally. Remove the pan from the heat and allow the liquid to cool to hand-hot. Without wringing the wool, gently squeeze out the excess moisture. To dye the wool straight away, treat this as the 'wet wool' stage and proceed as described. Or dry the wool in a towel and store it in plastic bags containing moth repellent for dyeing later. Remember to wet the wool thoroughly again before dyeing.

To mordant with iron (ferrous sulphate, also known as copperas and green vitriol) measure the mordant in the proportion of 4g ($\frac{1}{8}$oz), just under 1 teaspoon, to each 125g (4oz) of wool. The iron is added to the dye for the last 15 to 30 minutes of the dyeing time. Lift out the wool on the stick, add the iron and stir it well before replacing the wool. Bring it back to simmering point slowly and then proceed as described above in the instructions for dyeing with a mordant.

The natural colours you can achieve

Yellow Turmeric powder and the outer skins of onion 'take' very quickly, yielding a pale yellow after a few minutes and a rich shade in 20 to 40 minutes. Other plant materials to dye direct are the tops and flowers of golden rod and of ragwort and the berries of white snowberries. Those which need a mordant are barberry twigs, the bark of black oak, the tips and flowers of yellow broom, the tops of queen of the meadow, the tops and flowers of St John's wort, the tops and flowers of tansy and the leaves and the tops of weld before they seed.

Blue The most popular and beautiful plant dye for blue is indigo. You can extract colour from most parts of the tree, or buy the plant extract. You can also use the leaves of woad, as ancient Britons did, and the berries of mahonia. They all need a mordant.

Brown Without a mordant, you can use the whole plant of grey wall lichen. With a mordant, you can use the bark and big bud of hickory, the hulls of black walnut (be prepared for them to take up to 3 hours to release the colour), larch needles, mahogany sawdust or wood chips, the leaves of mountain laurel, oak bark and pyracantha twigs.

Orange If simmered for longer, and mordanted, the outer skins of onion will give an orange extract. You can also use coreopsis flowers, orange dahlia flowers, the roots of lady's bedstraw and of madder.

Rose, pink and purple You can dye direct with the fruits of bilberry and sloe. With a mordant, try the fruits of blackcurrant, black huckleberry, blackberry, elder and wild grape vine.

Red For a successful red, one of the most luxurious-looking of natural colours, all the plant materials need a mordant. Try the roots of bloodroot, so aptly named, flowers of red dahlia and of geranium, the bark of hemlock, the roots of lady's bedstraw, madder roots, pokeweed berries and the fruity protruberances of prickly-pear cactus.

Green Use the young tops of bracken, the chip-wood of fustic, the tops and flowers of golden rod (mordanted with iron), the green part above the ground of horsetail, the black berries of ivy, lily of the valley leaves, nettle leaves and tops, privet leaves and the leaves and tops of weld.

Black or grey With suitable mordants, alder bark, buckthorn berries, butternut nuts, logwood bark and yellow flag iris roots will give shades varying from pale grey to almost black.

To test whether a plant material will give you a successful dye, simmer a little wool with the plant and watch as it turns colour. You will often find that you can achieve some pleasant surprises, and shades that even now cannot be prepared commercially.

SPICES IN YOUR KITCHEN

With a good selection of spices in your kitchen, the whole world of cooking is at your fingertips. You can bring constant interest and variety to your dishes, turn the cheaper types of meat and fish into delicacies, and give your family and friends all the culinary excitement of foreign travel. You can experience the splendour of a Medieval banquet with saffron-coloured fish dishes and hot, spiced wines, evoke all the gaiety and colour of South America with fiery, palate-tingling dishes and red-hot sauces, or present a perfectly balanced vegetarian meal in the Oriental manner, where the spices play an important but not dominating role.

So that you are always sure to extract the maximum possible flavour from your spices, it is important to follow a few simple rules about storing and using them. Most of the seeds, bark and roots we use as spices are dried. This means that they will have a fairly long shelf life and will actually keep almost indefinitely. But they gradually lose their aroma and in most cases are past their best after about three months. For this reason it is best to buy or grow your spices in small quantities, so that you are constantly replenishing your supply.

Whole spices retain their flavour much better than ground ones so the ideal is to buy whole spices little and often—never be afraid to ask for 15g or 25g (½oz or 1oz) of the ones you use least. Both light and heat affect the flavour, and so the least efficient means of storage is the decorative rows of glass jars that look so attractive on kitchen shelves. Since glass jars are so obviously practical and can be washed between each new supply, look for dark-coloured ones like old apothecary jars—if you want to keep them on show. Otherwise, put colourless glass containers away in a cupboard out of the light. If your kitchen is hot and steamy—and particularly if you have an all-night-burning oven—then it is in any case not the best place for your spices. Find a suitable place where the spices will be kept at a lower temperature. The effort of having to take extra paces to reach your spices will be more than rewarded in terms of flavour when you use them.

Buying ground spices

If, for quickness and convenience, you do choose to buy ground spices, it pays to buy a reputable branded make. Usually the higher price will be an

An assortment of ground and whole spices which are so necessary to everyone's kitchen. A mortar and pestle is especially useful in grinding spices.

indication that the product has been carefully graded and will be purer and more pungent. When you buy ground spices as fragrant, colourful powders, it is virtually impossible to be able to assess the quality when they are sealed into plastic bags, cardboard drums or glass containers. But because of the relatively high value of spices, the practice of dilution—or adulteration—with cheaper ingredients has been rife for centuries, and even now has not been stamped out entirely. However, the major spice importers who sell their products under brand names implement the strictest quality control. Not only do they, in a large number of cases, visit the spice plantations and buy the crop 'on the bush', but they also carry out tests at every stage thereafter. Delivery trucks are inspected, looking for any traces of impurities on the floor of the vehicle; then the spices are tested under laboratory conditions for impurities, moisture and acid content, colour and flavour. Only after a spice has passed with flying colours will such a firm accept the consignment.

Spices ground in the factories of these firms are subjected to analytical tests both during and after the process, too, and spice blends are constantly analyzed to check the balance of ingredients. And so, in terms of care, satisfaction and value for money, you generally get what you pay for.

Grinding your spices

Most spices are very easy to grind at home. An ordinary pepper mill will cope with most of the seeds (although the minute black poppy seeds slip through the teeth without a blemish!). A hand-operated rotary grinder, the type with a little drawer at the bottom to collect the powder, is also efficient, and gives the authentic aura of an Eastern spice market. These will cope with all your spices except poppy seeds, cinnamon and mace. For poppy seeds you need a special grinder, which you can buy in some countries abroad. Cinnamon and mace, along with all the other seeds, can be ground quite satisfactorily in a manual or electric coffee grinder.

If you find that your ground spices are not quite as finely powdered as you would wish, sift them before use, either through a metal or nylon strainer or through a piece of coarse cheesecloth or muslin.

Freshly-grated nutmeg, infinitely more aromatic than the ready-ground spice, is invaluable in many rich fruit cakes, baked puddings or as a last-minute garnish to soups and sweets. You can buy special little graters just for the purpose—or you might like to invest in an antique one if one of your hobbies is collecting old kitchen utensils and tableware. Otherwise, just use the smallest mesh of an ordinary kitchen grater, grating only the amount you need for the moment and storing the nutmeg away again in a lidded container.

When you want to crush the seeds without actually grinding them to a powder, a pestle and mortar are the traditional tools to use. Specialist kitchen shops usually sell the old-fashioned heavy stone ones, or you can buy them in decorative olive wood or even brass. These are particularly useful when you want to make a paste of pounded spices with a liquid such as lemon or lime juice, the 'wet masala' featured in many of the Southern Indian dishes. Another way to crush spices is by putting them in a heavy quality plastic bag, double sealing the ends, and giving them a good hard roll with a rolling pin.

A very good way to keep alive the flavour of your spices is to infuse vinegar and cooking oil with the flavours and to keep them, tightly corked, ready to use in salad dressings, marinades and to brush meat and fish before grilling (broiling).

To make flavoured vinegar

Use whole spice seeds such as coriander, fennel or fenugreek—one type of seed for each bottle of vinegar. Lightly bruise the seeds in a pestle and mortar or with a rolling pin. Use about 2 tablespoons of seed to 1.5 litres/

Below Dried ginger root is either crushed with a mortar and pestle or finely grated before use.
Bottom Fresh ginger is peeled and sliced or diced before use. It can occasionally be pounded.

210

2 pints (5 cups) of vinegar. White distilled vinegar will give you a purer impression of the spice flavour, while malt or cider is a much stronger brew. Put the crushed seeds into a jar, shake it well and put it in a warm, dark place such as an airing cupboard or linen closet for two weeks, shaking it occasionally. Taste the flavour at the end of this time—it should be fine. If you want a stronger spice, strain off and discard the seeds and start again, pouring the warmed vinegar onto a fresh batch. Finally, strain off the seeds and store the spiced vinegar in a tightly-corked bottle.

To make flavoured oil

You can flavour cooking oil in a similar way, keeping it on hand to give an unusual lift to marinades and salad dressings and to brush grilled (broiled) foods. Crush 2 tablespoons of spice seeds and put them in a jar. Pour on 250ml/½ pint (1¼ cups) of sunflower, corn or olive oil and 1 tablespoon of wine vinegar. Seal the bottle with a cork or screw cap and shake it well. Leave it in the sunlight to infuse for two or three weeks, shaking it

Where possible, spices should be bought loose and stored in airtight containers out of the light. If you have to buy them in ground form, buy in small quantities so as to avoid loss of freshness.

well twice each day. Strain off the seeds and pour the oil into a clean bottle. Cover it with the lid or a cork.

Heating spices for full flavour

Some spice seeds, such as fenugreek, coriander, cumin and poppy, improve in flavour if they are gently heated before being pounded, ground or used whole in cooking. To heat spice seeds, use a small non-stick pan over a low heat. Put in the seeds and shake the pan from time to time until the seeds are heated through and pop slightly. Then use them as directed in the recipes.

Some seeds—sesame is a good example—change their personality considerably if they are toasted over a higher heat or put into a medium oven. Seeds scattered on bread or cakes to be baked will, of course, toast as they are cooked; for seeds to garnish soups, mashed vegetables or mousses, toasting adds a nutty flavour and a contrastingly crunchy texture.

Spices in Indian cooking

The very smell of toasting spice seeds wafting through the kitchen brings to mind the great variety of regional Indian dishes, so much more subtle and delicious than our generic term 'curry' can ever imply. Curry powder is never used in authentic Indian cooking, though various blends of the sweeter spices, known as *garam masala*, are included, usually added to a dish towards the end of the cooking time. When the hotter spices—peppers and chillis—are included, they are added first, so that the heat is drawn off, as it were, into the main ingredients. An Indian cook would consider it an unpardonable sin to offer a dish in which any spice tasted raw.

Cloves, cardamom, cinnamon, fennel, cumin, nutmeg, mace and turmeric in any combination and varying proportions are usually used to make *garam masala* blends. You can mix together your own spices and grind them freshly, just before you use them, or a little in advance to save time at the last moment.

In Southern India where many people still follow a vegetarian diet, more fresh spices—coriander leaves, for example—are used, and the protein is largely made up of lentil dishes—*dhal*. Blends of spices are mixed to 'wet masalas' with lemon or lime juice or coconut oil, and plenty of rice is provided to soak up the sauce.

Tandoori chicken, now such a popular dish in restaurants in the Western world, emanated from the north of India, where many meat dishes absorb the flavour of the spices in marinades before being crisply cooked over glowing charcoal.

Chutneys and pickles are an important part of Indian cuisine, not only because they can provide perfect complements to the main dishes, but because they are a practical way of preserving fruit and vegetables that, in a tropical climate, have such a short season.

Spices for Chinese cuisine

There is a tendency to regard Chinese cooking as bland by comparison with Indian; or perhaps it would be more accurate to say there *was* such a tendency, before Szechuan dishes were introduced to restaurants in Europe and America. In this northern region of China, red-cooked dishes pulsating with Szechuan pepper are in complete contrast to the gentle dishes which rely for effect on an harmonious blend of soft and crisp textures, bright and pale colours, large and small ingredients. The equivalent of the Indian *garam masala* in China is called 'five-spice powder', a blend of finely ground anise, Szechuan pepper, fennel, cloves and cinnamon. The proportion of the hot pepper in the blend, of course, determines the 'heat' of a dish. Nothing about Chinese cooking is ever a hit and

miss affair, and the use of spices is no exception. The ancient cult of Taoism, the Way of Nature, determines the compatibility of foods with each other and in relation to spices. Followers of the cult would never, for example, serve lamb's liver spiced with pepper, nor flavour a dish containing rabbit with ginger in any form.

Latin American hot spices

If the word compatibility were to be applied to Latin American cooking, on the other hand, it might well be said that every ingredient—meat, fish, fruit, or tortillas, the daily bread of the Central American countries—is compatible with chilli peppers. When Columbus went in search of black pepper and other Oriental spices, and found America instead, he found a civilization already used to eating fire, with palate-stinging sauces sold by Indian peddlers in the markets, truly a downright lethal trap for the unwary traveller.

Experimenting with recipes from the countries where the spices originated, and from other parts of the world where they were traded over land and sea, it is fascinating to see how these aromatic plants have fitted in so many different ways into the various culinary cultures. With a selection of spices in the kitchen, you can capture in your own home the flavour of the Caribbean with lamb curry laced with mango, pumpkin and rum; of Spain with a paella succulent with shrimps, chicken, peas, beans and saffron; of the Middle East with honey cake enriched with cinnamon, allspice, cloves and candied peel, and of the Viennese Empire with traditional *sachertorte*, chocolate cake essentially flavoured with vanilla. Your cook's tour can take you to Russia with lamb and prunes gently simmered with cinnamon, nutmeg, coriander and lemon juice, or perhaps with bread dipped in allspice butter, or spread with quince and clove preserve. And for a taste of Scandinavia, you could try cardamom-flavoured waffles made with sour cream or, in a more lavish mood, *Gravlax*, pressed cured salmon with a sweet and sour mustard and dill sauce.

So many dishes in so many moods—and they can all be created from your store of spices.

SPICES YOU CAN GROW

Most spices grow in the hot, moist, tropical climates of the Eastern and Western Hemispheres, so in Northern gardens it is not possible to recreate all the exotic, pungent aroma of a plantation of cloves in the Moluccas or pepper vines rambling as far as the eye can see. However, on good, well-drained soil in a sunny position, you can grow several spices that favour a mild climate and, given a long, hot summer, can count on more successes; anise and sesame seeds, for example, will only ripen to their full pungency in a good long spell of hot sun.

With a greenhouse or cold frame you can widen the scope still further. In an unheated greenhouse you can sow and bring on seeds to plant out in the garden or greenhouse border later, and in a heated greenhouse, where conditions can be brought closer to the heat and humidity of the tropics, experiment with some of the real 'exotics'.

Obviously, the closer conditions are to their natural habitat, the more plants will flourish. Full details of the soil and cultivation requirements are given under the name of each individual spice in The Dictionary of Spices. When you read that a spice is indigenous to the Middle Eastern or Mediterranean countries, you will get an idea of the conditions it enjoys: generally speaking, a light, well-drained soil and a sunny position. Unfortunately, stodgy, heavy clay is no more a favourite with spice plants than it is with those of us who have to work on it. If that is your problem, it is best to plant your spices in troughs or large pots filled with light, specially prepared soil. Stand the troughs or pots against a south wall, or on a balcony rather than on a windowsill. Because of their largely straggling habits spice plants are not the neat little kitchen window decoration that some herbs can be.

Most of the spices we can grow produce generous quantities of seeds,

Coriander is very easy to grow and is a resilient annual plant.

on full, umbrella-shaped clusters or in tightly-packed pods, so two or three of each type of plant will usually produce enough seed to dry and use in one year. If, of course, you have space and want to turn your spice-growing hobby into a way of giving your friends an entirely personal, home-grown present, then go ahead and grow rows and rows. Don't be tempted, though, to grow a crop for about five years' use in your own kitchen. The dried seeds gradually lose their aroma completely, and there are few sadder sights in a kitchen than a spice rack without a single spicy smell.

Flowering spice plants
Many spice plants have such pretty flowers that it is a pity to consign them to the vegetable patch, along with the runner (snap) beans. The annuals give very good value in the flower garden before the seeds develop. Sesame has white flowers splashed with red or yellow, anise and fenugreek have creamy-white flowers, and the poppy grown for culinary seed, *Papaver somniferum*, rewards you with short-lived white, lilac or purple blooms. Coriander, a hardy annual which can be grown on slightly heavier soil than the others, has pale mauve flowers, and caraway, a biennial, great clusters of minute white flowers, rather like sheep's parsley. All these plants are of medium height, growing 60–90cm (2–3ft) high, and so should be planted towards the centre or back of a flower bed, depending on the other flowers you grow. If you have very tall flowers, such as hollyhock, foxglove and delphinium, of course, they will tower over your spices. Cumin, described as a low-growing annual, reaches about 30–60cm (1–2ft), and so could be in front of the others. With its white or rose-coloured flowers, it makes a pretty plant just behind, say, an edging of lavender or sweet-smelling pinks.

Another low-growing plant is the saffron crocus, which once established can be reproduced quite rapidly from the tiny cormlets which form at the base of the bulb. Plant the cormlets in rich, sandy, well-drained soil, 15cm (6in) apart, and be on the look-out, in the autumn (fall) for the splash of bluey-purple flowers that will suddenly burst out between the shiny green leaves. The golden stigmas are your treasure trove, and should be picked as soon as the flowers open.

Harvesting spice seeds
Harvesting spice seeds requires a certain amount of judgement. Clearly, you want to leave the seeds on the plant as long as possible to develop and ripen. But leave them too long and the plant will do the job that Nature intended for it, scattering the seed far and wide. Fine for next year's crop, but not so good for this year's spice jars! Cut all the umbrella-shaped clusters, such as anise and caraway, poppy, too, close to the ground. Tie the stems in bunches and hang them upside-down for the seeds to complete their ripening process. Avoid losing any falling seed by tying muslin or cheesecloth loosely round the seedheads, by hanging the bunches over a tray, or by standing them, head down, in a large crock or clean, dry bucket. Where necessary, shake out the remaining seed by hand or, in the case of cardamom, pick off the dried seed pods. They are best stored complete with the seeds inside, otherwise they quickly lose their aroma.

Other seeds need further drying before storing. The natural way to do this is to spread them on trays to dry in the sunshine, but the danger with this is that the wind might blow them away. A tray on a south-facing windowsill or in the airing cupboard or linen closet is usually the answer.

When the seeds are dry, store them in airtight jars or bottles, preferably away from the light and in a reasonably cool, dry room.

Sowing the seeds
You can plant some spice seeds straight into the ground where they are to grow.

Top *Saffron is best bought whole in little threads which are the dried stamens of the saffron crocus.* Above *The saffron crocus yields blue-purple flowers in the autumn (fall).*

Coriander likes soil well manured the previous year. Sow the seeds in spring, 6mm (¼in) deep; rows should be 30cm (1ft) apart. You can pick some of the fresh, pungent leaves to use in curries and chopped in salads. The seeds should ripen by late summer. Choose a damp day, when there is dew on the ground, to cut off the stems.

Anise seed, also sown in spring, likes light soil with plenty of lime and a sheltered, south-facing position. This is one of the spice seeds which will ripen only in a good summer; without a crystal ball, you can't actually know this when you plant them.

Fenugreek is one of the richest of spice aromas, indispensible in curry powder. The seed should be planted in spring in well-drained soil. The cream flowers bloom during early and late summer and are followed by long, flat pods, eaach one containing about sixteen seeds. Uproot the plants and hang them to dry before threshing the pods and drying out the seeds ready for storage.

Caraway seeds should be sown *in situ* and can take a light clay soil. Since the plants are biennial, and will not flower until the following year, be sure to mark the position where they are lying dormant, or you might accidentally dig them up. Plant the seed either in the late spring or the autumn (fall), and thin the seedlings to 15cm (6in) apart. Keep the patch well weeded and give the plants a light dressing of fertilizer the following spring. This will encourage them to produce flowers in late spring and ripe seeds in summer. Harvest the stems on a dull day, either by uprooting the whole plants or cutting the stems at ground level.

Mustard Although a field of mustard is one of the most marvellous sights of the countryside, the individual plants are rather disappointing, a bit like tall, scraggy cabbage plants. These really could be candidates for the vegetable patch. Both black and white mustard seed need a sunny position. Black mustard prefers light soil with plenty of moisture, and white mustard fares better in a heavy, sandy soil with less watering. Plant the seeds in the spring, thinning them to about 45cm (18in) apart, and take care to harvest them before the pods burst.

With a cold frame or greenhouse

If you have a cold frame or greenhouse, you can sow other spice seeds and bring them on for later repotting or transplanting into the open.

Cumin seed should be planted in pots or trays under glass in the spring, and transferred to a bed of warm, dry, rich soil in a sunny position. The plants develop in 3 to 4 months, producing slender, branching stems and

Bottom left *Caraway seeds should be sown in late spring or autumn (fall) and result in great clusters of tiny white flowers as illustrated by the photograph* Bottom Right.

long, narrow, deep green leaves. The small umbels of white or rose-coloured flowers are followed by the fruits, usually referred to as seeds, which develop to a yellowy-green colour and are covered with tiny hairs.

Sesame seeds should be sown in the greenhouse in spring. Prick out the seedlings as soon as they are large enough to handle. Pot them on into small pots, one per seedling, and then into 12–15cm (5–6in) pots in a temperate greenhouse. Alternatively, you can transplant them into rich soil in the warmest spot in the garden—ideally beneath a south-facing wall. You need luck with the weather for the seeds to ripen; without it, be grateful for the lovely flowers.

Capsicum is a favourite crop for greenhouse owners. Any one of the varieties of sweet peppers makes a delightful salad or vegetable. Though they are perennials, in temperate zones they are treated as half-hardy annuals. Sow the seed in the greenhouse in spring in potting soil, and keep the trays at a temperature of 16°C (60°F). Pot the seedlings singly into 7.5cm (3in) pots, then on again into 17.5cm (7in) pots or into well-fertilized soil in the greenhouse border—the growing bags you can buy in garden centres are ideal. Give the plants frequent dressings of nitrogenous fertilizer, and support the plants with canes as they grow. In a good summer, capsicum plants will thrive in a sunny border out of doors, but do not transplant them until early summer and keep them well watered. Cut the fruits when they are firm and a good size. It is usual to discard the seeds when preparing sweet peppers for salads or cooking, but you can enjoy them, fresh or dried, as an extra spicy seed.

Cardamom plants will flourish in a greenhouse where you can provide high humidity during the spring to autumn (fall) seasons and dryish conditions in the winter. The plants are grown from divided pieces of rhizomes planted in early spring in a soil made up of four parts turfy loam, one part sharp sand and one part leaf mould—any good gardening shop will advise you on this. The plants, perennial shrubs, will rarely reach more than 30cm (1ft) in height, but will reward you with beautiful spikes of flowers, white with a blue and yellow lip, and highly-scented pointed leaves. You can grow cardamom indoors as a house plant, away from direct sunlight in a warm room—the shuttered elegance of old country houses seems to be the right milieu!

Cinnamon It is interesting to try growing miniature cinnamon trees in a greenhouse. The temperature should be 21–27°C (70–80°F) from the spring right through until the autumn (fall) and then, when the growing season is over, down to about 16–21°C (60–70°F). Plant cuttings should be taken from young shoots in April and rooted in a closed propagating frame at a temperature of 27°C (80°F). They must have this initial heat if they are to flourish. Later on pot the young plants in a half-and-half mixture of turfy loam and peat to which a little sand has been added. The trees can be grown either in large pots or in the greenhouse border, and should be given plenty of water during the growing season. They will develop dark green, glossy leaves which are delightfully fragrant, and small yellow flowers before the dark purple berries.

Nutmeg If you are in an experimental mood you could try growing nutmeg trees in a warm greenhouse. The tree bears the male and female flowers on separate plants. As you need one of each for fruit to develop, plant several cuttings to be sure. Plant cuttings of ripened shoots in sand in a propagating frame with gentle heat underneath, then transplant the young plants into a mixture of sandy loam and fibrous peat. The greenhouse temperature must not drop below 13°C (55°F). Even if your trees do not bear the nutmeg and mace you would like to grate into your puddings or flavour your pickles, your efforts will be rewarded with the lovely scented evergreen leaves and pale yellow flowers in early summer.

Indoor spice seed crops
Some spice seeds are fun to grow indoors as quick salad crops.

Mustard As a slight graduation from growing white mustard seed on damp blotting paper or a piece of flannel, as everyone must have done at some time, you can grow the crop in bowls or seed trays filled with fine, sandy soil or bulb fibre. Weekly sowings between autumn (fall) and spring will give you an economical round-the-winter crop. Sprinkle the seed thinly on top of moist, well-firmed-down soil; do not cover with more soil. Either place the container in a drawer or closet or cover it with a piece of wood to exclude the light. Keep the seeds moist with a light sprinkling of water and bring them into the light once germination has started. Cut the crop when the sprouts are from about 7.5cm (3in) high.

Fenugreek is another indoor crop that gives marvellous value. The seeds take about 4 to 6 days to sprout and give a yield 6 to 8 times their original weight—a very good return on capital. Try growing the seed in jars; it works like a dream. Put 3 tablespoons of the seed in a large glass jar and cover it with a piece of clean old nylon or cheesecloth secured with an elastic band. Fill the jar with tepid water, drain it off through the covering and keep the jar on its side. Repeat the watering and draining treatment night and morning. When the sprouts are from about 5cm (2in) long, tip them into a colander and wash them well. They are an unusually spicy ingredient for salad, or can be served as a crisp vegetable. Plunge them into boiling salted water, bring it quickly to the boil again, and drain off the sprouts straight away. Serve them dotted with butter and sprinkled with ground black pepper.

A DICTIONARY OF SPICES

Most spices grow and reach their full, pungent maturity in the hot, sunny, moist climates of the tropical countries where they are harvested by hand, threshed and winnowed in ways that have not changed for centuries, and dried in the baking sun. More modern methods and machinery are gradually being introduced, but on the whole the spice harvest is still faithful to local tradition.

Some of the spices described on the following pages can be grown in our colder climates, and some can be successfully raised if a heated greenhouse is available to provide nearly-natural growing conditions. Those spices that can be grown in garden or greenhouse are marked with an asterisk. Some, such as caraway and sweet peppers, will produce a very satisfactory crop. Others, such as anise and sesame, will be rewarding only in a good summer. And still others—cinnamon is one—will produce a miniature tree and never reach full maturity.

But if you have space to spare, green fingers and a love of cooking, experiment by growing a few of your own spices. Even if they do not attain the full aroma of those grown in the tropics, you will have the satisfaction of achievement that will more than compensate.

Brassica hirta (or alba)

MUSTARD WHITE

Brassica nigra

MUSTARD BLACK

Both members of the cress family, and both having yellow flowers, black and white mustard are distinguished by the colour of the seed. Black mustard has reddish-black seed; white mustard seed is yellowish-orange. There is another type, known as brown, or wild mustard. These rather oily seeds are sometimes mixed with the cultivated ones in commercially prepared 'made' mustard or powders. The spice is one of the earliest known food preservatives and medicines.

Habitat A native plant of Southern European and Mediterranean countries, mustard is now extensively cultivated as a field crop in the United States and all over Europe. Black mustard is grown on light, sandy loam and white mustard on heavier sandy loam. Both plants need good sunshine. The plants are rather tall and straggly, and are not considered attractive garden crops.

White mustard seedlings are the ones grown with cress, a popular crop for children to cultivate on damp cotton. They can be grown out of doors, too, as a crop to be harvested a few days after germination.

Cultivation To grow the crop for seed, plant the seeds in spring and water well; white mustard needs more moisture than black. Both types of mustard will bear yellow flowers on straggly plants, then black mustard will develop smooth, narrow pods containing a row of small seeds and white mustard hairy pods with larger seeds.

To sow the seed for the salad crop, sprinkle it onto finely raked soil firmed down and lightly watered, but do not cover the seed with soil. In bad weather, protect both seed and seedlings under glass.

Black mustard has yellow flowers and its seeds are reddish-black. Only when liquid is added to dry mustard powder or the seeds does the characteristic 'hot' flavour evolve. White mustard seeds are added to the black and ground to provide commercial mustard powder.

Harvesting You must harvest the pods of both black and white mustard before they burst or they will scatter their contents everywhere. Wait until they are fully developed, but not quite ripe. Hang the plants to dry, then thresh out the seeds and dry them in the sun or a warm place.

To harvest the salad crop, cut the seedlings when they are about 7.5cm (3in) high.

Uses Black mustard seeds are used whole in pickling spice mixtures. White mustard seeds, much less aromatic, are mixed with the black and ground to provide the commercial mustard powder. A ground cereal such as wheat flour is added to act as a preservative and absorb the natural oils. Prepared or 'made' mustard, the ready-made condiment, is the dried powder mixed with salt, other spices and wine or vinegar. Dry mustard powder or seeds have no 'hot' flavour. It is not until liquid is added and enzyme activity takes place that the characteristic pungency is evident. Different countries and regions have their own traditional mustard recipes; for example, French mustard is made from the black seeds alone.

Made mustard can be spread on fish, poultry or meat before roasting or barbecuing for a 'devilled' finish, and a pinch of mustard powder added to salad dressings. It is used as a preservative in commerical salad creams and mayonnaise.

The leaves of field mustards can be cooked and served as a vegetable.

Salad mustard, often grown at home with cress, is used as a delicate garnish for savoury dishes, in mixed salads, or in sandwiches combined with egg, cheese or fish paste.

Capsicum annuum
CAPSICUM

Widely cultivated throughout the world, this half-hardy annual herbaceous plant grows from 30–90cm (1–3ft) high and bears fruit ranging from 1–24cm (½–11in) long. It includes all the red, yellow and green peppers, some long and thin and some small and round, which are eaten in salads and as a vegetable, and the red peppers which are ground and sold as paprika.

Habitat The plants require warm, moist conditions.

Cultivation Sow the seed under glass in potting soil in early spring, in a temperature of 16°C (60°F). Pot the seedlings singly first into 7.5cm (3in) pots and then into 17.5cm (7in) pots, or into a greenhouse border. Support the plants with sticks and feed them with nitrogenous fertilizer. The plants may be grown out of doors in sunny weather. Plant them out in summer and keep them well watered. In dry weather, spray them from above, too.

Harvesting Cut the fruits when they are firm and of a good size. This will depend on the variety.

Uses Remove the strips of white 'pith' and the small white seeds inside. Cut up the fruits to use in salad or in casserole dishes. Whole peppers can be stuffed with a rice and meat mixture and baked.

Dried, ground sweet pepper, paprika, is a feature of Hungarian cooking, especially goulash. It is not 'hot' in the way that chilli pepper is, and combines well with egg, fish and meat dishes, particularly pork, veal and chicken. A little paprika pepper is an attractive garnish on light-coloured cream soups such as potato or Jerusalem artichoke.

Capsicum frutescens
CHILLI PEPPER

The same family as the sweet peppers, chilli peppers are indigenous to Central and South America, Mexico, the West Indies, India and China. They have small red, orange or yellow pods which vary enormously in intensity of flavour; they are all more highly spiced than sweet pepper, and some are so hot that they can burn the skin—or the tongue.

Habitat Tropical and temperate climates.

Cultivation The perennial plants, wlth thick, woody stems, grow to a height of up to 2m (6ft). They are usually grown in dense rows.

Harvesting The mature fruits are harvested over a period of several months. They are dried in the sun, either on concrete areas or hanging on

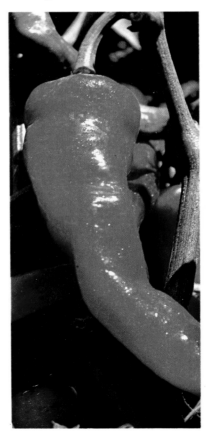

Chilli plants, besides producing a useful crop for the kitchen, are very decorative with their gaudy red hanging fruits. Care should be taken in handling certain varieties as they can leave an unpleasant burning sensation on the skin.

long strings, like colourful garlands.

Uses The various types of chillis cover a wide range of pungency. They are used both fresh and dried as a condiment in India, South-East Asia, Mexico and South America, even eaten raw. Ground chilli powder, or cayenne pepper, varies in strength, too, and should be used in such dishes as curries and chilli con carne with the utmost caution. A whole dish can be rendered quite unpalatable by the addition of too much of the spice. A very small pinch of the ground pepper is used to garnish egg dishes, cream soups, fish mousse and some shellfish dishes.

Carum carvi

CARAWAY

This biennial plant grows to about 60cm (2ft) high and has soft, fern-like leaves and white umbels of flowers. The fruits split into two seeds, which are considered as a spice. Caraway grows in Europe, North America, Russia and India.

Habitat A sunny position in any dry, well-drained light soil.

Cultivation Sow the seeds in a permanent position in the autumn (fall) and thin them to 23cm (9in) apart. Weed around the rows carefully and keep the plants watered in dry weather. They will flower and produce seed the following year. Caraway will re-establish itself with self-sown seed.

Harvesting Allow the seeds to ripen on the plant—usually in summer—then cut the plants off at ground level and hang them in a dry, airy place. When the seeds have dried, shake them on to a sheet of paper and store them in airtight jars away from heat and strong light.

Uses Caraway cakes, bread, biscuits or cookies, now enjoyed for their delicious, characteristic flavour, were served in Roman times to aid digestion. Caraway tea is said to have the same benefit. The seeds are used to flavour cheese, cabbage (particularly sauerkraut), dumplings and Hungarian goulash, and are added to rich game and meat dishes.

The young leaves can be chopped into green salad, and the roots boiled and served as a vegetable. Caraway seed oil is an important ingredient in the German liqueur, kümmel.

Cinnamomum zeylanicum   *Cinnamomum cassia*

CINNAMON  CASSIA

The two spices have similar properties, but cinnamon, always thought to be superior, has now almost replaced cassia. Cinnamon originated in Sri Lanka (Ceylon) and is now also cultivated in South India, the Malagasy Republic (Madagascar) and the Seychelles. The tree, a member of the laurel family, can grow to a height of 10–12m (30–40ft). It has long, aromatic leaves but is cultivated for the spice, the dried inner bark.

Habitat Wet forest areas.

Cultivation In the tropics, the seeds are planted in round clusters of four or five, with gaps of about 3.5m (10ft) between groups. The seeds germinate after about 3 weeks, but the first harvest does not take place until the fourth or fifth year. The trees are usually cut back to a height of 2–2.5m (6–8ft).

The trees can be raised in northern climates in a greenhouse, but will never reach full maturity. Put the plants in a 50/50 compost of peat and turfy loam with a little sand added, in large pots or a greenhouse border. Keep them warm and moist—21–27°C (70–80°F) during the spring and summer, and 16–21°C (60–70°F) for the rest of the year is ideal. Propaga-

tion is by cuttings, carefully taken from the young shoots of the plant, in mid-spring.

Harvesting The bark is peeled off in long strips with special curved knives. Bundles of bark are left for 24 hours to ferment, then the crumbly outer layer scraped off. As the inner bark dries, it curls like a quill.

Uses Pieces of stick cinnamon are used to spice pickling vinegar and in mulled wine drinks. Ground cinnamon is used in cakes, especially rich fruit cakes, biscuits (cookies), steamed puddings such as Christmas puddings, and in milk puddings.

Cinnamon trees can be grown in Northern climates in a greenhouse and although they will never fully mature, they will still produce an abundant supply of cinnamon. Stick cinnamon is used in pickling vinegar and mulled wines, while the ground variety is best in desserts.

223

Coriandrum sativum

CORIANDER

The plant is an umbelliferous hardy annual plant with fan-shaped feathery leaves and clusters of pale mauve flowers. The pungent leaves are used in Indian dishes, soups and stews, but the plant is mainly grown for the round, aromatic seeds, which are used as a spice. Coriander is a native of the Middle East and was grown in the Hanging Gardens of Babylon. It used to be cultivated on a large scale in the Eastern counties of England.

Habitat A sunny location with a medium or heavy soil, well manured from a previous year. Freshly-manured soil is not suitable.

Cultivation Sow seeds in spring or autumn (fall), 6mm (¼in) deep in rows 30cm (1ft) apart. The plants will grow about 30–90cm (1–3ft) high—autumn (fall) sowing produces stronger, healthier plants.

Harvesting Cut the clusters as soon as the seeds start to ripen, usually in summer or early autumn (fall). Hang them upside-down in a warm, airy place to dry, then shake them on to a sheet of paper. Store the seeds in airtight jars away from strong light and heat.

Uses The seeds, which are said to be an aid to digestion, are used in dishes as varied as sauces, pickles, chutneys, cakes and some confectionery and candy, and are the pungent ingredient in some spiced sausages and other meat products.

Coriander is a hardy annual; it is mainly grown for its seeds which are used in a wide variety of culinary dishes. The leaves, to a lesser extent, can be used in Indian dishes, soups and stews.

Crocus sativus

SAFFRON

The world's most expensive spice, costly because it takes about 250,000 stigmas from about 76,000 of the blue-violet autumn crocus flowers to yield 450g (1lb) of saffron. A native of Southern Europe and the Middle East, saffron was cultivated in Britain in the Middle Ages and a large industry grew up in East Anglia, where the growers were called 'crokers'. At the price it is, it is well worth trying to grow the crop and harvesting your own little gold mine!

Habitat The world's production now comes largely from Spain and Portugal. The saffron crocus favours a light, rich sandy or loamy soil with good drainage. It needs a sunny position and, since it does not flower until the autumn, might need protecting by cloches or Hotkaps from heavy rains or early frost, which would completely damage the crop.

Cultivation Carefully separate the young cormlets which form at the base of the bulb-like corms and plant them 15cm (6in) apart, in well-cultivated soil, in late summer or early autumn (fall).

Harvesting The crop should be harvested as soon as the flowers open. Each one has three bright orangey-red, funnel-like stigmas. Pick them carefully by hand and separate them from the flowers. Spread the stigmas on a tray and dry them in an airing cupboard or warm linen closet, away from draughts. Store them in airtight jars as soon as they are dry and thread-like.

Uses Saffron was one of the earliest known colourants, producing a beautiful range of yellow and orange shades for food, cotton, silk and wool, and was used as a cosmetic, notably by Cleopatra.

The spice is sold whole, the thin, thread-like strands packed in tiny sachets, or in ground form. But, because of the high cost of the spice, ground saffron is liable to be adulterated with additives. (In Germany in the fifteenth century people convicted of adulterating the spice were burned at the stake.)

The dried threads should be crushed with a pestle and mortar, then soaked in hot liquid—the stock or sauce that is to form part of the dish. Saffron is an essential colouring and flavouring ingredient in dishes such as Spanish paella, French bouillabaisse and traditional English saffron cakes and buns. A thread or a pinch of ground saffron added to the stock or water gives a beautiful golden colour to rice and is usually used in Indian biryanis.

Saffron is one of the world's most expensive spices as thousands of flowers are required to produce one pound of saffron. It has been in use for centuries in food, medicine and dyes, but nowadays its main function is in cooking.

Cuminum cyminum

CUMIN

A native of the Middle East, this delicate annual plant is mainly grown for the seed-like fruits, which are a pungent and highly aromatic spice, slightly reminiscent of caraway. Pliny, unwilling to make such a comparison, considered cumin the king among condiments.

Habitat Warm, sunny position in rich, well-drained sandy loam.

Cultivation Sow the seed in pots, then harden them off in a cold frame before transplanting to a warm, sunny bed. The plants grow 30–60cm (1—2ft) high on very slender stems and are delicate, so they should not be crowded by more vigorous ones.

Harvesting When the plants begin to wither, cut the stems just below the clusters of fruit, and hang them in a warm, airy place to dry. Store the seeds in airtight jars away from heat and strong light.

Uses The seed should be slightly warmed before use, to increase the aroma. Either whole or ground, it is an essential ingredient in curries; in the East it is known as 'jeera'. It is also used to flavour rye bread, pickles, chutneys, sausages and other meat products, and Dutch and Swiss cheeses. It is mixed with ground chilli powder in American spice blends called 'chilli seasoning'.

In the past, cumin seed was a symbol of fidelity, believed to keep lovers faithful and poultry from straying beyond the farmyard bounds!

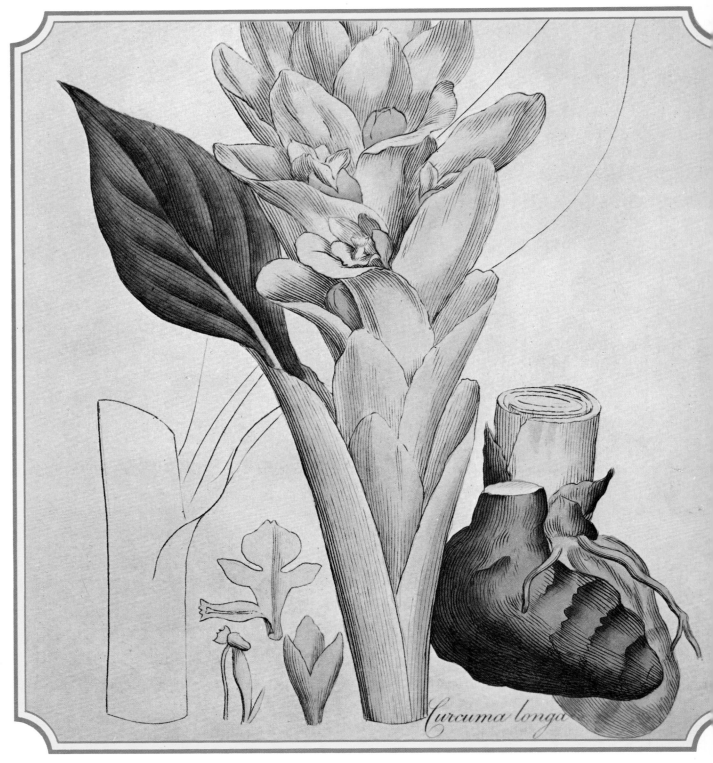

Curcuma longa

Derived from the dried root of a plant native to India, turmeric is ground to produce a vivid yellow powder. In certain dishes, it can be used as a substitute for saffron as it is so much cheaper. It also has successful dyeing propensities.

Curcuma longa
TURMERIC

A native of South Asia, turmeric is a perennial tropical plant of the ginger family. For many centuries it has been used not only as a spice but as a colourant, the bright yellow powder of the ground rhizomes being one of the earliest known vegetable dyes.

Habitat Humid, tropical hilly areas.

Cultivation The plant is propagated by dividing and planting small pieces of the round, orange rhizomes.

Harvesting Turmeric has large lily-type leaves and pale yellow flowers. It is harvested about 10 months after planting, when the stems begin to fade. During processing, in which the rhizomes are cured, boiled, cleaned and dried in the sun, they lose three-quarters of their original weight.

Uses Turmeric is sold already ground to a fine powder. Since it is so much cheaper than saffron, it is most unlikely to be adulterated. It is an essential spice in curry powder and is also used in Indian sweet dishes for both its colour and flavour. It is used in mixed pickles, particularly the mustard pickle known as 'piccalilli', chutneys and rice dishes such as pilaffs. Turmeric is said to have certain medical properties and is used to treat ulcers and liver disorders. Externally, it is used as a cosmetic by Eastern women, who prefer to give their cheeks a golden rather than a rosy glow.

Ellettaria cardamomum

CARDAMOM

A native of South India and Sri Lanka (Ceylon), the plant can grow 2–6m (6–18ft) tall. Cultivated in the colder climates of northern countries, however, it would rarely reach a height of more than 30cm (1ft). The flowers, in loose spikes, are white, edged with yellow and blue. The small, ovoid green fruit capsules contain 15 to 20 hard, almost black seeds which quickly lose their aroma when released from the capsule. This is why cardamom seeds are marketed inside the capsule.

Habitat The plants can be cultivated in a very warm, shaded greenhouse. The humidity must be high during the spring and summer, but the plants need to be dry during winter.

Cultivation Propagation is by division of the creeping rhizomes. Plant them in pots in early spring in a mixture of one part of sharp sand, one part of leaf mould and four parts of turfy loam. If no greenhouse is available, the plants may be grown as houseplants in a warm, shady room free from draughts.

Harvesting In plantations, the three-sided, beige-coloured capsules are harvested by hand, five or six times a year, when they are three-quarters ripe. They are washed, then dried in the sun or in artificially-heated rooms.

Uses The small black cardamom seeds are the essential flavouring ingredient in Danish pastries and are used in a wide range of cakes. In Arab countries they are infused in strong black coffee to offset the bitterness and sometimes chewed as a confection, and to aid digestion. They are also used in some Indian spice blends and to flavour pulaos and biryanis. The seeds are very hard and should be pounded before use in cooking.

Juniperus communis

JUNIPER

A hardy, perennial shrub which can grow to the size of a small tree, juniper grows wild in North America, Europe and Asia. The whole plant —reddish-brown stems, needle-like leaves and pungent berries—is aromatic.

Habitat A sloping situation on well-drained, chalky or lime soil is ideal. The plant does not do well in intense shade, but will tolerate barren conditions.

Cultivation Each berry contains three seeds. Sow the seed, or set out small plants 1.2m (4ft) apart in the spring. As male and female flowers rarely grow on the same shrub, you need at least two trees for fertilization. The male flowers are like green catkins and the female ones like cones. Occasional dressings of organic fertilizer will help to promote growth. You can propagate the plants by cuttings. The plants can also be grown in tubs or large pots.

Harvesting The berries are green at first and may not mature for two or three years. Pick them when they are black.

Uses Juniper berries are used to flavour gin and to make beer. They can be used fresh or dried and should be lightly crushed to extract the flavour. They are used in marinades for pork, veal, beef, venison and other game and poultry. They are also an essential ingredient in the Alsatian dish Choucroûte Garni which is a dish composed of sauerkraut, pork and various vegetables.

A tisane of the berries infused in hot water is said to be helpful in promoting activity of the kidneys. Juniper berries were burned as a form of disinfectant.

Myristica fragrans
NUTMEG  MACE

This evergreen tree, a native of the Moluccas and other East Indian islands, and for the past 150 years extensively cultivated in the West Indies, produces two spices. It has a yellow fleshy fruit, rather like an apricot. Inside the ripe fruit, the nutshell is covered by an interlaced membrane, the mace, and inside the shell, the 'kerneal' of the fruit is the nutmeg. When it is harvested, the mace is bright red, but it mellows to golden yellow when dried. Nutmegs, thimble-sized and almost egg-shaped, have been the subject of flagrant imitation, wooden shapes having been passed off for them by unscrupulous pedlars in America. Mace and nutmeg are the only two spices found growing on the same plant.

Habitat The trees are said to thrive best where they are within sight of the sea. In the tropics, they grow in sheltered valleys up to 300m (1500ft) above sea level, in rich, sandy, well-drained soil.

The trees can be cultivated in a heated greenhouse with a minimum winter temperature of 13°C (55°F). They will bear pale yellow flowers in early summer.

Cultivation The trees are propagated by seed, and in the tropics the seedlings are transplanted to the fields, where they can bear fruit for as long as 90 years.

Plant seed in a 50/50 mixture of sandy loam and fibrous peat. The male and female flowers are borne on separate plants so, to achieve fruit, you will need at least one of each. You can graft shoots from the trees of one sex to trees of the other, and can propagate by taking cuttings of ripened shoots. Insert these in sand in a propagating frame.

Harvesting In the tropics, gathering the spice crop takes place over many months, sometimes by collecting the fallen ripened fruits. Traditionally, the fruits are shaken into baskets attached to long poles. The nuts are spread out to dry in the sun, then the mace is removed by hand, flattened and dried separately. When the nuts are dry enough for the kernel to rattle in the shells, they are cracked open and the pungent nutmeg removed. They are then carefully graded according to quality.

Uses Nutmegs are sold whole and the most aromatic way to use the spice is by grating it freshly as it is needed, using either a nutmeg grater or the small, fine holes on a cheese grater. The spice is added to mulled wine drinks, eggnog, egg and fish dishes, hot and cold milk drinks, milk puddings, cakes and biscuits (cookies), boiled green vegetables, soups, sauces, Christmas puddings, spiced breads, pies, pastries and doughnuts. Ground nutmeg is also available but is never as aromatic, so for the best

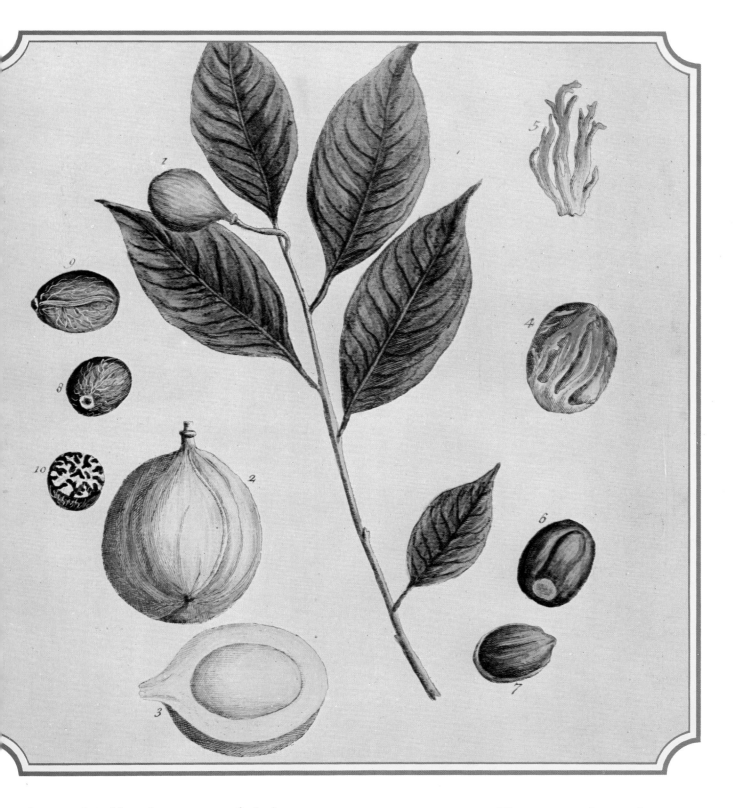

results it is advisable to have a store of whole nutmegs.

Mace is sold whole, when it is called blade mace, or ground. It is particularly suitable in savoury egg, cheese and vegetable dishes, and gives the characteristic spiciness to Bechamel sauce. Blade mace is often included in pickling spice blends. Ground mace sparingly added to the cocoa or chocolate ingredient of chocolate cakes or desserts can deliciously enhance the flavour. It is also an essential ingredient of potted shrimps and many other potted meat and fish dishes. It is useful to remember that Mace can be subsituted for Nutmeg in most sweet recipes.

The same tropical tree produces both nutmeg and mace, the former being a hard, dry seed which is light brown. It is better to buy nutmeg whole as it keeps for a long time and ground nutmeg is never as aromatic. Mace can be bought whole (blade mace) or ground.

229

Papaver somniferum

POPPY SEED

The poppy from which the tiny blue-black culinary seeds are taken is the opium poppy, an annual which is native to Asia. The drug was—and still is—taken from the milky juice in the unripe heads of plants grown in sunny climates. It is no longer present when the seeds are ready to harvest, so these are in no way narcotic. And it does not develop in plants grown in colder regions.

Habitat Poppies grow well in herbaceous borders where not only the short-lived purple, pale lilac or white flowers but also the greyish-green leaves are attractive. Soil should be moist, rich and well cultivated. Poppies like a position in full sun.

Cultivation Sow the seeds in spring in clumps or rows towards the back of the herb garden or border, because they grow to a height of 60–90cm (2–3ft). Cut off the urn-shaped seedheads before the seeds ripen, or they will scatter and take over the entire patch the following year.

Harvesting The seeds will be ready to harvest in late summer. Cut off the stalks below the seedheads and hang them in bundles to dry, with a tray beneath to catch any seeds as they fall. Shake the remaining seeds out and store them in airtight jars away from strong light and heat. There will be about 900,000 seeds to 450g (1lb).

Uses Poppy seeds are scattered on some breads, buns, cakes and biscuits (cookies) as both decoration and flavouring, and used extensively in Jewish and Central European cooking in dishes such as noodles and desserts. They are generally used whole but can be ground—in some countries you can buy a special grinder for the exceptionally fine, hard seeds. Without one, soak the seeds in water overnight, then put them in a plastic bag and roll them heavily with a rolling pin. To bring out the full flavour, toast the seeds lightly in the oven or in a frying pan over a low heat for a few minutes.

Pimenta dioica

ALLSPICE

Exclusively grown in the Western hemisphere, the spice is a native of Latin America and the West Indies, where it was discovered by Spanish explorers in the sixteenth century. Although the tree will grow in other parts of the world, it will not bear fruit. The name allspice recognizes the fact that the berries smell like a blend of cinnamon, cloves and nutmeg.

Habitat Limestone hills.

Cultivation In Jamaica, the trees are planted 6.5m (20ft) apart. They reach full maturity after 15 years and may bear fruit for over 100 years. In Mexico and Central America the trees are almost all wild.

Harvesting The unripe but fully-grown fruits are harvested 3 to 4 months after flowering, when they are reddish-brown. They are dried in the sun for 7 to 10 days before being cleaned and packed for export.

Uses Allspice berries have a long history as a food preservative, especially of meat. They are one of the ingredients in mixed pickling spice and are packed with barrels of fish shipped from Scandinavia. They are used to flavour cakes, soups, meat, vegetables, especially sauerkraut, and in the manufacture of Benedictine and Chartreuse liqueurs.

Allspice is sometimes known as Jamaica pepper or pimento and it derives its name from the fact that its flavour is similar to a mixture of cinnamon, cloves and nutmeg. Its berries have long been used to preserve and flavour Benedictine and Chartreuse liqueurs.

Pimpinella anisum

ANISE

The plant is a medium-tall annual herb of the parsley family, but is usually grown for the minute oil-bearing seeds, called aniseed, which are classed as a spice. There are about 100,000 seeds to every 450g (1lb) weight. Anise is a native of the Middle East and grows wild in Greece and Egypt.

Habitat Anise will grow well in a good summer in light, dry, loamy soil, in a sunny position.

Cultivation Sow the seeds in mid-spring. The plants will produce small white flowers and delicate, fern-like leaves.

Harvesting The seeds will ripen only in a hot summer, when they will turn greyish-green. Carefully cut the whole flower stems and hang them upside down in an airy place to dry. Shake the seeds over a sheet of paper and store them in airtight jars away from heat or strong light, which would affect the flavour.

Uses The seeds give the liquorice-like flavour to the liqueur anisette, as well as to Pernod and the Greek aperitif, ouzo. They are used in salads, to garnish root vegetables, and in cakes, biscuits (cookies) and bread. Anise tea is reputed to soothe indigestion.

Piper nigrum

PEPPER

The world's most important spice, both black and white pepper are produced from a climbing vine which is a native of India and the East Indies. The spice was one of the earliest trading commodities between the Orient and European countries and many seafaring expeditions were launched in search of it.

Habitat The pepper vine, a perennial evergreen climber, grows in damp jungle and is now extensively cultivated in the tropics of both hemispheres.

Cultivation The vine is propagated by cuttings grown in nurseries, then planted 2.75m (8ft) apart with posts or small trees to support the 10m (30ft) long climbing shoots.

Harvesting The first small spice crop may be gathered in the third year. The black pepper is the entire peppercorn, or berry, which includes the

Pepper, a native of India and the East Indies, comes from a climbing vine. Black peppercorns are picked while unripe and left to dry and darken. White peppercorns are left on the vine to mature and the husk is then removed, revealing a smooth core.

dark outer hull. The berry clusters are harvested 9 months after flowering and, for black pepper, picked in their unripe, green state. It is only in the natural drying process that they darken. For white pepper, the berries are left to mature on the vine, then soaked to soften the outer hull. This is then rubbed off to reveal the greyish-white inner peppercorn, which lightens in colour as it is dried.

Uses One of the best-known of all spices and condiments, both black and white peppercorns are used in mixtures of pickling spice, added to the stock in which meat or fish is cooked, and freshly ground to flavour all kinds of savoury dishes. Both black and white pepper are available ready ground, but the flavour is less pungent. Whole green peppercorns, which have not been dried, can be bought in jars, preserved in brine.

Sesamum indicum
SESAME

The annual plant, native to Africa and Indonesia, was immortalized by Ali Baba in his famous command, 'Open, Sesame', which revealed a cave of priceless jewels. The value of the plant is in the versatile seeds it produces, which vary in colour from almost white, through golden-brown and pale orange to greyish-black. The seeds are sold whole, either raw or toasted, as a ground meal, and as a paste, *tahina*, whigh features in many Middle Eastern dishes. Sesame oil is a high-protein vegetable oil.

Habitat Light, friable soil, preferably a sandy loam, with a warm climate and moderate rainfall. In a good summer, the plant should grow more than 60cm (2ft) high and produce white, mauve or pink flowers.

Cultivation Sow the seeds in a greenhouse in spring and prick them out singly into pots when they are big enough to handle. To continue growing in a greenhouse, pot on into 12–15cm (5–6in) pots containing a well-drained potting mixture. To grow outside, plant the hardened seedlings in rich soil, ideally near a south wall.

Harvesting The plants will flower in the late summer. Harvest the seeds when the upper pods are fully developed but still green and spread them on a tray in a warm, dry place to dry. Shake the seeds out and store them in airtight jars away from heat and strong light.

Uses The seeds are sprinkled on breads, cakes, biscuits and cookies where they give a pleasant nutty texture. *Tahina* is used extensively in Middle Eastern cooking and as a spread instead of butter—it tastes a little like peanut butter. Sesame oil can be used as a salad or cooking oil, and is a good skin moisturizer; Cleopatra is said to have found it so.

Syzygium aromaticum or *Eugenia aromatica*
CLOVES

A native of the Moluccas, or Spice Islands, and now cultivated in the Malagasy Republic (Madagascar), Tanzania and the West Indies, this large, evergreen tree—or at least its highly-prized flower buds—caused many voyages, adventures and battles.

Habitat The trees grow best in volcanic, loamy soil in areas with an average rainfall of 250cm (100in) a year.

Cultivation The seeds germinate within 4 to 6 weeks, and the trees are planted 6.5m (20ft) apart.

Harvesting The spice crop is the unopened flower bud, which must be picked before the pinky-green blossom opens. The buds are literally harvested by hand—by brushing clusters against the palm. When dried, the buds turn dark brown and retain only one-third of their original weight—it takes 5,000 to 7,000 dried cloves to 450g (1lb) weight. The best grade have round, capped domes.

Uses Whole cloves are natural partners to apple dishes of all kinds; they are used to decorate and flavour whole baked ham, and mixed with other spices for pickling and mulled wine drinks. Ground cloves are used with dried fruit in cakes, steamed puddings and mincemeat, and in milk puddings and sauces. In Indonesia, cloves are mixed with tobacco in a thriving cigarette industry.

Sesame has been immortalized for ever in the legend of Ali Baba and his famous command. For centuries, it has been valued as a spice and also for the oil it produces. It is high in protein and also makes an effective skin moisturizer.

A leguminous tree native to Africa, tamarind is valued for its leaves which produce a yellow or red dye, its timber, and the seeds and pulp from the brown pod which are used in cooking.

Tamarindus indica

TAMARIND

Known as the Indian date, tamarind is a leguminous tree which grows freely in India, tropical East Africa and the West Indies.
Habitat Damp, humid tropical regions.
Cultivation The tree can grow to a height of about 2.75m (8ft), bearing seed pods 15–20cm (6–8in) long which ripen to dark brown.
Harvesting The leaves, flowers and pods are all harvested for their separate uses.
Uses Tamarind leaves are used to make a red or yellow dye, and both the leaves and flowers are eaten in salads. The main culinary use, however, is of the pods once the seeds have been removed. This pulp, which forms a black sticky mass, is sold in Indian food shops and is invaluable in the preparation of some curries and chutneys. The pulp contains about 10 to 12 per cent of tartaric acid, and it is this that gives tamarind the sourness for which it is valued. To obtain the souring agent without the tough fibres of the broken pods, infuse the pulp in a little hot water, then press it through a strainer to squeeze out the juice. The pulp is said to have mildly laxative properties.

Trigonella foenum-graecum

FENUGREEK

This annual leguminous plant of the pea family, a native of South-Eastern Europe and Western Asia, has also been cultivated in India, Mediterranean countries and North Africa, both for the seed, a spice, and as a forage for cattle.

It can be grown in other mild climates, and indoors as a sprouting salad crop.
Habitat A mild climate, well-drained loamy soil and a sunny position.
Cultivation Sow the seed in spring, either in seed boxes or under glass. Transplant the seedlings in light soil in a sunny spot. The plants should bear cream-coloured flowers, beautifully scented, in mid-summer and then develop long, flat pods, each one containing about 15 seeds. To grow the spicy seeds as a salad crop, sprinkle the seed in light potting soil in seed boxes or on damp flannel or cotton.
Harvesting When the seed pods are fully developed, pull up the plants and hang them upside-down to dry—as one does with dwarf bean plants. Break open the pods and dry the seeds in the sun if there is no wind, on a tray in the airing cupboard, linen closet or a warm, south-facing windowsill. To use the seedlings as a salad crop, cut them after a few days' growth, at the two-leaf (cotyledon) stage, using sharp scissors and cutting just above the seeds.
Uses Rich in vitamins and protein, the reddish-yellow seeds are an important part of Oriental vegetarian diets. Ground fenugreek seed—methi —is an ingredient in curry spice blends, and in America is used to flavour imitation maple syrup. Middle Eastern women eat the roasted seed to make them plump, and it flavours the calorie-packed sweetmeat, *halva*. Fenugreek tea is said to aid digestion.

The salad crop, cut after a few days' growth, has a slightly pungent and light taste and can be eaten raw or quickly blanched in boiling, salted water. The leaves of the fully-grown plant are too bitter to eat as a vegetable, but are sometimes served with a curry sauce.

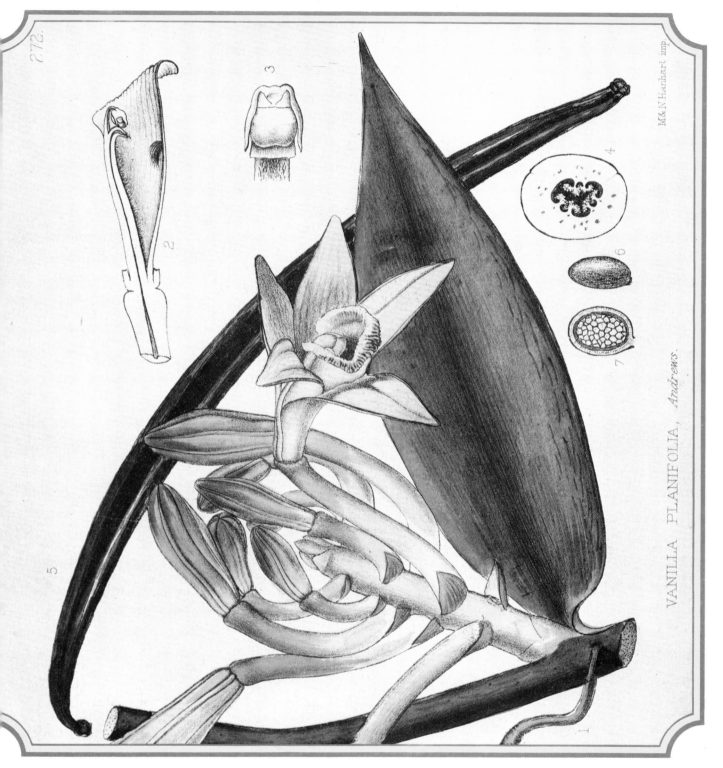

Vanilla planifolia
VANILLA

A native of the humid forests of tropical America, vanilla is one of the flavourings discovered by early explorers of the New World. It was brought to Europe by the Spaniards, who had found the Aztecs using it as a flavouring for chocolate. Now 80 per cent of the world's crop is grown in the Malagasy Republic (Madagascar).
Habitat Hot, humid, tropical regions with good drainage. The plants

Vanilla, a perennial climbing vine, produces pods which are either dried or made into a liquid extract. Vanilla pods can be used several times and pieces of the pod may be infused in milk in the making of cakes and custards.

235

must be protected from the wind.

Cultivation The vine is grown on supports of posts or trellis, and propagated by cuttings 30–120cm (1–4ft) long. The crop will not bear fruit unless pollinating insects are present, as in Mexico and Central America. In other regions, pollination must be done by hand. In these plantations, therefore, the vines are pruned and trained to a convenient height. The first crop is harvested after 3 years and the vines replaced after ten years.

Harvesting Each vine may bear up to 1,000 pale yellow flowers. These are nipped out to leave clusters of about seven flowers, and no more than fifty on each vine. The pods are picked when they are 15–25cm (6–10in) long, before they are ripe, when they are beginning to turn from green to yellow. They are matured by being alternately sweated and dried. The curing process takes about six months.

Uses One of the most versatile of flavourings, vanilla is used commercially in the manufacture of chocolate, ice cream, puddings and tobacco.

A pod of vanilla stored in an airtight jar of sugar subtly flavours it. To flavour sweet sauces, boil a pod with the milk, remove it, wash and dry and store to use again.

True vanilla extract is made from the cured pods chopped and percolated with alcohol and water, and is very expensive. Cheap synthetic substitutes sold as vanilla flavouring can be made from wood pulp, waste paper pulp, coal tar, oil of sassafras and chemicals.

Zingiber officinale

GINGER

Originating in South Asia and cultivated in ancient China and India, ginger now grows in most tropical countries. It is an erect, perennial plant growing to a height of 60–120cm (2–4ft) from thick, knobbly rhizomes, and was the first spice imported into Europe.

Habitat Ginger plants need heavy rain and plenty of sun—a warm, moist tropical climate and a situation up to 850m (2500ft) above sea level.

Cultivation Propagation is by dividing the rhizome into pieces 2.5–5cm (1–2in) long. The shoots grow up to about 1m (3ft) high and bear highly-scented flowers.

Harvesting The ginger is ready to harvest 9 months to 1 year after planting, when the plant begins to wither. The rhizomes are dug up with a hoe. The spice is obtained from the rhizomes, which are marketed fresh, dried, ground or preserved. You can buy fresh root ginger in most Oriental foodstores and keep it moist by burying it in soil in a pot or in

the garden.

Uses Dried root (green) ginger, which is hard and shrivelled, needs lightly crushing, or 'bruising', to extract the flavour for use in chutneys, pickles and curries. Ground ginger is the dried rhizome which is scraped, boiled and peeled. This is used in cakes, especially gingerbread, puddings, biscuits (cookies) and candy. Preserved, candied and crystallized ginger are processed from the fresh green rhizome and are eaten as sweetmeats or as a garnish for cakes and desserts. Stem ginger, preserved in a thick sugar syrup, is a popular dessert after a Chinese meal.

Ginger is the root of a perennial plant and is available ground, dried, preserved, candied, fresh and crystallized. It is used for a wide variety of purposes ranging from curries and chutneys to cakes and candy, and is popular in Oriental cooking.

237

AT-A-GLANCE

	SPICE	PART OF PLANT	FLAVOUR
	Allspice	Dried berry, whole or ground. Berries retain freshness if stored whole and crushed or pounded when needed	Fragrant, like mixture of cinnamon, cloves and nutmeg (hence name)
	Aniseed	Whole dried seed	Faintly liquorice
	Caraway	Whole dried seed	Slightly sharp and peppery
	Cardamom	Usually bought as dried seed capsules, still containing very hard black seed. Remove seeds and crush before using	Slightly lemony and bitter-sweet
	Chillis	Whole dried pod; ground, as chilli pepper or cayenne pepper. Use very sparingly. Also sold mixed with other spices as chilli seasoning—less hot	The hottest of all peppery spices. Can be very fiery indeed
	Cinnamon and Cassia	Cinnamon—dried inner bark, in curled sticks, or ground. When infusing sticks in cooked dishes, remove before serving. Cassia buds, dried leaves and ground powder available	Gentle, sweet, musky flavour
	Cloves	Dried unopened bud. Whole or ground. To impart flavour in savoury dish, stud cloves into an onion, then they are easy to remove	Sweet and tangy

SPICE CHART

MEAT AND FISH DISHES	VEGETARIAN	FRUIT AND DESSERTS	BAKING
Whole, in stock for poaching meat and fish, pot roasts, marinades. Ground, in beef and game casseroles	Whole, in pickles, chutneys, when cooking beetroot (beets). Crushed in sauerkraut, and cabbage dishes. Ground, with cream cheese, cream soups	Whole, in fruit pickles and stewed apples, pears, rhubarb. Ground, in mincemeat and in rose-flavoured confections	Ground, in cakes, especially fruit cakes, buns and biscuits (cookies), and in baked sponge puddings
Rich meat dishes, such as beef stews, casserole of hare or pigeon, or with sausages	Sparingly in cheese dishes, with braised red cabbage, carrots, parsnips. In salad dressings	With stewed apples, apple and other fruit pies	The seeds are used in cakes, especially coffee cake, bread, biscuits (cookies)
In Hungarian goulash, rich game, meat and offal dishes, to offset fattiness. Good with pork and goose	As a flavouring in some manufactured cheeses. Used in pickling vegetables and in vegetable soups and to garnish potato, cabbage, swede. In sauerkraut and coleslaw salad. In dumplings and cheese dips	With apple dishes of all kinds. Traditional with baked apples	Caraway cake (said to aid digestion) is traditional farm fare. Seeds used in other cakes, bread, biscuits (cookies), as ingredient or garnish. Particularly in rye bread. Eaten on bread and butter
In curry powder, and added to curries. Good with beef, pork and goose. Used to flavour pickled herrings	Used in pickling vegetables. In Indian rice dishes, with sauerkraut, in vegetable soups	With stewed fruit, in rice pudding and moulds, infused to make custards. Add lightly crushed seeds to black coffee and mulled wine and ale	Crushed seeds in Danish pastries, and in cakes and buns, especially gingerbread and coffee cakes
Whole, in classic, highly-spiced Mexican dishes, curries and some Chinese cooking. Ground, in beef casseroles, sprinkled on meat for grilling (broiling) or barbecue. With seafood such as prawn (shrimp) cocktail or grilled (broiled) lobster	Whole, in pickling spices, for onions, red cabbage. Infused in oil and vinegar for salad dressings and in barbecue sauces. Ground, as a garnish for egg and cheese dishes, especially mousses, soufflés and some cream soups. In tomato and pasta dishes		
Cinnamon sticks in pickling. Ground, sprinkled on meat for grilling (broiling) and in casseroles. Cassia leaves crumbled into curries. Whole cassia buds used in curries. Ground cassia sometimes sold as cinnamon	Cinnamon sticks in pickling. Ground, in vegetable curries and as garnish to mashed potatoes and some cream soups	Cinnamon sticks with stewed fruit such as apples, pears, rhubarb. And in mulled wine and ale. Ground, with fruit salad, bananas, peaches, and stirred into whipped cream. Sprinkled on milk puddings— rice and junket. In steamed puddings, especially Christmas pudding	Ground cinnamon in cakes, especially fruit cake, buns, biscuits (cookies). Mixed with sugar and sprinkled on hot, buttered toast or buns
Whole, used in brine to souse herrings, studded in ham and gammon. In stock, to pickle meat such as pork or beef, and in beef stew and *coq au vin*	Whole, in pickling vegetables such as onions, beetroot (beets). Infused in milk to make savoury sauces. Ground, as garnish to mashed vegetables and cream soups	Whole, in pickled and bottled fruits, with apples and pears, especially in pies and puddings. In mulled wine and ale and fruit punch. Ground, to garnish milk puddings. In mincemeat	Whole, as decoration for children's fancy confections, such as eyes on sugar mice, buttons of gingerbread men. Ground in cakes, especially fruit cakes, buns, biscuits (cookies). Often combined with ginger

239

SPICE	PART OF PLANT	FLAVOUR
Coriander (dhania)	Dried seed, whole or ground. Whole seeds are more aromatic if lightly toasted before use. Are usually lightly crushed	Mild, sweet and pungent
Cumin (jeera)	Dried seed, whole or ground. Flavour of whole seeds improved by lightly toasting	Strong and aromatic with lingering flavour
Curry powder	A blend of ground spices, can be turmeric, coriander, ginger, cloves, cinnamon, mustard, cardamom, fenugreek, cayenne, cumin, salt and others, according to region	The taste varies from mild to hot according to proportion of different spices
Fenugreek (methi)	Whole dried seed. The flavour is improved by lightly toasting	Slightly bitter and caramel-like
Garam masala	A spice blend (not the same as curry powder) which could contain any of the following: cumin, black pepper, cloves, cardamom and others, ground together. They are added towards the end of cooking	Blends vary but are never hot
Ginger	Fresh or dried rhizome, 'root' ginger, can be bought in pieces; ground ginger is made from the dried rhizome	Hot, rich flavour. Ground ginger less pungent than the root
Juniper	Dried berries. Lightly crush the whole berries before use	Sweet, aromatic and pine-like
Mace	Dried outer shell of nut, whole or ground	An exotic spice with strong nutmeg flavour
Mixed spice	A blend of ground spices, usually cinnamon, cloves, allspice, sometimes with ginger	Flavour depends on the proportions used of each spice
Mustard seed	Whole seeds of black or white mustard; or ground to a yellow powder	Seed has slightly sharp and hot flavour. Strength of powder depends on proportion of the different seeds

MEAT AND FISH DISHES	VEGETARIAN	FRUIT AND DESSERTS	BAKING
Crushed in casseroles, stuffings, curries. Often used in spiced sausages and in meat loaf. Ground, peppery addition to seasoned flour	Crushed seeds in thick vegetable soups such as green pea, lentil, carrot. In chutney, and Greek rice dishes and stuffings. As garnish on egg and cheese dishes. With mushrooms *à la grecque*. Infused in oil and vinegar for salad dressing	Crushed, in apple pie or pudding, fruit crumbles, with quince. Can be added to preserves such as marrow or rhubarb jam	Crushed, in apple cake, cakes, fruit breads
An ingredient of curry powder and chilli seasoning. In marinades for lamb and beef kebabs, and to spice seasoned flour	Whole, with cream cheese in dips, and with cabbage, carrots and savoury rice. Used in pickles and chutneys and sweet and sour sauce	Ground, used sparingly in fruit pies	Whole, in rye bread
Apart from curries, can be used to season flour, and lightly season meat and fish, and garnish rice dishes	Apart from curries, can be used to flavour cottage or cream cheese dips, omelettes and other egg dishes, and as a garnish to cream soups		In sweet and savoury breads and biscuits (cookies), particularly cheese straws
Whole, in stock for poaching fish. Ground, in meat casseroles, curries and sauces	Whole, in pickles and chutneys, and with boiled rice	Seeds are used to flavour imitation maple syrup. In Middle Eastern sweetmeat, *halva*	
Use in meat and fish curries, with other spices in varying proportions according to taste, or in seasoned flour in Western cooking. Also as a garnish	Use with other spices in egg or vegetable curries, in *dhal* (lentils) and in savoury rice, or as a light garnish to cheese and egg dishes (e.g. mousse) and cream soups		
Whole, in pickling. Ground, in curries and meat dishes, especially beef, and sprinkled on grilled (broiled) and baked white fish	Whole, in pickling and chutneys, and in Chinese dishes	The fresh, whole root is used to make ginger beer. Whole, in marrow and rhubarb jams, and in baked and stewed fruit, especially mixed dried fruits. Ground, with melon and to flavour steamed sponge puddings and treacle tart	Ground, in cakes. Specialities, gingerbread, ginger snaps (cookies), and brandy snaps. Usually added to fruit cakes and to spice some sweet pastries
Good with all game, poultry and pork, and in stuffings for them. In pâté, meat loaf, and all meat and fish marinades	Used in vegetable dishes, especially sauerkraut. Whole, in pickles, chutneys, infused in Béchamel sauce	A few berries infused in milk to make puddings and sauces— e.g. chocolate sauce	
Whole, in soups and casseroles, with pork, veal, sausages. Ground, in meat loaf, pâté, with minced beef	In savoury rice, egg and cheese dishes, and with root vegetables	Whole, in fruit preserves and stewed fruit. Ground, in fruit salads and sprinkled on milk puddings	Ground, in light fruit cakes, chocolate cakes, buns and biscuits (cookies)
Rubbed into pickled spiced beef, and used in rich beef and game casseroles and meat loaf	As a garnish for egg and cheese dishes and some cream soups	With stewed apples, pears and rhubarb. In steamed sponge puddings. With fresh melon	In cakes, especially fruit cakes, buns, biscuits (cookies)
Whole seed in pickling meat and fish, especially herring and mackerel, in fish dishes and sauces. In casserole of pork, veal, rabbit and in offal dishes. Mustard powder rubbed into meat and fish before grilling (broiling) or baking. Used to flavour sauce to serve with ham	Whole seed in pickling and chutneys, and in vegetable dishes such as braised celery. With cabbage, broccoli, and in coleslaw. Mustard powder in sauce to serve with cauliflower, and in cheese and egg dishes. With cream cheese in savoury dips		

241

	SPICE	PART OF PLANT	FLAVOUR
	Nutmeg	Dried kernel, whole (to be grated before use), or can be bought ground	Exotic, sweet, musky flavour
	Paprika	Dried ground sweet red peppers	Mild and slightly sweet. Not at all hot
	Pepper, black	Whole, dried peppercorns more pungent if freshly ground in a mill. Can be bought ready-ground	Strong, pungent, spicy
	Pepper, white	Whole dried inner peppercorns best if freshly ground. Can be bought ready-ground	Milder and less 'exotic' than black pepper
	Pickling spice	Can be bought ready-mixed, a selection of dried black and white whole peppercorns, chillis, mustard seed, cloves, allspice, ginger, mace, coriander	The flavour depends on the proportions of the various ingredients. Better to control it by mixing your own
	Poppy seed	Whole dried seed. Lightly toast before grinding. Needs special grinder, or firm rolling with rolling pin	Scant flavour, nutty texture
	Saffron	Whole dried strands, or ground (buy a reputable brand to avoid adulteration). Crush dry threads before infusing in hot liquid	Exotic golden colour, slightly sweet taste
	Sesame	Whole seed, dried or toasted	Sweet, nutty flavour and crunchy texture
	Tamarind	Bought as fibrous black, sticky pulp, broken seed pods. Extract sour flavour by soaking in hot water, then squeezing	Sour, acidy flavour
	Turmeric (haldi)	Ground yellow rhizome, sold as powder. Is slight thickening agent	Bright yellow colour, rather bitter
	Vanilla	Whole, dried pod, or pure bottled extract	Sweet, chocolate-like flavour

MEAT AND FISH DISHES	VEGETARIAN	FRUIT AND DESSERTS	BAKING
Grated into fish cakes, fish sauces, and 'white' chicken dishes. To spice pâté and meat loaf	Grated over broad (lima) beans, potatoes, cabbage, and egg and cheese dishes, cheese sauce, cream soups	Grated on to milk puddings, custard and ice cream, and in stewed fruit such as apples or pears	In fruit cakes, spiced buns and biscuits (cookies)
In Hungarian goulash (beef stew), with pork and chicken. Meat dishes with tomatoes. As a garnish to canapés. With shellfish, especially prawns (shrimp), crab, lobster	As a garnish to potatoes, cauliflower, celery. In sauce to cook potatoes or mixed vegetables. In tomato, egg or cheese dishes, and cream soups. And in Waldorf salad		Used in cheese shortbread, cheese straws and biscuits (cookies)
Whole peppercorns for pickling and in boiling meat and fish, and in marinades. Ground black pepper in all 'dark' meat dishes, some fish dishes, sauces. Crushed on steak *au poivre*	Whole peppercorns for pickling and chutneys. Ground black pepper in almost all vegetable, egg and cheese dishes, salads and salad dressings		
Whole white peppercorns in pickled meat and fish. Ground, in 'white' fish and poultry dishes where dark pepper would affect appearance	Whole white peppercorns in pickles. Ground, in cream soups, white sauces, egg and cheese dishes where paler colour is preferred		
Use to pickle beef and pork and to souse or pickle fish, and in liquor to boil fish or meat, particularly ham	Use to pickle single or mixed vegetables and in chutneys	To pickle fruit and nuts, omit hot spices such as red chillis	
Whole seed used in some curries and in savoury rice	Used whole to give nutty texture to cream cheese dips and spreads; some egg and cheese dishes. Sprinkled on carrots, potatoes, parsnips, and to garnish vegetable soups		Whole seed sprinkled on bread, buns, cakes, sweet and savoury biscuits (cookies). Crushed seed used in some baked goods
A powerful colourant. For colour alone, turmeric is cheaper. Saffron is used in rice dishes, particularly *paella*, and with fish. Is essential in *bouillabaisse*	Saffron transforms rice dishes, in both colour and flavour. Good in cheese and egg dishes and cream of vegetable soups		Ground saffron used in traditional saffron cakes and buns
Toasted, as topping to creamed fish dishes, and chicken	Gives nuttiness to cream cheese dips, and as a garnish to cream soups and some vegetables	Toasted, as topping to fruit crumble and cobbler, and on chocolate sauce to serve with ice cream	Toasted, sprinkled on bread, buns, biscuits (cookies) before baking
Authentic sour taste in meat and fish curries. Stronger than lemon or lime juice	Use in vegetable and egg curries, too		
Used in most curries and in rice-and-fish dishes such as kedgeree (but *not paella*)	Especially used in vegetable curries. Very small pinch adds colour to egg and cheese dishes. Essential in mustard pickles		Used very sparingly to colour cakes and buns. Too much will give a bitter taste
		Infuse whole dry pods in jar of sugar or in milk for sauces, puddings, ice cream, custards. More subtle than flavour of the extract	Vanilla sugar (see previous column) used in all baked goods, fillings, frostings, toppings and baked puddings, especially with chocolate

COOKING WITH SPICES

SOUPS & STARTERS
FISH & SHELLFISH
POULTRY & GAME
MEAT & MAIN COURSES
VEGETABLES & SALADS
ETHNIC DISHES
PUDDINGS & DESSERTS
BREADS & CAKES
PRESERVES

SOUPS & STARTERS

Marinated artichoke hearts

	Metric/UK	US
Cooked or canned and drained artichoke hearts, quartered	6	6
Juice of 2 lemons		
Salt	½ tsp	½ tsp
Black peppercorns, crushed	3	3
White wine vinegar	4 Tbs	¼ cup
Olive oil	75ml/3floz	6 Tbs
Coriander seeds, crushed	2 Tbs	2 Tbs
Chopped parsley	1 Tbs	1 Tbs
Garlic clove, crushed	½	½
Onion, thinly sliced into rings	1	1

Put the artichoke hearts in a bowl and add the lemon juice, salt, peppercorns, vinegar, oil, coriander seeds, parsley and garlic. Fold together gently until the ingredients are well combined. Fold in the onion rings.

Cover and leave to marinate in a cool place for 2 hours, basting occasionally.

Transfer the artichoke hearts and onion rings to a serving dish using a slotted spoon. Sprinkle over about 4 tablespoons of the marinade and discard the remainder. Serve at room temperature or lightly chilled.

6 Servings

Potted salmon

	Metric/UK	US
Fresh salmon	½kg/1lb piece	1lb piece
Salt	1½ tsp	1½ tsp
Black pepper	1½ tsp	1½ tsp
Ground mace	½ tsp	½ tsp
Ground cloves	¼ tsp	¼ tsp
Butter	150g/5oz	10 Tbs
Black peppercorns	4	4
Bay leaves	2	2

Preheat the oven to moderate 180°C (Gas Mark 4, 350°F).

Rub the salmon with half the salt and pepper and the mace and cloves. Put the fish in a baking dish. Cut 25g/1oz (2 tablespoons) of the butter into small pieces and dot them over the fish. Sprinkle over the peppercorns and lay the bay leaves on top. Bake for 30 to 40 minutes or until the fish is cooked.

Remove the fish from the baking dish and allow to cool slightly. Strain the liquid from the dish and reserve.

Skin the fish and remove all bones. Pound the fish with a wooden spoon or using a mortar and pestle, gradually work in 50g/2oz (¼ cup) of the remaining butter and the reserved cooking liquid. Alternatively, purée the fish with the butter and liquid in a blender. Beat in the remaining salt and pepper.

Pack the fish into small pots or ramekins, leaving space at the top. Allow to cool.

Melt the remaining butter. Allow to cool slightly, then pour it over the salmon mixture in the pots. Cover with foil and chill for at least 2 hours before serving.

6 Servings

Chicken liver pâté

	Metric/UK	US
Celery stalk	1	1
Parsley sprigs	3	3
Peppercorns	8	8
Salt		
Chicken livers	½kg/1lb	1lb
Tabasco sauce	½ tsp	½ tsp
Butter or rendered chicken fat	225g/8oz	1 cup
Grated nutmeg	¼ tsp	¼ tsp
Dry mustard	2 tsp	2 tsp
Ground cloves	¼ tsp	¼ tsp
Onion, finely minced	1	1
Garlic clove, minced	1	1
Brandy or dry sherry	2 Tbs	2 Tbs
Stuffed olives, sliced	50g/2oz	¼ cup

Bring a saucepan of water to the boil and add the celery, parsley, peppercorns and salt. Simmer for 10 minutes. Add the chicken livers, cover and simmer gently for 10 minutes.

Drain the livers, then mince (grind) them, or purée in a food mill or blender. Transfer to a bowl and beat in the Tabasco, butter or chicken fat, nutmeg, mustard, cloves, onion, garlic and brandy or sherry. Add salt to taste.

Put the pâté into a serving dish and make a decorative pattern on top with the prongs of a fork. Garnish with the

Mace, the outer covering of nutmeg, is an essential ingredient in potted salmon.

olive slices. Chill for at least 6 hours before serving.

5-8 Servings

Spiced fish

	Metric/UK	US
Flour	75g/3oz	$\frac{3}{4}$ cup
Salt and black pepper		
Cod fillets, skinned and cut into 5cm/2in pieces	1$\frac{1}{2}$kg/3lb	3lb
Oil	4 Tbs	4 Tbs
SAUCE		
Flour	1 Tbs	1 Tbs
Green chilli (chili pepper), seeded and finely chopped	1	1
Hot chilli powder	$\frac{1}{4}$ tsp	$\frac{1}{4}$ tsp
Ground coriander	$\frac{1}{2}$ tsp	$\frac{1}{2}$ tsp
Ground cumin	$\frac{1}{2}$ tsp	$\frac{1}{2}$ tsp
Ground cardamom	$\frac{1}{2}$ tsp	$\frac{1}{2}$ tsp
Ground ginger	$\frac{1}{2}$ tsp	$\frac{1}{2}$ tsp
Ground cloves	$\frac{1}{4}$ tsp	$\frac{1}{4}$ tsp
Turmeric	1 tsp	1 tsp
Garlic cloves, crushed	2	2
Salt and black pepper		
Soft brown sugar	2 Tbs	2 Tbs
White wine vinegar	450ml/15floz	2 cups
Water	450ml/15floz	2 cups
Large onions, sliced	2	2
Bay leaves	2	2
Fennel seeds	$\frac{1}{2}$ tsp	$\frac{1}{2}$ tsp
Black peppercorns	12	12

Mix the flour with salt and pepper and use to coat the fish pieces. Heat the oil in a frying pan. Add the fish pieces, in batches, and fry for 3 to 4 minutes on each side or until well browned and cooked through. Drain on paper towels and place in a deep serving dish.

Mix together the flour, chilli, spices, garlic, salt and pepper to taste and the sugar in a saucepan. Stir in 4 tablespoons of the vinegar to make a smooth paste. Gradually stir in the remaining vinegar and the water. Add the remaining sauce ingredients and bring to the boil, stirring occasionally. Cover and simmer for 30 minutes.

Strain the sauce over the fish and leave to cool. Cover and chill in the refrigerator for at least 24 hours before serving.

8 Servings

Avocados with prawns (shrimp)

	Metric/UK	US
Large avocados	2	2
Lemon juice	1 Tbs	1 Tbs
Mayonnaise	75ml/3floz	6 Tbs
Double (heavy) cream	2 Tbs	2 Tbs
Salt and black pepper		
Cayenne pepper	$\frac{1}{4}$ tsp	$\frac{1}{4}$ tsp
Mild curry powder	2 tsp	2 tsp
Canned pineapple rings, drained and finely chopped	2	2
Shelled prawns (shrimp)	125g/4oz	4 oz

Spiced Fish, a cold dish soused in a piquant sauce, is an appetizing first course.

Cut the avocados in half lengthways and remove the stones (seeds). Rub the cut surfaces with the lemon juice to prevent discolouration. Place the halves in serving dishes.

Mix together the mayonnaise, cream, salt and pepper to taste, the cayenne, curry powder and pineapple. Fold in the prawns (shrimp). Spoon the prawn (shrimp) mixture into the avocado hollows and serve.

4 Servings

Hot spiced grapefruit

	Metric/UK	US
Soft brown sugar	50g/2oz	⅓ cup
Ground allspice or mixed spice	¼ tsp	¼ tsp
Ground cinnamon	¾ tsp	¾ tsp
Butter, softened	1 Tbs	1 Tbs
Dark rum	1 Tbs	1 Tbs
Large grapefruit, halved and flesh loosened	2	2

Preheat the grill (broiler) to fairly hot.

Mix together the sugar, spices, butter and rum, and cream to a smooth paste. Divide the paste between the grapefruit halves, spreading it evenly over the cut surfaces. Arrange the grapefruit halves in the grill (broiler pan, cut sides up. Grill (broil) for 6 to 8 minutes or until the tops are browned and bubbling. Serve hot.

4 Servings

Baked stuffed aubergines (eggplants)

	Metric/UK	US
Medium aubergines (eggplants)	2	2
Salt		
Olive oil	6 Tbs	6 Tbs
Large onion, finely chopped	1	1
Mushrooms, sliced	½kg/1lb	1lb
Cooked pork, minced (ground)	175g/6oz	¾ cup
Sour cream	6 Tbs	6 Tbs
Black pepper		
Ground allspice	½ tsp	½ tsp
Fresh breadcrumbs	25g/1oz	½ cup
Parmesan cheese, grated	25g/1oz	¼ cup
Paprika	½ tsp	½ tsp
Butter, cut into small pieces	1 Tbs	1 Tbs

Cut the aubergines (eggplants) in half lengthways and sprinkle the cut sur-

Refreshing as a first course, Hot Spiced Grapefruit can also be served as an unusual breakfast dish.

faces with salt. Set aside for 30 minutes.

Squeeze the aubergines (eggplants) to remove as much liquid as possible, then rinse and pat dry with paper towels.

Heat 4 tablespoons of the oil in a frying pan. Put in the aubergine (eggplant) halves, cut sides down, and cook for 7 to 8 minutes or until lightly browned. Turn over and cook the other sides for 8 to 10 minutes. Remove from the pan and allow to cool slightly.

Preheat the oven to fairly hot 190°C (Gas Mark 5, 375°F).

Heat the remaining oil in the pan. Add the onion and fry until softened. Add the mushrooms and fry for 2 minutes. Stir in the pork, sour cream, salt and pepper to taste and the allspice and cook for a further 3 minutes. Remove from the heat.

Scoop out the aubergine (eggplant) flesh, leaving the skins intact. Finely chop the flesh and add it to the pork mixture. Stir well, then stuff the aubergine (eggplant) skins with the pork mixture. Arrange the stuffed aubergines (eggplants) in a greased baking dish.

Mix together the breadcrumbs, cheese and paprika and sprinkle over the aubergines (eggplants). Dot the tops with the pieces of butter. Bake for 10 to 15 minutes or until the topping is golden brown. Serve hot.

4 Servings

Roquefort mousse

	Metric/UK	US
Roquefort cheese, crumbled	½kg/1lb	1lb
Single (light) cream	250ml/8floz	1 cup
Ground cinnamon	½ tsp	½ tsp
Double (heavy) cream, whipped until thick	350ml/12floz	1½ cups
Unflavoured gelatine dissolved in 4 Tbs hot water	15g/½oz	2 envelopes
Mustard and cress (garden cress) to garnish		

Rub the cheese through a strainer with the back of a wooden spoon into a heatproof bowl. Beat in the single (light) cream and cinnamon and place the bowl over a pan of hot water. Stir the mixture until it is smooth and creamy, then remove from the heat. Allow to cool, then chill for 1 hour.

Fold the double (heavy) cream and gelatine into the cheese mixture. Divide between eight dishes or moulds and chill for 1 hour or until the mousse is firm.

Serve cold garnished with the cress.

8 Servings

Turkish lamb and lemon soup

	Metric/UK	US
Lean lamb, cut into cubes	½kg/1lb	1lb
Flour	50g/2oz	½ cup
Olive oil	3 Tbs	3 Tbs
Water	1¼l/2 pints	5 cups
Onions, quartered	2	2
Carrots, quartered	2	2
Salt and black pepper		
Cayenne pepper	½ tsp	½ tsp
Egg yolks	3	3
Lemon juice	2 Tbs	2 Tbs
Butter, melted	50g/2oz	4 Tbs
Paprika	2 tsp	2 tsp
Ground cinnamon	½ tsp	½ tsp
Chopped mint	2 Tbs	2 Tbs

Coat the lamb cubes with the flour. Heat the oil in a saucepan. Add the lamb cubes and brown on all sides. Stir in the water and bring to the boil. Skim any scum from the surface, then add the onions, carrots, salt and pepper to taste and the cayenne. Cover and simmer for 1½ to 2 hours or until the meat is tender.

Beat the egg yolks and lemon juice together. Beat in a few spoonfuls of the hot soup, then add this egg yolk mixture to the pan. Heat very gently, stirring. Do not allow the soup to boil or it will curdle. Pour the soup into a warmed tureen.

Mix together the melted butter, paprika and cinnamon. Pour this over the soup and sprinkle with the mint. Serve hot.

6 Servings

Iced carrot and orange soup

	Metric/UK	US
Butter	25g/1oz	2 Tbs
Large onion, thinly sliced	1	1
Flour	3 Tbs	3 Tbs
Chicken stock	900ml/1½ pints	3¾ cups
Orange juice	600ml/1 pint	2½ cups
Chopped chives	2 Tbs	2 Tbs
Salt and pepper		
Grated nutmeg	¼ tsp	¼ tsp
Ground allspice	¼ tsp	¼ tsp
Carrots, cut into 2.5cm/1in pieces	½kg/1lb	1lb

Melt the butter in a saucepan. Add the

onion and fry until softened. Stir in the flour and cook, stirring, for 1 minute. Gradually stir in the stock and orange juice, then add the remaining ingredients with salt and pepper to taste and stir well.

Bring to the boil, stirring. Cover and simmer for 1 hour, stirring occasionally.

Purée the soup in a blender or with a food mill or strainer. Allow to cool, then chill for at least 2 hours before serving.

6 Servings

Mulligatawny soup

	Metric/UK	US
Water	3l/5 pints	6 pints
Salt		
Chicken, cut into 6 pieces and giblets removed (excluding liver)	1 × 1½kg/3lb	1 × 3lb
Root ginger, peeled and bruised	5cm/2in piece	2in piece
Bay leaves	2	2
Creamed coconut	4cm/1½in slice	1½in slice
Butter	40g/1½oz	3 Tbs
Onions, finely chopped	2	2
Garlic cloves, crushed	2	2
Hot chilli powder	½ tsp	½ tsp
Ground coriander	1 Tbs	1 Tbs
Ground cumin	1 tsp	1 tsp
Black pepper		
Ground almonds	25g/1oz	¼ cup
Gram or chick-pea flour	1½ Tbs	1½ Tbs

Put the water, 1 teaspoon salt, the chicken pieces and giblets, ginger and bay leaves in a saucepan and bring to the boil. Cover and simmer for 45 minutes or until the chicken is cooked. Remove the chicken pieces from the pan.

Continue to simmer the stock, uncovered, until it is reduced to about 1¼l/3 pints (4 pints). Strain the stock, discarding all the giblets and flavourings. Add the coconut to the stock and mix well.

Skin the chicken pieces and remove the meat from the bones. Cut the meat into dice.

Melt the butter in the cleaned-out saucepan. Add the onions and garlic and fry until the onions are golden. Stir in the chilli powder, coriander, cumin and salt and pepper to taste and fry for 5 minutes. Add the ground almonds and flour and cook, stirring, for 1 minute. Gradually stir in the stock and coconut mixture and bring

to the boil, stirring. Add the diced chicken. Cook, stirring occasionally, for 15 minutes longer.

Serve hot.

6 servings

Pumpkin soup

	Metric/UK	US
Butter	25g/1oz	2 Tbs
Onions, chopped	2	2
Flour	2 Tbs	2 Tbs
Chicken stock	1¼l/2 pints	5 cups
Pumpkin flesh, chopped	½kg/1lb	1lb
Grated nutmeg	¼ tsp	¼ tsp
Ground cloves	1/8 tsp	1/8 tsp
Salt and black pepper		
Tomatoes, skinned, seeded and chopped	225g/8oz	8oz
Milk	300ml/10floz	1¼ cups
Sour cream (optional)	4 Tbs	4 Tbs

Melt the butter in a saucepan. Add the onions and fry until softened. Stir in the flour and cook, stirring, for 1 minute. Gradually stir in the stock and bring to the boil, stirring. Add the pumpkin, spices, salt and pepper to taste, tomatoes and milk and stir well. Cover and simmer for 30 minutes.

Purée the soup in a blender or using a food mill or strainer and return to the saucepan. Heat through gently until the soup is piping hot. Serve hot, with croûtons, or allow to cool and serve chilled, topped with a spoonful of sour cream.

4-6 Servings

Chilled fruit soup

	Metric/UK	US
Mixed fruit, peeled and chopped	1kg/2lb	2lb
Sugar	50g/2oz	¼ cup
Salt	pinch	pinch
Clove	1	1
Cinnamon stick	1 × 5cm/2in	1 × 2in
Juice and grated rind of 1 lemon		
Water	1¼l/2 pints	5 cups

Put all the ingredients in a large saucepan and bring to the boil, stirring occasionally. Cover and simmer for 10 to 15 minutes or until the fruit is tender.

Discard the cinnamon stick and clove and purée the soup in a blender or with a food mill or strainer. Chill for at least 1 hour before serving.

4 Servings

Lentil and fish chowder

	Metric/UK	US
Lentils, soaked overnight and drained	225g/8oz	1 cup
Water	900ml/ 1½ pints	3¾ cups
Salt	2 tsp	2 tsp
Lemon sole fillets	6	6
Turmeric	1 tsp	1 tsp
Butter	50g/2oz	4 Tbs
Large onions, finely chopped	2	2
Garlic clove, crushed	1	1
Ground ginger	½ tsp	½ tsp
Mild chilli powder	½ tsp	½ tsp
Ground coriander	1 tsp	1 tsp
Black pepper		
Large green pepper, pith and seeds removed and cut into rings	1	1
Celery stalks, cut into 5cm/2in pieces	2	2
Creamed coconut dissolved in 500ml/ 16floz (1 pint) water	5cm/2in slice	2in slice

Put the lentils in a saucepan with the water and 1 teaspoon salt. Bring to the boil, then cover and simmer for 40 minutes or until all the water has been absorbed. Purée the lentil mixture in a blender.

Rub the sole fillets with the turmeric and remaining salt. Melt the butter in another saucepan. Add the fillets, in batches, and fry for about 2 minutes on each side. Remove from the pan and cut the fillets into 5cm/ 2in pieces.

Add the onions, garlic and ginger to the pan and fry until the onions are softened. Stir in the chilli powder, coriander and pepper to taste and cook for a further 4 minutes. Add the green pepper, and celery, then gradually stir in the coconut mixture. Add the lentil purée in spoonfuls, stirring well. Bring to the boil, then add the fish pieces. Cover and simmer for 10 to 15 minutes.

Serve hot.

6-8 Servings

Iced Fruit Soup is just the thing to serve on hot, summer days either as a starter or as a dessert.

FISH & SHELLFISH

Herrings with mustard sauce

	Metric/UK	US
Herrings, filleted and halved	8	8
Lemon juice	1 Tbs	1 Tbs
Eggs, lightly beaten	2	2
Dry mustard	2 tsp	2 tsp
Salt and black pepper		
Flour	50g/2oz	½ cup
Butter	75g/3oz	6 Tbs
Lemon wedges	6	6
MUSTARD SAUCE		
Butter	125g/4oz	8 Tbs
Salt	½ tsp	½ tsp
White pepper	¼ tsp	¼ tsp
Dry mustard	1 tsp	1 tsp

Sprinkle the herring fillets with the lemon juice and set aside.

Mix together the eggs, mustard and salt and pepper to taste. Dip the fillets in the egg mixture, then coat with the flour.

Melt the butter in a frying pan. Add the fillets and fry for 2 to 3 minutes on each side or until cooked through.

Meanwhile, melt the butter for the sauce in a saucepan. Add the salt, pepper and mustard and stir well.

Arrange the herring fillets on a warmed serving platter and pour over the mustard sauce. Garnish with the lemon wedges and serve hot.

8 Servings

Cold seafood salad

	Metric/UK	US
RICE		
Long-grain rice	350g/12oz	2 cups
Canned sweetcorn kernels, drained	300g/10oz	10oz
Cooked peas	225g/8oz	1 cup
SAUCE		
Mayonnaise	300ml/10floz	1¼ cups
Cayenne pepper	⅛ tsp	⅛ tsp
Tomato purée (paste)	1 Tbs	1 Tbs
Hot chilli powder	¼ tsp	¼ tsp
Salt and white pepper		
SEAFOOD		
Cooked lobster meat, diced	½kg/1lb	1lb
Shelled prawns (shrimp)	225g/8oz	8oz
Cooked white crabmeat, flaked	225g/8oz	8oz
Large unshelled prawns (shrimp), to garnish	6	6

Cook the rice in boiling salted water until it is tender. Drain, if necessary, and allow to cool. Stir in the corn and peas and pile the mixture on a serving platter.

Mix the mayonnaise with the cayenne, tomato purée (paste), chilli powder and salt and pepper to taste. Chill well.

Arrange the seafood on top of the rice and pour over the sauce. Garnish with the unshelled prawns (shrimp) and serve.

6 Servings

Polynesian mullet

	Metric/UK	US
Grey mullet, filleted	1 × 2kg/4lb	1 × 4lb
Salt and black pepper		
Root ginger, peeled and finely chopped	1cm/½in piece	½in piece
Garam masala	1 tsp	1 tsp
Butter	50g/2oz	4 Tbs
Onion, finely chopped	1	1
Medium pineapple, peeled, cored and thinly sliced	1	1
Flaked almonds	50g/2oz	½ cup
Bananas, cut into 4 slices lengthways	4	4
Sesame seeds, blanched	50g/2oz	¼ cup
Creamed coconut dissolved in 250ml/ 8floz (1 cup) water	5cm/2in slice	2in slice

Preheat the oven to moderate 180°C (Gas Mark 4, 350°F).

Rub the mullet fillets with salt and pepper, the ginger and garam masala.

Melt the butter in a frying pan. Add the onion and fry until softened. Add the fillets and fry for 5 minutes on each side. Remove from the heat.

Arrange half the pineapple slices in a greased baking dish. Place the fillets on top, skin sides down. Cover the fish with the onion, remaining pineapple, almonds, banana slices and sesame seeds. Pour over the dissolved coconut mixture.

Cover the dish and bake for 20 minutes. Uncover and bake for a further 15 minutes or until the fish is cooked through.

Serve hot.

4-6 Servings

Snapper with tomato chilli sauce

	Metric/UK	US
Flour	50g/2oz	½ cup
Salt and black pepper		
Mild chilli powder	1 tsp	1 tsp
Red snapper fillets	1kg/2lb	2lb
Olive or peanut oil	75ml/3floz	6 Tbs
Onion, finely chopped	1	1
Garlic cloves, crushed	2	2
Canned pimientos, drained and finely chopped	125g/4oz	4oz
Red chilli (chili pepper), finely chopped	1	1
Canned tomatoes	425g/14oz	14oz
Pimiento-stuffed olives, chopped	50g/2oz	⅔ cup
Ground coriander	1 tsp	1 tsp
Hard-boiled egg yolks, sieved (strained)	2	2

Preheat the oven to moderate 180°C (Gas Mark 4, 350°F).

Mix the flour with salt and pepper and the chilli powder and use to coat the fillets. Heat 4 tablespoons of the oil in a frying pan. Add the fillets, and fry until golden on both sides.

Add the remaining oil to the pan. When it is hot, add the onion, garlic, pimientos and chilli and fry until the onion is softened. Stir in the tomatoes, olives, coriander and salt and pepper to taste. Bring to the boil, then simmer for 5 minutes.

Arrange the fillets in a baking dish and pour over the tomato chilli sauce. Bake for 10 to 15 minutes or until the fish is cooked through. Sprinkle over the egg yolks and serve hot, in the dish.

4-6 Servings

Snapper with Tomato Chilli Sauce is a spicy dish from Mexico.

Shrimp baked with lettuce

	Metric/UK	US
Double (heavy) cream	250ml/8floz	1 cup
Prepared French mustard	2 tsp	2 tsp
Worcestershire sauce	1 tsp	1 tsp
Cayenne pepper	⅛ tsp	⅛ tsp
Grated nutmeg	¼ tsp	¼ tsp
Salt and black pepper		
Tabasco sauce	⅛ tsp	⅛ tsp
Cornflour (cornstarch) dissolved in 1 Tbs cream	1 tsp	1 tsp
Small lettuces, shredded	2	2
Shelled shrimp	225g/8oz	8oz
Tomatoes, skinned, seeded and chopped	4	4
Lemon juice	2 tsp	2 tsp
Parmesan cheese, grated	50g/2oz	½ cup

Preheat the oven to fairly hot 190°C (Gas Mark 5, 375°F).

Put the cream, mustard, Worcestershire sauce, cayenne, nutmeg, salt and pepper to taste, Tabasco and dissolved cornflour (cornstarch) in a saucepan and heat gently, stirring, until the mixture thickens. Remove from the heat and fold in the shredded lettuces.

Spread half the lettuce mixture on the bottom of a greased baking dish (or use four individual ovenproof dishes). Make a layer of the shrimp on top and cover with the tomatoes. Spread over the remaining lettuce mixture. Sprinkle with the lemon juice and cheese.

Bake for 35 to 40 minutes or until the top is lightly browned. Serve hot.

4 Servings

Haddock morsels

	Metric/UK	US
Flour	75g/3oz	¾ cup
Salt	1 tsp	1 tsp
Dry mustard	½ tsp	½ tsp
Ground ginger	½ tsp	½ tsp
Egg, separated	1	1
Egg yolk	1	1
Oil	1 Tbs	1 Tbs
Milk	225ml/7floz	Scant 1 cup
Sufficient oil for deep-frying		
Smoked haddock fillets, cut into small pieces	700g/1½lb	1½lb

Sift the flour, salt, mustard and ginger into a mixing bowl. Add the egg yolks,

A subtle combination of shrimps, cream, lettuce and spices, Shrimp Baked with Lettuce is delicious either on its own or as an accompaniment to roast main courses.

1 tablespoon oil and 4 tablespoons of the milk. Beat well, gradually beating in the remaining milk to form a smooth batter. Beat the egg white until stiff and fold into the batter.

Heat the oil in a deep-frying pan (deep fat fryer) until it is 185°C/360°F, or until a small cube of stale bread dropped into the oil turns golden in 50 seconds.

Coat the haddock pieces in the batter, then fry them, a few at a time, in the hot oil until they are deep golden brown. Drain on paper towels and serve hot with a piquant sauce.

4 Servings

Salmon kedgeree

	Metric/UK	US
Canned salmon, drained and flaked	700g/1½lb	1½lb
Béchamel or white sauce	450ml/15floz	2 cups
Grated nutmeg	¾ tsp	¾ tsp
Butter	50g/2oz	4 Tbs
Small onion, finely chopped	1	1
Cooked rice	300g/10oz	4 cups
Hard-boiled eggs, finely chopped	2	2
Salt and black pepper		
Curry powder	2 tsp	2 tsp

Mix together the salmon, sauce and nutmeg in a saucepan and heat through gently, stirring occasionally.

Meanwhile, melt the butter in another pan. Add the onion and fry until softened. Stir in the rice and half the chopped eggs, then stir in the salmon mixture, salt and pepper to taste and the curry powder. When the mixture is very hot, pile it on a warmed serving platter and sprinkle over the remaining egg. Serve hot.

4 Servings

Soused mackerel

	Metric/UK	US
Dry white wine	1l/1¾ pints	4½ cups
Carrots, thinly sliced	2	2
Onions, thinly sliced	2	2
Mackerel, filleted and rolled with the skins outside	8	8
Dried marjoram	2 tsp	2 tsp
Cloves	2	2
Bay leaves	4	4
Black peppercorns	1 tsp	1 tsp
Allspice berries	1 tsp	1 tsp
Salt	1 tsp	1 tsp
Lemon, sliced	1	1

Preheat the oven to cool 150°C (Gas Mark 2, 300°F).

Put the wine, carrots and onions in a saucepan and bring to the boil. Simmer for 10 minutes.

Put the fish rolls in a baking dish. Strain over the wine and sprinkle with the marjoram, cloves, bay leaves, peppercorns, allspice berries and salt. Arrange the lemon slices around the edge of the dish.

Bake for 1½ to 2 hours or until the fish is thoroughly cooked. Allow to cool completely and serve at room temperature.

8 Servings

Carp in paprika sauce

	Metric/UK	US
Carp, cut into 6 serving pieces	1 × 1½kg/3lb	1 × 3lb
Salt		
Butter	40g/1½oz	3 Tbs
Onions, finely chopped	2	2
Green peppers, pith and seeds removed and chopped	3	3
Tomatoes, skinned and chopped	8	8
Paprika	1 Tbs	1 Tbs
Oil	3 Tbs	3 Tbs

Sprinkle the carp pieces with salt and set aside.

Preheat the oven to moderate 180°C (Gas Mark 4, 350°F).

Melt the butter in a saucepan. Add the onions and fry until softened. Stir in the green peppers, tomatoes, paprika and salt to taste and cook for 20 to 25 minutes or until the sauce is thick.

Meanwhile, heat the oil in a frying pan. Add the carp pieces and brown on all sides. Transfer the carp pieces to a baking dish and pour over the paprika sauce. Bake for 30 to 40 minutes or until the fish is cooked through. Serve hot, in the dish.

4 Servings

Paprika is the ingredient which adds pungency to this recipe for Carp in Paprika Sauce.

POULTRY & GAME

West African chicken and peanut butter stew

	Metric/UK	US
Peanut oil	2 Tbs	2 Tbs
Onion, chopped	1	1
Garlic clove, crushed	1	1
Green pepper, pith and seeds removed and chopped	1	1
Chicken, cut into serving pieces	1 × 2kg/4lb	1 × 4lb
Peanut butter	225g/8oz	1 cup
Chicken stock	600ml/1 pint	2½ cups
Salt and black pepper		
Turmeric	1 tsp	1 tsp
Ground coriander	1 Tbs	1 Tbs
Ground cumin	1 tsp	1 tsp
Hot chilli powder	½ tsp	½ tsp
Tomatoes, skinned and chopped	2	2
Chopped parsley	1 Tbs	1 Tbs

Heat the oil in a saucepan. Add the onion, garlic and green pepper and fry until the onion is softened. Add the chicken pieces and brown on all sides. Mix together the peanut butter, stock, salt and pepper to taste, the turmeric, coriander, cumin and chilli powder and add to the pan. Stir well, then stir in the tomatoes. Bring to the boil. Cover and simmer for 30 minutes.

Uncover and simmer for a further 15 minutes or until the chicken is cooked through. Serve hot, sprinkled with the parsley.

4 Servings

Venezuelan chicken

	Metric/UK	US
Chicken pieces, skinned	8	8
Butter	50g/2oz	4 Tbs
Green beans	175g/6oz	1 cup
Canned sweetcorn kernels, drained	225g/8oz	8oz
MARINADE		
Orange juice	175ml/6floz	¾ cup
Grapefruit juice	4 Tbs	¼ cup
Grated rind of 1 large orange		
Garlic cloves, crushed	2	2
Shallots, chopped	2	2
Cumin seeds, crushed	½ tsp	½ tsp
Ground allspice	¼ tsp	¼ tsp
Ground mace	¼ tsp	¼ tsp
Salt and black pepper		
Mild chilli powder	¼ tsp	¼ tsp

Put all the ingredients for the marinade in a shallow dish and mix well. Add the chicken pieces and turn over to coat. Leave to marinate for 8 hours or overnight, turning occasionally.

Preheat the oven to moderate 180°C (Gas Mark 4, 350°F).

Remove the chicken pieces from the marinade and pat them dry with paper towels. Reserve the marinade.

Melt the butter in a flameproof casserole. Add the chicken pieces and brown on all sides. Add the reserved marinade, green beans and corn and stir gently to mix. Bring to the boil.

Cover the casserole and transfer it to the oven. Bake for 1 hour or until the chicken is cooked through. Serve hot, in the casserole.

4 Servings

Greek chicken in tomato and cinnamon sauce

	Metric/UK	US
Chicken pieces, skinned	8	8
Salt and black pepper		
Butter	50g/2oz	4 Tbs
Olive oil	2 Tbs	2 Tbs
Small onion, finely chopped	1	1
Garlic clove, crushed	1	1
Prepared mustard	1 tsp	1 tsp
Tomato purée (paste)	2 Tbs	2 Tbs
Canned tomatoes, chopped	425g/14oz	14oz
Chicken stock	4 Tbs	¼ cup
Juice of ½ lemon		
Ground cinnamon	1 tsp	1 tsp
Dried marjoram	½ tsp	½ tsp

Rub the chicken pieces with salt and pepper. Melt the butter with the oil in a flameproof casserole. Add the chicken pieces and brown them on all sides. Remove them from the pot.

Add the onion and garlic to the pot and fry until golden. Stir in the mustard, tomato purée (paste), tomatoes, stock, lemon juice, cinnamon and marjoram. Bring to the boil and simmer for 10 minutes.

Return the chicken pieces to the casserole, cover and simmer for 40 minutes or until tender.

Serve hot, with boiled noodles.

4 Servings

Hawaiian chicken

	Metric/UK	US
Butter	25g/1oz	2 Tbs
Oil	1 Tbs	1 Tbs
Chicken pieces, skinned	8	8
Medium onions, sliced into rings	2	2
Flour	2 Tbs	2 Tbs
Chicken stock	450ml/15floz	2 cups
Green peppers, pith and seeds removed and chopped	2	2
Large red pepper, pith and seeds removed and chopped	1	1
Canned pineapple chunks, drained	425g/14oz	14oz
Salt and black pepper		
Caraway seeds	1 Tbs	1 Tbs
Double (heavy) cream	150ml/5floz	$\frac{2}{3}$ cup
RICE		
Long-grain rice	350g/12oz	2 cups
Butter	40g/1½oz	3 Tbs
Lean cooked ham, diced	4 slices	4 slices
Canned sweetcorn kernels, drained	425g/14oz	14oz
Cayenne pepper	$\frac{1}{4}$ tsp	$\frac{1}{4}$ tsp
Grated nutmeg	$\frac{1}{8}$ tsp	$\frac{1}{8}$ tsp

Melt the butter with the oil in a flame-proof casserole. Add the chicken pieces and brown them on all sides.

Remove them from the pot. Add the onions to the pot and fry until softened. Stir in the flour and cook, stirring, for 1 minute. Gradually stir in the stock.

Return the chicken pieces to the casserole with the peppers, pineapple chunks, salt and pepper to taste and the caraway seeds. Stir well and bring to the boil. Cover and simmer for 40 minutes or until the chicken pieces are tender.

Meanwhile, prepare the rice. Cook the rice in plenty of boiling salted water until it is tender.

Melt the butter in a saucepan. Add the ham, corn, cayenne and nutmeg and cook gently for 5 minutes, stirring occasionally. Stir in the rice, mixing thoroughly, and continue to cook until the rice is hot.

Spread the rice on a warmed serving platter. Arrange the chicken pieces on top and keep hot.

Stir the cream into the cooking liquid in the casserole and heat through gently. Pour this sauce over the chicken and rice and serve hot.

4 Servings

Hawaiian Chicken is a filling main course made from a combination of pineapple, chicken, peppers and rice.

Spiced honey chicken

	Metric/UK	US
Butter	50g/2oz	4 Tbs
Clear honey	125ml/4floz	½ cup
Prepared German mustard	4 Tbs	4 Tbs
Salt	1 tsp	1 tsp
Mild curry powder	1 tsp	1 tsp
Chicken pieces, skinned	8	8

Preheat the oven to moderate 180°C (Gas Mark 4, 350°F).

Melt the butter in a saucepan. Remove from the heat and stir in the honey, mustard, salt and curry powder. Mix well.

Arrange the chicken pieces in one layer in a roasting pan and pour over the honey mixture. Turn the chicken pieces so they are coated on all sides.

Bake for 1 hour, turning the chicken pieces at least once during that time. Serve hot.

4 Servings

Danish Christmas goose

	Metric/UK	US
Goose	1 × 3½–4kg/ 8–9lb	1 × 8– 9lb
Lemon	½	½
Salt and black pepper		
Cooking apples, peeled, cored and chopped	4	4
Prunes, stoned (pitted)	350g/12oz	2 cups
Dry breadcrumbs	50g/2oz	⅔ cup
Ground cardamom	1 tsp	1 tsp
GARNISH		
Prunes, soaked for 3 hours in 300ml/10floz (1¼ cups) port	225g/8oz	1⅓ cups
Sugar	125g/4oz	½ cup
Water	300ml/10floz	1¼ cups
Cooking apples, peeled, cored and halved	4	4
Cornflour (cornstarch) dissolved in 1 Tbs port	1 tsp	1 tsp
Double (heavy) cream	250ml/8floz	1 cup

Preheat the oven to very hot 230°C (Gas Mark 8, 450°F).

Rub the goose, inside and out, with the lemon, then sprinkle all over with salt and pepper. Mix together the apples, prunes, breadcrumbs and cardamom and use to stuff the goose. Secure the opening with trussing needle and string or skewers. Prick the skin of the goose all over.

Place the goose, on its breast, on a rack in a roasting pan. Roast for 15 minutes, then reduce the oven temperature to moderate 180°C (Gas Mark

A fragrant dish made with honey, German mustard and chicken pieces, Spiced Honey Chicken should be served with fresh vegetables.

4, 350°F). Continue roasting for 3 to 3¼ hours, removing the fat from the pan occasionally. After 1½ hours roasting, turn the goose onto the other side.

Just before the goose is ready, prepare the garnish. Put the prunes and port mixture into a saucepan and simmer for 15 minutes.

Meanwhile, in another saucepan dissolve the sugar in the water. Bring to the boil and boil for 3 minutes or until this syrup has thickened slightly. Add the apples to the mixture and poach gently for 10 minutes or until just tender.

Transfer the goose to a warmed serving platter. Arrange the poached apple halves around it, cut sides up, and fill the hollows with the prunes. Stir the cornflour (cornstarch) and cream into the port in which the prunes were soaked and cooked, and simmer until thick and smooth. Pour this sauce into a sauceboat and serve at once, as an accompaniment to the goose.

6-8 Servings

Devilled turkey drumsticks

	Metric/UK	US
French mustard	2 tsp	2 tsp
Prepared English mustard	2 tsp	2 tsp
Tomato ketchup	1 Tbs	1 Tbs
Ground ginger	¼ tsp	¼ tsp
Salt and black pepper		
Cayenne pepper	¼ tsp	¼ tsp
Turkey drumsticks, cooked	4	4
Butter, melted	25g/1oz	2 Tbs

Mix together the mustards, ketchup,

Right Cayenne pepper should be used sparingly as it has a hot flavour. It is suitable for cheese dishes, meat stews, fish and game. Below Serve Devilled Turkey Drumsticks with a refreshing salad to offset the piquant, spicy coating.

ginger, salt and pepper to taste and the cayenne. Score the drumsticks on both sides. Brush them with the melted butter, then coat with the mustard mixture. Leave for 30 minutes.

Preheat the grill (broiler) to moderate.

Place the drumsticks on the grill (broiler) rack and cook for about 10 minutes or until crisp and golden brown. Serve hot.

4 Servings

Normandy duck

	Metric/UK	US
Fresh white breadcrumbs	225g/8oz	4 cups
Strong (hard) cider	300ml/10floz	1¼ cups
Butter	50g/2oz	4 Tbs
Olive oil	2 Tbs	2 Tbs
Cooking apples, peeled, cored and sliced	1kg/2lb	2lb
Celery stalks, finely chopped	3	3
Ground cinnamon	½ tsp	½ tsp
Ground cloves	½ tsp	½ tsp
Salt and black pepper		
Duck	1 × 3kg/6lb	1 × 6lb
Calvados or applejack	75ml/3floz	⅓ cup
Double (heavy) cream	175ml/6floz	¾ cup

Preheat the oven to moderate 180°C (Gas Mark 4, 350°F).

Put the breadcrumbs in a bowl and sprinkle over 4 tablespoons of the cider. Squeeze the breadcrumbs gently so that they become completely moistened.

Melt the butter with the oil in a saucepan. When hot, add the apples and celery. Cook for about 10 minutes or until just tender. Stir in the cinnamon, cloves and salt and pepper to taste. Remove the saucepan from the heat and stir in the breadcrumb mixture.

Spoon the stuffing into the duck and secure the opening with trussing needle and string or skewers. Place the duck on a rack in a roasting pan and prick it all over. Roast for about 15 minutes.

Pour the rest of the cider over the duck and continue roasting for 1¾ hours or until the duck is tender, basting every 15 minutes with the juices in the pan.

Transfer the duck to a warmed serving platter. Remove the string or skewers, set the platter aside and keep hot.

Skim the fat from the surface of the cooking juices and place the pan over heat on top of the stove. Bring to the boil and boil until reduced to half the original quantity. Stir in the Calvados or applejack and cream and heat through gently. Pour this sauce into a sauceboat and serve at once with the duck.

4 Servings

Pigeons with chestnuts

	Metric/UK	US
Butter	25g/1oz	2 Tbs
Pigeons	4	4
Dried chestnuts, soaked overnight and cooked until almost tender	16	16
Garlic clove, crushed	1	1
Grated nutmeg	¼ tsp	¼ tsp
Ground allspice	¼ tsp	¼ tsp
Flour	1 Tbs	1 Tbs
Salt and black pepper		
Dry red wine	250ml/8floz	1 cup
Beef stock	250ml/8floz	1 cup

Preheat the oven to moderate 180°C (Gas Mark 4, 350°F).

Melt the butter in a frying pan. Add the pigeons and brown on all sides. Transfer the pigeons to a casserole. Add the chestnuts to the casserole.

Add the garlic, nutmeg and allspice to the frying pan and cook, stirring, for 2 minutes. Stir in the flour with salt and pepper to taste and cook, stirring, for a further 2 minutes. Gradually stir in the wine and stock and bring to the boil, stirring. Simmer until thickened, then pour over the pigeons in the casserole.

Cover the casserole and bake the pigeons for 1 hour or until they are cooked through. Serve hot.

4 Servings

Nutmeg is a popular spice since it can be used in many sweet and savoury dishes.

MEAT & MAIN COURSES

Spiced steak

	Metric/UK	US
Salt	1 tsp	1 tsp
Black peppercorns, crushed	4	4
Garlic clove, crushed	1	1
Turmeric	1 tsp	1 tsp
Cardamom seeds, crushed	2	2
Cayenne pepper	$\frac{1}{4}$ tsp	$\frac{1}{4}$ tsp
Ground cumin	$\frac{1}{2}$ tsp	$\frac{1}{2}$ tsp
Butter, melted	25g/1oz	2 Tbs
Soy sauce	1 Tbs	1 Tbs
Medium steaks (sirloin, porterhouse, rump, etc)	4	4

Preheat the grill (broiler) to high.

Mix together the salt, peppercorns, garlic, turmeric, cardamom, cayenne, cumin, butter and soy sauce.

Put the steaks on the rack in the grill (broiler) pan and brush with the spice mixture. Grill (broil) for 5 to 6 minutes on each side (for rare steaks), basting frequently with the spice mixture. Serve hot.

4 Servings

Empanadas

	Metric/UK	US
PASTRY		
Flour	175/6oz	$1\frac{1}{2}$ cups
Salt	$\frac{1}{4}$ tsp	$\frac{1}{4}$ tsp
Butter	140g/4$\frac{1}{2}$oz	9 Tbs
Iced water	3–4 Tbs	3–4 Tbs
FILLING		
Oil	2 Tbs	2 Tbs
Onion, finely chopped	1	1
Tomatoes, skinned, seeded and chopped	2	2
Small green pepper, pith and seeds removed and chopped	$\frac{1}{2}$	$\frac{1}{2}$
Minced (ground) beef	225g/8oz	8oz
Raisins	50g/2oz	$\frac{1}{3}$ cup
Salt and black pepper		
Hot chilli powder	$\frac{1}{2}$ tsp	$\frac{1}{2}$ tsp
Ground cumin	$\frac{1}{4}$ tsp	$\frac{1}{4}$ tsp

To make the pastry, sift the flour and salt into a mixing bowl. Add the butter and cut it into small pieces. Mix in enough water just to bind the mixture to a dough, which will be lumpy.

Turn out the dough onto a floured surface and roll it out into an oblong. Fold it in three and turn it so that the open edges face you. Roll it out again into an oblong, then fold and turn as before. Repeat this once again to make three folds and turns in all. Chill for 30 minutes.

Preheat the oven to fairly hot 190°C (Gas Mark 5, 375°F).

To make the filling, heat the oil in a frying pan. Add the onion, tomatoes and green pepper and fry until the onion is softened. Add the beef and cook until browned.

Stir in the raisins, salt and pepper to taste, the chilli powder and cumin and cook for 10 minutes. Remove from the heat and allow the mixture to cool slightly.

Roll out the dough into a large square and cut it into eight 13cm/5in circles. Divide the filling between the dough circles. Fold over the circles to enclose the filling.

Dampen the dough edges and press together to seal.

Arrange the empanadas on a greased baking sheet and bake for 35 minutes or until the pastry is golden brown. Serve hot.

4 Servings

Hungarian goulash

	Metric/UK	US
Butter	40g/1$\frac{1}{2}$oz	3 Tbs
Oil	2 Tbs	2 Tbs
Lean stewing (chuck) steak, cut into cubes	1kg/2lb	2lb
Onions, sliced	$\frac{1}{2}$kg/1lb	1lb
Garlic clove, crushed	1	1
Paprika	2 Tbs	2 Tbs
Salt and black pepper		
Water	150ml/5floz	$\frac{2}{3}$ cup
Bay leaf	1	1
Potatoes, peeled and sliced	$\frac{1}{2}$kg/1lb	1lb
Sour cream	150ml/5floz	$\frac{2}{3}$ cup

Melt the butter with the oil in a saucepan. Add the beef cubes and brown them on all sides. As the cubes brown, remove them from the pan. Add the onions to the pan and fry until golden. Stir in the garlic, paprika, salt and pepper to taste, the water and bay leaf. Return the beef cubes to the pan and

turn to coat them thoroughly with the sauce.

Bring to the boil, then cover and simmer for 1 hour.

Stir in the potatoes and continue simmering the mixture for a further 1 hour.

Remove the bay leaf and spoon the goulash into a warmed serving bowl. Spoon the sour cream on top and serve hot.

4 Servings

German beef and clove casserole

	Metric/UK	US
Lean topside (top round) beef, in one piece	1 × 1½kg/3lb	1 × 3 lb
Garlic clove, crushed	1	1
Dried marjoram	1 tsp	1 tsp
Salt and black pepper		
Salt pork	25g/1oz	1 oz
Cloves	8	8
Butter	50g/2oz	4 Tbs
Oil	4 Tbs	¼ cup
Red wine	250ml/8floz	1 cup
Beef stock	250ml/8floz	1 cup
Onion, chopped	1	1
Carrots, chopped	3	3
Celery stalk, chopped	1	1

Lay the meat on a working surface and pound it flat with a meat mallet. Mix together the garlic, marjoram and a little salt and pepper. Cut the salt pork into thin strips and coat the strips with the garlic mixture. Make incisions in the beef and insert the pork strips and cloves. Roll up the meat and tie with string.

Melt the butter with the oil in a flameproof casserole. Add the meat and brown it on all sides. Add the remaining ingredients with salt and pepper to taste and bring to the boil. Cover and simmer for 1¾ to 2 hours or until the beef is cooked through and tender.

Transfer the beef to a warmed serving platter. Skim the fat from the cooking liquid and strain some of it over the meat. If you like, the remainder may be thickened with cornflour (cornstarch) and served as a gravy with the meat. Serve hot.

6 Servings

A delicious dish of beef spiced with cloves, German Beef and Clove Casserole makes an appetizing lunch or supper.

263

Chilean meat and corn pie

	Metric/UK	US
Oil	3 Tbs	3 Tbs
Onions, thinly sliced	2	2
Red chilli (chili pepper), seeded and finely chopped	1	1
Garlic clove, crushed	1	1
Minced (ground) beef	350g/12oz	¾lb
Minced (ground) pork	350g/12oz	¾lb
Salt	1 tsp	1 tsp
Ground cumin	1 tsp	1 tsp
Hot chilli powder	½ tsp	½ tsp
Flour	1 Tbs	1 Tbs
Black olives, stoned (pitted)	50g/2oz	½ cup
Raisins, soaked in water for 15 minutes and drained	75g/3oz	½ cup
TOPPING		
Oil	2 Tbs	2 Tbs
Onion, finely chopped	1	1
Canned sweetcorn kernels, drained and puréed in a blender or food mill	350g/12oz	12oz
Salt	½ tsp	½ tsp

Preheat the oven to fairly hot 190°C (Gas Mark 5, 375°F).

Heat the oil in a frying pan. Add the onions, chilli and garlic and fry until the onions are softened. Add the beef and pork and fry until browned. Stir in the salt, cumin, chilli powder and flour, then mix in the olives and raisins. Spoon the mixture into a greased 1¼l/2 pint (2½ pint) baking dish.

To make the topping, heat the oil in another frying pan. Add the onion and fry until softened. Stir in the sweetcorn purée and salt and cook, stirring, for 5 minutes.

Spoon the topping over the meat mixture in the dish. Bake for 20 to 25 minutes or until the top is golden brown. Serve hot, in the dish.

4 Servings

Chillis should always be used with great caution in cooking as they have a very hot flavour and over-zealous use can ruin carefully prepared dishes.

Marinated beef fillet (tenderloin)

	Metric/UK	US
Beef fillet (tenderloin roast)	1 × 2kg/4lb	1 × 4lb
Salt and black pepper		
Streaky bacon rashers (slices)	8	8
MARINADE		
Red wine	300ml/10floz	1¼ cups
Tarragon vinegar	125ml/4floz	½ cup
Grated nutmeg	1 tsp	1 tsp
Ground cloves	1 tsp	1 tsp
Bay leaves	2	2
Onion, sliced into rings	1	1
Lemon, thinly sliced	½	½
Large carrot, thinly sliced	1	1
SAUCE		
Oil	2 Tbs	2 Tbs
Onions, finely chopped	2	2
Large carrot, finely chopped	1	1
Brandy	4 Tbs	¼ cup
Beef stock	350ml/12floz	1½ cups
Bouquet garni	1	1
Black peppercorns	6	6
Butter	40g/1½oz	3 Tbs
Flour	2 Tbs	2 Tbs
Salt	¼ tsp	¼ tsp

Rub the beef with salt and pepper and place it in a shallow dish. Mix together all the marinade ingredients and pour over the meat. Turn to coat, then leave to marinate for 24 hours.

Preheat the oven to hot 220°C (Gas Mark 7, 425°F).

Remove the beef from the marinade and dry with paper towels. Put the beef in a roasting pan. Strain the marinade and reserve 125ml/4floz (½ cup).

Lay the rashers (slices) of bacon over the beef and roast for 1 hour for rare meat; increase the time by 30 minutes if you prefer it well done.

Meanwhile, make the sauce. Heat the oil in a saucepan. Add the onions and carrot and fry until the onions are softened. Stir in the reserved marinade and the brandy and bring to the boil. Boil until reduced to one-third. Add the stock and bouquet garni, stir well, cover and simmer for 30 minutes.

Add the peppercorns to the sauce. Mix 1 tablespoon of the butter with the flour to form a paste and add to the sauce in small pieces. Simmer, stirring, until thickened. Add the salt and remaining butter. Stir until the butter melts, then pour the sauce into a sauceboat. Keep hot.

Transfer the beef to a warmed serving platter. Remove the bacon. Carve and serve with the sauce.

8 Servings

Pakistani lamb chops

	Metric/UK	US
Juice of ½ lemon		
Salt	2 tsp	2 tsp
Cayenne pepper	1 tsp	1 tsp
Lamb chops	8	8
Butter	50g/2oz	4 Tbs
Onion, finely chopped	1	1
Garlic cloves, crushed	2	2
Root ginger, peeled and finely chopped	2.5cm/1in piece	1in piece
Ground cumin	1 tsp	1 tsp
Ground fenugreek	½ tsp	½ tsp
Ground pomegranate seed	1 Tbs	1 Tbs
Hot chilli powder	½ tsp	½ tsp
Plain yogurt	150ml/5floz	⅔ cup
Saffron threads soaked in 2 Tbs boiling water	½ tsp	½ tsp
Chopped fresh coriander leaves	1 Tbs	1 Tbs

Mix together the lemon juice, salt and cayenne and rub into the chops. Leave them for 30 minutes.

Melt the butter in a frying pan. Add the chops, in batches, and brown on both sides. Remove the chops from the pan.

Add the onion, garlic and ginger to the pan and fry until the onion is golden. Mix together the cumin, fenugreek, pomegranate seed, chilli powder, yogurt and saffron-coloured water. Add to the pan and stir well. Bring to the boil.

Return the chops to the pan and turn them over in the sauce. Cover and cook gently for 15 minutes. Uncover and continue cooking for 20 to 25 minutes or until the chops are tender and the sauce is thick. Serve hot, sprinkled with the coriander leaves.

4 Servings

Arabian stewed lamb

	Metric/UK	US
Oil	2 Tbs	2 Tbs
Boned lamb leg or shoulder, cut into large cubes	1kg/2lb	2lb
Large onion, sliced	1	1
Garlic clove, crushed	1	1
Turmeric	1 tsp	1 tsp
Cinnamon stick	1 × 5cm/2in	1 × 2in
Salt and pepper		
Flour	1 Tbs	1 Tbs
Beef stock	350ml/12floz	1½ cups
Brown sugar	1 Tbs	1 Tbs
Prunes, stoned (pitted) and soaked in water for 2 hours	16	16

Heat the oil in a large saucepan. Add the lamb cubes, in batches, and fry until evenly browned. As the cubes are browned, remove them from the pan.

Add the onion and garlic to the pan and fry until softened. Stir in the turmeric, cinnamon and salt and pepper to taste and cook, stirring, for 5 minutes. Stir in the flour, cook for 1 minute, then gradually stir in the stock. Bring to the boil, stirring.

Return the lamb cubes to the pan and simmer for 1 hour or until the meat is tender. Ten minutes before the lamb is ready, stir in the sugar and prunes. Remove the cinnamon stick and serve hot.

4 Servings

Lamb pie

	Metric/UK	US
Lemon juice	1 tsp	1 tsp
Dessert apples, peeled, cored and sliced	1kg/2lb	2lb
Best end of neck of lamb (rib chops), boned and cut into slices	1kg/2lb	2lb
Soft brown sugar	2 Tbs	2 Tbs
Prunes, stoned (pitted) and chopped	10	10
Large onions, chopped	2	2
Grated nutmeg	2 tsp	2 tsp
Ground mace	1 tsp	1 tsp
Ground cinnamon	1 tsp	1 tsp
Salt and black pepper		
Beef stock	175ml/6floz	¾ cup
PASTRY		
Flour	225g/8oz	2 cups
Salt	¼ tsp	¼ tsp
Butter, lard or vegetable fat	75g/3oz	6 Tbs
Iced water	4-6 Tbs	4-6 Tbs
Egg, lightly beaten	1	1

To make the pastry, sift the flour and salt into a bowl. Add the fat and cut into small pieces, then rub the fat into the flour until the mixture resembles breadcrumbs. Mix in enough of the water to bind the ingredients to a dough. Chill for 20 minutes.

Preheat the oven to fairly hot 190°C (Gas Mark 5, 375°F).

Meanwhile, mix the lemon juice into the apple slices. Put one-third of the meat on the bottom of a pie dish (casserole) and cover with one-third of the apples. Sprinkle over a little of the sugar and about one-third of the prunes. Top with one-third of the onions. Mix together the spices and salt and pepper to taste and sprinkle about one-third of this mixture over the onions. Continue making layers in this way until all the ingredients are used up. Pour in the stock.

Delicious Syrian Stuffed Lamb Breasts is an exotic main course.

Roll out the dough and use to cover the dish (casserole). Make a large cross in the centre to allow steam to escape and decorate the top with leaves made from the dough trimmings. Brush with the beaten egg.

Bake for 1¼ to 1½ hours or until the pastry is golden brown. Serve hot.

4 Servings

Syrian stuffed lamb breasts

	Metric/UK	US
Large, whole breasts of lamb, boned	2	2
Salt and pepper		
Olive oil	2 Tbs	2 Tbs
Dried apricots, soaked in water overnight	275g/9oz	1½ cups
Sugar	2 Tbs	2 Tbs
STUFFING		
Oil	2 Tbs	2 Tbs
Large onion, finely chopped	1	1
Minced (ground) beef	225g/8oz	8oz
Long-grain rice	1½ Tbs	1½ Tbs
Ground cumin	1 tsp	1 tsp
Turmeric	1 tsp	1 tsp
Water	175ml/6floz	¾ cup
Chopped parsley	3 Tbs	3 Tbs
Salt and black pepper		
Almonds, chopped	50g/2oz	½ cup
Raisins	50g/2oz	⅓ cup

To make the stuffing, heat the oil in a saucepan. Add the onion and fry until golden. Add the beef and fry until browned. Stir in the rice and cook for 4 minutes. Stir in the cumin, turmeric, water, parsley, and salt and pepper to taste and bring to the boil. Cover and simmer for 25 minutes or until the rice is tender and all the water has been absorbed. Remove from the heat and add the almonds and raisins. Allow to cool.

Preheat the oven to moderate 180°C (Gas Mark 4, 350°F).

Lay the lamb breasts flat on a working surface and spread them with the stuffing. Roll up each breast and tie securely with string. Rub the meat with salt and pepper and brush with the oil.

Place the breasts in a roasting pan and roast for 1½ hours or until the meat is well browned and tender.

Meanwhile, put the apricots in a saucepan with the water in which they were soaked and the sugar. Bring to the boil and simmer for 30 minutes or until the apricots are pulpy.

When the lamb is cooked, pour off the liquid from the roasting pan. Increase the oven temperature to very hot 230°C (Gas Mark 8, 450°F). Pour the apricot mixture over the lamb breasts and roast for a further 10 minutes or until glazed and golden brown. Serve hot.

6 Servings

Leg of lamb with coriander and garlic

	Metric/UK	US
Leg of lamb	1 × 3kg/6lb	1 × 6lb
Garlic cloves	6	6
Crushed coriander seeds	1 Tbs	1 Tbs
Salt and black pepper		
Butter, cut into small pieces	25g/1oz	2 Tbs

Preheat the oven to fairly hot 190°C (Gas Mark 5, 375°F).

Make shallow incisions in the lamb and insert the garlic cloves and crushed coriander seeds. Rub the lamb with salt and pepper and place it in a roasting pan. Dot with the butter.

Roast for 20 minutes, then reduce the heat to moderate 180°C (Gas Mark 4, 350°F) and roast for a further 1½ hours, or a little longer if you do not like lamb to be pink. Serve hot.

6-8 Servings

Moussaka

	Metric/UK	US
Medium aubergines (eggplants), sliced	3	3
Salt		
Flour	50g/2oz	½ cup
Oil	175ml/6floz	¾ cup
Butter	25g/1oz	2 Tbs
Shallots, finely chopped	4	4
Lean lamb, minced (ground)	½kg/1lb	1lb
Tomatoes, skinned, seeded and chopped	2	2
Red wine	4 Tbs	¼ cup
Lemon juice	1 tsp	1 tsp
Dried sage	¼ tsp	¼ tsp
Black pepper		
Ground allspice	½ tsp	½ tsp
Fresh white breadcrumbs	50g/2oz	1 cup
SAUCE		
Mizithra or ricotta cheese	175g/6oz	6oz
Egg yolks	3	3
Single (light) cream	350ml/12floz	1½ cups
Salt		
Ground allspice	½ tsp	½ tsp
Kefalotiri or Parmesan cheese, grated	50g/2oz	½ cup

Put the aubergine (eggplant) slices in a colander and sprinkle with salt. Leave for 30 minutes, then rinse and pat dry with paper towels. Coat the aubergine (eggplant) slices with the flour.

Heat 4 tablespoons of the oil in a frying pan. Add the aubergine (eggplant) slices, in batches, and fry until they are golden brown on each side. Drain the slices on paper towels.

Preheat the oven to fairly hot 190°C (Gas Mark 5, 375°F).

Melt the butter in the cleaned-out frying pan. Add the shallots and fry until they are softened. Stir in the lamb and cook, stirring, until it is browned. Add the tomatoes, wine, lemon juice, sage, salt and pepper to taste and the allspice and mix well. Cook for 4 minutes, remove from the heat and stir in the breadcrumbs.

To make the sauce, mash the mizithra or ricotta cheese until it is smooth. Beat in the egg yolks, then gradually stir in the cream. Add salt to taste, the allspice and kefalotiri or Parmesan cheese.

Make alternate layers of aubergine (eggplant) slices and meat mixture in a baking dish. Pour over the sauce. Bake for 45 to 50 minutes or until the top is golden. Serve hot.

4-6 Servings

Hungarian veal escalopes (scallops)

	Metric/UK	US
Veal escalopes (scallops), pounded thin	4	4
Lemon juice	2 Tbs	2 Tbs
Flour	2 Tbs	2 Tbs
Salt and black pepper		
Butter	75g/3oz	6 Tbs
Onions, finely chopped	2	2
Paprika	1 Tbs	1 Tbs
Dry white wine	75ml/3floz	⅓ cup
Sour cream	125ml/4floz	½ cup

Put the escalopes (scallops) in a shallow dish and sprinkle with the lemon juice. Leave to marinate for 30 minutes, turning occasionally. Pat the veal dry with paper towels.

Mix the flour with salt and pepper and use to coat the veal. Melt 50g/2oz (¼ cup) of the butter in a frying pan. Add the escalopes (scallops), two at a time, and brown on both sides. Cook gently until the veal is cooked through. Remove from the pan and arrange on a warmed serving platter. Keep hot.

Add the remaining butter to the pan. When it has melted, add the onions and fry until they are softened. Stir in the paprika, then the wine. Bring to the boil, stirring. Simmer for 3 to 4 minutes.

Remove the pan from the heat and stir in the sour cream. Pour this sauce over the veal and serve hot.

4 Servings

Allspice has great versatility and can be used in a number of sweet and savoury dishes.

Right A dish fit to grace any dinner table, Allspice Veal Roll looks and is mouth-wateringly good.

Allspice veal roll

	Metric/UK	US
Fresh white breadcrumbs	50g/2oz	1 cup
Raisins or sultanas	1 Tbs	1 Tbs
Grated rind of 1 orange		
Finely chopped parsley	1 Tbs	1 Tbs
Dried sage	¼ tsp	¼ tsp
Dried thyme	¼ tsp	¼ tsp
Finely chopped onion	1 Tbs	1 Tbs
Salt and pepper		
Boned breast of veal, trimmed of excess fat	1 × 1kg/2lb	1 × 2lb
Butter	125g/4oz	8 Tbs
Ground allspice	1 Tbs	1 Tbs
Orange juice	3 Tbs	3 Tbs

Preheat the oven to moderate 180°C (Gas Mark 4, 350°F).

Mix together the breadcrumbs, raisins or sultanas, orange rind, parsley, sage, thyme, onion and salt and pepper to taste. Lay the veal flat on a work surface, fat side down, and spread with the breadcrumb mixture. Cut 40g/1½oz (3 tablespoons) of the butter into small pieces and dot them over the stuffing. Roll up the meat tightly and tie with string at 2.5cm/1in intervals.

Cream 25g/1oz (2 tablespoons) of the remaining butter with the allspice. Grease a baking dish with the remaining butter and place the veal roll in it. Rub the veal with the allspice butter. Sprinkle over the orange juice.

Cook for 1¼ hours, basting occasionally and adding more orange juice if necessary. Remove the string and serve hot.

4 Servings

Pork chops with apricots

	Metric/UK	US
Large pork chops	6	6
Garlic cloves, crushed	2	2
Ground coriander	½ tsp	½ tsp
Ground ginger	½ tsp	½ tsp
Grated nutmeg	½ tsp	½ tsp
Salt and black pepper		
Butter	125g/4oz	8 Tbs
Onions, finely chopped	2	2
Potatoes, peeled and cut into 1cm/½in thick slices	6	6
Canned apricot halves	½ kg/1lb	1lb
Soft brown sugar	1 Tbs	1 Tbs

Preheat the oven to moderate 180°C (Gas Mark 4, 350°F).

Rub the chops with the garlic, coriander, ginger, nutmeg and salt and pepper. Melt half the butter in a frying pan. Add the onions and potatoes and fry until the onions are golden. Transfer the vegetables to a casserole.

Add the remaining butter to the pan. When it has melted, add the chops and fry until browned on both sides. Arrange the chops on top of the onions and potatoes in the casserole and cover them with the apricot halves. Pour the syrup from the can of apricots over the top and sprinkle with the sugar.

Cover and bake for 30 minutes. Uncover and bake for a further 15 minutes or until the chops are cooked through. Serve hot, in the casserole.

6 Servings

Pork with grapes

	Metric/UK	US
Seedless green grapes	1¼kg/2½lb	2½lb
Boned loin of pork, trimmed of excess fat, rolled and tied	1 × 2½kg/5lb	1 × 5lb
Salt and black pepper		
Ground coriander	1 tsp	1 tsp
Juniper berries, crushed	16	16
Garlic clove, crushed	1	1
Shallots, finely chopped	2	2
Worcestershire sauce	4 tsp	4 tsp
Butter	50g/2oz	4 Tbs
Dry white wine	150ml/5floz	⅔ cup
Cayenne pepper	⅛ tsp	⅛ tsp
Gin	4 Tbs	¼ cup
Cornflour (cornstarch) dissolved in 1 Tbs white wine	1 Tbs	1 Tbs
GARNISH		
Butter	50g/2oz	4 Tbs
Seedless green grapes	1kg/2lb	2lb

Purée the grapes in a blender or food mill and strain. Put the pork in a shallow dish and rub with salt and pepper and the coriander. Pour over the grape juice and add the juniper berries, garlic, half the shallots and 3 teaspoons of the Worcestershire sauce. Leave to marinate for 8 hours or overnight, turning occasionally.

Remove the pork from the marinade and pat dry with paper towels. Reserve the marinade.

Melt the butter in a flameproof casserole. Add the remaining shallot and fry until softened. Put the pork in the casserole and brown on all sides. Add half the reserved marinade with all the juniper berries, the wine, cayenne and remaining Worcestershire sauce. Discard the remaining marinade.

Pork Meatballs with Spicy Sauce should be served on a bed of pasta or rice for a substantial meal.

Bring to the boil, then cover and simmer for 2½ hours or until the pork is cooked through.

Ten minutes before the pork is ready, prepare the garnish. Melt the butter in a frying pan. Add the grapes and fry until they are lightly browned all over. Remove from the heat and keep warm.

Warm the gin, pour it over the pork and set alight. When the flames die down, transfer the pork to a warmed serving platter. Arrange the grape garnish around the meat and keep the mixture hot.

Skim the fat from the surface of the cooking liquid in the casserole. Stir in the dissolved cornflour (cornstarch) and bring back to the boil. Simmer, stirring, until thickened. Strain the sauce into a sauceboat. Pour a little over the pork.

Serve hot.

8–10 Servings

Pork meatballs with spicy sauce

	Metric/UK	US
Minced (ground) pork	1kg/2lb	2lb
Large onion, finely grated	1	1
Garlic cloves, crushed	2	2
Ground almonds	50g/2oz	½ cup
Fresh breadcrumbs	50g/2oz	1 cup
Egg, lightly beaten	1	1
Chopped parsley	1 Tbs	1 Tbs
Ground cinnamon	¾ tsp	¾ tsp
Salt and black pepper		
Medium dry sherry	3 Tbs	3 Tbs
Butter	1 Tbs	1 Tbs
Olive oil	2 Tbs	2 Tbs
SAUCE		
Large onion, finely chopped	1	1
Garlic clove, crushed	1	1
Soft brown sugar	1½ tsp	1½ tsp
Tomatoes, skinned, seeded and chopped	6	6
Green pepper, pith and seeds removed and thinly sliced	1	1
Red pepper, pith and seeds removed and thinly sliced	1	1
Green chilli (chili		

pepper), finely	Metric/UK	US
chopped	1	1
Cayenne pepper	¼ tsp	¼ tsp
Paprika	1 tsp	1 tsp
Chopped parsley	1 Tbs	1 Tbs
Beef stock	150ml/5floz	⅔ cup
Cornflour (cornstarch)		
dissolved in 4 Tbs		
dry sherry	2 tsp	2 tsp

Mix together the pork, onion, garlic, almonds, breadcrumbs, egg, parsley, cinnamon, salt and pepper to taste and the sherry. Combine the ingredients thoroughly, then shape the mixture into about 36 walnut-sized balls.

Melt the butter with the oil in a frying pan. Add the meatballs, in batches, and fry until well browned. Remove the balls from the pan.

Add the onion, garlic and brown sugar for the sauce to the pan and fry until the onion is golden. Stir in the tomatoes, green and red peppers, chilli, cayenne, paprika and parsley and cook for a further 3 minutes. Add the stock and salt and pepper to taste and bring to the boil, stirring occasionally. Stir in the dissolved cornflour (cornstarch) and simmer, stirring until the sauce thickens.

Add the meatballs to the sauce and coat well. Cover and cook gently for 20 to 25 minutes or until the meatballs are cooked through. Serve hot.

4–6 Servings

Pork and beef loaf

	Metric/UK	US
Fresh breadcrumbs	75g/3oz	1½ cups
Milk	250ml/8floz	1 cup
Minced (ground) pork	½kg/1lb	1lb
Minced (ground) beef	½kg/1lb	1lb
Large onions, finely chopped	2	2
Canned pimientos, drained and chopped	125g/4oz	4oz
Prepared French mustard	3 Tbs	3 Tbs
Dried basil	1 tsp	1 tsp
Cayenne pepper	¼ tsp	¼ tsp
Paprika	1 Tbs	1 Tbs
Salt and black pepper		
Eggs, lightly beaten	2	2

Preheat the oven to moderate 180°C (Gas Mark 4, 350°F).

Soak the breadcrumbs in the milk for 15 minutes. Add the remaining ingredients, with salt and pepper to taste, to the breadcrumb mixture and knead well together with your fingers. Pack the mixture into a greased 1kg/2lb loaf pan and smooth the top.

Place the loaf pan in a roasting pan and pour enough boiling water into the roasting pan to come halfway up the loaf pan. Bake for 1½ hours, or until a skewer comes out clean.

Turn the meat loaf out of the pan and serve hot or cold.

4–6 Servings

Serve Pork and Beef Loaf hot surrounded by an elegant layer of creamed potatoes or cold with a mixed salad.

Loin of pork with oranges and pineapple

	Metric/UK	US
Boned loin of pork, trimmed of excess fat, rolled and tied	1 × 2kg/4lb	1 × 4lb
Oil	2 Tbs	2 Tbs
Large oranges, peeled and sliced	2	2
Small pineapple, peeled, cored and cut into chunks	1	1
MARINADE		
Root ginger, peeled and finely grated	2.5cm/1in piece	1in piece
Ground allspice	½ tsp	½ tsp
Crushed coriander seeds	1 tsp	1 tsp
Salt	1 tsp	1 tsp
Crushed black peppercorns	1 tsp	1 tsp
Prepared French mustard	1 tsp	1 tsp
Grated rind of 1 orange		
Garlic cloves, crushed	2	2
Soy sauce	5 Tbs	5 Tbs
Lemon juice	4 Tbs	¼ cup

Mix together the ingredients for the marinade in a shallow dish. Add the pork and turn to coat. Leave to marinate for about 3 hours, turning occasionally.

Preheat the oven to fairly hot 190°C (Gas Mark 5, 375°F).

Remove the pork from the marinade and pat it dry with paper towels. Reserve the marinade.

Put the oil in a roasting pan and place it in the oven. When the oil is hot, put the pork in the pan, fat side up. Roast for 1¾ hours. While the pork is roasting, put the marinade in a saucepan and bring it to the boil. Baste the pork with the hot marinade every 20 minutes during the roasting period.

Cover the pork with the orange slices and add the pineapple chunks to the pan. Continue roasting for 45 minutes, basting as before.

Carve the pork and arrange the slices on a warmed serving platter. Add the fruit. Skim any fat from the cooking liquid in the pan and pour over the pork.

Serve hot.

8 Servings

A highly seasoned dish originating from Central America, Mexican Pork and Veal Stew is delicious accompanied by crunchy, salted popcorn.

Peruvian pork stew

	Metric/UK	US
Oil	4 Tbs	4 Tbs
Pork fillet (tenderloin), cut into 5cm/2in pieces	1kg/2lb	2lb
Onions, thinly sliced	2	2
Garlic clove, crushed	1	1
Dried red chillis (chili peppers), chopped	2	2
Cumin seeds, crushed	1½ tsp	1½ tsp
Canned sweetcorn kernels, drained	425g/14oz	14oz
Canned tomatoes	425g/14oz	14oz
Orange juice	175ml/6floz	¾ cup
Grated orange rind	1 tsp	1 tsp
Salt and black pepper		
Sweet potatoes, parboiled for 15 minutes, peeled and cubed	½kg/1lb	1lb

Heat the oil in a saucepan. Add the pork cubes and brown on all sides. Remove the pork from the pan.

Add the onions, garlic, chillis and cumin to the pan and fry until the onions are softened. Stir in the sweetcorn, tomatoes, orange juice, orange rind and salt and pepper to taste. Bring to the boil.

Return the pork to the pan and stir well. Cover and simmer for 50 minutes.

Stir in the sweet potatoes and continue to cook, covered, for 20 minutes or until the pork is cooked through. Serve hot.

4 Servings

Mexican pork and veal stew

	Metric/UK	US
Butter	50g/2oz	4 Tbs
Oil	2 Tbs	2 Tbs
Boneless veal, cut into cubes	1kg/2lb	2lb
Boneless pork, cut into cubes	1kg/2lb	2lb
Onions, finely chopped	2	2
Garlic cloves, crushed	3	3
Green tomatoes, skinned, seeded and chopped (if unavailable substitute ordinary ones)	1kg/2lb	2lb
Green peppers, pith and seeds removed and chopped	3	3
Green chillis (chili peppers), chopped	4	4
Tomato purée (paste)	2 Tbs	2 Tbs
Dried marjoram	2 tsp	2 tsp
Chopped chives	1 Tbs	1 Tbs
Dried basil	2 tsp	2 tsp
Grated nutmeg	2 tsp	2 tsp
Salt and black pepper		
Sugar	1 tsp	1 tsp
Chicken stock	250ml/8floz	1 cup
Dry sherry	250ml/8floz	1 cup
Double (heavy) cream	6 Tbs	6 Tbs

Melt the butter with the oil in a saucepan. Add the veal and pork, in batches, and brown on all sides. Remove the meat from the pan.

Add the onions and garlic to the pan and fry until softened. Stir in the tomatoes, green peppers, chillis, tomato purée (paste), herbs, nutmeg, salt and pepper to taste and the sugar. Cook, stirring, for 5 minutes. Stir in the stock and sherry.

Return the meat to the pan and bring to the boil. Cover and simmer for 1½ hours or until the meat is tender.

Remove from the heat and stir in the cream. Serve hot.

8 Servings

Left To bring out the flavour of cumin, heat gently without fat and then use accordingly.

Pork and ham balls

	Metric/UK	US
Fresh breadcrumbs soaked in 2 Tbs milk	25g/1oz	½ cup
Lean pork, minced (ground)	350g/12oz	12oz
Uncooked ham, minced (ground)	300g/10oz	10oz
Hard-boiled eggs, finely chopped	2	2
Chopped parsley	1½ Tbs	1½ Tbs
Dry mustard mixed with 2 tsp milk	1 tsp	1 tsp
Salt and black pepper		
Ground cinnamon	¼ tsp	¼ tsp
Egg, lightly beaten	1	1
Flour	25g/1oz	¼ cup
Butter	25g/1oz	2 Tbs
Oil	2 Tbs	2 Tbs
Red wine	125ml/4floz	½ cup
Chicken stock	125ml/4floz	½ cup

Mix together the breadcrumbs, pork, ham, eggs, parsley, mustard, salt and pepper to taste and the cinnamon. Add the beaten egg and combine thoroughly. Form the mixture into 24 balls and coat them with all but 2 teaspoons of the flour.

Melt all but 1 teaspoon of the butter with the oil in a frying pan. Add the balls, in batches, and fry for 8 minutes or until they are brown on all sides. Drain the balls on paper towels and transfer them to a baking dish.

Preheat the oven to moderate 180°C (Gas Mark 4, 350°F).

Put the wine and stock in a saucepan and bring to the boil. Mix together the remaining flour and butter to make a paste and add to the liquid in small pieces, stirring constantly. Simmer until thickened.

Pour the wine mixture over the ham balls and bake for 15 minutes or until the ham balls are thoroughly cooked. Serve hot.

4–6 Servings

Tunisian scrambled eggs and sausages

	Metric/UK	US
Olive oil	2 Tbs	2 Tbs
Spicy sausage, such as Spanish chorizo, cut into 2.5cm/1in thick slices	½ kg/1lb	1lb
Garlic clove, finely chopped	1	1
Cayenne pepper	½ tsp	½ tsp
Ground cumin	¼ tsp	¼ tsp
Salt and pepper		
Canned tomatoes	425g/14oz	14oz
Cold water	4 Tbs	¼ cup
Green peppers, pith and seeds removed and cut into strips	4	4
Eggs, lightly beaten	6	6

Heat the oil in a frying pan. Add the sausage slices and fry until they are evenly browned. Stir in the garlic, cayenne, cumin, salt and pepper to taste, tomatoes and water and bring to the boil. Simmer until the mixture is thick, stirring occasionally.

Stir in the pepper strips, cover and cook gently for a further 5 minutes.

Pour over the beaten eggs and cook gently, stirring lightly, until the eggs are just set and scrambled. Serve hot.

4 Servings

Ox tongue with hot raisin sauce

	Metric/UK	US
Butter	50g/2oz	4 Tbs
Flour	25g/1oz	¼ cup
Beef stock	125ml/4floz	½ cup
Water	425ml/14floz	1¾ cups
Raisins	125g/4oz	⅔ cup
Salt and black pepper		
Juice of ½ lemon		
Soft brown sugar	1 tsp	1 tsp
Hot chilli powder	¼ tsp	¼ tsp
Ground cinnamon	¼ tsp	¼ tsp
Ground ginger	¼ tsp	¼ tsp
Ground cloves	⅛ tsp	⅛ tsp
Salted ox tongue, soaked for 36 hours, cooked, skinned and kept warm	1×2–2½kg/ 4–5lb	1×4– 5lb
Single (light) cream	2 Tbs	2 Tbs

Melt the butter in a saucepan. Add the flour and cook, stirring, for 1 minute. Gradually stir in the stock and water and bring to the boil, stirring. Simmer until smooth and thickened.

Stir in the raisins, salt and pepper to taste, the lemon juice, sugar, chilli powder, cinnamon, ginger and cloves. Continue to cook gently for 10 minutes.

Slice the tongue into 6mm/¼in thick slices, discarding the bones and gristle. Arrange the slices on a warmed serving platter. Stir the cream into the sauce and pour a little over the tongue.

Put the rest into a sauceboat and then serve hot.

8–10 Servings

VEGETABLES & SALADS

Algerian carrots

	Metric/UK	US
Carrots, cut into 1cm/½in slices	1kg/2lb	2lb
Olive oil	5 Tbs	5 Tbs
Salt and pepper		
Ground cinnamon	½ tsp	½ tsp
Cumin seeds	½ tsp	½ tsp
Garlic cloves, finely chopped	2	2
Dried thyme	½ tsp	½ tsp
Bay leaf	1	1
Lemon juice	1 tsp	1 tsp

Put the carrot slices into a saucepan and just cover with water. Bring to the boil and simmer until the carrots are just tender but still firm. Drain the carrots, reserving 150ml/5floz (⅔ cup) of the cooking liquid. Keep the carrots warm.

Put the oil, salt and pepper to taste, cinnamon, cumin, garlic and thyme in the saucepan and cook gently for 10 minutes. Stir in the reserved cooking liquid and the bay leaf and simmer the mixture for a further 15 minutes or until it has thickened slightly.

Add the carrots to the pan and fold them into the sauce. Reheat for 2 to 3 minutes. Remove the bay leaf from the pan and turn the carrots into a warmed serving dish.

Sprinkle over the lemon juice and serve hot.

4 Servings

Israeli pumpkin

	Metric/UK	US
Sweet potatoes, peeled	½kg/1lb	1lb
Pumpkin, sliced, peeled and seeded	½kg/1lb	1lb
Salt and black pepper		
Grated nutmeg	½ tsp	½ tsp
Ground cloves	¼ tsp	¼ tsp
Orange marmalade	6 Tbs	6 Tbs
Large cooking apples, peeled, cored and sliced	3	3
Lemon juice	2 Tbs	2 Tbs
Water	125ml/4floz	½ cup
White wine	125ml/4floz	½ cup
Grated lemon rind	2 Tbs	2 Tbs
Brown sugar	1 Tbs	1 Tbs
Butter, cut into small pieces	1 Tbs	1 Tbs

Put the sweet potatoes in a saucepan, cover with water and bring to the boil. Cook for 30 minutes or until tender but not too soft.

Meanwhile, put the pumpkin slices in another saucepan, cover with water and bring to the boil. Cook for 10 minutes.

Preheat the oven to warm 170°C (Gas Mark 3, 325°F).

Drain the sweet potatoes and pumpkin and allow to cool, then cut into thin slices. Mix together salt and pepper to taste, the nutmeg and cloves.

Arrange half the sweet potato slices in a greased baking dish. Cover with about 1 tablespoon of the marmalade

A spiced vegetable dish, Algerian Carrots are delicious with roasted or boiled meat dishes.

and sprinkle with a little of the spice mixture. Top with half the apples, then a little more marmalade and spice mixture. Add a layer of half the pumpkin, then marmalade and spices. Repeat each layer once more.

Mix together the lemon juice, water and wine and pour into the baking dish. Sprinkle the lemon rind and sugar on top and dot with the pieces of butter. Bake for 1 hour and serve hot, in the dish.

6-8 Servings

Braised red cabbage with apples

	Metric/UK	US
Small red cabbage, cored and shredded	1	1
Grated nutmeg	¼ tsp	¼ tsp
Ground cinnamon	¼ tsp	¼ tsp
Salt and black pepper		
Vinegar	3 Tbs	3 Tbs
Butter	25g/1oz	2 Tbs
Cooking apples, peeled, cored and quartered	4	4
Brown sugar	1 Tbs	1 Tbs

Mix together the cabbage, nutmeg, cinnamon, salt and pepper to taste and vinegar. Melt the butter in a saucepan

and add the cabbage mixture. Cover and cook gently for 1½ hours, stirring occasionally.

Stir in the apples and brown sugar and continue cooking for 30 minutes. Serve hot.

4 Servings

Jugged celery

	Metric/UK	US
Lean bacon rashers (slices)	8	8
Large cooking apples, halved	10	10
Water	450ml/15floz	2 cups
Sugar	2 Tbs	2 Tbs
Ground cloves	⅛ tsp	⅛ tsp
Grated nutmeg	½ tsp	½ tsp
Salt and black pepper		
Large head of celery, cut into 15cm/6in pieces	1	1
Chopped walnuts	50g/2oz	½ cup

Preheat the oven to moderate 180°C (Gas Mark 4, 350°F).

Lay half the bacon rashers (slices) on the bottom of a greased casserole.

Put the apple halves in a large saucepan with the water and cook until the apples are soft. Strain the apples into a mixing bowl, pressing down on the

Jugged Celery, a succulent, flavourful accompaniment, should be served with plain, grilled (broiled) meat or egg dishes.

peel and core to push the pulp through to make a purée. Discard the peel and core. Stir the sugar, cloves, nutmeg and salt and pepper to taste into the apple purée. Spoon the purée over the bacon slices in the casserole.

Arrange the celery pieces in the purée so they stand upright. Sprinkle over the chopped walnuts and lay the remaining bacon slices on top. Cover and bake for 1½ to 2 hours or until the celery is cooked. Serve hot, in the casserole.

4-6 Servings

Creole potatoes

	Metric/UK	US
Sufficient oil for deep-frying		
Small new potatoes, parboiled and drained	1kg/2lb	2lb
Prepared French or German mustard	2 tsp	2 tsp
Butter, melted	40g/1½oz	3 Tbs
Cayenne pepper	¼ tsp	¼ tsp
Hot chilli powder	¼ tsp	¼ tsp
Salt and black pepper		
Chilli vinegar	2 tsp	2 tsp

Heat the oil in a deep-frying pan (deep fat fryer) until it is 185°C/360°F, or until a small cube of stale bread dropped into the oil turns golden in 50 seconds.

Deep-fry the potatoes, in batches, for 4 minutes or until golden. Drain on paper towels and keep hot.

Mix together the remaining ingredients, with salt and pepper to taste, in a saucepan. Cook, stirring, for 2 minutes. Add the fried potatoes and turn well to coat with the sauce. Continue cooking for 5 minutes, stirring frequently.

Serve hot.

4 Servings

Nut and fruit pilaff

	Metric/UK	US
Butter	75g/3oz	6 Tbs
Onion, chopped	1	1
Green pepper, pith and seeds removed and chopped	1	1
Turmeric	½ tsp	½ tsp
Grated nutmeg	¼ tsp	¼ tsp
Salt	1 tsp	1 tsp
Dried apricots, soaked for 30 minutes, drained and chopped	175g/6oz	1 cup
Raisins	75g/3oz	½ cup
Long-grain rice	350g/12oz	2 cups
Chicken stock, boiling	900ml/1½ pints	3¾ cups
Flaked almonds, toasted	125g/4oz	1 cup

Melt the butter in a saucepan. Add the onion and green pepper and fry until the onion is softened. Stir in the turmeric, nutmeg and salt, then add the apricots and raisins. Cook, stirring, for 2 minutes.

Add the rice and cook, stirring, for 5 minutes. Stir in the stock and bring to the boil. Cover and simmer for 20 to 25 minutes or until the rice is tender and has absorbed all the stock. Add a little oil to the simmering stock if the rice seems in danger of sticking to the bottom of the pan. Stir in the almonds.

Serve hot.

6-8 Servings

Jamaican beans

	Metric/UK	US
Dried white haricot (navy) beans, soaked overnight and drained	350g/12oz	2 cups
Salt pork, diced	50g/2oz	2oz
Oil	2 Tbs	2 Tbs
Onions, thinly sliced	2	2
Green pepper, pith and seeds removed and chopped	1	1
Celery stalk, thinly sliced	1	1
Canned tomatoes, drained and chopped	425g/14oz	14oz
Dark rum	6 Tbs	6 Tbs
Black treacle or molasses	3 Tbs	3 Tbs
Dry mustard	1 tsp	1 tsp
Dried thyme	½ tsp	½ tsp
Hot chilli powder	¼ tsp	¼ tsp
Salt and black pepper		

Put the beans in a saucepan and cover with plenty of water. Bring to the boil, cover and simmer for 45 to 50 minutes or until just tender.

Drain the beans well and place them in a casserole.

Preheat the oven to moderate 180°C (Gas Mark 4, 350°F).

Blanch the salt pork dice for 5 minutes, then drain well. Heat the oil in a frying pan. Add the salt pork dice, onions and green pepper and fry until the onions are softened. Stir in the celery and tomatoes, then stir this vegetable mixture into the beans in the casserole. Add the rum, treacle or molasses, mustard, thyme, chilli powder and salt and pepper to taste and mix well.

Bake for 30 to 40 minutes or until the beans are very tender. Serve hot.

4 Servings

Korean vegetable salad

	Metric/UK	US
Small turnip, peeled and cut into strips	1	1
Salt		
Oil	4 Tbs	4 Tbs
Small onion, finely chopped	1	1
Mushrooms, sliced	125g/4oz	1 cup
Celery stalks, thinly sliced	2	2
Spring onions (scallions), chopped	3	3
Carrot, cut into strips	1	1
Finely chopped pine nuts	1 Tbs	1 Tbs
DRESSING		
Soy sauce	3 Tbs	3 Tbs
Brown sugar	1 Tbs	1 Tbs
Vinegar	1 Tbs	1 Tbs
Black pepper	$\frac{1}{4}$ tsp	$\frac{1}{4}$ tsp
Ground ginger	$\frac{1}{4}$ tsp	$\frac{1}{4}$ tsp

Sprinkle the turnip strips with salt and leave for 15 minutes.

Heat half the oil in a frying pan. Add the turnip strips and fry until crisp. Drain on paper towels and leave to cool.

Add the onion to the pan and fry until golden brown. Drain on paper towels and leave to cool.

Add the mushrooms to the pan and fry until tender, adding the remaining oil if necessary. Drain on paper towels and leave to cool.

Fry the celery until golden, then drain on kitchen paper towels and leave to cool.

Mix all the fried vegetables together with the spring onions (scallions) and carrot. Combine the ingredients for the dressing and add to the vegetables. Toss well, then spoon into a serving dish. Sprinkle with the finely chopped pine nuts and serve.

4 Servings

Coleslaw with caraway

	Metric/UK	US
Large white cabbage, cored and shredded	1	1
Onion, finely chopped	1	1
Green pepper, pith and seeds removed and finely chopped	$\frac{1}{2}$	$\frac{1}{2}$
Lemon juice	$\frac{1}{2}$ tsp	$\frac{1}{2}$ tsp
Caraway seeds	1 Tbs	1 Tbs
DRESSING		
Double (heavy) cream	175ml/6floz	$\frac{3}{4}$ cup
Sour cream	75ml/3floz	$\frac{1}{3}$ cup
Prepared French mustard	1 Tbs	1 Tbs
Lemon juice	3 Tbs	3 Tbs
Sugar	1 Tbs	1 Tbs
Salt and white pepper		

Put the cabbage, onion, green pepper and lemon juice in a mixing bowl. In another bowl, mix together the dressing ingredients with salt and pepper to taste. Add the dressing to the cabbage mixture and toss well until all

Korean Vegetable Salad can be served either with roast meats or on its own as a crunchy first course.

the vegetables are well coated. Fold in the caraway seeds until well mixed into the salad.

Chill for at least 1 hour before serving.

8 Servings

Tunisian aubergines (eggplants)

	Metric/UK	US
Aubergines (eggplants), cut into cubes	4	4
Salt		
Olive oil	4 Tbs	¼ cup
Onions, sliced	2	2
Garlic clove, chopped	1	1
Cayenne pepper	¼ tsp	¼ tsp
Ground cloves	¼ tsp	¼ tsp
Ground cumin	½ tsp	½ tsp
Tomatoes, skinned and chopped	½ kg/1lb	1lb
Ground coriander	1 tsp	1 tsp
Chopped fresh mint	1 Tbs	1 Tbs
Raisins	2 Tbs	2 Tbs
Black pepper		
Chopped parsley	2 Tbs	2 Tbs

Put the aubergine (eggplant) cubes into a colander and sprinkle with salt. Leave for 20 minutes, then drain, rinse and pat dry with kitchen paper towels.

Heat the oil in a frying pan. Add the onions and garlic and fry until softened. Stir in the cayenne, cloves and cumin and cook for 2 minutes. Add the aubergine (eggplant) cubes and brown carefully on all sides, stirring well.

Stir in the tomatoes, coriander, mint, raisins, and salt and pepper to taste. Cook gently until almost all the liquid has evaporated and the aubergines (eggplants) are tender. Stir in the parsley. Serve hot or cold.

4 Servings

Tunisian Aubergines (Eggplants), accompanying an eastern dish such as lamb kebabs, creates a meal with a foreign flavour.

ETHNIC DISHES

Seekh kabab

	Metric/UK	US
Minced (ground) meat	700g/1½lb	1½lb
Fresh white breadcrumbs	50g/2oz	1 cup
Root ginger, peeled and grated	2.5cm/1in piece	1in piece
Green chilli (chili pepper), finely chopped	1	1
Garlic cloves, crushed	2	2
Ground cumin	1 tsp	1 tsp
Hot chilli powder	½ tsp	½ tsp
Salt	½ tsp	½ tsp
Finely grated lemon rind	1 tsp	1 tsp
Lemon juice	1 tsp	1 tsp

Mix together all the ingredients, using your fingers to combine them thoroughly. Divide the mixture into 16 portions. With dampened hands, mould each portion into a sausage shape. Thread the sausages onto greased skewers (two or three to a skewer), pressing them on well.

Preheat the grill (broiler) to high.

Grill (broil) the kebabs for 6 minutes or until they are cooked through and browned on all sides.

Serve hot.

4 Servings

Tandoori chicken

	Metric/UK	US
Chicken, skinned	1 × 1½kg/3lb	1 × 3lb
Hot chilli powder	1 tsp	1 tsp
Salt and black pepper		
Lemon juice	2 Tbs	2 Tbs
Butter, melted	50g/2oz	4 Tbs
MARINADE		
Plain yogurt	3 Tbs	3 Tbs
Garlic cloves	4	4
Raisins	1 Tbs	1 Tbs
Root ginger, peeled and chopped	5cm/2in piece	2in piece
Cumin seeds	1 tsp	1 tsp
Coriander seeds	1 Tbs	1 Tbs
Dried red chillis (chili peppers)	2	2
Red food colouring	½ tsp	½ tsp

Make gashes all over the chicken. Mix together the chilli powder, salt and pepper to taste and the lemon juice and rub all over the chicken. Leave for 20 minutes.

Meanwhile, put all the marinade ingredients, except the food colouring, into a blender and blend to a smooth purée. Mix in the red food colouring.

Place the chicken in a large bowl and spread it with the yogurt marinade. Cover and leave in the refrigerator for 24 hours.

Preheat the oven to fairly hot 200°C (Gas Mark 6, 400°F).

Put the chicken, on its back, on a rack in a roasting pan. Put enough water in the tin just to cover the bottom. Spoon all the marinade from the bowl over the chicken, then 1 tablespoon of the melted butter. Roast for 1 hour, basting frequently with the remaining melted butter and the drippings in the pan.

Carve the chicken and serve hot.

3 Servings

Marinated lamb kebabs

	Metric/UK	US
Root ginger, peeled and finely chopped	10cm/4in piece	4in piece
Onions, chopped	3	3
Small bunch fresh coriander leaves	1	1
Coriander seeds	1 Tbs	1 Tbs
Juice of 1 lemon		
Green chillis (chili peppers)	2	2
Black peppercorns	½ tsp	½ tsp
Boned leg of lamb, cut into 2.5cm/1in cubes	1kg/2lb	2lb
Salt	1 tsp	1 tsp
Butter, melted	25g/1oz	2 Tbs

Put the ginger, onions, coriander leaves and seeds, lemon juice, chillis and peppercorns in a blender and blend to a purée. Add a little more lemon juice, if necessary. Put the spice mixture in a shallow dish and add the lamb cubes. Turn to coat well. Leave to marinate for 4 hours, turning occasionally.

Preheat the grill (broiler) to high.

Thread the lamb cubes onto skewers and sprinkle with the salt and melted butter. Grill (broil) for 8 to 10 minutes, turning occasionally.

Serve hot.

4 Servings

Marinated Lamb Kebabs is a subtly flavoured meat dish from India.

Samosas, savoury meat-filled parcels, are ideal either as a pre-dinner snack with drinks or as a piquant side dish to a main course.

Samosas

	Metric/UK	US
PASTRY		
Flour	225g/8oz	2 cups
Salt	½ tsp	½ tsp
Butter	25g/1oz	2 Tbs
Water	4-6 Tbs	4-6 Tbs
FILLING		
Butter	25g/1oz	2 Tbs
Onion, finely chopped	1	1
Garlic cloves, crushed	2	2
Green chillis (chili peppers), chopped	2	2
Root ginger, peeled and finely chopped	2.5cm/1in piece	1in piece
Turmeric	½ tsp	½ tsp
Hot chilli powder	½ tsp	½ tsp
Lean minced (ground) meat	350g/12oz	12oz
Salt	1 tsp	1 tsp
Garam masala	2 tsp	2 tsp
Juice of ½ lemon		
Sufficient oil for deep-frying		

To make the pastry, sift the flour and salt into a bowl. Rub in the butter until the mixture resembles breadcrumbs. Mix in enough of the water to bind the ingredients to a dough. Knead well for about 10 minutes, then set aside.

To make the filling, melt the butter in a frying pan. Add the onion, garlic, chillis and ginger and fry until the onion is golden. Stir in the turmeric and chilli powder, then add the meat and salt. Fry until the meat is well cooked and all the moisture has evaporated. Stir in the garam masala and lemon juice and cook for a further 5 minutes. Remove from the heat and allow to cool.

Divide the dough into 15 portions and roll each into a ball. Flatten the balls and roll out each into a circle about 10cm/4in in diameter. Cut each circle in half. Dampen the edges of each circle with water and shape them into cones. Fill the cones with the filling, then pinch them together to seal.

Heat oil in a deep-frying pan (deep-fat fryer) until it is 185°C/360°F or until a cube of stale bread dropped into the hot oil turns golden brown in 50 seconds.

Deep-fry the samosas in batches for 2 to 3 minutes or until they are golden brown. Drain on paper towels and serve hot.

30 Samosas

282

Vegetable kitcheri

	Metric/UK	US
Long-grain rice	225g/8oz	1⅓ cups
Moong dhal (yellow lentils)	75g/3oz	⅓ cup
Tur dhal (orange lentils)	50g/2oz	¼ cup
Masoor dhal (salmon-pink lentils)	75g/3oz	⅓ cup
Butter	50g/2oz	4 Tbs
Onions, sliced	2	2
Green chillis (chili peppers), finely chopped	2	2
Root ginger, peeled and chopped	2.5cm/1in piece	1in piece
Garlic cloves, crushed	2	2
Ground coriander	1 Tbs	1 Tbs
Turmeric	½ tsp	½ tsp
Potatoes, peeled and cubed	125g/4oz	1 cup
Carrots, cubed	125g/4oz	1 cup
Aubergine (eggplant), cubed	1	1
Green peas	125g/4oz	½ cup
Small cauliflower, broken into flowerets	½	½
Large tomatoes, skinned and chopped	2	2
Salt	1 tsp	1 tsp
Chicken stock or water, boiling	500ml/16floz	2 cups
Butter, melted	25g/1oz	2 Tbs

Cook the rice in boiling salted water for 3 minutes, then drain. Cook the dhals (lentils) in boiling salted water for 5 minutes, then remove from the heat and drain.

Melt the butter in a frying pan. Add the onions and fry until golden. Stir in the chillis, ginger and garlic and fry for 2 minutes. Add the spices and fry, stirring, for 1 minute. Add the vegetables and salt and mix thoroughly. Cover and cook the mixture gently for 20 minutes.

Preheat the oven to very cool 140°C (Gas Mark 1, 275°F).

Make layers of the vegetable mixture, rice and dhals in a greased baking dish beginning with vegetables and ending with a layer of dhal. Pour in the boiling chicken stock or water, cover and bake for 45 minutes to 1 hour or until the rice and dhals are cooked and tender and all the liquid has been absorbed.

Serve hot, straight from the dish, liberally sprinkled with the melted butter.

4-6 Servings

Vegetable Kitcheri uses three types of lentils (dhal).

Dry beef curry

	Metric/UK	US
Oil	4 Tbs	4 Tbs
Green chillis (chili peppers), finely chopped	2	2
Onions, finely chopped	2	2
Stewing (chuck) steak, cut into small cubes	1kg/2lb	2lb
Salt	½ tsp	½ tsp
Tomatoes, skinned and chopped	2	2
Turmeric	1 tsp	1 tsp
Ground cumin	1 tsp	1 tsp
Ground coriander	2 tsp	2 tsp
Garam masala	1½ tsp	1½ tsp
Plain yogurt	300ml/10floz	1¼ cups

Heat the oil in a saucepan. Add the chillis and fry for 1 minute. Add the onions and fry until softened. Add the beef cubes and salt and fry until the beef cubes are evenly browned. Stir in the tomatoes and continue cooking gently for 10 minutes.

Mix together the turmeric, cumin, coriander, 1 teaspoon of the garam masala and the yogurt. Add to the meat mixture and stir well. Half cover the pan and simmer for 1½ hours.

Remove the lid and continue cooking for 30 minutes or until the meat is covered with a thick gravy. If the curry becomes too dry, cover the pan.

Spoon the curry into a warmed serving dish and sprinkle over the remaining garam masala.

Serve hot.

4-6 Servings

Aviyal (Vegetable curry)

	Metric/UK	US
Oil	4 Tbs	4 Tbs
Mustard seeds	1 tsp	1 tsp
Root ginger, peeled and minced	5cm/2in piece	2in piece
Garlic cloves, quartered	2	2
Onion, minced	1	1
Green chilli (chili pepper), minced	1	1
Turmeric	1½ tsp	1½ tsp
Ground coriander	1 Tbs	1 Tbs
Mixed vegetables (carrots, beans, aubergines (eggplants), turnips, cauliflower, green peppers, potatoes, okra, etc.), sliced	700g/1½lb	1½lb
Salt	1 tsp	1 tsp
Fresh coconut, puréed in a blender with 175ml/6floz (¾ cup) water, or 2.5/1in slice creamed coconut	225g/8oz	8oz
Chopped coriander leaves	2 Tbs	2 Tbs

Heat the oil in a saucepan. Add the mustard seeds, ginger and garlic and fry for 30 seconds. Add the onion and chilli and fry until the onion is golden. Stir in the turmeric and coriander and fry for 1 minute.

Add the vegetables and stir well to mix with the spices. Stir in the salt and coconut purée or creamed coconut. If the mixture is too dry, add a little water. Cover and simmer for 30 minutes or until the vegetables are cooked and tender.

Serve hot, sprinkled with the coriander.

4 Servings

Pork korma

	Metric/UK	US
Butter	50g/2oz	4 Tbs
Root ginger, peeled and finely chopped	4cm/1½in piece	1½in piece
Garlic cloves, crushed	3	3
Onions, finely chopped	2	2
Hot chilli powder	½ tsp	½ tsp
Ground coriander	2 Tbs	2 Tbs
Pork fillet (tenderloin), cut into 4cm/1½in cubes	1kg/2lb	2lb
Salt	1 tsp	1 tsp
Plain yogurt	300ml/10floz	1¼ cups
Ground almonds	125g/4oz	1 cup
Double (heavy) cream	300ml/10floz	1¼ cups
Ground cinnamon	½ tsp	½ tsp
Ground mace	¼ tsp	¼ tsp
Ground cardamom	½ tsp	½ tsp
Saffron threads soaked in 2 Tbs boiling water	¼ tsp	¼ tsp
GARNISH		
Onions, thinly sliced into rings and fried until golden brown	2	2

Melt the butter in a saucepan. Add the ginger, garlic and onions and fry until the onions are golden. Stir in the chilli powder and coriander and fry for 1 minute. Add the pork cubes and brown on all sides. Continue cooking briskly until all the moisture in the pan evaporates.

Reduce the heat to moderate and add the salt and 4 tablespoons of the yogurt. Cook, stirring, until the yogurt evaporates. Add 4 more tablespoons and cook until it evaporates. Continue in this way until all the yogurt has been added and there is no liquid in the pan.

Mix together the almonds and cream and stir into the pork mixture. Add the spices and bring to the boil, stirring. Cover the pan and simmer for about 25 minutes, stirring occasionally

to prevent sticking.

Preheat the oven to moderate 180°C (Gas Mark 4, 350°F).

Transfer the pork mixture to a casserole and stir in the saffron-coloured water. Transfer to the oven and bake for 15 minutes. Serve hot, straight from the casserole, generously garnished with the onions.

4 Servings

Fruit curry

	Metric/UK	US
Apricots, peeled, stoned (pitted) and chopped	4	4
Pears, peeled, cored and chopped	4	4
Bananas, sliced	3	3
Small honeydew melon, peeled, seeded and chopped	½	½
Canned mangoes, drained and chopped	125g/4oz	½ cup
Canned pineapple chunks, drained	50g/2oz	⅓ cup
Clear honey mixed		
with 300ml/10floz (1¼ cups) boiling water	4 Tbs	¼ cup
Ground cumin	½ tsp	½ tsp
Ground coriander	½ tsp	½ tsp
Turmeric	½ tsp	½ tsp
Ground cloves	½ tsp	½ tsp
Ground fenugreek	½ tsp	½ tsp
Hot chilli powder	pinch	pinch
Lemon juice	1 tsp	1 tsp
Plain yogurt	150ml/5floz	⅔ cup
Creamed coconut	2.5cm/1in slice	1in slice

Put the fruit in a saucepan with the honey mixture. Cover and poach gently for 15 minutes. Mix together the spices, lemon juice and yogurt and stir into the fruit mixture. Continue cooking gently for 25 minutes.

Add the creamed coconut and stir until it dissolves and the liquid thickens. Simmer for a further 3 minutes.

Remove from the heat and allow to cool, then chill for at least 3 hours before serving.

Serve cold.

4 Servings

Yogurt, pork, cream and spices are the basic ingredients in Pork Korma.

Lamb and cashew nut curry

	Metric/UK	US
Root ginger, peeled and chopped	4cm/1½in piece	1½in piece
Garlic cloves	3	3
Green chillis (chili peppers)	2	2
Unsalted cashew nuts	50g/2oz	½ cup
Water	4-6 Tbs	4-6 Tbs
Cloves	4	4
Cardamom seeds	¼ tsp	¼ tsp
Coriander seeds	1 Tbs	1 Tbs
White poppy seeds	1 Tbs	1 Tbs
Butter	50g/2oz	4 Tbs
Onions, finely chopped	2	2
Boned leg or shoulder of lamb, cut into cubes	1kg/2lb	2lb
Plain yogurt	300ml/10floz	1¼ cups
Saffron threads soaked in 2 Tbs boiling water	¼ tsp	¼ tsp
Salt	1 tsp	1 tsp
Juice of ¼ lemon		
Chopped coriander leaves	1 Tbs	1 Tbs
Lemon, sliced	1	1

Put the ginger, garlic, chillis, nuts and half the water in a blender and blend to a purée. Add the cloves, cardamom seeds, coriander seeds and poppy seeds and blend again until smooth, adding just enough of the remaining water to prevent blender from sticking.

Melt the butter in a saucepan. Add the onions and fry until golden. Stir in the spice purée and fry, stirring, for 3 minutes. Add the lamb cubes and fry for 5 minutes, turning to coat them with the spice mixture.

Mix together the yogurt, saffron-coloured water and salt. Add this to the pan and stir well. When the mixture begins to bubble, reduce the heat and cook gently for 1 hour, stirring occasionally.

Stir in the lemon juice and sprinkle over the coriander leaves. Cover and continue cooking for 20 minutes. Serve hot, garnished with the lemon slices.

4 Servings

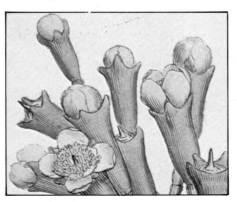

Cloves have a strong flavour and should be used with restraint.

286

Chicken with almonds and raisins

	Metric/UK	US
Chicken, skinned	1 × 2kg/4lb	1 × 4lb
Juice of ½ lemon		
Coriander seeds	1 Tbs	1 Tbs
Black peppercorns	1 tsp	1 tsp
Cardamom seeds	1 tsp	1 tsp
Cloves	6	6
Root ginger, peeled and very finely chopped	4cm/1½in piece	1½in piece
Salt	1 tsp	1 tsp
Hot chilli powder	½ tsp	½ tsp
Butter	75g/3oz	6 Tbs
Onions, very finely chopped	2	2
Double (heavy) cream	300ml/10floz	1¼ cups
Saffron threads soaked in 2 Tbs boiling water	¼ tsp	¼ tsp
Slivered almonds	50g/2oz	½ cup
Raisins	50g/2oz	⅓ cup

Preheat the oven to fairly hot 200°C (Gas Mark 6, 400°F).

A luxurious dish seasoned with saffron, Chicken with Almonds and Raisins is a splendid party dish.

Prick the chicken all over with a fork, then rub it all over with the lemon juice.

Crush or grind the coriander seeds, peppercorns, cardamom seeds and cloves. Sift the crushed spices, then stir in the ginger, salt and chilli powder. Cream in half the butter to make a smooth paste. Rub this spice paste over the chicken. Put the chicken in a casserole and bake for 15 minutes.

Meanwhile, melt the remaining butter in a saucepan. Add the onions and fry until golden. Stir in the cream, saffron-coloured water, almonds and raisins and remove from the heat.

Reduce the oven temperature to moderate 180°C (Gas Mark 4, 350°F). Continue roasting the chicken for 1 hour, basting every 10 minutes with the cream mixture.

Remove the chicken from the casserole and carve it. Arrange the pieces on a warmed serving platter. Keep hot.

Skim any fat from the surface of the cooking liquid in the casserole. Pour the cooking liquid into a saucepan and stir in any remaining cream mixture. Cook the sauce on top of the stove for 2 to 3 minutes or until it is very hot. Pour the sauce over the chicken and serve.

4 Servings

The pungency of chillis can be lessened by removing the small white seeds found inside the peppers.

287

Cantonese roast pork

	Metric/UK	US
Pork fillet (tenderloin), cut into strips 15cm/ 6in long and 4cm/1½in thick	1½kg/3lb	3lb
Oil	2 Tbs	2 Tbs
MARINADE		
Onion, very finely chopped	1	1
Soy sauce	5 Tbs	5 Tbs
Sugar	1 Tbs	1 Tbs
Dry sherry	1 Tbs	1 Tbs
Ground ginger	1½ tsp	1½ tsp
Hoisin sauce (optional)	1 Tbs	1 Tbs

Mix together the ingredients for the marinade in a shallow dish. Add the pork strips and leave to marinate for 2 hours, turning occasionally.

Preheat the oven to moderate 180°C (Gas Mark 4, 350°F).

Remove the pork from the marinade, reserving the marinade, and arrange the strips in a roasting pan in one layer. Baste with half the marinade and 1 tablespoon of the oil. Roast for 15 minutes.

Turn the pork strips over and baste with the remaining marinade and oil. Roast for a further 15 minutes. Cut the pork strips into 6mm/¼in thick slices and serve hot.

6-8 Servings

Beef in Chinese sauce

	Metric/UK	US
Walnut-size tamarind, soaked in 125ml/4floz (½ cup) water for 30 minutes, or 1 Tbs vinegar	1	1
Groundnut oil	4 Tbs	4 Tbs
Onions, sliced	2	2
Garlic cloves, crushed	3	3
Root ginger, peeled and finely chopped	4cm/1½in piece	1½in piece
Cloves	3	3
Grated nutmeg	¼ tsp	¼ tsp
Black pepper	¼ tsp	¼ tsp
Chuck steak, cut into 4cm/1½in cubes	1kg/2lb	2lb
Salt	1 tsp	1 tsp
Brown sugar	2 tsp	2 tsp
Black treacle or molasses	1 Tbs	1 Tbs
Dark soy sauce	2 Tbs	2 Tbs
Water	150ml/5floz	⅔ cup

Squeeze the tamarind in the water, then strain the liquid, pressing down on the pulp to extract all the liquid.

Heat the oil in a saucepan. Add the onions and fry until softened. Add the garlic, ginger, cloves, nutmeg and pepper and cook, stirring, for 3 minutes. Add the beef and fry until browned on all sides.

Stir in the salt, sugar, treacle or molasses, soy sauce, tamarind water or vinegar, and the water. Bring to the boil, then cover and simmer for 2 to 2½ hours or until the beef is cooked through and tender. Serve hot.

4 Servings

Gingered beef

	Metric/UK	US
Ground ginger	2 tsp	2 tsp
Soy sauce	5 Tbs	5 Tbs
Cornflour (cornstarch)	2 tsp	2 tsp
Sugar	½ tsp	½ tsp
Rump (sirloin) steak, thinly sliced across the grain	700g/1½lb	1½lb
Oil	4 Tbs	¼ cup
Root ginger, peeled and finely chopped	5cm/2in piece	2in piece
Canned bamboo shoots, drained and diced	125g/4oz	4oz
Large dried Chinese mushrooms, soaked for 30 minutes, drained and sliced	4	4

Mix together the ginger, soy sauce, cornflour (cornstarch) and sugar. Use to coat the steak slices and leave to marinate for 1 hour.

Remove the meat from the marinade and pat dry with paper towels. Heat the oil in a frying pan. Add the root ginger and fry for 3 minutes. Add the meat, bamboo shoots and mushrooms and cook for 6 to 8 minutes or until the meat is cooked through. Serve hot.

4 Servings

Honeyed ham with bean sprouts

	Metric/UK	US
Ham, soaked overnight (if necessary) and drained	1 × 1kg/2lb	1 × 2lb
Carrot, sliced	1	1
Onion, sliced	1	1
Star anise	1	1
Peppercorns, coarsely crushed	6	6
Unsalted peanuts	50g/2oz	½ cup
Clear honey	4 Tbs	¼ cup
Chicken stock	125ml/4floz	½ cup
Oil	3 Tbs	3 Tbs
Sesame seeds (optional)	1 tsp	1 tsp
Beansprouts	½kg/1lb	1lb
Cornflour (cornstarch) dissolved in 3 Tbs water	2 tsp	2 tsp

Put the ham, carrot, onion, anise and peppercorns in a saucepan and cover with water. Bring to the boil, then cover and simmer for 50 minutes. Remove the ham from the pan and allow to cool. Reserve the cooking liquid.

Preheat the oven to moderate 180°C (Gas Mark 4, 350°F).

Cut the ham into 2.5cm/1in cubes. Skim any fat from the surface of the cooking liquid, then strain it and reserve 125ml/4floz (½ cup).

Put the ham cubes, peanuts, honey and chicken stock in a casserole and stir well. Cover and bake for 30 minutes.

Five minutes before the ham is ready, heat the oil in a frying pan. Add the sesame seeds, if using, and fry for 1 minute. Add the bean sprouts and fry, stirring, for 2 minutes. Stir in the reserved ham cooking liquid and cook for a further 2 minutes. Transfer the beansprouts to a warmed serving dish, using a slotted spoon. Keep hot. Reserve the cooking liquid in the frying pan.

Remove the ham cubes from the casserole using a slotted spoon and pile them on top of the beansprouts. Keep hot.

Pour the mixture from the casserole into the frying pan. Bring to the boil, stirring well. Stir in the dissolved cornflour (cornstarch) and simmer, stirring, until thickened. Pour this sauce over the ham and beansprouts and serve hot.

4 Servings

Chinese red-cooked chicken

	Metric/UK	US
Spring onions (scallions), cut into 5cm/2in pieces	2	2
Root ginger, peeled and sliced	4cm/1½in piece	1½in piece
Chicken	1 × 1½kg/3lb	1 × 3lb
Oil	6 Tbs	6 Tbs
Soy sauce	6 Tbs	6 Tbs
Water	300ml/10floz	1¼ cups
Chicken stock cube, crumbled	½	½
Sugar	2 tsp	2 tsp
Sherry	3 Tbs	3 Tbs

Gingered Beef, made with Chinese mushrooms, beansprouts, spices and steak, is a delicious mixture of textures and flavour.

Dindings duck

	Metric/UK	US
Ground coriander	1 Tbs	1 Tbs
Ground fenugreek	2 tsp	2 tsp
Ground cumin	2 tsp	2 tsp
Turmeric	1 tsp	1 tsp
Ground cinnamon	1 tsp	1 tsp
Ground cardamom	½ tsp	½ tsp
Ground cloves	¼ tsp	¼ tsp
Grated nutmeg	¼ tsp	¼ tsp
Mild chilli powder	1 tsp	1 tsp
Salt	½ tsp	½ tsp
Black pepper	1 tsp	1 tsp
Root ginger, peeled and finely chopped	1cm/½in piece	½in piece
Juice of 1 lemon		
Small onions, minced	2	2
Garlic cloves, crushed	2	2
Desiccated (shredded) coconut, soaked in 175ml/6floz (¾ cup) boiling water	125g/4oz	½ cup
Duck, split open through the breastbone	1 × 2½kg/5lb	1 × 5lb

Stuff the spring onions (scallions) and ginger slices into the cavity in the chicken and secure the opening with trussing needle and string or skewers.

Heat the oil in a saucepan. Add the chicken and brown lightly on all sides. Pour off the excess oil from the pan and add the soy sauce, water, stock cube, sugar and sherry. Bring to the boil, then cover and simmer for 30 minutes. Turn the chicken over and continue to cook, covered, for a further 45 minutes.

Carve the chicken and serve with the cooking liquid as a sauce.

Preheat the oven to fairly hot 190°C (Gas Mark 5, 375°F), or prepare the barbecue fire.

Mix together the spices, salt and pepper, ginger, lemon juice, onions garlic and coconut mixture to form a thick paste.

Tie the duck wings and legs to

Below *Barbecued Dindings Duck.*   *4 Servings*

gether and open the duck so that it will lie flat. Place it on a rack in a roasting pan, or on the barbecue grid, skin side down. Spread with some of the spice paste. Roast for 45 minutes, basting with the spice paste every 15 minutes, then turn the duck over and continue roasting and basting for a further 45 minutes.

If you are using a barbecue, the total cooking time will be about half that for roasting, depending on how hot the fire is and how near you place the grid. The duck will need to be turned and basted more frequently.

Serve hot.

4 Servings

Malaysian fish

	Metric/UK	US
Fish fillets	700g/1½lb	1½lb
Turmeric	2 tsp	2 tsp
Salt	1½ tsp	1½ tsp
Oil	3 Tbs	3 Tbs
Onions, finely chopped	2	2
Root ginger, peeled and grated	2.5cm/1in piece	1in piece
Green or red chillis (chili peppers), finely chopped	2	2
Blachan or anchovy paste	1 tsp	1 tsp
Sereh powder or finely grated lemon rind	1 tsp	1 tsp
Sugar	1 tsp	1 tsp
Tomatoes, skinned and chopped	4	4
Small pineapple, peeled, cored and cut into chunks	1	1

Cut the fillets into finger-size pieces and rub them with 1 teaspoon each of the turmeric and salt. Heat the oil in a frying pan. Add the fish pieces and fry for 1 to 2 minutes on each side or until beginning to brown. Remove the fish pieces from the pan.

If necessary, add more oil to the pan so that the bottom is just covered. Heat the oil, then add the onions and fry until golden. Stir in the ginger, chillis, blachan or anchovy paste, sereh or lemon rind and the remaining turmeric. Fry gently for 5 minutes, stirring. Add the sugar, tomatoes and remaining salt.

Return the fish pieces to the pan with the pineapple chunks. Stir well, then cover and cook for 20 to 25 minutes or until the fish is cooked through. Serve hot.

4 Servings

Bali tamarind fish

	Metric/UK	US
Tamarind soaked in 125ml/4floz (½ cup) hot water for 20 minutes	2 Tbs	2 Tbs
Red mullet, cleaned	4	4
Peanut oil	4 Tbs	¼ cup
Red chillis (chili peppers), seeded	4	4
Onion, quartered	1	1
Garlic cloves	2	2
Root ginger, peeled	1cm/½in piece	½in piece
Water	175ml/6floz	¾ cup
Soy sauce	1 tsp	1 tsp
Salt	½ tsp	½ tsp

Strain the tamarind, pushing through as much pulp as possible. Discard all the seeds remaining in the strainer. Rub the fish all over with the tamarind pulp. Heat the oil in a frying pan. Add the fish and cook for 7 minutes on each side.

Meanwhile, put the chillis, onion, garlic, ginger and 4 tablespoons of the water in a blender and blend to a purée.

Remove the fish from the pan and set aside. Add the chilli mixture to the pan and cook, stirring, for 2 minutes. Stir in the soy sauce, salt and remaining water and bring to the boil.

Return the fish to the pan and continue cooking for 10 minutes or until cooked through. Serve hot.

4 Servings

Indonesian mackerel

	Metric/UK	US
Fresh lime juice	300ml/10floz	1¼ cups
White wine vinegar	4 Tbs	¼ cup
Salt	1 tsp	1 tsp
Black peppercorns	6	6
Mackerel, filleted	2 × 1kg/2lb	2 × 2lb
Turmeric	1 tsp	1 tsp
Peanut oil	4 Tbs	4 Tbs

Mix together the lime juice, vinegar, half the salt and the peppercorns in a shallow dish. Add the mackerel fillets and turn to coat well. Leave to marinate for 1 hour, turning occasionally.

Remove the fish from the marinade and pat dry with paper towels. Strain the marinade and reserve 4 tablespoons (¼ cup). Rub the fish all over with the remaining salt and the turmeric.

Heat the oil in a frying pan. Add the fish fillets and fry for 4 to 5 minutes on each side or until cooked through. Arrange on a warmed serving platter and sprinkle over the reserved marinade. Serve hot.

4 Servings

PUDDINGS & DESSERTS

Pineapple soufflé

	Metric/UK	US
Butter	50g/2oz	4 Tbs
Flour	50g/2oz	½ cup
Ground allspice	1 tsp	1 tsp
Single (light) cream	250ml/8floz	1 cup
Kirsch	4 Tbs	¼ cup
Sugar	50g/2oz	¼ cup
Egg yolks	4	4
Small pineapple, peeled, cored and finely chopped	1	1
Egg whites	5	5

Preheat the oven to fairly hot 190°C (Gas Mark 5, 375°F).

Melt the butter in a saucepan. Add the flour and allspice and cook, stirring, for 1 minute. Gradually stir in the cream and kirsch and bring to the boil, stirring. Simmer, stirring, until very thick and smooth. Remove from the heat and allow to cool.

Beat the sugar and egg yolks into the cooled sauce, then fold in the pineapple. Beat the egg whites until stiff and fold gently but thoroughly into the pineapple mixture. Spoon into a greased 1.8l/3 pint (2 quart) soufflé dish fitted with a paper collar. Bake for 35 to 40 minutes or until the soufflé has risen and is golden on top.

Remove the paper collar and serve immediately.

4 Servings

Apple noodle pudding

	Metric/UK	US
Eggs, lightly beaten	2	2
Milk	2 Tbs	2 Tbs
Sugar	2 Tbs	2 Tbs
Salt	¼ tsp	¼ tsp
Ground cinnamon	¼ tsp	¼ tsp
Ground allspice	¼ tsp	¼ tsp
Large cooking apples, peeled, cored and grated	2	2
Raisins	50g/2oz	⅓ cup
Fine noodles, cooked and drained	350g/12oz	12oz
Butter, melted	25g/1oz	2 Tbs

Preheat the oven to moderate 180°C (Gas Mark 4, 350°F).

Mix together the eggs, milk, sugar, salt, cinnamon and allspice. Add the apples, raisins and noodles and fold together thoroughly. Turn into a deep baking dish and pour the melted butter on top.

Bake for 45 minutes or until the pudding is firm to the touch and lightly browned on top. Serve hot.

4-6 Servings

Armenian dried fruit dessert

	Metric/UK	US
Dried apricots, soaked overnight	225g/8oz	1⅓ cups
Prunes, stoned (pitted) and soaked overnight	225g/8oz	1⅓ cups
Sultanas or raisins, soaked overnight	125g/4oz	⅔ cup
Large cooking apples, peeled, cored and sliced	2	2
Clear honey	6 Tbs	6 Tbs
Pared rind of 1 lemon		
Grated nutmeg	½ tsp	½ tsp
Ground cinnamon	½ tsp	½ tsp
Ground ginger	½ tsp	½ tsp
Brandy	2 Tbs	2 Tbs

Drain the dried fruit, reserving 125ml/4floz (½ cup) of the soaking liquid. Put the fruit and reserved liquid in a saucepan and add the apples, honey, lemon rind, nutmeg, cinnamon and ginger. Stir well and bring to the boil. Simmer for 25 minutes or until the mixture is pulpy.

Discard the lemon rind and allow the fruit to cool, then beat the fruit with a wooden spoon to form a purée. Stir in the brandy. Chill for at least 30 minutes before serving.

6 Servings

Ginger cream-filled horns

	Metric/UK	US
Butter, melted	75g/3oz	6 Tbs
Sugar	50g/2oz	¼ cup
Flour, sifted	50g/2oz	½ cup
Ground ginger	1 tsp	1 tsp
Large egg whites	4	4
Double (heavy) cream, whipped	250ml/8floz	1 cup
Madeira	1 Tbs	1 Tbs
Chopped preserved ginger	2 Tbs	2 Tbs

Preheat the oven to fairly hot 200°C (Gas Mark 6, 400°F).

Mix together the melted butter,

sugar, flour and ginger to make a smooth batter. Beat the egg whites until stiff and fold into the batter. Drop teaspoonfuls of the batter onto a greased baking sheet, leaving space around each. Gently flatten the batter mounds. Put the baking sheet into the oven and bake gently for 3 to 5 minutes or until golden.

Shape each biscuit (cookie) into a horn with your fingers before baking the next batch. When all the horns have been baked and shaped, allow them to cool.

Whip the cream and fold in the Madeira and preserved ginger. Fill the horns with the cream mixture and serve.

38 Horns

Pears baked with cardamom

	Metric/UK	US
Large pears, peeled, cored and sliced	3	3
Soft brown sugar	2 Tbs	2 Tbs
Orange-flavoured liqueur	125ml/4floz	½ cup
Ground cardamom	2 tsp	2 tsp

Preheat the oven to moderate 180°C (Gas Mark 4, 350°F).

Arrange the pear slices in a baking dish and sprinkle with the sugar, liqueur and cardamom. Bake for 35 to 40 minutes or until cooked and very tender.

Allow the pears to cool and serve at room temperature with whipped cream.

4-6 Servings

Pears baked with Cardamom is a refreshing dessert to serve after a filling main course.

An elegant recipe to round off a dinner party, Cinnamon Flavoured Layer Cake is light pastry filled with almond cream and topped by a chocolate-covered layer garnished with slivered almonds.

Danish cinnamon layer cake

	Metric/UK	US
PASTRY		
Butter	225g/8oz	1 cup
Sugar	125g/4oz	½ cup
Flour	225g/8oz	2 cups
Ground cinnamon	2 tsp	2 tsp
FILLING		
Dark (semi-sweet) cooking chocolate, broken into small pieces	50g/2oz	2 squares
Rum	1 Tbs	1 Tbs
Double (heavy) cream	300ml/10floz	1¼ cups
Ground almonds	75g/3oz	¾ cup
Slivered almonds	1 Tbs	1 Tbs

Preheat the oven to fairly hot 200°C (Gas Mark 6, 400°F).

To make the pastry, cream the butter and sugar together until the mixture is pale and fluffy. Sift in the flour and cinnamon and knead in thoroughly. Divide the dough into six portions and roll out each between two sheets of greaseproof or wax paper into a 20cm/8in circle. Remove the top sheet of paper, but leave each circle on the bottom sheet. Place two circles on a baking sheet and bake for 6 to 8 minutes or until the pastry is pale golden brown. Allow to cool on the paper. Bake the remaining circles in the same way. When the pastry circles are completely cold, carefully peel off the paper.

Melt the chocolate with the rum. Spread the chocolate over one of the pastry circles. Leave to set.

Whip the cream until it begins to thicken. Gradually beat in the ground almonds until the cream is stiff. Sandwich together the remaining five pastry circles with the almond cream. Place the chocolate-covered circle on top and garnish decoratively with the slivered almonds. Serve immediately.

6 Servings

Flummery

	Metric/UK	US
Round-grain rice	125g/4oz	⅔ cup
Milk	300ml/10floz	1¼ cups
Double (heavy) cream	300ml/10floz	1¼ cups
Sugar	50g/2oz	¼ cup
Grated lemon rind	1 Tbs	1 Tbs
Ground cinnamon	1 tsp	1 tsp

Put all the ingredients in the top of a double saucepan (boiler) and place over the heat. Cover and cook gently for 50 to 55 minutes, or until the rice is soft and has absorbed all the liquid. Stir occasionally during cooking and add more milk if necessary.

Pour the flummery into a serving bowl, or individual dishes, and allow to cool. Chill until set and serve cold.

4 Servings

Rhubarb and ginger compote

	Metric/UK	US
Sugar	225g/8oz	1 cup
Water	125ml/4floz	½ cup
Rhubarb, cut into 5cm/2in pieces	1kg/2lb	2lb
Gin	250ml/8floz	1 cup
Grated orange rind	1 Tbs	1 Tbs
Grated nutmeg	¼ tsp	¼ tsp
Ground ginger	½ tsp	½ tsp
Preserved ginger, finely chopped	1 Tbs	1 Tbs

Dissolve the sugar in the water in a saucepan, then bring to the boil. Add the rhubarb, gin, orange rind and spices and simmer for 20 to 30 minutes or until the rhubarb is tender, stirring occasionally. Transfer the rhubarb to a serving dish using a slotted spoon.

Return the cooking liquid to the boil and boil until reduced to about one-third. Pour the liquid over the rhubarb and stir gently. Sprinkle the preserved ginger over the top and allow to cool. Chill for at least 30 minutes before serving.

4 Servings

Oranges with cinnamon

	Metric/UK	US
Large oranges, peeled, white pith removed and thinly sliced	4	4
Sugar	2 tsp	2 tsp
Ground cinnamon	1 tsp	1 tsp
Orange-flavoured liqueur	2 Tbs	2 Tbs

Arrange the orange slices in a serving dish. Sprinkle with the sugar, cinnamon and liqueur. Chill for at least 30 minutes before serving.

4 Servings

Rhubarb and Ginger Compote is a delectable blend of gin and rhubarb.

Coriander fruit crumble

	Metric/UK	US
Cooking apples, peeled, cored and thinly sliced	700g/1½lb	1½lb
Blackberries	225g/8oz	8oz
Brown sugar	2 Tbs	2 Tbs
Ground cinnamon	1 tsp	1 tsp
TOPPING		
Flour	125g/4oz	1 cup
Sugar	125g/4oz	½ cup
Butter	125g/4oz	8 Tbs
Ground coriander	2 tsp	2 tsp

Preheat the oven to moderate 180°C (Gas Mark 4, 350°F).

Put the apples and blackberries in a greased baking dish and fold in the sugar and cinnamon.

Sift the flour into a mixing bowl and stir in the sugar. Add the butter and rub it into the flour until the mixture resembles breadcrumbs. Stir in the coriander.

Sprinkle the topping on the fruit. Bake for 45 minutes, or until the topping is golden. Serve hot.

4-6 Servings

Grumble pie

	Metric/UK	US
PASTRY		
Flour	175g/6oz	1½ cups
Sugar	1 tsp	1 tsp
Salt	pinch	pinch
Butter	50g/2oz	4 Tbs
Vegetable fat or lard	50g/2oz	¼ cup
Iced water	1-2 Tbs	1-2 Tbs
FILLING		
Raisins	75g/3oz	½ cup
Brown sugar	175g/6oz	1 cup
Water	125ml/4floz	½ cup
Eggs, lightly beaten	3	3
TOPPING		
Stale cake crumbs	50g/2oz	1 cup
Flour	50g/2oz	½ cup
Ground cinnamon	½ tsp	½ tsp
Ground ginger	¼ tsp	¼ tsp
Butter, cut into small pieces	50g/2oz	4 Tbs

First make the pastry. Sift the flour, sugar and salt into a mixing bowl. Add the butter and vegetable fat or lard and cut into small pieces, then rub the fat into the flour until the mixture resembles breadcrumbs. Mix in enough water to bind the mixture to a dough. Chill for 20 minutes.

Preheat the oven to fairly hot 200°C (Gas Mark 6, 400°F).

Roll out the dough and use to line a 23cm/9in pie dish (pan). Line the dough with foil and weigh down with dried beans. Bake for 10 minutes, then remove the foil and beans and bake for a further 5 minutes. Remove from the oven and set aside. Reduce the oven temperature to moderate 180°C (Gas Mark 4, 350°F).

Sprinkle the raisins over the bottom of the pastry shell. Dissolve the brown sugar in the water over gentle heat. Beat in the eggs and cook very gently, stirring, until the mixture thickens. Remove from the heat and cool.

To make the topping, mix together the cake crumbs, flour, cinnamon and ginger. Rub in the butter until the mixture resembles fine breadcrumbs.

Pour the cooled filling into the pastry shell and sprinkle over the topping. Bake for 30 minutes or until the topping is golden. Serve warm.

6 Servings

Green grape and apple pie

	Metric/UK	US
PASTRY		
Flour	300g/10oz	2½ cups
Salt	¼ tsp	¼ tsp
Vegetable fat or lard	125g/4oz	½ cup
Butter	50g/2oz	4 Tbs
Iced water	6 Tbs	6 Tbs
Egg, lightly beaten	1	1
FILLING		
Sugar	125g/4oz	½ cup
Salt	¼ tsp	¼ tsp
Ground cinnamon	½ tsp	½ tsp
Grated nutmeg	¼ tsp	¼ tsp
Large cooking apples, peeled, cored and thinly sliced	2	2
Seedless green grapes	350g/12oz	12oz
Cornflour (cornstarch) dissolved in 2 Tbs water	1 Tbs	1 Tbs
Butter, cut into small pieces	25g/1oz	2 Tbs

To make the pastry, sift the flour and salt into a mixing bowl. Add the vegetable fat or lard and butter and cut into small pieces, then rub the fat into the flour until the mixture resembles crumbs. Mix in enough water to bind to a dough. Chill.

Roll out about two-thirds of the dough to line a deep pie dish (pan).

Preheat the oven to hot 220°C (Gas Mark 7, 425°F).

To make the filling, mix together the sugar, salt, cinnamon and nutmeg. Add the apples, grapes and dissolved cornflour (cornstarch) and fold together thoroughly. Spoon into the pie dish (pan) and dot with the butter.

Roll out the remaining dough and use to cover the pie. Press the edges together to seal and cut two slits in the centre to allow the steam to escape. Brush with the beaten egg.

Bake for 10 minutes, then reduce the oven temperature to moderate

180°C (Gas Mark 4, 350°F). Continue baking for 45 minutes or until the crust is golden brown. Serve warm.

6-8 Servings

Italian cherries

	Metric/UK	US
Canned Morello (Bing) cherries, drained and stoned (pitted)	1kg/2lb	2lb
Marsala	150ml/5floz	⅔ cup
Grated nutmeg	½ tsp	½ tsp
Sugar	1 Tbs	1 Tbs
Double (heavy) cream, whipped	150ml/5floz	⅔ cup

Put the cherries, Marsala, nutmeg and sugar in a saucepan and bring to the boil, stirring thoroughly to dissolve the sugar. Simmer gently for 10 minutes.

Transfer the cherries to a serving bowl using a slotted spoon. Continue simmering the cooking syrup for 3 to 4 minutes or until it is thick and syrupy. Pour the syrup over the cherries.

Allow to cool, then chill for at least 1 hour. Serve at once topped with the whipped cream in individual glass dessert bowls.

4 Servings

BREADS & CAKES

Lardy cake

	Metric/UK	US
Fresh (compressed) yeast	15g/½oz	½ cake
Sugar	50g/2oz	¼ cup
Lukewarm water	300ml/10floz	1¼ cups
Flour	½kg/1lb	4 cups
Salt	1 tsp	1 tsp
Oil	1 tsp	1 tsp
Lard, cut into small pieces	125g/4oz	½ cup
Grated nutmeg	½ tsp	½ tsp
Ground cinnamon	½ tsp	½ tsp
Ground ginger	½ tsp	½ tsp
Currants	350g/12oz	2 cups
GLAZE		
Sugar	3 Tbs	3 Tbs
Water	3 Tbs	3 Tbs

Crumble the yeast into a bowl and mash in ½ teaspoon of the sugar and 1 tablespoon of the water. Leave in a warm place for 15 to 20 minutes or until puffed up and frothy.

Sift the flour and salt into another bowl. Make a well in the centre and pour in the yeast mixture, oil and remaining water. Gradually draw the flour into the liquids and mix to a dough. Turn the dough out onto a floured surface and knead until it is smooth and elastic—about 10 minutes.

Return the dough to the bowl, cover and leave to rise in a warm place for 1 to 1½ hours or until doubled in bulk.

Knead the dough lightly, then roll it out into an oblong about 6mm/¼in thick that is three times as long as it is wide. Sprinkle the upper two-thirds of the oblong with half the lard, remaining sugar, spices and currants. Fold the bottom, uncovered, third up and the top third down. Turn the dough so the open ends face you. Lightly press the open ends with the rolling pin to seal them, then roll out again into an oblong. Repeat the process with the remaining lard, sugar, spices and currants and fold and turn as before. Roll out the dough to fit a 20cm/8in round loose-bottomed cake tin (springform pan). Put the dough in the tin (pan), cover and leave to rise in a warm place for 40 to 45 minutes or until almost doubled in bulk.

Preheat the oven to fairly hot 200°C (Gas Mark 6, 400°F).

Bake for 35 minutes. Mix together the sugar and water for the glaze and brush over the cake. Continue baking for 10 minutes or until well risen and golden brown. Allow to cool on a wire rack before serving.

20cm/8in Cake

Spice and nut cake

	Metric/UK	US
Butter	75g/3oz	6 Tbs
Black treacle or molasses	3 Tbs	3 Tbs
Sugar	75g/3oz	6 Tbs
Egg	1	1
Egg white	1	1
Flour	175g/6oz	1½ cups
Baking powder	2 tsp	2 tsp
Ground allspice	¼ tsp	¼ tsp
Ground cinnamon	¼ tsp	¼ tsp
Ground ginger	¼ tsp	¼ tsp
Ground cloves	⅛ tsp	⅛ tsp
Juice of ½ lemon		
Milk	1 Tbs	1 Tbs
Walnuts, chopped	175g/6oz	1½ cups
Grated lemon rind	2 tsp	2 tsp
TOPPING		
Flour	2 Tbs	2 Tbs
Soft brown sugar	2 Tbs	2 Tbs
Grated lemon rind	1 tsp	1 tsp
Grated nutmeg	½ tsp	½ tsp
Butter	25g/1oz	2 Tbs
Walnuts, chopped	50g/2oz	½ cup

Preheat the oven to moderate 180°C (Gas Mark 4, 350°F).

First make the topping. Mix together the flour, sugar, lemon rind and nutmeg. Add the butter and rub into the flour mixture until the mixture resembles breadcrumbs. Stir in the walnuts.

Cream the butter until it is pale and fluffy. Beat in the treacle or molasses and sugar, then beat in the egg and egg white. Sift together the flour, baking powder and spices and fold into the creamed mixture. Stir in the lemon juice, milk, walnuts and lemon rind. Pour the batter into a greased and lined 18cm/7in loose-bottomed cake tin (springform pan). Sprinkle over the topping.

Bake for 1 hour or until a skewer inserted into the centre of the cake comes out clean. Cool in the tin for 5 minutes, then turn out onto a wire rack to cool completely.

18cm/7in Cake

A traditional British bread, Lardy Cake makes an excellent accompaniment to morning coffee.

Parkin

	Metric/UK	US
Flour	½kg/1lb	4 cups
Bicarbonate of soda (baking soda)	1 tsp	1 tsp
Salt	1 tsp	1 tsp
Ground ginger	2 tsp	2 tsp
Rolled oats	½ kg/1lb	4 cups
Butter	225g/8oz	1 cup
Black treacle or molasses	250ml/8floz	1 cup
Golden (light corn) syrup	250ml/8floz	1 cup
Clear honey	4 Tbs	¼ cup
Soft brown sugar	2 Tbs	2 Tbs
Milk	350ml/12floz	1½ cups

Preheat the oven to moderate 180°C (Gas Mark 4, 350°F).

Sift the flour, soda, salt and ginger into a bowl. Stir in the oats.

Melt the butter in a saucepan. Add the treacle or molasses, syrup, honey and sugar and stir well. Cook, stirring, for 1 minute. Add to the flour mixture with the milk and mix together thoroughly. Pour the batter into two greased and lined 25cm/10in square cake tins (pans).

Bake for 45 to 50 minutes or until the parkins feel firm when pressed with a fingertip. Allow to cool in the tins (pans) for 15 minutes, then cool completely on a wire rack. Store the parkins in airtight tins for at least a week before eating.

2 × 25cm/10in Square cakes

German spice cake

	Metric/UK	US
Eggs	3	3
Sugar	175g/6oz	¾ cup
Clear honey	300ml/10floz	1¼ cups
Almonds, finely chopped	125g/4oz	1 cup
Grated rind of ½ lemon		
Grated rind of ½ orange		
Chopped mixed candied peel	50g/2oz	⅓ cup
Flour	300g/10oz	2½ cups
Baking powder	1 tsp	1 tsp
Ground cloves	¼ tsp	¼ tsp
Ground cinnamon	½ tsp	½ tsp
Grated nutmeg	¼ tsp	¼ tsp

Preheat the oven to fairly hot 190°C (Gas Mark 5, 375°F).

Beat the eggs and sugar together until the mixture is pale and fluffy. Stir in the honey, almonds, grated lemon and orange rind and candied peel. Sift in the flour, baking powder and spices and mix well. Pour the batter into a greased 20cm/8in square baking tin (cake pan). Bake for 40 to 45 minutes or until a skewer inserted into the centre of the cake comes out clean. Allow the cake to cool in the tin (pan) for 15 minutes before turning it out onto a cake rack to cool completely.

20cm/8in Square cake

Hermits

	Metric/UK	US
Butter	225g/8oz	1 cup
Soft brown sugar	175g/6oz	1 cup
Eggs	2	2
Strong black coffee	125ml/4floz	½ cup
Flour	225g/8oz	2 cups
Ground cinnamon	1 tsp	1 tsp
Grated nutmeg	½ tsp	½ tsp
Baking powder	½ tsp	½ tsp
Raisins	75g/3oz	½ cup
Walnuts, chopped	50g/2oz	½ cup

Preheat the oven to fairly hot 190°C (Gas Mark 5, 375°F).

Cream the butter and sugar together until the mixture is fluffy. Beat in the eggs, then beat in the coffee. Sift in the flour, spices and baking powder and fold in thoroughly. Stir in the raisins and walnuts.

Drop heaped teaspoonfuls of the mixture onto a greased baking sheet, leaving space around each. Bake for 10 to 15 minutes or until the biscuits (cookies) are golden brown. Cool on a wire rack.

50 Biscuits(Cookies)

Genoese sweet bread

	Metric/UK	US
Fresh (compressed) yeast	25g/1oz	1 cake
Sugar	175g/6oz plus ½ tsp	¾ cup plus ½ tsp
Lukewarm milk	425ml/14floz	1¾ cups
Flour	1kg/2lb	8 cups
Salt	1 tsp	1 tsp
Orange-flower water	3 Tbs	3 Tbs
Butter, melted	75g/3oz	6 Tbs
Pine nuts	50g/2oz	⅓ cup
Pistachio nuts	50g/2oz	⅓ cup
Raisins, soaked in 3 Tbs Marsala for 30 minutes and drained	175g/6oz	1 cup
Fennel seeds, crushed	2 tsp	2 tsp
Aniseed, crushed	½ tsp	½ tsp
Candied citron, chopped	50g/2oz	⅓ cup
Candied lemon peel, chopped	50g/2oz	⅓ cup
Grated rind of 1 orange		

Crumble the yeast into a bowl and mash in the ½ teaspoon sugar and 4 tablespoons of the milk. Leave in a warm place for 15 to 20 minutes or

until puffed up and frothy.

Sift the flour, salt and remaining sugar into another bowl. Make a well in the centre and pour in the yeast mixture, remaining milk, orange-flower water and butter. Gradually draw the flour mixture into the liquids and mix to a dough. Turn the dough onto a floured board and knead until it is elastic and smooth—about 10 minutes.

Return the dough to the bowl, cover and leave to rise in a warm place for 1 to 1½ hours or until doubled in bulk.

Knead the dough lightly, then shape it into a square about 1cm/½in thick on a floured surface. Mix together the remaining ingredients and sprinkle them evenly over the dough square. Roll it up like a Swiss (jelly) roll, then shape it into a round. Place it on a baking sheet, cover and leave to rise in a warm place for 1 hour or until almost doubled in bulk.

Preheat the oven to fairly hot 190°C (Gas Mark 5, 375°F).

Make three cuts in the top of the dough round in the shape of a triangle.

Bake for 20 minutes, then reduce the oven temperature to warm 170°C (Gas Mark 3, 325°F). Continue baking for 1 hour.

Cool the bread on a wire rack before serving.

1¼kg/2½lb Bread

An unusual bread from Northern Italy, Genoese Sweet Bread is delicately flavoured with pine nuts, fennel seeds and orange-flower water.

Treacle or molasses loaf

	Metric/UK	US
Butter, melted	125g/4oz	8 Tbs
Black treacle or molasses	125ml/4floz	½ cup
Large eggs	2	2
Flour	225g/8oz	2 cups
Baking powder	1½ tsp	1½ tsp
Ground ginger	1½ tsp	1½ tsp
Ground allspice	½ tsp	½ tsp
Ground cinnamon	¼ tsp	¼ tsp
Salt	¼ tsp	¼ tsp
Rolled oats	125g/4oz	1 cup
Sour cream	150ml/5floz	⅔ cup
Sultanas or raisins	4 Tbs	4 Tbs
Chopped walnuts	2 Tbs	2 Tbs

Preheat the oven to moderate 180°C (Gas Mark 4, 350°F).

Mix together the butter, treacle or

Black Bun is a rich pastry case filled with a choice selection of fruit and assorted spices.

molasses and eggs. Sift the flour, baking powder, spices and salt into another bowl. Stir in the oats. Gradually mix in the treacle or molasses mixture and sour cream, then fold in the sultanas or raisins and walnuts.

Spoon the batter into a greased 1kg/2lb loaf pan. Bake for 1 hour or until a skewer inserted into the centre of the loaf comes out clean. Cool in the pan for 10 minutes and then turn out on to a wire rack to cool completely.

700g/1½lb Loaf

Cumin and raspberry buns

	Metric/UK	US
Butter	175g/6oz	¾ cup
Sugar	225g/8oz	1 cup
	plus 2 Tbs	plus 2 Tbs
Eggs	2	2
Ground cumin	1 tsp	1 tsp
Self-raising flour	350g/12oz	3 cups
Salt	pinch	pinch
Raspberry jam	125g/4oz	½ cup

Preheat the oven to fairly hot 190°C (Gas Mark 5, 375°F).

Cream the butter and all but 2 tablespoons of the sugar together until the mixture is pale and fluffy. Beat in the eggs and cumin. Sift in the flour and salt and fold into the butter mixture thoroughly. Chill for 30 minutes.

Roll the dough into walnut-sized balls. Make an indentation in each with your thumb, fill with a little jam, and seal up the dough to enclose the jam completely. Roll the balls in the remaining sugar to coat on all sides.

Place the balls in greased patty or cup cake pans and bake for 20 minutes or until risen and golden. Allow to cool before serving.

24 Buns

Black bun

PASTRY	Metric/UK	US
Flour	350g/12oz	3 cups
Salt	¼ tsp	¼ tsp
Butter	75g/3oz	6 Tbs
Sugar	2 Tbs	2 Tbs
Small eggs, lightly beaten	3	3
Iced water	4-6 Tbs	4-6 Tbs
FILLING		
Flour	225g/8oz	2 cups
Bicarbonate of soda (baking soda)	1 tsp	1 tsp
Baking powder	1½ tsp	1½ tsp
Soft brown sugar	125g/4oz	⅔ cup
Ground allspice	1 tsp	1 tsp
Ground cinnamon	½ tsp	½ tsp
Ground ginger	½ tsp	½ tsp
Ground mace	¼ tsp	¼ tsp
Sultanas or raisins	350g/12oz	2 cups
Currants	350g/12oz	2 cups
Almonds, chopped	125g/4oz	1 cup
Walnuts, chopped	125g/4oz	1 cup
Chopped mixed candied peel	125g/4oz	⅔ cup
Grated rind and juice of 1 lemon		
Milk	175ml/6floz	¾ cup
Brandy	1 Tbs	1 Tbs

To make the pastry, sift the flour and salt into a bowl. Add the butter and cut it into small pieces, then rub the butter into the flour until the mixture resembles breadcrumbs. Stir in the sugar. Mix in the beaten eggs with enough of the water to bind the ingredients to a dough. Chill for 20 minutes.

Roll out two-thirds of the dough and use to line a deep 18cm/7in cake pan.

Preheat the oven to fairly hot 200°C (Gas Mark 6, 400°F).

To make the filling, sift the flour, soda, baking powder, sugar and spices into a bowl. Stir in the sultanas or raisins, currants, almonds, walnuts, candied peel and lemon rind and juice. When the ingredients are thoroughly combined, moisten with the milk and brandy. Spoon the filling into the pastry case and smooth the top.

Roll out the remaining dough and use to cover the top of the cake. Cut a large cross in the centre. Brush the dough with the remaining beaten egg.

Bake for 15 minutes, then cover with foil and reduce the oven temperature to warm 170°C (Gas Mark 3, 325°F). Continue baking for 3½ hours or until a skewer inserted into the centre of the cake comes out clean.

Carefully turn the cake out onto a wire rack and leave to cool. Wrap in foil and keep for at least 1 week before eating.

18cm/7in Cake

German dried fruit bread

	Metric/UK	US
Fresh (compressed) yeast	25g/1oz	1 cake
Sugar	125g/4oz plus ½ tsp	½ cup plus ½ tsp
Lukewarm water	750ml/1 pint 8floz	3½ cups
Flour	1½kg/3lb	12 cups
Ground coriander	½ tsp	½ tsp
Ground fennel seeds	¼ tsp	¼ tsp
Ground cloves	¼ tsp	¼ tsp
Salt	1 tsp	1 tsp
Butter, melted	125g/4oz	8 Tbs
Dried apricots, chopped	50g/2oz	⅓ cup
Dried pears, chopped	50g/2oz	⅓ cup
Dried apples, chopped	50g/2oz	⅓ cup
Whole hazelnuts	300g/10oz	2 cups
Raisins	175g/6oz	1 cup
Chopped mixed candied peel	125g/4oz	⅔ cup

Crumble the yeast into a bowl and mash in the ½ teaspoon sugar and 125ml/4floz (½ cup) of the water. Leave in a warm place for 15 to 20 minutes or until puffed up and frothy.

Sift half the flour into a mixing bowl with the spices and salt. Make a well in the centre and pour in the yeast mixture, the butter and the remaining water. Gradually draw the flour mixture into the liquids and mix to a dough.

In another bowl, mix together the remaining flour with the dried fruits, nuts, raisins and candied peel. Add to the dough and knead together thoroughly to distribute the fruits and nuts evenly. Continue kneading until the dough is smooth and elastic. Cover and leave to rise in a warm place for 1½ hours or until doubled in bulk.

Knead the dough lightly and cut it into three pieces. Shape each piece into a ball. Place the balls on greased baking sheets, cover and leave to rise in a warm place for 30 to 40 minutes or until almost doubled in bulk.

Preheat the oven to hot 220°C (Gas Mark 7, 425°F).

Bake the breads for 15 minutes, then reduce the oven temperature to fairly hot 190°C (Gas Mark 5, 375°F). Continue baking for 30 minutes or until crusty and golden brown. Cool on a wire rack.

3 × 1kg/2lb Loaves

Chocolate cinnamon biscuits (cookies)

	Metric/UK	US
Butter	225g/8oz	1 cup
Sugar	125g/4oz	½ cup
Self-raising flour	225g/8oz	2 cups
Cocoa powder	50g/2oz	½ cup
Ground cinnamon	¾ tsp	¾ tsp
Vanilla essence (extract)	1 tsp	1 tsp

Preheat the oven to moderate 180°C (Gas Mark 4, 350°F).

Cream the butter until it is pale and fluffy. Beat in the sugar gradually, then sift in the flour, cocoa powder and cinnamon. Fold into the butter until the mixture is smooth. Stir in the vanilla.

Roll small spoonfuls of the dough into balls and place them on a greased baking sheet, about 5cm/2in apart. Flatten the balls using the prongs of a fork.

Bake for 12 minutes. Allow to cool slightly before removing from the baking sheet.

25 Biscuits (Cookies)

Spice doughnuts

	Metric/UK	US
Fresh (compressed) yeast	15g/½oz	½ cake
Brown sugar	50g/2oz plus ½ tsp	⅓ cup plus ½ tsp
Lukewarm milk	150ml/5floz plus 2 Tbs	⅔ cup plus 2 Tbs
Flour	½kg/1lb	4 cups
Ground allspice	1 tsp	1 tsp
Ground cinnamon	½ tsp	½ tsp
Ground cloves	½ tsp	½ tsp
Ground mace	½ tsp	½ tsp
Butter, melted	25g/1oz	2 Tbs
Currants	50g/2oz	⅓ cup
Sufficient oil for deep-frying		

Crumble the yeast into a bowl and mash in the ½ teaspoon sugar and 2 tablespoons milk. Leave in a warm place for 20 minutes or until frothy.

Sift the flour and spices into another bowl. Make a well in the centre and pour in the yeast mixture, remaining milk and butter. Gradually draw the flour mixture into the liquids and mix to a dough. Cover and leave to rise in a warm place for 1 to 1½ hours or until doubled in bulk.

Knead the dough lightly, then work in the currants until they are distributed evenly. Shape the dough into about 30 balls. Cover and leave to rise in a warm place for 30 minutes.

Heat oil in a deep-frying pan (deep fat fryer) until it is 180°C/350°F, or until a small cube of stale bread dropped into the oil turns golden in 55 seconds. Deep-fry the doughnuts, a few at a time, for 5 to 6 minutes or until golden brown. Drain on paper towels and serve hot.

30 Doughnuts

Hot cross buns

	Metric/UK	US
Fresh (compressed) yeast	15g/½oz	½ cake
Sugar	50g/2oz plus ¼ tsp	¼ cup plus ¼ tsp
Lukewarm milk	250ml/8floz plus 2 Tbs	1 cup plus 2 Tbs
Flour	½kg/1lb	4 cups
Salt	½ tsp	½ tsp
Ground mixed spice or allspice	1 tsp	1 tsp
Ground cinnamon	1 tsp	1 tsp
Eggs	2	2
Unsalted butter, melted	50g/2oz	4 Tbs
Raisins	50g/2oz	⅓ cup
Chopped mixed candied peel	50g/2oz	⅓ cup
CROSSES		
Butter	1 Tbs	1 Tbs
Flour	25g/1oz	¼ cup
Cold water	1 tsp	1 tsp
GLAZE		
Milk	2 Tbs	2 Tbs
Sugar	1 tsp	1 tsp

Crumble the yeast into a bowl and mash in the ¼ teaspoon sugar and 2 tablespoons milk. Leave in a warm place for 15 to 20 minutes or until puffed up and frothy.

Sift the flour, remaining sugar, salt and spices into another bowl. Make a well in the centre and pour in the yeast mixture, remaining milk, the eggs and butter. Gradually draw the flour mixture into the liquids and mix

o a dough. Turn the dough out onto a
loured board and knead until it is
mooth and elastic—about 10 minutes.

Return the dough to the bowl, cover
nd leave to rise in a warm place for 1
our or until doubled in bulk.

Knead the dough lightly and work in
he raisins and candied peel. Divide
he dough into 16 portions and shape
ach into a bun. Arrange the buns,
bout 5cm/2in apart, on greased bak-
g sheets. Cover and leave to rise in a
varm place for 15 to 20 minutes or
ntil almost doubled in bulk.

Preheat the oven to very hot 230°C
Gas Mark 8, 450°F).

Make the dough for the crosses by
ubbing the butter into the flour until
he mixture resembles breadcrumbs.
dd the water and mix to a firm dough.
oll out the dough thinly and cut it
nto thin strips 5cm/2in long. Press the
ough strips into the tops of the buns
1 the shape of a cross.

Mix together the milk and sugar for
he glaze and brush over the buns.
ake for 15 minutes or until golden
rown. Cool on a wire rack.

5 Buns

Apple muffins

	Metric/UK	US
Flour	225g/8oz	2 cups
Salt	½ tsp	½ tsp
Baking powder	2 tsp	2 tsp
Sugar	50g/2oz	¼ cup
Ground cinnamon	½ tsp	½ tsp
Grated nutmeg	¼ tsp	¼ tsp
Ground allspice	¼ tsp	¼ tsp
Eggs, lightly beaten	2	2
Butter, melted	50g/2oz	4 Tbs
Buttermilk	150ml/5floz	⅔ cup
Lemon juice	1 Tbs	1 Tbs
Medium dessert apples, peeled, cored and grated	2	2

Preheat the oven to very hot 230°C
(Gas Mark 8, 450°F).

Sift the flour, salt, baking powder,
sugar and spices into a mixing bowl.
Beat together the eggs, butter, buttermilk and lemon juice and add to the
flour mixture. Stir but do not over-
mix. Fold in the apples.

Spoon the batter into greased muffin
tins and bake for 15 to 20 minutes or
until cooked through.

Allow to cool in the tins for 5
minutes, then serve warm, or cool
completely on a wire rack.

12 Muffins

*Traditionally eaten at Easter, Hot
Cross Buns are delicious toasted and
served with butter and jam.*

PRESERVES

Pickled cucumbers

	Metric/UK	US
Small pickling cucumbers	1kg/2lb	2lb
Fresh dill sprigs	4	4
White wine vinegar	600ml/1 pint	2½ cups
Dill seed	1 tsp	1 tsp
Allspice berries, bruised	½ tsp	½ tsp
Mace blade	1	1
Mustard seeds, bruised	1 tsp	1 tsp
Mixed black and white peppercorns, bruised	1 tsp	1 tsp
Celery seed	½ tsp	½ tsp
Garlic cloves	2	2
Dried red chillis (chili peppers)	4	4
Bay leaf, crumbled	1	1
Rock salt	2 Tbs	2 Tbs

Prick the cucumbers all over with a fork. Pack them tightly into four preserving (canning) jars. Put a dill sprig in each jar.

Put the vinegar, dill seed, allspice berries, mace blade, mustard seeds, peppercorns, celery seed, garlic, chillis, bay leaf and salt in a saucepan and bring to the boil. Boil for 5 minutes. Remove from the heat and allow to cool, then remove the garlic cloves.

Half fill each preserving (canning) jar with water, then top up with the spiced vinegar. The liquid should cover the cucumbers completely. Leave the jars, covered but not sealed, in a warm place for 4 days, then seal and label. Store in a cool dark place for at least 3 or 4 weeks before serving.

About 2kg/4lb

Mushroom ketchup

	Metric/UK	US
Button mushrooms, chopped	1½kg/3lb	3lb
Salt	125g/4oz	½ cup
Small onion, finely chopped	1	1
Pickling spices	2 tsp	2 tsp
Black peppercorns, crushed	6	6
Ground mace	1 tsp	1 tsp
Ground allspice	¼ tsp	¼ tsp
Juice of 2 lemons		
Brandy	6 Tbs	6 Tbs

Make layers of mushrooms and salt in a casserole. Cover and leave for 24 hours, stirring occasionally.

Preheat the oven to cool 150°C (Gas Mark 2, 300°F).

Stir the onion into the mushrooms. Re-cover the casserole and bake for 30 minutes.

Purée the mushrooms and onion in a blender or with a food mill. Pour the purée into a saucepan and add the pickling spices, peppercorns, mace, allspice and lemon juice. Bring to the boil, stirring, and simmer for 3 to 5 minutes or until the purée is thick.

Allow the ketchup to cool completely, then stir in the brandy. Use immediately, or store in tightly sealed bottles.

About 900ml/1½ pints (2 pints)

Orange pickle

	Metric/UK	US
Oranges	6	6
Salt	1 tsp	1 tsp
Sugar	½kg/1lb	2 cups
Golden (light corn) syrup	2 Tbs	2 Tbs
Malt vinegar	175ml/6floz	¾ cup
Water	500ml/16floz	2 cups
Seeds of 6 cardamoms		
Black peppercorns, crushed	6	6
Ground cinnamon	½ tsp	½ tsp
Ground allspice	¼ tsp	¼ tsp
Cloves	12	12

Put the oranges and salt into a saucepan and cover with hot water. Bring to the boil and simmer for 50 minutes or until the oranges are tender. Drain the oranges and allow to cool.

Put the remaining ingredients in the cleaned-out saucepan and bring to the boil, stirring occasionally. Simmer for 10 minutes, then remove from the heat and leave to cool for 20 minutes.

Thinly slice the oranges.

Strain the cooled spice mixture into another saucepan. Add the orange slices and bring to the boil. Simmer for 20 minutes. Remove from the heat and allow to cool for 5 minutes before ladling into warm jars.

Seal and label and store in a cool dry place.

About 2kg/4lb

It is always useful to have a variety of sauces to hand such as those illustrated here: Mushroom Ketchup, Mustard, Tomato, Horseradish, Mint, and Worcestershire sauces.

Piccalilli

	Metric/UK	US
Medium cauliflower, broken into flowerets	1	1
Cucumber, cut into 1cm/½in pieces	1	1
Pickling (pearl) onions	225g/8oz	8oz
Large Spanish (Bermuda) onion, chopped	1	1
Green tomatoes, skinned and chopped	4	4
Coarse salt	175g/6oz	1½ cups
Malt vinegar	600ml/1 pint	2½ cups
SAUCE		
Malt vinegar	600ml/1 pint	2½ cups
Mustard seed, bruised	3 Tbs	3 Tbs
Root ginger, peeled and chopped	5cm/2in piece	2in piece
Garlic cloves, halved	4	4
Black peppercorns, bruised	1 Tbs	1 Tbs
Turmeric	1 Tbs	1 Tbs
Dry mustard	1 Tbs	1 Tbs
Sugar	125g/4oz	½ cup
Flour dissolved in 4 Tbs water	3 Tbs	3 Tbs

Put the vegetables in a bowl. Sprinkle them with the salt and leave for 4 hours. Drain the vegetables well and pat dry with paper towels.

Bring the vinegar to the boil in a saucepan. Add the vegetables, cover and simmer for 15 minutes or until almost tender. Remove from the heat and drain the vegetables. Put them in a bowl.

To make the sauce, put the vinegar, mustard seed, ginger, garlic, peppercorns, turmeric, mustard and sugar in the cleaned-out saucepan and bring to the boil, stirring to dissolve the sugar and spices. Simmer for 15 minutes.

Strain the sauce and return it to the saucepan. Bring back to the boil and stir in the dissolved flour. Simmer, stirring, until smooth and thickened.

Pour the sauce over the vegetables and turn and toss gently so they become well coated. Spoon the piccalilli into warm jars. Allow to cool completely before sealing and labelling. Store in a cool, dry place.

About 1½kg/3lb

Fruit chutney

	Metric/UK	US
Apricots, stoned (pitted) and chopped	1kg/2lb	2lb
Cooking apples, peeled, cored and chopped	1kg/2lb	2lb
Peaches, peeled, stoned (pitted) and chopped	4	4
Onions, finely chopped	2	2
Raisins	225g/8oz	1⅓ cups
Root ginger, peeled and diced	5cm/2in piece	2in piece
Grated nutmeg	¾ tsp	¾ tsp
Ground allspice	¾ tsp	¾ tsp
Dry mustard	¾ tsp	¾ tsp
Finely grated rind of 1 large lemon		
Finely grated rind and juice of 2 oranges		
White wine vinegar	750ml/1¼ pints	1½ pints
Sugar	½kg/1lb	2 cups
Soft brown sugar	½kg/1lb	2⅔ cups

Put the apricots, apples, peaches, onions, raisins, ginger, nutmeg, allspice, mustard, lemon rind, orange rind and juice and 600ml/1 pint (2½ cups) of the vinegar in a saucepan. Stir well and bring to the boil. Simmer, stirring occasionally, for 1 to 1½ hours

Far Left *Piccalilli is a delicious, pungent pickle usually served with cold meats. It owes its bright colouring to turmeric and mustard, two of its ingredients.*

Near Top Left and Bottom Right *Black and white mustard are the two basic varieties, the seeds either being ground to provide the ready-made mustard or used bruised in Indian cooking and pickles. Whole seeds are more aromatic than the ready-made variety.*

or until the mixture is very soft and pulpy.

Stir in the sugars and the remaining vinegar and continue simmering, stirring occasionally, for 40 to 50 minutes or until the chutney is very thick.

Ladle the chutney into jars, cover and seal. Label and store in a cool dry place for 6 weeks before serving.

About 4kg/8lb

Nectarine chutney

	Metric/UK	US
Large nectarines, peeled, stoned (pitted) and quartered	10	10
Large dessert apples, peeled, cored and chopped	2	2
Grated rind and juice of 3 lemons		
Soft brown sugar	175g/6oz	1 cup
Walnuts, chopped	175g/6oz	1½ cups
Sultanas or raisins	275g/9oz	1½ cups
Root ginger, bruised	5cm/2in piece	2in piece
Garlic cloves, crushed	2	2
Black peppercorns	6	6
Cayenne pepper	¼ tsp	¼ tsp
Ground cinnamon	1 tsp	1 tsp
White wine vinegar	175ml/6floz	¾ cup

Put the nectarines, apples, lemon rind and juice, sugar, walnuts, sultanas or raisins, ginger, garlic, peppercorns, cayenne, cinnamon and half the vinegar in a saucepan. Stir well and bring to the boil. Simmer for 30 minutes, stirring occasionally.

Stir in the remaining vinegar and continue simmering, stirring occasionally, for 1½ hours or until the chutney is thick.

Ladle the chutney into jars, cover and seal. Label and store in a cool dry place.

About 2kg/4lb

Coconut chutney

	Metric/UK	US
Desiccated (shredded) coconut, soaked in 150ml/5floz (⅔ cup) plain yogurt for 1 hour	50g/2oz	½ cup
Juice and grated rind of 1 lemon		
Root ginger, peeled and sliced	2.5cm/1in piece	1in piece
Green chilli (chili pepper), chopped	1	1
Garlic clove, sliced	1	1
Onion, chopped	1	1

Put the coconut mixture and lemon juice in a blender and blend to a smooth purée. Add the lemon rind, ginger, chilli, garlic and onion and blend until smooth again.

If you do not have a blender, very finely chop or mince (grind) all the ingredients.

Serve immediately, or keep, covered, in the refrigerator. This chutney will keep for 2 to 3 days.

About 125g/4oz (1 cup)

Apple chutney

	Metric/UK	US
Cooking apples, peeled and cored	2kg/4lb	4lb
Sultanas or raisins	½kg/1lb	2⅔ cups
Onions	4	4
Chilli (chili pepper), chopped	1	1
Mustard seeds	1 Tbs	1 Tbs
Lemon juice	3 Tbs	3 Tbs
Chopped lemon rind	3 Tbs	3 Tbs
Ground ginger	2 tsp	2 tsp
Vinegar	900ml/1½ pints	3¾ cups
Brown sugar	1kg/2lb	5⅓ cups

Mince (grind) the apples, sultanas or raisins, onions and chilli into a preserving pan. Add the mustard seeds, lemon juice and rind, ginger and 600ml/1pint (2½ cups) of the vinegar. Stir well and bring to the boil. Simmer for 1 to 1½ hours, stirring occasionally, or until very soft and pulpy.

Dissolve the sugar in the remaining vinegar in another saucepan, then add to the apple mixture. Continue to simmer, stirring occasionally, until the chutney is thick.

Ladle the chutney into jars, cover and seal. Label and store in a cool dry place.

About 2kg/4lb

Peach jam

	Metric/UK	US
Medium cooking apple, chopped	1	1
Thinly pared rind of 2 lemons		
Cloves	2	2
Peaches, stoned (pitted) and sliced	1½kg/3lb	3lb
Water	300ml/10floz	1¼ cups
Ground allspice	1 tsp	1 tsp
Sugar	1½kg/3lb	3lb (6 cups)

Tie the apple, lemon rind and cloves in a double piece of muslin or cheese-

cloth. Skin the peaches and put the peaches, water and flavourings bag in a preserving pan and bring to the boil, stirring.

Simmer until the peaches are just soft but be careful not to overcook.

Remove the flavourings bag and press it against the side of the pan to extract all the liquid. Add the allspice and sugar and stir continuously until the sugar has dissolved. Return to the boil and boil rapidly for 15 to 20 minutes or until setting point (jell point) is reached.

To test for setting, put a spoonful of the jam on a saucer. Allow it to cool, then push it with your finger. If the jam is ready, it will crinkle and the surface should feel set. If it is still runny, continue boiling and testing as described.

Leave the jam off the heat for 10 minutes, then ladle it into jars, cover, seal and label. Store in a cool, dry place.

About 2½kg/5lb

Quince jelly

	Metric/UK	US
Ripe quinces, sliced	2kg/4lb	4lb
Water	600ml/1 pint	2½ cups
Allspice berries, bruised	6	6
Lemon juice		
Sugar		

Put the quinces, water and allspice berries in a preserving pan and bring to the boil. Simmer for 50 minutes or until tender. Pour into a jelly bag and drain overnight. Discard the pulp.

Measure juice and return to the pan. Add 1 tablespoon of lemon juice and 425g/14oz (1¾ cups) of sugar to every 600ml/1 pint (2½ cups) of liquid. Place over low heat and stir until the sugar has dissolved. Bring to the boil and boil for 10 minutes or until setting (jell) point is reached.

Skim surface of jelly with a metal spoon. Ladle into hot pots, cover, label and store in a dark, cool place.

About 1.2kg/2½lb

Peach jam is delicious either on hot toast at breakfast or thickly spread on pieces of bread.

INDEX – HERBS

INDEX – SPICES

HERBS

Picture Credits

A-Z Botanical Collection 82(tr); D. Arminson 86(r); Barnaby's Picture Library 103(b); Walter Bauer 67; Carlo Bevilacque 87; Steve Bicknell 14, 29(b), 31(l & br), 37, 44, 46, 52; Bodleian Library 20, 24(b); Brian Lake Books 61(t); Camera Press 53, 57, 145; Colonial Williamsburg 54; A. Cooke 73(b); R. J. Corbin 35(c), 45(t), 79(r), 96(r); J. Cowley 96(c); C. Dawkins 62(t); DELU PAF/International 115; Anthony Denney 33, 65(br), 150(tl); J. Downard 73(c); Alan Duns 35(b), 117. 118, 120, 130, 138, 150(br), 152, 160; Mary Evans 17(b), 19(tr & l); Derek Fell 84(tr); V. Finnis 29(t), 55, 56(t), 59(t), 73(t); Brian Furner 74(t); P. Genereux 39; Melvin Grey 139, 150(bl); Graeme Harris 34, 38; P. Hunt 99(c); A. J. Huxley 76; G. Hyde 23(b), 61(b), 65(bl), 70; Jacana 84(tl); L. Johns 64; Paul Kemp 113, 119, 123(b), 159; Don Last 127; David Lewin 153; Chris Lewis 50; Maison de Marie Claire/Godeaut 27; Mansell Collection 18, 22, 35(tr), 36, 62(b), 63; J. Markham 24(t), 25, 82(tl); Bill McLaughlin 12/13, 48; David Meldrum 129, 147, 148; H. Morrison 94(t); Key Nilson 141; M. Nimmo 79(bl); S. J. Orme 79(tl); Pharmaceutical Society of Great Britain 106(r); Roger Phillips 47, 74(b), 109, 110/1, 114, 123(t), 124, 136, 142, 143, 149, 154, 155, 157, 158/9; Iain Reid 135, 156; Royal Horticultural Society 65(t), 66, 68, 71, 72, 75, 77, 78, 80, 81, 83, 85, 88(r), 89, 90(t), 92, 93, 95, 97, 98, 100, 102, 104; Red Saunders 133; Scala 21; Harry Smith Horticultural Photographic Agency 31(tr), 32, 79(r), 86(l), 90(b), 94(b), 99(l); Snark 17(t); Tourist Photo Library 88(l); M. Warren 103(t); Michael Wickham 56(l & b); C. Williams 45(b); D. Woodland 69; George Wright 116.

SPICES

Picture Credits

A-Z Collection 234; D. Arminson 175(tl), 233; Rex Bamber 175(tr), 177, 178, 179, 180(lb), 181, 182, 183, 184(tl), 185(br), 190(tl), 196, 201(tr), 209, 215(tr), 216(bl), 246, 255, 264, 268, 274, 290(t); I.B.B. Barton 215(cr); Steve Bicknell 207(br); R. Boston & Sons 194; Camera Press 207(tr); Patrick Cocklin 213; Bruce Colman Ltd/Jane Burton 214; DELU/PAF International 275; Alan Duns 186/7, 192/3, 195(tr), 247, 251, 266, 269, 302; Mary Evans Picture Library 169, 176; Valerie Finnis 224; Geoffrey Frosh 202, 203(bl & br), 205; Gascoigne/R. Harding Associates 174; Denis Hughes-Gilby 260; M. Holford/Kings College Chapel 170; George E. Hyde 185(cr); Paul Kemp 199, 248, 253, 257, 263, 278, 297; David Lean 190(tr), 210(cl & bl); Linnean Society Library 180(lc), 201(cr); Max Logan 197; J. Maddams 208(tl); The Mansell Collection 172, 184(cl), 208(bl); John Markham 261; Marshall Cavendish/Clay Perry 216(br); The Pierport Morgan Library 171; Roger Phillips 189, 191, 211, 244, 254, 258/9, 270, 272/3, 267, 279, 280/1, 282, 285, 286/7, 289, 290(b), 293, 294, 295, 298, 301, 307, 308, 309(tl & br), 311; Iain Reid 188, 271, 283; Royal Horticultural Society 220, 221, 223, 225, 226, 229, 230, 232, 235, 237; H. Smith 195(cr), 217.

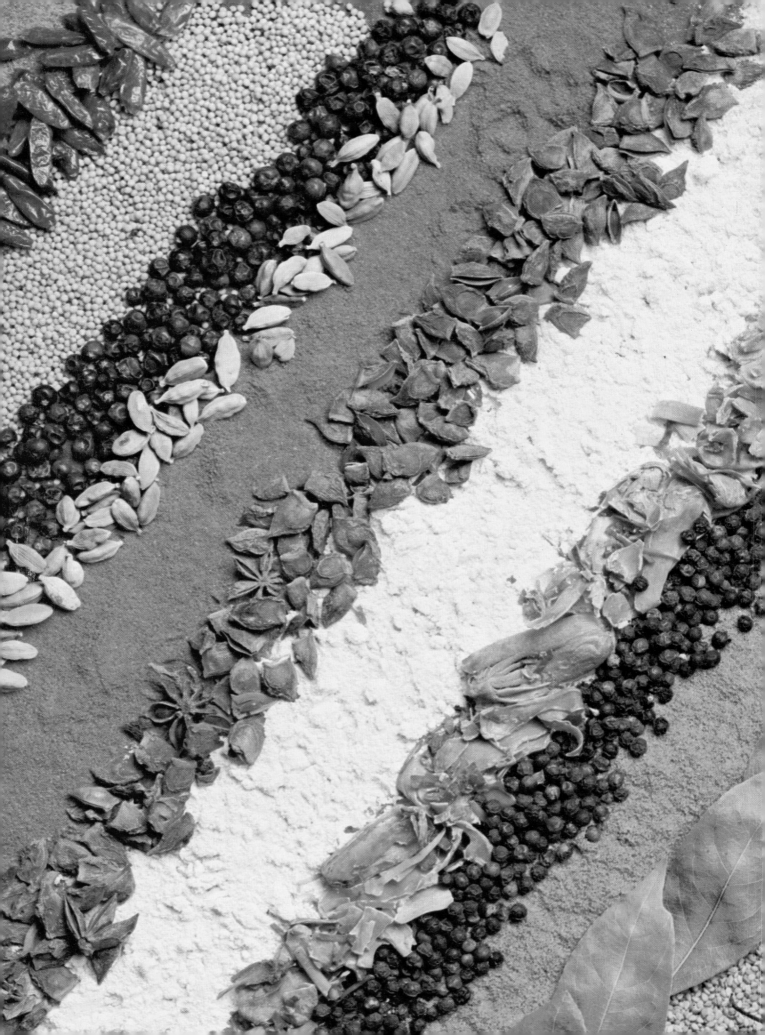